INSECTS THAT FEED ON TREES AND SHRUBS

AN ILLUSTRATED PRACTICAL GUIDE

INSECTS THAT FEED ON

COMSTOCK PUBLISHING ASSOCIATES, a division

CORNELL UNIVERSITY PRESS | ITHACA AND LOND

TREES AND SHRUBS

An Illustrated Practical Guide

By WARREN T. JOHNSON

Professor of Entomology,
Cornell University

and HOWARD H. LYON

Photographer, Department of Plant Pathology,
Cornell University

607-256-3284

With the Collaboration of

C. S. KOEHLER
University of California, Berkeley

N. E. JOHNSON
Weyerhaeuser Company

J. A. WEIDHAAS
Virginia Polytechnic Institute and State University

First published 1976 by Cornell University Press
Published in the United Kingdom by Cornell University Press Ltd.,
2-4 Brook Street, London W1Y 1AA.
Third printing 1979

International Standard Book Number 0-8014-0956-x
Library of Congress Catalog Card Number 75-12255
Printed in the United States of America by Simpson/Milligan Printing Company, Inc.

Contents

5

Preface

Entomological investigations in the United States over the past century have been directed mainly toward the many pests that feed on food and fiber crops. The efficient production of foodstuffs and the resulting increased productivity of American agriculture today is attributable in no small way to the contributions of early entomologists and their successors. Efficiency of agricultural production has reached the point where only a small fraction of our population is now directly engaged in farming. But as the rural population diminishes, the urban and suburban populations acquire greater voting power. It seems inevitable that the increased strength of the urban and suburban vote will in the years ahead bring about changes in the research and extension orientation of land-grant institutions and other publicly funded agencies within which most entomologists operate. Clear signs of change have already been indicated in several states. Rather than continue to commit nearly all entomological talent to areas of traditional agriculture, state and federal governments can be expected to place greater emphasis on the quasi-agricultural problems of the urban and suburban resident and his recreational lands.

This book is an attempt to add one brick to the foundation upon which "urban entomology" must be built. Entomology's success in the future—as has been the case in the past—will depend to a considerable degree on service to a clientele that expresses a need. The need is no less than it was a century ago; only the clientele has changed.

As cities and suburbs grow, increased value is being placed on greenbelts and parks and on the plants that occupy these spaces. People are becoming more aware that trees and other green plants are a part of their life-support system. Vegetation supplies oxygen, filters out dust from the air, and reduces noise pollution. Shade trees can lower the temperature of an urban street by ten or more degrees (the cooling effect results from transpiration as well as the sun-shielding action of the leaves). A properly placed row of trees can serve as an effective windbreak, reducing either hot or cold air movement. Trees and shrubs increase the quality of life in other ways. The flowering cherry trees of Washington, D.C., attract visitors from all over the world, as do the fall-colored hardwoods of the Northeast and the redwoods of California. The benefits provided by trees and other woody ornamentals are available to everyone.

One of the greatest challenges confronting the urban entomologist is appraising the actual importance of the innumerable insects and mites that attack ornamental plants. In agriculture, a species is usually termed an economic pest when the expected monetary loss it may cause, if the crop attacked is left unprotected, is greater than the cost of the usual treatment needed to prevent or mitigate that loss. In the case of ornamentals, however, it is more difficult to identify "pests," since no economic loss (in the agricultural sense) is involved. Pest-caused damage to ornamentals, then, must be measured in terms of the reduced aesthetic value of the plants, the loss of shade, or the cost of replacement of the afflicted plant. Loss may entail inconvenience, as in the case of pest-induced premature leaf drop, requiring the frequent raking of leaves, or even embarrassment (falling caterpillars—or their droppings—at a social affair held under shade trees). The point is that, regardless of what constitutes loss in the case of ornamentals, it is extremely difficult to measure. Yet it is important that appraisal be made.

Current trends in agricultural pest-control philosophy favor reduction of pest numbers to a level just below the so-called economic injury level in cases in which the pest's natural enemies are thereafter capable of containing the infestation. The urban entomologist must not only establish the importance of a pest but also determine the level at which the pest is of no concern to those who make use of the tree or shrub in the landscape. This level must be expected to vary according to the location of the plant and the uses for which it is intended.

This reference work has been in preparation since 1965. Though predating the present "environmental crisis" by several years, it is appropriate for the book to appear at this time because of the widespread attention that has recently been focused on pest control. It is hoped that this book will be regarded as contributing to a rational approach to pest-control problems as they relate to woody ornamental vegetation.

C. S. Koehler

University of California
Berkeley, California

Acknowledgments

The research and preparation of the manuscript were sponsored by the New York State College of Agriculture and Life Sciences at Cornell University, Ithaca, New York, and the University of California at Berkeley, California.

Private funds helped subsidize the publication costs, which the authors gratefully acknowledge. Among those contributing support are:

J. M. McDonald Foundation
Kenneth Post Foundation
Grace H. Griswold Fund
International Shade Tree Conference
New York State Nurserymen's Association
National Arborist Association
Davey Tree Expert Company
New York State Arborists' Association

The following people made important technical contributions to the development of this book: W. W. Allen, University of California, Berkeley; Roxanna Barnum, Cornell University, Ithaca, New York; L. R. Brown, University of California, Riverside; G. M. Buxton, California Department of Food Agriculture; C. S. Davis, University of California, Cooperative Extension, Berkeley; G. W. Dekle, Florida Department of Agriculture; J. E. Dewey, Cornell University, Ithaca, New York; Robert Dirig, Cornell University, Ithaca, New York; J. G. Franclemont, Cornell University, Ithaca, New York; Gordon Gunter, Gulf Coast Research Laboratory, Ocean Springs, Mississippi; D. D. Jensen, University of California, Berkeley; Marilyn A. Johnson, Ithaca, New York; J. L. Joos, California Cooperative Extension, Santa Rosa, California; Tokuwo Kono, California Department of Food Agriculture; Michael Kosztarab, Virginia Polytechnic Institute and State University, Blacksburg, Virginia; J. N. Layne, Archbold Biological Station, Lake Placid, Florida; M. D. Leonard, USDA, Washington, D. C.; F. W. Mead, Florida Department of Agriculture; J. A. Powell, University of California, Berkeley; Louise M. Russell, USDA, Washington, D.C.; L. W. Schneski, Nurseryman, Williamstown, Massachusetts, formerly Cornell University, Ithaca, New York; F. F. Smith, USDA, Beltsville, Maryland; H. G. Walker, Los Angeles City and County Arboretum; R. F. Wilkey, Arthropod Slide Mounts, Bluffton, Indiana, formerly California Department of Agriculture; M. L. Williams, Auburn University, Alabama.

Warren T. Johnson
Cornell University
Ithaca, New York

Reader's Aid to Identification of Insects

(Numbers refer to plates)

Insects That Feed on Conifers

Leaf-consuming insects
    Defoliators and needle chewers, 1–5, 9, 12, 18, 67, 68
    Leaftiers and webbers, 6, 9, 12
    Needle-miners and casebearers, 7, 8, 10, 11
Boring insects
    Bark beetles, 16, 17, 19
    Cambium miners, 197 and Figure 13 (cambium borers)
    Other borers, 18, 21–23
    Tip and shoot borers, 5, 11, 13–15, 20
Sucking insects
    Aphids and adelgids, 24–27, 40, 41
    Mealybugs, 29, 30
    Scale insects, 29, 31–39
    Spittlebugs, 28
Gall makers, 9, 40–42
Mites, 43–45, 204

Insects That Feed on Broad-leaved Evergreens and Deciduous Plants

Leaf- or flower-consuming insects
    Defoliators and leaf or flower chewers, 46–70, 84–95
    Leaf miners, bagworms, and shield bearers, 67, 68, 71–82, 95
    Skeletonizers, 61, 81, 84–88, 91
    Webworms, tentmakers and leaf rollers, 60, 62–66, 69, 70, 82
Root-feeding and root- crown-feeding insects, 89, 90, 93, 94
Boring insects
    Bark beetles, bark and cambium borers, and cambium miners, 99–101, 103, 108, 111, 112, 197
    Stem, shoot, petiole, or fruit borers, girdlers, miners, or pruners, 48, 83, 95–98
    Wood borers, 104–107, 109–113
Sucking insects
    Aphids, 116–127, 190–192
    Lace bugs, 179–181
    Leafhoppers, 171, 175–177
    Mealybugs, 131–135, 140
    Plant bugs, 167–171
    Plant hoppers and treehoppers, 172–174, 178
    Psyllids, 114, 115, 168, 181, 192–196
    Scale insects, 135–166
    Whiteflies, 128–131
Thrips, 177, 182–184
Gallmakers, 95, 96, 112, 185–200, 205–207
Mites, 96, 183, 190, 201–208

Miscellaneous pests

Birds, 212
Mammals, 212
Slugs and snails, 211

Introduction

The Book and Its Use

This book is a reference manual. It covers essential information about many of the important insects, mites, and other animals associated with woody ornamental plants. Its audience is intended to be the agricultural advisor, teacher, student, nurseryman, arborist, forester, gardener, scientist, as well as any other person having direct or peripheral responsibility for the maintenance of trees and shrubs. It deals in a pragmatic way with the science of entomology, and provides assistance in the identification of insects and related animals often considered pests. Scientific information has been interpreted in nontechnical language to make it more useful to those interested in plant protection and natural history. The metric system of measurement has been used throughout. Transition to this international system has already started and in a few years "millimeter," "centimeter," "liter" and "Celsius" will be a part of our everyday language.

The plants considered in this volume are either aesthetically pleasing or serve some environmental function important to man. The number of species of insects and mites destructive to ornamental plants in the United States alone is conservatively estimated to be about 2,500. There are over 700 insects and mites discussed, listed, or illustrated in this book. They are the most important pest species occurring on ornamental plants in the United States and Canada at the present time. All color photographs except thirteen were taken by the authors and collaborators. While these photographs represent specific examples, many are sufficiently generalized to enable one to recognize closely related species not illustrated. By comparing the actual specimen with the photograph and by reading the text and legend, the reader should, by close inspection, be able to identify the specimen.

The writers, in preparing this volume, assumed that the user would have at least general knowledge about the identification of his ornamental plants and would know the common names. Common names of both plants and pests are used throughout the book where meaningful, but to avoid confusion both common (if recognized) and latinized names have been used for pests and most plants. It is important also to know what constitutes the normal and the abnormal—in many instances, not as simple as it may seem. The more knowledge one has about trees and shrubs and their normal growing habits, the more useful this book will be. The process of elimination is a major means of identifying the cause or causes of plant disorders under field conditions; such an empirical method is the tool of the scientist was well as the laymen. The index also is an important tool. Make effective use of it! The Reader's Aid to Identification of Insects is a simplified key, based in part upon plant groups and in part upon where or how an insect feeds. A list of selected references has been prepared for those desiring more detailed information about specific insects covered in this manual. When reference in the text has been made to the work of a specific scientist, a number (0) has been placed by his/her name for ease in locating the work in the list of references. Also, reference numbers are listed at the end of each text unit. A glossary defines the more technical terms.

Pest Control

Pest control is a dynamic field and changes in its technology come about frequently. New chemical compounds are continually being made available and these usually displace older materials. Recommendations or other guidelines for the control of pests of ornamentals are prepared and distributed by agricultural agencies in most states and Canadian provinces (see "Sources of Information on Pest Control," page 443). Such recommendations, based in most cases on local conditions and experience, are always to be preferred over those that attempt to generalize over a broad area. These statements are by no means intended to imply that chemical control is the sole means available to combat all pests that attack woody ornamental plants. Although insecticides and acaricides (miticides) have been heavily relied upon in the past, and their continued use in the foreseeable future is a certainty, many interesting new approaches to insect control are being investigated. Nearly all of these involve control of pests of traditional food and fiber agriculture, although in time they may also be applied to the control of pests of ornamental plants. Even discounting chemical control and the new approaches, there are proven procedures which could markedly change the traditional chemical control picture for many ornamental plants, if entomological talent were devoted to adapting them for use with ornamentals. For example, the principles of host plant resistance, used successfully to combat a number of important pests of agriculture, could be put to even greater use in searching out or developing ornamentals which pests would choose not to attack or which would be tolerant to the effects of attack.

Diagnosis and Identification

With each change of seasons a plant must adjust to a new set of living conditions. In fact there are daily changes in the total environment, some subtle, some abrupt. The growing plant must adjust to each new set of conditions if it is to survive. Each new day can present the plant with a set of conditions too harsh

POSSIBLE CAUSES OF INJURY TO PLANTS

Biotic Environment		Physical Environment	
Animal	**Plants (including microorganisms)**	**Man-controlled**	**Natural**
Nematodes	Viruses and "viroids"	Industrial wastes	Mineral deficiencies
Insects	Mycoplasma-like organisms "spiroplasma"	Air pollution	Frost/Freeze
Mites	Bacteria	Phytotoxicity (pesticides)	Sun scorch
Millipedes	Rickettsia-like organisms	Salt (chemical) accumulations	Drought
Slugs and snails	Fungi	Concrete and macadam	Lightning
Birds (woodpeckers)	Dodder	Soil compaction	Wind
Rabbits, mice, moles and	Mistletoe	Changes in soil level	Hail
other rodents	Algae	Changes in ground water level	Blowing sand
Dogs	Moss	Mechanical injury by auto, machinery	Flood
Man	Weeds	and vandalism	
	Strangling vines		
	Strangling roots		

for its normal development or too extreme for its survival without man's help. The failure of the plant to adjust brings about distress symptoms. Sometimes the problem is obvious, but frequently one must search for specific and subtle symptoms.

Symptoms are produced from two general sources: the living agents (biotic), and the physical environment (abiotic). The living agents are parasites, that is, animal pests and plant pathogens. The physical environmental factors are soil, climate, weather conditions, and man-modified atmospheric and soil conditions. All of these factors must be taken into account by those who attempt to diagnose the ills of plants (see table). In this volume we deal exclusively with animals, mainly insects and mites, that injure trees and shrubs.

Certain information must be obtained before diagnosis or identification of a plant pest problem can be made. Much of this information is obtained by discriminating observation to detect the symptoms. The diagnostician should be, of course, well aware that plants have a characteristic life expectancy and that this may vary from place to place. Thus, decline and death of trees and shrubs come about as a result of old age, as with animals. In certain locations gray birch or mimosa may be old at forty years. A fifty-year-old birch could be senile and therefore difficult, if not impossible to save from the bronze birch borer. The sequoia, on the other hand, may live for thirty centuries.

General health and vigor can often be determined by examining the distance between nodes, and by comparing them with plants of the same species that are growing nearby. Short internodes express stress or poor growing conditions. A history of annual growing conditions can be visually determined in many tree species—white pine, for example. Likewise, growing conditions often can be determined from week to week by observing the internode length on new twigs and the distance between leaves (see Figure 1).

Climate of course is a major limiting factor in the distribution of plant species. The orange tree and the palm, for example, will not survive the winter out-of-doors in Michigan. Neither will many northern conifers survive or do well in southern latitudes. People are experimenters and continually attempt to introduce plants where they normally will not grow. The plants may survive, and in some cases may thrive until the one-in-ten-year freeze or drought occurs. Knowing the climatic zones that favor various plant species is an important aid to diagnosis of disorders.

Trees or shrubs growing in situations where they are exposed to fumes, salt, natural gas or other hydrocarbon vapors can produce symptoms difficult to diagnose. Drought symptoms may be delayed or not fully apparent until after the dry period has passed. Similarly, it may take more than a year for the symptoms of water-logged soils to become evident.

When sufficient observable information is obtained, and adequate references are used, the exact pest species can often be determined. This may be a long process. The plant, of course, must be identified first. Sometimes broad identification categories such as oak or maple are acceptable, and it is not necessary to identify an oak more specifically as, for example, a white oak or a valley oak. The diagnostician must know, however, whether or not he is dealing with a normal plant. Some years ago certain galls on plants were considered normal growth rather than symptoms of parasitic attack. One must always search carefully for signs and symptoms. A sign is the actual organism, skeleton, or other part of a pest, used to identify the cause of a symptom; the symptom is the injury or plant response to an offender (see Figure 2). Diagnosis is based largely upon symptoms. Symptomatic evidence of insect or mite attack takes the forms shown in the list below.

Death of the tree or bush is, of course, a symptom. In the case of certain bark beetles, symptoms from a dead plant are useful. But for the most part post-mortem diagnosis is not very useful because many secondary organisms enter dead plants and erase or subdue the symptoms that are essential to understanding why the plant died.

The same symptom may be produced by two or more organisms that are in no way related, or may be caused by the physical environment. Verticillium, a disease-causing fungus, may induce a maple branch or an entire tree to wilt in mid-summer. Hidden bark beetles or wood borers may cause the same symptom. Drought conditons or a lightning strike may do the same. Thus no firm conclusion can be made on the basis of only a single symptom. Another symptom must be found or the sign (organism) must be located. Often, a tree may be damaged by

Leaves	Twigs and Buds	Stems	Roots	Fruit
Discoloration	Girdled	Mines in cambium	Girdled	Mines or borer channels
Curl	Galls	Mines in outer bark	Galls	Premature drop
Spots	Mines	Borer channels into wood	Mines	Damaged seed
Galls	Pruned	Chewed bark	Chewed	Chewed
Notches	Chewed	Galls	Engraved or borer tunnels	Galls
Circular to irregular holes	Wilted twigs	Mass of pitch		Holes
Mines in blade or petiole	Discolored twigs or buds	Mass of fine sawdust		Abnormal shape
Skeletonization	Holes	Holes		
Defoliation	Enlarged buds			
Disfiguration with				
excrement				

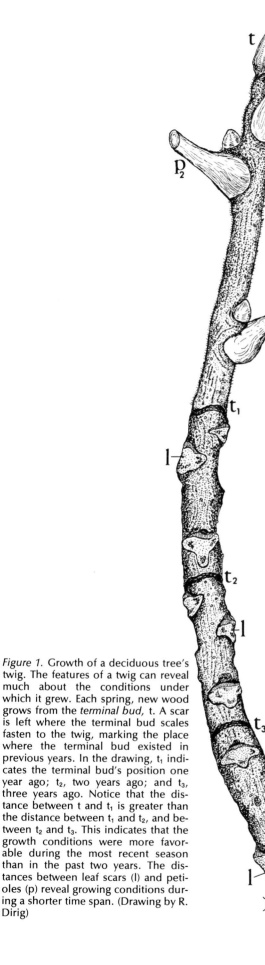

Figure 1. Growth of a deciduous tree's twig. The features of a twig can reveal much about the conditions under which it grew. Each spring, new wood grows from the *terminal bud,* t. A scar is left where the terminal bud scales fasten to the twig, marking the place where the terminal bud existed in previous years. In the drawing, t_1 indicates the terminal bud's position one year ago; t_2, two years ago; and t_3, three years ago. Notice that the distance between t and t_1 is greater than the distance between t_1 and t_2, and between t_2 and t_3. This indicates that the growth conditions were more favorable during the most recent season than in the past two years. The distances between leaf scars (l) and petioles (p) reveal growing conditions during a shorter time span. (Drawing by R. Dirig)

several factors working together or in sequence. For example, a tree may be weakened by some activity of man, or climate, resulting in greater susceptibility to an insect, which in feeding may inoculate the tree with a pathogen that actually kills the plant. If sequential events have been in effect, the diagnostician should follow the symptoms of injury back in time, to determine the initial event (or pest) that caused the problem. Only then can the proper preventative measure be prescribed.

Symptoms of injury resulting from nonliving environmental factors may be similar in appearance to symptoms of injury caused by living entities. A severe frost during the time a maple leaf bud is in a critical stage of development will cause a series of holes to form in the developing leaf. Certain caterpillars can chew holes of similar size and shape.

The diagnostician must have access to the expertise of the taxonomist, an identification specialist. Even after the sign or signs have been characterized, or a sample has been collected, exact identification may require weeks or months. Some insects such as aphids, scale crawlers, and certain caterpillars cannot be fully identified in their immature stage. If they are to be identified they must be reared through to the adult stage. Certain species of leafhoppers can be positively determined only if the male insect is present, and then only by a specialist. The male must be killed and dissected to reveal internal structures that will permit identification.

The information in this volume capitalizes on the diagnostic sleuthing, symptom interpretation, and taxonomic prowess of many scientists. The plates are illustrations of signs and symptoms. The text and legends help to interpret the symptoms and identify the signs. This system is admittedly a short cut in which there are many pitfalls. It will, however, permit identification of the more important pests. Also, it will eliminate some of the gross errors that can result from faulty word interpretation and that can lead to the wrong approach to insect or disease control by readers. The aim is to eliminate unwitting contributions to environmental pollution.

When you, the reader, suspect that something is wrong with a plant, examine it carefully for the causative agent or symptoms. Compare your specimen with those illustrated. In most instances there is more than one picture of the symptom or insect. If the pest or one of its stages is not illustrated, the text may describe it sufficiently for a tentative identification. The plant's growing situation is often illustrated. With a series of pictures, the subject is brought closer and closer so that symptoms or the insect can be seen clearly, and can be identified without further help or interpretation from a specialist.

Natural History

A pictorial study of plant or animal life is usually a nontechnical approach to natural history. Volumes on birds, mammals, fish, reptiles, and flowers are much used by the layman, student, and professional. Pictorial representations reduce the use of, and help the nonprofessional understand, technical jargon. Insect natural history can be interesting and exciting to those who have economic reasons for learning it as well as to those who simply have a natural curiosity about animal life.

Insects affect human life and comfort daily. They are the most abundant group of animals on the earth. We need to go no further than our own premises to explore their natural history. Their activities and behavior are nothing less than phenomenal, but one must be a careful observer to appreciate them.

Certain insects have evolved to the point where separate sexes are unnecessary for the multiplication of the species. Males of certain species are unknown. Thus the female produces more females without fertilization (see Asiatic Weevils, Plate 89). A phenomenon common to gall-producing wasps and certain aphids is alternation of generations. One generation

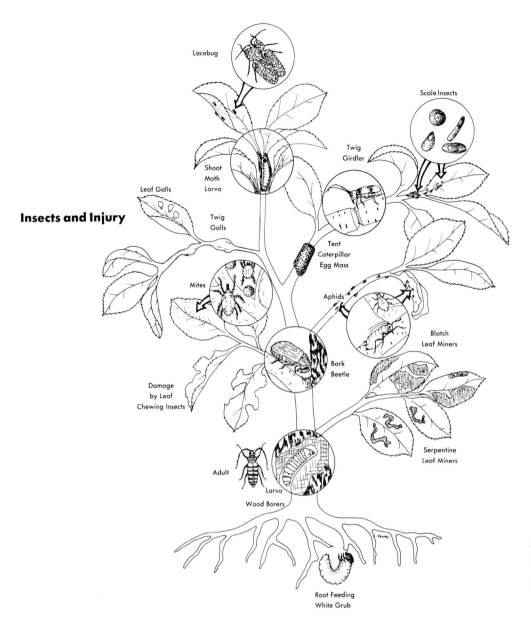

Insects and Injury

Lacebug

Scale Insects

Twig
Girdler

Shoot
Moth
Larva

Leaf Galls

Twig
Galls

Tent
Caterpillar
Egg Mass

Mites

Aphids

Blotch
Leaf Miners

Bark
Beetle

Damage
by Leaf
Chewing Insects

Serpentine
Leaf Miners

Adult

Larva

Wood Borers

Root Feeding
White Grub

Figure 2. A generalized relationship between insect and plant injury. No matter how or where on a plant an insect feeds, a symptom is produced. Sometimes, however, it may be difficult to see or interpret.

may be produced sexually, have a very characteristic appearance, and feed in a very precise way. Its offspring may be only females, may look entirely different, and may feed on a plant unrelated to the one used as a host by the parent (see Plate 118). Insects have unique ways of communicating with one another. Chemical communication by odor is a means by which certain insects convey messages. These chemicals, called pheromones, are currently of much interest to those studying insect biochemistry and behavior. Pheromones aid a species in finding food (Plate 19) and in finding a mate (Plate 49).

The range of longevity of insects and related arthropods is great. The adult males of many species (scale insects) live only a few hours, just long enough for mating to take place. Likewise, some adult females live only a few hours or days. The bagworm female (Plate 67) has no functional mouthparts. Her only role is to produce eggs. When her eggs are laid she dies. For the most part adult insects live for a short time—three days to eight

weeks. Certain beetles such as the pales weevil (Plate 21) live nine to eighteen months. In warm regions, a cycle from birth to death may occur in ten days or less (Plate 204). In the temperate zone, the pattern of many insects is a one-year cycle with a long hibernation period. Life is longer for the wood-boring insects; some live as long as four years under normal conditions (Plate 107). The insect with the longest life-span in North America is the periodical (seventeen-year) cicada (Plate 209).

Protective coloration is illustrated in Plate 21. Defense adaptation with stinging hairs is illustrated in Plate 61. Sexual dimorphism is illustrated in Plate 173. And so it goes—endless examples of strange and interesting insect natural history.

The reader will note a frequent statement in the text describing the plates: "Little is known about this insect's biology and habits." There is much that needs to be learned about insects for our own well being. There is no shortage of work left to be done.

14

Sawfly Defoliators (Plates 1, 2, 3)

Sawflies are not flies at all but non-stinging wasps. The female has a saw-like apparatus (see Figure 3) at the tip of its abdomen, which accounts for the name sawfly. The "saw" is used to slit or cut plant tissue. It aids in the insertion of eggs into these slits (Plate 2, section C). There are a great number of species of sawflies in the United States. Probably a hundred species, in the larval stage, feed on conifer foliage. Some species feed only on the old needles, others only on the new. Sawflies in the first larval stages eat only the outer portion of the needles; later the entire needle may be consumed. Partially eaten needles look like fine straw hanging on twigs (Plate 3, section A and B). Some species occur only in the spring, others in the summer, and others throughout the growing season. The larvae of typical defoliating sawflies look much like the caterpillars of moths and butterflies; they may be differentiated from them, however, by the number of prolegs on the abdomen. Sawfly larvae have more than five pairs. Caterpillars have two to five pairs. Sawflies that attack broad-leaved trees may be defoliators, leaf rollers, webformers, skeletonizers, leaf miners, bud miners, stem borers or gall makers (see Plates 46, 47, 71, 83, 198).

The life cycle of the redheaded pine sawfly, *Neodiprion lecontei* Fitch, will be used to illustrate a typical sawfly life cycle. This sawfly is an important pest of ornamental, forest and especially plantation trees. It attacks jack, shortleaf, loblolly, slash, red, Scots and other two- and three-needle pines. This sawfly may feed on five-needle pines, Norway spruce, deodar cedar and larch, if these trees are growing among other, preferred hosts.

The winter is spent as a prepupa (stage between a larva and pupa) in a cocoon spun on the ground or duff under the trees (Plate 3, section E). Pupation is completed in the spring and the adults emerge a few weeks later. Some prepupae may wait until the second or third season before transforming into adults. This phenomenon, called diapause, is probably a mechanism to allow some sawflies to survive in case all those that emerge in a particular season should die.

The female deposits over 100 eggs in rows of slits in the edges of several needles. Egg-laying may take place without mating, but unfertilized eggs produce only males. The fertilized eggs produce either sex.

The larvae hatch from the eggs after about a month and feed gregariously for another month or so, before dropping from the host to the ground to spin their cocoons. In Canada and the northern United States a single generation occurs each year. In the latitude of southern Michigan and New York a second generation may develop, and in parts of South Carolina, Georgia and the Gulf states three generations occur annually.

The rapid decline of a population of redheaded pine sawflies is often due to rodents that feed on the pupae, and diseases that kill large numbers of larvae. The redheaded pine sawfly is shown in Plate 1, sections D and E.

The introduced pine sawfly, *Diprion similis* (Hartig), is an unintentional import from Europe. It feeds on a wide range of pines including white, red, Scots, and jack. Austrian pine is somewhat resistant. The sawfly is found from Maine to Virginia, in the Central and Great Lakes states, in parts of Ontario and Quebec, and as far west as Minnesota. Two generations occur per year. A mature larva is shown in Plate 1, section F. Eggs are laid in series in old needles (Plate 2, section B).

Neodiprion excitans Roh. is an important pest of pines in the South where it attacks all the southern pines and has been known to cause widespread damage in young pine plantations. Four or five generations may occur in a year. The mature larvae have glossy black heads, and olive-green bodies. Two longitudinal black stripes run along the back of the body, and a row of conspicuous black spots can be found on each side.

The European pine sawfly, *Neodiprion sertifer* (Geoff.), is an important pest of red, Scots, Japanese red, jack, Swiss mountain, and mugho pines. The larvae are gregarious and feed on

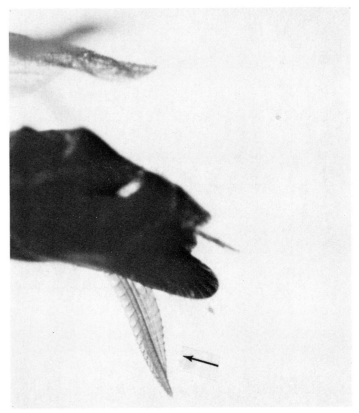

Figure 3. The abdomen of a female sawfly. Arrow indicates the "saw" or ovipositor, used to cut plant tissue and to insert eggs.

mature foliage (Plate 2, section A). The mature larva is grayish-green with markings that allow it to be distinguished from other species (Plate 2, sections D and E).

The European pine sawfly is found in northeastern United States and Canada. One generation occurs annually.

From Anderson (1) we have this list of common spring-and summer-feeding sawflies that attack pine.

1. Loblolly sawfly, *Neodiprion taedae linearis* Ross; south-central United States; loblolly and shortleaf pines.

2. Spotted loblolly pine sawfly, *N.t. taedae* Ross; southeastern United States (Virginia); loblolly, shortleaf, and Virginia pines.

3. Jack pine sawfly, *N. pratti banksianae* Roh.; eastern Canada and the Great Lakes region; jack pine and occasionally other pines.

4. *N. p. pratti* (Dyar); southeastern United States; loblolly, shortleaf and scrub pine.

6. *N. p. paradoxicus* Ross; northeastern United States, from Maine to North Carolina; jack, Virginia, pitch, and shortleaf pines.

A. Branch of *Larix decidua* partially defoliated by larch sawfly larvae.
B. Close-up of mature larvae of larch sawfly.
C. Adult larch sawfly.
D. Branch of *Pinus nigra* partially defoliated by larvae of the redheaded pine sawfly.
E. Mature larvae of the redheaded pine sawfly.
F. Mature larva of the introduced pine sawfly.
G. Larch sawfly eggs embedded in larch twig. (Photo courtesy H. Tashiro, New York State Agricultural Experiment Station, Geneva, New York)

16

PLATE 1

7. European pine sawfly, *N. sertifer* (Geoff.); northeastern North America west to Illinois; red, pitch, shortleaf, and occasionally other pines.

8. Hetrick's sawfly, *N. hetricki* Ross; southeastern United States; loblolly and possibly other pines.

9. Redheaded pine sawfly, *N. lecontei* Fitch; eastern half of North America; all hard (two- or three-needle) pines (sometimes the foliage of other conifers is eaten by older larvae). Usually infests smaller-sized trees up to about fifteen feet tall.

10. White pine sawfly, *N. pinetum* Nort.; northeastern and north-central North America; white pine. See Figures 4-6.

11. Pitch pine sawfly *N. pinirigidae* Nort.; northeastern United States; pitch pine.

Figure 4 (left). Adult male sawfly, *Neodiprion pinetum.* x5. (Photo courtesy United States Department of Agriculture) *Figure 5 (right).* Adult female sawfly, *Neodiprion pinetum.* x5. Note difference in size and antennae between female and male shown in Figure 4. (Photo courtesy United States Department of Agriculture)

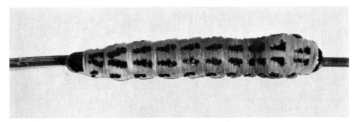

Figure 6. The larva of the sawfly *Neodiprion pinetum* feeds on the needles of eastern white pine. x4. (Photo courtesy United States Department of Agriculture)

12. Lodgepole pine sawfly, *N. burkei* Midd.; western North America; lodgepole pine.

13. Abbott's sawfly, *N. abbottii* Leach.; eastern North America; all hard pines.

14. Swaine jack pine sawfly, *N. swainei* Midd.; southeastern Canada and the Great Lakes states; jack pine.

15. *N. excitans* Roh.; southeastern United States; most hard pines.

16. Introduced pine sawfly, *Diprion similis* (Hartig); northeastern North America west to the Great Lakes states; chiefly the soft five-needle pines.

17. *D. frutetorum* Fab.; northeastern North America; red and Scots pines.

In addition, there are several species of the genus *Acantholyda* that are called pine-webbing sawflies because of their habit of spinning fine webs which become filled with excrement and needle fragments. These are discussed on page 32.

One might get the impression that only pines have sawfly enemies. Other conifers have their sawfly pests, too, but not as many as do the pines. Following is a list of some of the more important species, their ranges and hosts:

1. Larch sawfly, *Pristiphora erichsonii* Hartig; across North America and southern Canada; all species of larch. (Plate 1)

2. Two-lined larch sawfly, *Anoplonyx occidens* Ross; northwestern United States; western larch.

3. Western larch sawfly, *A. laricivorus* Roh. and Midd; western United States; western larch.

4. European spruce sawfly, *Diprion hercyniae* Hartig; northeastern United States, eastern Canada; spruces.

5. Yellowheaded spruce sawfly, *Pikonema alaskensis* Roh.; Canada, northern United States, south to latitude of Colorado; spruces.

6. Hemlock sawfly, *Neodiprion tsugae* Midd.; western United States; western hemlock, Pacific silver fir.

7. Cypress sawfly, *Susana cupressi* Roh. and Midd.; California; Monterey cypress.

Sawflies are hosts to many kinds of parasites, and are subject to various virus and fungus diseases. Rodents and birds have been shown to be important predators. But even with these natural controls, outbreaks of sawflies occur in their range every year and cause severe injury to forests and homeground ornamentals.

References: 1, 50, 80, 94, 153, 174, 248, 283, 316, 317, 319

A. Scots pine needles being devoured by European pine sawfly larvae.
B. Eggs of European pine sawfly in Scots pine needles.
C. Close-up of eggs on pine needle. Note that eggs are partially embedded in the needle.
D,E. Fully grown European pine sawfly larvae.

PLATE 2

A. Injury to Colorado blue spruce by the larvae of an undertermined sawfly. Note the straw-like appearance of the damaged needles.
B. A single needle from Colorado blue spruce injured by early instar sawfly larvae. Only the major vascular bundles (midrib) remain in the injured area.
C. Sawfly larva on white fir, *Abies concolor.*
D. Close-up of damage on white fir.
E. Typical sawfly cocoons.

PLATE 3

Moth Larvae Defoliators (Plate 4)

Pines are subject to serious attack by several kinds of caterpillar defoliators. Since needles normally remain on the tree and are functional for from two to five years, defoliation of conifers is serious. When pine or other conifers are completely stripped of needles they usually die.

Lambdina athasaria pellucidaria (G & R) can be a serious defoliator of pitch and red pine. It overwinters in the pupal stage in the duff beneath its host tree. The moths emerge in May and June to lay eggs on the needles. The young larvae chew notches out of the needles, which, after a few days, turn to a straw-like brown color (A). This change in color is often the first symptom of the presence of the larvae. Later they devour the entire needle. The larvae are loopers (D) (Geometridae) and have only two pair of prolegs. Fully grown larvae are about 30 mm long. One generation occurs each year.

Lambdina athasaria pellucidaria is known only in the Atlantic coast states where outbreaks are usually locally distributed. On Cape Cod, Massachusetts, outbreaks occurred in ten-year cycles for a period of about 40 years. In 1970 there was an outbreak on Long Island.

Related species, *Lambdina fiscellaria* (Guenée) and *L. athasaria* (Walker), are defoliators of hemlock and are more widely distributed than *Lambdina athasaria pellucidaria*. They can be found from Canada to Georgia and west to Wisconsin. *L. fiscellaria lugubrosa* Hulst attacks and does serious damage to hemlock in Oregon, Washington and California.

The looper larva shown in section E is a species of *Semiothisa* (Geometridae). A solitary feeder on several species of pine, it is never abundant. Larvae may be found during July and August. One generation occurs each year. Several other species are found mostly in northern or mountainous states and in Canada.

The caterpillar shown in section F is a species of *Zale*. It is the larva of one of the noctuid moths and has five pairs of abdominal prolegs. It is a solitary feeder. Rarely are larvae of this genus abundant enough to cause economic injury, though they have a wide geographical range. The one whose photograph appears here was found on red pine in New York State in August. Larvae may be found from mid-June to late August. One generation is believed to occur each year.

References: 12, 50, 153

A. Twigs of *Pinus rigida*. The straw-like needles of the twig on the left are a symptom of attack by young caterpillars of *Lambdina athasaria pellucidaria*.

B. A close-up view of green needles notched by larvae. Later they will turn brown.

C,D. The measuring worm posture of *Lambdina athasaria pellucidaria*.

E. The larva of a species of *Semiothisa*, about 22 mm when fully grown.

F. The larva of a species of *Zale*.

PLATE 4

Moth Larvae Defoliators and *Dioryctria* Bark Feeder (Plate 5)

A great number of insects consume conifer needles. Two groups are of particular importance—moths and sawflies. The sawflies (Plates 1–3) belong to the same order of insects as the wasps and bees, both of whose larvae are similar in appearance to moth larvae. Only a few examples of the many conifer defoliators are discussed here.

The spruce budworm, *Choristoneura fumiferana* (Clem.) (Torticidae), and its several variants, is the most important conifer defoliator in North America. It is responsible for the destruction of billions of board feet of balsam fir and spruce in the East, and Douglas fir, lowland white and subalpine firs in the West. A closely related species, or subspecies, of the budworm, found in the Great Lakes states, prefers Scots and jack pine; another in the West feeds on sugar pine. At times, ornamental conifers are attacked, especially in those regions where an epidemic on forest trees is occurring.

SPRUCE BUDWORM

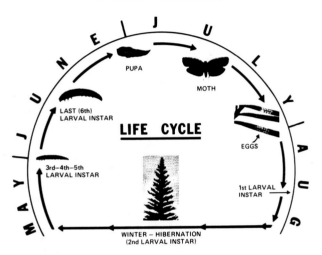

Adult spruce budworm moths (G) are small (22 mm wing expanse) and are variously marked. These markings may be the result of long association with host trees—an example of protective coloration. The female moths lay their oval, pale-green eggs on the foliage in a fish-scale-like manner (J). The larvae reach about 25 mm in length at maturity and are reddish brown with conspicuous, whitish or yellowish, raised spots. They spin fine silk strands that intertwine the foliage (H). In the West, there is a green form that feeds primarily on white fir, *Abies concolor*. The pupae are 16 mm long and have the typical shape and color of many moth pupae (H).

The blackheaded budworm, *Acleris variana* (Fern.), the adult of which has even more varied markings than the spruce budworm, causes similar damage to hemlock, true fir and spruce in western United States, Canada and Alaska. The Pacific silver fir twigs shown in section I were probably fed upon by mature larvae of this species, or the silver-spotted tiger moth, *Halisidota argentata* Pack, shown in section K. The silver-spotted tiger moth is a common defoliator of Douglas fir and occasionally other conifers in the West. Damage is usually confined to individual branches because of the many parasites and diseases that attack it.

Douglas fir tussock moth, *Orgyia* (=*Hemerocampa*) *pseudotsugata* (McD.), populations occasionally occur in such numbers in the western United States that Douglas fir, true firs, spruce, pine and larch found in forests, parks and yards are completely defoliated. The female moths are wingless (E). After mating they lay their eggs in a mixture of a frothy substance and the hairy covering of the cocoon from which they emerged. They spend the winter as eggs; the small larvae hatch in the

spring and feed on new foliage. The mature larva (F) is about 25 mm long with distinctive markings and tan tufts. When the larval population is high, pellets (larval excrement) "rain" from the trees and cover the ground (F). The hairs on the larvae, and the hairy covering of cocoons and eggs, break off and become airborne. When the drifting hairs touch human skin they may cause severe itching and other allergic reactions.

Of importance, but not illustrated, is the pine tussock moth, *Dasychira plagiata* (Walker), believed to be distributed from Nova Scotia south to Pennsylvania and west to Minnesota. Occasionally it has been found as far south as Florida, and as far west as British Columbia. One generation occurs yearly. The small larvae overwinter under bark scales on the trunk, and become active in the spring, completing their development in Wisconsin by the middle of July. The most severe injury to their hosts occurs during June and early July while the insects are in their fifth and sixth larval stages. The larvae are colorful. Like many other tussock moth larvae (see Plate 58, section A), they have four tufts of hair on their backs. The primary host plants are jack, red and occasionally white pine. Several species of fir, spruce and larch are also attacked.

Dioryctria abietivorella Grote larvae frequently take up residence where other boring insects have been. They also feed on soft, smooth bark and bore into terminal twigs, cones and galls of pine, spruce, Douglas fir and arborvitae (A). They do not feed on foliage. When bark is damaged, the terminal portion of the twig, past the injury site, usually dies. A dead "flag" remains as a symptom. Partly grown larvae overwinter inside the host and complete their growth in the spring. Fully grown larvae are about 18 mm long. Adults are present in New York in early July. There is little information about their biology or distribution in the United States, but they are presumed to be found throughout the United States. The larvae of related species (Zimmerman pine moth and others) are among the most serious pests of cones and conifer seed in the South and West. In the Northeast the larvae of *Dioryctria zimmermani* (Grote) or related species bore into the terminal shoots of Japanese black pine as well as Scots, Austrian and native pines. Injured twigs often exude pitch mixed with sawdust-like frass at the entrance site. The twig tip turns brown. The larvae are dark with black heads and up to 15 mm long. Larvae in the same genus feed in the trunk cambium where pitch masses accumulate. The adult moth looks much like the one illustrated in D.

References: 50, 153, 275

A. A twig of *Thuja occidentalis* showing bark injury caused by the larva of *Dioryctria abietivorella*.
B. Mature *Dioryctria* larva.
C. Webbing and needle injury made by Douglas fir tussock moth larvae on white fir.
D. *Dioryctria abietivorella* adult, approximately 15 mm long.
E. Wingless female tussock moths and egg masses at arrows. (Females are 10–12 mm long.)
F. Mature tussock moth larvae walking on forest floor covered with excrement pellets. Pencil shows size relationship.
G. Spruce budworm moth.
H. Silvery appearance of silk strands made by larvae of the spruce budworm. A pupa is at the twig juncture.
I. Damage to Pacific silver fir by an unknown defoliator, probably blackheaded budworm or silver-spotted tiger moth, *Halisidota argentata* Pack.
J. Spruce budworm egg mass greatly enlarged.
K. The silver-spotted tiger moth larva hanging from the branchlet has died from a viral disease.

PLATE 5

Juniper Webworm (Plate 6)

The juniper webworm, *Dichomeris marginella* (D & S), is a moth and belongs to the family Gelechiidae. It was first reported in the United States in 1910 and is European in origin. The species is known from Maine to North Carolina, west to Michigan and Missouri, and also in California. *D. marginella* has been found only on juniper, especially the species or cultivars *hibernica, horizontalis, depressa, aurea,* and *suecica,* and also on Chinese juniper, although *Juniperus chinensis* var. *pfitzeriana* and *J. sabina* apparently are immune.

The juniper webworm larvae are well protected within masses of webbing and dead needles; the larvae cause extensive damage (see section A). Early signs of infestation often go unnoticed because larvae tend to inhabit the thicker, inner parts of a host plant. It is not uncommon for larvae to consume 80 percent or more of the foliage if control measures are not applied early.

One generation of this pest occurs annually. The adult moth is active during May in the southern parts of its range, and during June farther north. It lays an average of 132 eggs at a time in the axils of the leaves. Adults live for two to two and one-half weeks. They are brownish with a wingspan of about 14 mm. The front wing is brown; the front and rear margins are white. The hind wing is uniformly gray. Eggs hatch in 9–16 days and larvae are present from June or July until the following April or May when pupation occurs. When first hatched the larvae are about 1 mm long, and grow to a length of 10–14 mm. A newly hatched larva constructs a tiny white web in the axil of a leaf and feeds initially as a leaf miner. As the larva grows it begins feeding on other leaves but uses the mined leaf as a "retreat cell" for a time. In late summer, larger larvae are gregarious, and produce much webbing in the foliage. Most of the webbing, however, is produced in the spring by mature larvae.

Chemical control measures are often of no avail because the life history of the pest is not well understood. Small larvae are most susceptible to chemicals before they produce masses of webs.

The juniper webworm has several natural enemies including a mite predator, *Pediculoides ventricosus,* and several parasites, *Tetrastichus* sp. *Catoloccus aeneoviridis (Gir.), Itoplectis conquisitor* (Say), *Ephialtes aequalis* (Prov.), and *Microbracon gelechiae* (Ashm.).

Another species, *Dichomeris ligulella* (Hbn.), occurs on apple, cherry, pear, plum, hazel, and oak in the Northeast, and west through Minnesota including parts of Canada.

References: 12, 216, 308

A. Brown needles show the extent of damage done by juniper webworms on a large columnar juniper.
B. A mature larva, about 13 mm long. Strands of silk are evident.
C. Characteristic webbing of needles on a single branch.
D. Larval feeding and webbing tend to leave some foliage untouched.

PLATE 6

Spruce Needle-Miners (Plate 7)

At least two species of moth larvae mine in spruce needles and cause similar kinds of damage.

The spruce needle-miner, *Endothenia albolineana* (Kearf.), is widely distributed in the spruce-growing regions of the United States and Canada. In the West it has been found attacking Engelmann, blue and Sitka spruces. In the northeastern United States and eastern Canada it attacks primarily Norway and blue spruces.

The adult moths emerge in May and June to mate. The female deposits a group of pale-green eggs, shingle fashion, on the base of a needle. The larva develops and cuts a hole near the base of a needle and then mines the interior. Sometimes several larvae mine a single needle. When the interior of the needle has been consumed, the larva often cuts off the needle. The needle remains attached to other dead needles by silk strands. Typical damage is shown in sections A, B, and C. Feeding continues until the first heavy frost, when each larva enters a hollowed-out needle and spins a web over the opening. In this protected location the larva spends the winter. It emerges again in the spring and resumes feeding until ready for pupation in mid-April.

Epinotia nanana (Treit.) is a smoky brown moth with blunt wing tips (E). It was introduced from Europe and is now known to occur in the United States from Maine westward to Ohio and Michigan. The hosts are red, white, Norway and blue spruces. The moths fly during June. Eggs are deposited singly on needles in June, and hatch in July. The newly hatched larva mines in the base of the previous year's needles. More than ten needles may be mined by a single larva before feeding is stopped by cold weather. The winter is spent in the last hollowed-out needle. Feeding resumes in April. An additional fifteen needles may be killed before the larva completes its growth. Pupation occurs with the mass of mined needles held loosely together by silk strands.

Even with light infestations, both *E. nanana* and *T. albolineana* can give ornamental spruces an unhealthy and unsightly appearance. At times they can cause severe defoliation of both ornamental and forest trees.

Epinotia subviridis Hein. is known in all the Pacific coast states as the cypress webber but it feeds on both cypress and arborvitae. In the spring, caterpillars feed by burrowing through the leaflets and form a nest from pieces gnawed from twigs and leaves. Damage symptoms appear in the spring in the form of brown foliage.

References: 50, 153

A. Damage to blue spruce caused by *Endothenia albolineana*.
B. Close-up of photograph in section A.
C,D. Damage by *Epinotia nanana* to foliage of Norway spruce.
E. An adult *Epinotia nanana*.
F. Adult *Endothenia albolineana;* wing spread is 11 to 15 mm.

PLATE 7

29

Larch Casebearer (Plate 8)

Larch is only occasionally used as an ornamental. In certain parts of the United States, however, it grows into a beautiful yard tree. Larch has an uncommon trait for a conifer—it loses its foliage in the winter. Only bald and pond cypress, and dawn redwood do the same. The casebearer sometimes causes larch to lose its foliage before winter comes.

Coleophora laricella (Hubner), derives its name from the case constructed by the larva (C, D). The case provides camouflage that allows larvae to go undetected by nearly all but trained observers. The case is formed by part of a mined-out larch needle lined with silk spun by the larva. It is the color of a dead needle and shaped somewhat like a miniature cigar. The casebearer overwinters within its case, which is firmly attached to a branch often near the base of a bud (C). The larva resumes feeding in the spring as soon as the foliage begins to appear. Damaged needles look as though they have been bleached or scorched (A, B).

When the larva finishes feeding in late May or June it pupates within the case. Adults emerge during June and early July. Dispersal takes place at this time. The adult moths are silvery gray and have a wing expanse of only 8 mm. The distinctively shaped eggs are deposited one or more to a needle. Under magnification, the reddish brown eggs resemble inverted jelly molds with 12–14 ridges. When the egg hatches, the larva burrows directly into the needle where it feeds as a miner for about two months.

The most conspicuous damage occurs in the spring when the foliage may shrivel and die. Heavy defoliation retards both height and diameter growth. If defoliation occurs during two or more consecutive years the host may be killed.

The casebearer, an unfortunate introduction from Europe, was first reported in Massachusetts in 1886. It was known only in the eastern United States until the late 1950's when it was found in the western United States. It is now ravaging the larch forests in the northern Rocky Mountains. A number of native and introduced parasites such as *Agathis pumila* (Ratz.), *Bassus pumilio* Nees and *Chrysocharis laricinellae* (Ratz.) attack the casebearer but are unable to hold it completely in check. In some localities birds play an important role in the control of this insect.

References: 50, 73, 129, 153, 238

A,B. Typical damage by the larch casebearer, *Coleophora laricella*, to foliage of *Larix decidua*.
C. Larch casebearer larvae overwintering in cases at the base of a bud.
D. Larch casebearer larva in its strange walking position.

PLATE 8

31

Pine Webworm and Balsam Needle Gall (Plate 9)

Insects described as webworms have a habit of tying foliage together with silk. This process provides the insect with an abundance of food, and serves as protection from enemies. An important webworm on pine is *Tetralopha robustella* Zell. It is of considerable importance to home owners and growers of Christmas trees. Ugly web nests are made on terminal twigs. The loose webbing contains dead needles and brown frass (B). Usually the injury has been done and the nest vacated before the pest is noticed.

The biology of this insect was studied in detail in Wisconsin in 1959. One generation occurs each year in its northern range. It is believed that two generations occur each year in Virginia, and three or more in Florida. The larva overwinters inside a cocoon in the soil. The moths begin to emerge in June and others follow through July and part of August. Eggs are commonly laid in single rows along the length of pine needles. A needle may contain as few as one but up to 20 or more eggs.

Upon hatching from their eggs, the young larvae wander about spinning silk threads among the needles. They then select a needle and begin feeding as miners. When they become too large to mine needles they begin constructing a nest of frass and silk. The larvae live in colonies ranging in size from a few to 78 individuals. Colonies are covered by loosely webbed needles. The nests are usually 5 cm long but occasionally reach 15 cm in length, depending upon the number of larvae in the colony. As the larvae devour the needles, the web becomes loosely filled with brown, nearly oblong, fecal pellets wrapped around the twig. Fully grown larvae are about 15 mm long, and are yellowish brown with dark brown longitudinal stripes. They crawl or drop from the nest to pupate in the soil in late September. On Long Island in New York, their webs are found in late June and July; in Florida, the webs of the year's first generation are found in April.

This insect is found from New England to Florida and west to Wisconsin and Minnesota. The hosts by region are: Great Lakes states—jack pine, red pine, eastern white pine, Scots pine; Northeast—mugho pine, pitch pine, red pine, Scots pine, Virginia pine; South—slash pine, shortleaf pine, longleaf pine, loblolly pine. Parasites include *Apanteles* sp., *Trachysphyrus albitaris* Cress., and *Mesostenus thoracicus* Cress., all of which are wasps; and *Phorocera* sp., a tachinid fly. Birds such as chickadees and nuthatches tear at the nests to obtain the larvae.

The three species of webbing sawflies discussed here make similar nests and may easily be confused. The larvae of the pine false webworm, *Acantholyda erythrocephala* (Linnaeus), live gregariously in a web. They cut needles off at the sheath and pull them inside the web to eat. Larvae may be found from early May to late June. Fully grown larvae are about 20 mm long, and are a pale greenish-gray with longitudinal purplish-red stripes and a yellow head. They pupate in the soil. Distribution is essentially limited to the Northeast and the Great Lakes states.

Acantholyda zappei (Rohwer) larvae also appear from early May to late June and feed in the same manner as the pine false webworm. Both sawflies occur over the same geographical area and feed on red, white, Scots, mugho, jack and Austrian pines.

The balsam gall midge larva, *Dasineura* (=*Itonida*) *balsamicola* (Lintner), causes a gall on the needles of balsam fir and Frazier fir. It is occasionally found on ornamentals and Christmas trees, and is frequently found in the Adirondack region of New York, in Maine, and in New Hampshire. It probably exists throughout the range of balsam fir. Little is known about the biology of this midge. The galls which form on the spring needles become evident by midsummer. Those shown in section F were collected on the second day of November in New York. Wasp parasites of the genus *Platygaster* help keep the midge population low. Other conifer needle galls may be seen on Plate 42.

References: 12, 45, 258, 298

A. A mugho pine with the abandoned nest of the pine webworm, *Tetralopha robustella*.

B. A white pine twig with a nest of the pine webworm. The needles were removed and eaten by larvae.

C. The six instars of the pine webworm. (Courtesy D. M. Benjamin, University of Wisconsin)

D. A close-up of the frass, web and dead needles—leftovers from a colony of pine webworms.

E. A close-up of a galled balsam fir needle.

F. A balsam fir twig with needle galls caused by the midge *Dasineura balsamicola*.

PLATE 9

Needle-Miners (Plate 10)

The pine needle-miner, *Exoteleia pinifoliella* (Chamb.), is a native insect which feeds on red, mugho, jack, Virginia, short-leaf, loblolly and perhaps other hard pines. It is known throughout the eastern half of the United States and eastern Canada. This insect can be a serious pest. Up to 85% of the needles on a single tree may be mined. Where infestations are heavy, the needles of the affected tree acquire a brownish cast.

In the North, the adult moth emerges in June and lays its eggs early in July. Eggs are laid singly on twig bark. The newly hatched larva enters its first needle by cutting a hole in the flat side, usually within the needle sheath. After molting several times, the larva overwinters within the needle. The following spring other needles are mined until the larva is mature and 6 mm long. Pupation occurs (E) in early June.

The lodgepole needle-miner, *Coleotechnites* (*Recurvaria*) *milleri* (Busck), does similar damage to lodgepole pine in the West and has been a troublesome pest in Yosemite National Park in California. Other species of *Recurvaria* mine needles of ponderosa pine in the West. A number of related species mine the needles of spruce, fir and other conifers throughout the United States.

References: 50, 153

A,B. Needles killed by the caterpillar mines of *Exoteleia pinifoliella*.
C. Close-up of damaged needles, easily recognizable by the brown tips. Adult moths emerge through characteristic holes.
D. An exposed larva mine in a needle. Larva is at arrow.
E. Pupa of the pine needle-miner inside a mined needle.

PLATE 10

Cypress Tip Moth and Arborvitae Leaf Miner (Plate 11)

Several species of *Argyresthia* (among them *A. cupressella* Walsingham and *A. franciscella* Busck) are commonly known as cypress tip moths. They attack the foliage tips of cypress (*Cupressus*), juniper (*Juniperus*) and arborvitae (*Thuja*) in the coastal western region of the United States. The larvae tunnel within the growing points of the host, and kill back the foliage an inch or so (F). Entire plants may appear brown as a result of the activities of these insects.

The adult is a silvery tan moth with a wingspan of about 6 mm. The moth (I) of *A. cupressella* is present only in the spring and early summer. The exact time of its occurrence depends upon the amount of time the infested plant is exposed to the sun and upon the latitudinal location of the plant. In the vicinity of Corvallis, Oregon, moths occur from early May until late June. In the San Francisco Bay area, the cypress tip moth occurs from mid-April until late June, with the peak of activity in May and early June. In southern California, adults are most numerous in April but can be found from mid-March until late in July.

Eggs are laid by the females on the green tips of twigs of susceptible host plants. Upon hatching, the tiny larvae tunnel into the leaf scales and feed by mining within the foliage until late winter or spring of the following year. Relatively little foliage discoloration is associated with the young larvae. Beginning in late winter, however, a yellowing and then a browning of the infested tips can easily be seen. The dead twigs can be readily broken off because of their shell-like condition.

After their feeding period has been completed, the larvae (6 mm long when mature) of *A. cupressella* leave their mines and spin a white paper-like cocoon among the living or dead foliage. The pupal state is passed within this cocoon. *A. franciscella,* on the other hand, spends its pupal stage within the hollowed-out, dead but formerly growing point. Several weeks later the adult moths emerge, mate, and begin laying eggs. One complete generation occurs each year.

Other western species which cause similar damage include *A. trifasciae* Braun, *A. libocedrella* Busck and *A. arceuthobiella* Busck. The latter two mine the tips of incense cedar, *Calocedrus decurrens,* found in Oregon. Several species of *Recurvaria,* including *R. stanfordia* Keif, and *R. juniperella,* mine the tips of Monterey cypress, *Cupressus macrocarpa,* and Sierra juniper, *Juniperus occidentalis,* respectively.

In northeastern North America there are four species of leaf miners that attack arborvitae; *Argyresthia thuiella* (Pack.), *A. freyella* Wlshm., *A. aureoargentella* Brower and *Recurvaria thujaella* Kft. The arborvitae leaf miner, *A. thuiella,* is the most abundant species and has a much greater known range than the other species. *A. thuiella* is found not only in New England and eastern Canada but also in the mid-Atlantic states and as far west as Missouri.

Moths appear from mid-June to mid-July and lay their eggs between the leaf scales. These insects overwinter as half-grown larvae inside the mine. All four species may occur together in mixed populations over their respective ranges. The damage (A) caused by all eastern species is virtually identical to that described for *A. cupressella.* According to Silver (260), trees may lose 80 per cent of their foliage from leaf miner attack and still survive. Twenty-seven parasites of pupa and larva have been recovered from New Brunswick, Canada. *Pentacnemus bucculatricis* How., a wasp parasite, is the most widely abundant and important for natural control.

A. freyella Wlshm. infests red cedar, *Juniperus virginiana,* as well as arborvitae in the northeastern United States and Canada. *Coleotechnites juniperella* (Kearf.) mines the tips of red cedar and juniper in the northeastern states. Like the western leaf miner species, one generation of *Coleotechnites* occurs each year.

References: 36, 50, 153, 243, 260, 261

A. An arborvitae heavily infested by the arborvitae leaf miner, *Argyresthia thuiella.* The tree has lost about half its leaves.
B. Loss of foliage on arborvitae following attack by *Argyresthia thuiella.* The brown foliage drops from the twig leaving it bare.
C. An exposed arborvitae leaf miner. Tunnels made by the larva are visible.
D. Healthy foliage seen with mined foliage.
E. Browning of foliage on Monterey cypress resulting from attack by *Argyresthia franciscella.*
F,G. Close-up of tip damage caused by *Argyresthia cupressella.* Black spots in section G are exit holes where the larvae emerged.
H. The adult arborvitae leaf miner, *Argyresthia thuiella.*
I. *Argyresthia cupressella* adult.

PLATE 11

37

Pine Tube Moth (Plate 12)

Nature often provides its creatures with a home. If not, it provides them with the capability for building a home. The pine tube moth, *Argyrotaenia pinatubana* (Kearfott), builds its own protection by webbing from five to twenty needles together into the form of a tube. The larva, nestled inside, is surrounded by soft white silk fabric it has spun. Eastern white pine, *Pinus strobus,* is its major, if not sole, host plant.

The pine tube moth's biology is not well known but it is believed to overwinter as a pupa. Adult moths emerge in early May and lay eggs on the needles. The young larvae feed on the tips of needles and become fully grown by mid-June (A). A new generation of moths appears in July. Eggs are laid soon thereafter. The adult moths, male (B) and female (C), are shown as pinned specimens. In fresh specimens the hind wings are pearl-gray.

This insect is not considered to be a serious pest. When abundant, however, it can cause needles to turn brown, thus reducing the ornamental value of the tree. Injury may go unnoticed until the second generation appears.

The pine tube moth is likely to be found throughout the native range of eastern white pine. It has been found from Florida north to Canada and west to Wisconsin.

References: 50, 129

A. Larva of the pine tube moth, *Argyrotaenia pinatubana,* and two bundles of needles showing the internal webbing inside the "tube." The larva is about 12 mm long.
B. Male moth, pinned specimen.
C. Female moth, pinned specimen. Wingspan is about 14 mm.
D. Evidence of damage after the insect has vacated the tube.

PLATE 12

Pine Tip Moths (Plates 13, 14)

Larvae of one or more species of small moths bore into the tips of pines wherever they are grown in the United States. The most damaging species belong to the genus *Rhyacionia*. Some of the more important species and their hosts are listed below:

Scientific Name	Common Name	Principal Hosts	Range
R. frustrana	Nantucket pine tip moth	all two- and three-needle pines except slash pine and longleaf pine	East, South and South-central
R. frustrana bushnelli	Western pine tip moth	ponderosa pine	Nebraska, Great Lakes states and Dakotas
R. buoliana	European pine shoot moth	red, mugho, Scots, Austrian, ponderosa and other pines	Northern United States from coast to coast
R. pasadenana	Monterey pine tip moth	Monterery, Bishop pines	Coastal California
R. zozana	none	ponderosa, Jeffrey pines	Far West
R. montana	none	lodgepole pine	Rocky Mountains
R. neomexicana	none	ponderosa pine	Southwest

The damage inflicted on hosts by all such species is similar: the tips of terminals and laterals are killed as a result of larval boring, initially into the base of the needles or buds, and then into the twig itself. *R. frustrana* may kill back shoots of loblolly and shortleaf pine as much as one foot. At times trees that are heavily infested by this species appear reddish in color as a result of the many dead branches. Small trees may be killed. Both this species and *R. buoliana* are troublesome pests in nurseries and Christmas tree plantations. The western species cause similar damage. Repeated infestations leave the trees distorted and unsightly. Light infestations may, however, actually improve the form of some ornamental pines, giving them a bushier appearance.

A single generation of the European pine shoot moth occurs annually. The Nantucket pine tip moth may undergo four or more generations in the deep South with injury symptoms appearing numerous times during the growing season. The adult European pine shoot moth lays small flattened eggs on new shoots near the base of the needles or bud scales. When the eggs hatch, the larvae bore into the bases of the needles. As the larvae mature they begin to tunnel into the shoot tip. Some species overwinter as pupae within the shoot; others drop to the ground and spend the winter there.

All species are attacked by a number of parasites which at times, seem to keep the moth populations in check. Dry weather and poor soil conditions are thought to encourage damage by tip moths.

Moths of the genera *Eucosma*, *Petrova*, *Dioryctria* and *Exoteleia* cause similar damage to pines in various parts of the United States.

References: 36, 50, 86, 129, 153

A. Brown, stunted needles at the tip of a pine twig, caused by the larva of the European pine shoot moth.
B. Pitch accumulation at the site of larval activity.
C. European pine shoot moth larvae exposed in a pitch mass.
D. A European pine shoot moth pupa in a tunneled twig.
E. The European pine shoot moth.

PLATE 13

A. A mugho pine "candle" (shoot) damaged by the European pine shoot moth.
B. Several new pine shoots (candles) showing symptoms of *Rhyacionia buoliana* larval injury.
C. The "crook" symptom of European pine shoot moth injury. The leader recovered but the tree will remain disfigured.
D. A black pine showing the characteristic bushy growth after repeated attack by the European pine shoot moth.
E. A close-up of one of the injured candles from section B.
F. A close-up of an injured twig caused by the European pine shoot moth larva.

PLATE 14

Pine Shoot Borers (Plate 15)

Nine or more species of tip and shoot moths attack pine. The eastern pine shoot borer, *Eucosma gloriola* Heinrich, is a native North American moth. It may be found throughout the natural range of white pine, including eastern Canada south to New Jersey and West Virginia and west to Minnesota and Manitoba. The major host plants are four- to ten-year-old white, Scots, and red pine. Other hosts include the Austrian, jack, mugho and pitch pines and, on occasion, Douglas fir and other conifers.

Damage to the plant is caused by larval feeding and tunneling in the pith of new shoots (C). Either the leader or lateral shoots are attacked, but more often the latter. Mined shoots fade and turn red in the summer, although smaller twigs may redden earlier (G). Such injury may be confused with that of the white pine weevil (Plate 20).

As the larva develops, it cuts into the wood at the base of the burrow but leaves the bark intact. The weakened shoot droops or breaks—this is often the first symptom of attack by the pest.

The loss of needles, and the reduced size of the terminal leader is quite important to the Christmas tree grower. A leader size of eight to fourteen inches is desirable. After a white pine shoot borer attacks its host, only a three- to four-inch stub may remain.

The shoot borer overwinters as a pupa in the soil. Adults emerge any time from late April to early June, depending on the geographical location. Moth emergence in some areas seems to occur shortly after the Scots pine buds burst open. The adult moth has a wingspan of 14–15 mm (D). During the day, the insect rests on the shaded inner foliage of the pine. Eggs are laid on twigs or on needle sheaths, and can be found singly or in twos and threes. These eggs are round, flattened, pale yellow, ½ mm in diameter, and hatch in 10–15 days. The newly hatched larva enters the shoot behind a needle fascicle and develops through five instars (stages) within the shoot over a period of 42–55 days. The larva is of a dirty white color and has a dark head. It can be as long as 13 mm. When fully developed, the larva chews an exit hole and drops to the ground. A light brown pupa is then formed in a loosely woven cocoon either in the top few inches of the soil or in debris.

The jack pine shoot borer, *Eucosma sonomana* Kft., is a western species and occurs throughout the range of ponderosa pine. Feeding habits and damage caused are similar to *E. gloriola*. *E. sonomana* has a wingspan of 20–21 mm. In some areas of the West, larvae of this species cause growth reduction in the leaders of ponderosa and lodgepole pines without causing evident tissue injury. Some insects belonging to the genus *Eucosma* attack cones, thus interfering with seed production.

One parasite has been found to overwinter as a mature larva in its own cocoon which in turn is located inside the host's cocoon. This parasite is an ichneumon wasp of the genus *Glypta*.

References: 50, 63, 64, 65, 66, 81, 153

A. Damage inflicted by the larva of *Eucosma gloriola* to the terminal leader of eastern white pine.
B. The leader of an eastern white pine with the "shepherds crook" symptom.
C. An exposed tunnel in the pith of a new shoot with a shoot borer larva.
D. Pinned specimens of *Eucosma gloriola* (top) and *E. sonomana*. Note the similar color pattern and difference in size.
E. Pupae and a larva of *Eucosma gloriola*.
F,H. Infested Scots pine shoots that have dropped their needles.
G. Red needles on a shoot are a symptom of the presence of the shoot borer larva.

PLATE 15

Cypress Bark Beetles (Plate 16)

Several species of bark beetles, all of the genus *Phloeosinus*, attack trees of the families Cupressaceae and Taxodiaceae. These two families include cypress, juniper, redwoods, and certain other cedar-like trees. In fact, bark beetles found tunneling beneath the bark of limbs or trunks of such trees almost certainly are *Phloeosinus*, for this group of trees has virtually no other bark beetle enemies.

The biology and life history of these pests are quite similar to those of the pine bark beetles (see Plate 19). However, many newly emerged cypress bark beetles have the curious habit of feeding on the twigs of cypresses and certain other plants of the two plant families mentioned above. Twigs are usually attacked at a location between six and twelve inches from their tip. During feeding, the adult beetle hollows out, or deeply grooves, slender twigs which then break easily in the wind. (B). The dead tips, called "flags," often remain on the trees for long periods of time, making them unsightly (A). "Flagging" is very common on Monterey cypress, *Cupressus macrocarpa*, in coastal California.

Flagging, if caused by cypress bark beetles, is not an indication that the tree is declining in health. It does indicate that somewhere in the area a dead or dying cedar-like tree is serving as a breeding place for the beetles. Flagging may continue for many months each year. In the vicinity of San Francisco Bay, however, it occurs mostly during the spring.

Important eastern species of *Phloeosinus* include *P. canadensis* Swaine (about 2 mm long), known as the northern cedar bark beetle, which attacks arborvitae (*Thuja*) in eastern Canada and the northeastern United States (see Plate 17); *P. dentatus* (Say), called the eastern juniper bark beetle, which infests eastern red cedar, *Juniperus virginiana*, and several related trees from Massachusetts to Florida and west to Texas. *P. taxodii* Blackman, the southern cypress bark beetle, attacks bald cypress, *Taxodium distichum*, in the southern United States. In the West, the cypress bark beetles, *P. cupressi* Hopk. and *P. cristatus* Lec., feed on Monterey and other cypresses in California.

References: 1, 36, 50, 153

A. A Monterey cypress with many "flagged" twigs caused by *Phloeosinus cristatus*.
B. Three "flagged" twigs of Monterey cypress. One twig has not yet turned brown.
C. The adult *Phloeosinus cristatus*, 3.5 mm long, on a Monterey cypress twig.
D. A twig showing the nature of adult injury—bark chewed away by the beetle.
E. Gallery systems of *Phloeosinus* beneath the bark of Monterey cypress. Vertical channels were made by the adult beetles. Each lateral channel was made by a single larva.

PLATE 16

Cedar Bark Beetles (Plate 17)

Northern white cedar, commonly called arborvitae, is subject to injury by a small bark beetle, *Phloeosinus canadensis* Sw., also sometimes called the northern cedar bark beetle. This group of beetles (see Plate 16) is quite host-specific, often attacking only a single species, or plants closely related to it. *P. canadensis* occurs in the northeastern part of the United States and throughout eastern Canada. This species is not usually considered a major pest since it attacks mainly twigs, branches, and the bark of weakened trees. After Hurricane Hazel in 1954, when there was a great deal of windthrown and damaged timber in woods and parks, and during the years 1963 through 1967, when the Northeast was plagued by drought during the growing seasons, *P. canadensis* invaded weakened arborvitae trees. Although many tree deaths could have been prevented by sound cultural practices such as the cabling, bracing and watering of injured trees, and the pruning of twisted limbs, a high mortality rate resulted.

Both the larva and adult (C) northern cedar bark beetle injure trees. Each horizontal tunnel is the work of a single larva (D). There were at least 72 larvae in this brood gallery. Another brood gallery on the opposite side of this trunk would have been adequate to kill the tree. Injury to *Juniperus virginiana* resulting from the feeding of adult beetles is limited primarily to the bark (C,E), and, occasionally, the foliage. The beetle, shown at the arrow point in section C, chews holes at twig crotches to produce the "flagged" (or dead) twig as shown in section B. In section E a small quantity of sap has collected and solidified in an attempt to heal the wound. This is an example of a protective mechanism found in many coniferous trees.

The female beetle lays her eggs in a groove cut deeply into the sapwood. The brood develops through the autumn and resumes feeding in the spring. For more details on bark beetles, see Plate 19.

Several other species are found in the East. *Phloeosinus dentatus* (Say) feeds principally on eastern red cedar. *P. taxodii* Blackman is known only in the southern states and feeds on bald cypress, *Taxodium distichum*. Western *Phloeosinus* bark beetles are shown in Plate 16.

Woodpeckers often work in trees infested by bark beetles. In section A, two vertical rows of holes were punched in the bark in a previous season by a woodpecker. Note that the bird has followed one side of the gallery pattern.

References: 1, 12

A. Pit-like scars were caused by woodpeckers in pursuit of *Phloeosinus* larvae in the bark.
B. Dead twigs caused by *Phloeosinus canadensis* adults feeding at the twig crotch.
C. A beetle feeding at a twig crotch.
D. Adult and larval galleries of *Phloeosinus canadensis*. The adult gallery is vertical.
E. The reddish material at the base of the twig is sap that has collected and solidified at the wound site.

PLATE 17

Pine Needle Weevils and Juniper Twig Girdler (Plate 18)

A number of weevils of the genus *Scythropus* feed on the needles of pines in western states. Their damage is distinctive in that the needles are notched intermittently along their length (B). Usually the needle dies beyond the point of damage. Under severe conditions the tree may assume a generally browned appearance.

The best known of these weevils is *S. californicus* Horn which attacks Monterey and Bishop pines and occurs along the Pacific coast. In coastal central California the adults (D) appear in late winter and begin feeding on needles produced the previous year. By May or June the adults have completed their activities and are not seen until the following year. Eggs are laid on year-old growth in an egg chamber. To construct it, the female draws together three adjacent needles and cements them together along their length (C). Upon hatching, the young larvae drop to the ground where they begin tunneling. They sustain themselves throughout this stage on the rootlets of pine. Pupation also occurs in the soil. The life cycle is believed to require two years.

S. californicus attacks only foliage that is two years old or older. It always leaves part of the needle uneaten. The damage done by *Scythropus* can thus be distinguished from that caused by other insect pests such as sawflies.

Although the juniper twig girdler, *Periploca nigra* Hodges, has been known in the eastern United States for more than 50 years, it has never been reported as a pest there. In the mid-1950's the cause of dieback of juniper twigs in California was found to be the twig girdler. The insect is not known to cause damage outside California.

Virtually all species and cultivars of ornamental juniper are attacked. Serious damage seems to be restricted to the junipers with slender stems, such as Tam (Tamariscifolia).

The adult insect is a tiny, black moth. In the San Francisco Bay area moths are active in May, June and July whereas in southern California moths fly during March, April and May. Eggs are laid on the woody stems of juniper. Eggs hatch into tiny larvae which tunnel into the stems. In eight or nine months the larval stage is completed. After a short pupal period, spent in a tunnel beneath the bark, the adult moths appear and emerge from the twigs to begin the cycle again.

Damage is caused by the larval stage of the insect which mines and girdles the stems of juniper beneath the bark (I). The first sign of damage is the appearance of scattered yellow shoots which later die and turn brown. Plants may be infested for two or three years before damage becomes apparent. Entire plants are never killed.

To determine if the insects are present, remove the bark from the lower part of affected juniper twigs and look for the characteristic girdling tunnels (H). Symptoms of twig girdler activity are sometimes confused with those caused by mice which find the thick cover of the juniper planting an ideal place to live. Mice chew the bark from the twigs which then die as a result of this girdling injury. The juniper twig girdler leaves the bark intact and girdles beneath the bark.

Once the twig girdler larva is beneath the bark there are no practical means of killing it. Sprays for control therefore must be applied only during the brief period when the moths are active and laying eggs. The clipping and removing of yellowed or dead twigs will improve the appearance of the juniper planting, but will not control the twig girdler.

References: 36, 93, 145, 158

A. A terminal of Monterey pine showing the dead needle symptom caused by the weevil, *Scythropus californicus*.

B. The notches chewed in the brown needle are another symptom of damage caused by *Scythropus californicus*.

C. *S. californicus* lays its eggs between needles. These two needles were forced apart to show the eggs.

D. An adult *Scythropus californicus*.

E. A view of the head of *Scythropus californicus* showing the long sharp mandibles.

F. Dead or dying twigs in a mass planting of *Juniperus sabina* 'Tamariscifolia' (Tam juniper) caused by *Periploca nigra*.

G. Twig girdler moth exit holes in a juniper twig.

H. Twigs of *Juniperus sabina* girdled by *Periploca nigra*; Arrow 1: loose bark not removed; arrow 2: bark removed to show the depth of the channel.

I. A portion of the bark removed to show the larva of *Periploca nigra*.

PLATE 18

Conifer Bark Beetles (Plate 19)

Over 600 species of beetles are commonly referred to as bark beetles. Some of these are extremely destructive to coniferous forest trees and, at times, to conifers used in parks or around homes. Bark beetles are important enemies of older mature conifers, especially pines. They are more likely to be a problem in areas such as the West and South where suburbs intermingle with large tracts of mature and overmature conifers. The beetles may be attracted to yard trees, especially those weakened by excavation and filling associated with home building.

Certain similarities exist in the life cycle and habits of bark beetles. The beetles usually overwinter beneath the bark of the host tree as larvae (C,F), pupae, or adults (I) depending on the species involved. In the spring, the adult beetles tunnel their way to the bark surface, emerge and fly in search of other trees to attack. Some beetles are attracted to the resinous odors of injured or weakened host trees. The adult (in some species the female, in others the male) initiates the egg-laying gallery after first tunneling through the bark. This gallery lies mostly in the phloem—the spongy inner white bark—though it sometimes involves the xylem or wood. The first beetles to attack a host produce and emit powerful volatile chemicals called pheromones which attract other beetles to the host. Sometimes by sheer numbers alone the beetles are able to overwhelm and kill healthy trees.

Mating of male and female usually occurs in the gallery. Eggs are laid on the sides of the gallery in characteristic patterns for each species. When the eggs hatch the larvae form individual feeding galleries which may radiate out from the egg-laying gallery (G). Other species, *Dendroctonus brevicomis* Leconte in particular form sinuous tunnels which appear to meander aimlessly in the phloem (B).

When feeding is completed the larvae pupate in the inner or outer bark. Emergence from the tree and initiation of a new generation follows. There may be one to six or more generations each year depending on species and geography.

As a general rule, bark beetles attack trees that are dying or in a state of decline due to a variety of stress factors such as drought, mechanical injury, compaction of soil in the root zone, smog, alteration of the water table level by cuts or fills, root rots, etc. Some species apparently are able to attack healthy trees, especially if the healthy tree is near an unhealthy one. Healthy pines located near one that has been struck by lightning often begin to die for this reason. Lightning-struck trees should be removed from the yard as soon as possible, especially in the South where few of them would survive, even if not removed.

Attacks by the various bark beetles characteristically occur in one particular part of the tree. The red turpentine beetle, *Dendroctonus valens* Leconte, and its close relative, the black turpentine beetle, *Dentroctonus terebrans* (Oliv.), restrict their activities to the lower bole (stem). Attack sites are conspicuous in that reddish tubes of pitch and dust protrude an inch or more from the infested tree. The western pine beetle, *Dendroctonus brevicomis* Leconte, attacks the upper mid-bole of the tree though it may subsequently infect the bole above and below that site. Other bark beetles, among them species of *Ips, Pityogenes* and *Pityophthorus*, attack the tops and twigs. *Hylastes* infests the root collar of newly transplanted or weakened young pines. Members of the bark beetle group *Phloeosinus* attack cypress and junipers, where they feed for a short time as adults on the small twigs. See Plates 16 and 17.

References: 36, 50, 153

A. Pines killed by bark beetles.
B. Wandering galleries made by the western pine beetle.
C. Eggs and young larvae of Douglas fir beetle, *Dendroctonus pseudotsugae* Hopkins.
D. A southern pine beetle "pitched out" by a healthy pine.
E. Western pine beetle.
F. Typical bark beetle larva.
G. Typical gallery of Douglas fir beetle. Note the egg-laying gallery at the arrow. Larvae are at the left, at the ends of the feeding galleries.
H. A healed-over Douglas fir beetle gallery that eventually will lead to deterioration of the stem.
I. Adult *Ips* beetles under bark.

PLATE 19

Conifer Twig Weevils (Plate 20)

Taxonomists have now classified the white pine weevil, the Engelmann spruce weevil and the Sitka spruce weevil as members of one species, *Pissodes strobi* (Peck), a name which formerly referred to only the white pine weevil. This species is without doubt the most important one limiting the production of timber from eastern white pine, *Pinus strobus,* and Sitka spruce, *Picea sitchensis.* It also causes serious damage to landscape plantings and Christmas tree plantations of Norway spruce, *Picea abies.* It is known to attack a wide variety of pines and spruces in addition to those listed above, and occasionally even Douglas fir.

This weevil, which kills the top two year's growth of the host tree, causes homeowners a great deal of concern. Weevil attack does not, however, kill the entire tree, although it may become crooked and limby as a result of repeated top killing. To some, the affected tree may be more aesthetically pleasing than a normal one.

A number of related weevils attack the tips and lateral branches of conifers. In the West, *Pissodes terminalis* Hopping attacks various species of pine, occasionally causing extensive damage to young lodgepole pine (1½-3 M in height) in the central Rocky Mountain region. Some very small weevils (about 4 mm) of the genus *Cylindrocopturus* attack and kill small branches and tips of pines and Douglas fir. They are particularly troublesome to Christmas tree plantings. Weevils of the genus *Magdalis* and *Scythropus* (Plate 18) feed on the needles of various conifers. The black vine weevil, *Otiorhynchus sulcatus* (Fab.), feeds on the foliage and causes considerable damage to yew as well as to a number of other conifer and broad-leaved ornamentals (Plate 94). In the South and East, the deodar weevil, *Pissodes nemorensis* Germar, attacks deodar, Atlas cedars and cedar of Lebanon, all well established exotic tree species. A native insect, this weevil is considered a minor pest of the southern pines *Pinus taeda, P. echinata* and *P. palustris.* Adult weevils look much like the white pine weevil and *P. approximatus* (Plate 21) and cause injury during both adult and larval stages. Adult weevils feed on the inner bark, often girdling a stem or twig. Needles turn brownish red and may curl on lightly damaged trees. Adult weevils appear in April or May.

Although the biology of the twig weevils varies by species, a description of that of *Pissodes strobi* follows here as an example.

Adults usually overwinter in the litter on the ground. In the spring, adults fly or crawl to the leaders of suitable host trees. Mating takes place on the leader where from one to a dozen or more pairs may gather. The female excavates a round hole in the bark and deposits from one to five eggs into the cavity (H). She then fills the hole with a plug of mascerated bark. Hundreds of eggs may be deposited in a single leader. The eggs hatch and the larvae feed in the bark, killing the leader of the previous year. While they are feeding, the current year's flush of growth starts, but soon droops over, producing the symptom known as "shepherd's crook" (see Plate 15). The larvae bore into the wood and produce pupal chambers filled with shredded wood and bark. The new adults leave the host by late summer and do some feeding on twigs prior to overwintering. In British Columbia some adult weevils live up to 4 years.

References: 50, 153, 218

A. Drooping tip of Norway spruce, an early indication of attack by the white pine weevil, *Pissodes strobi.*
B. Dead top in pine resulting from weevil attack.
C. Hardened pitch exuded from weevil punctures in the leader of Norway spruce.
D. Adult *Pissodes strobi.*
E. Monterey pine twig has been split to show damage by *Pissodes radiatae.*
F. Evidence of external feeding of *Pissodes radiatae* on Monterey pine.
G. Weevil larva within spruce leader. In larger leaders the larvae do not bore into the pith.
H. Egg-laying punctures at arrow 1; punctures open to show eggs at arrow 2.

PLATE 20

Trunk and Root Collar Weevils (Plate 21)

The pales weevil, *Hylobius pales* (Herbst), is probably the most important pest of newly planted pines in the South(I). Young trees planted in recently cut-over areas are the hosts most likely to be damaged by its activities. The adult weevils are attracted to freshly cut pine stumps in which they lay their eggs. Once the weevils are in an area, however, they feed on living pines, often stripping them clean of bark. Under certain circumstances ornamental pine could be damaged. In the South, if a pine-covered lot is to be cleared for home construction, it is wise to wait a year before planting ornamental pines. There are instances when fresh pine bark and sawdust have attracted enough weevils into a yard to cause damage to young pines.

After feeding on pines the adults mate and the females lay their eggs in the roots of fresh pine stumps or weakened trees. The larvae feed in the roots and reach maturity by fall. When they emerge as adults they (as did their parents) feed on pine bark, buds and needles before entering the soil to overwinter. In most of the southern states, the adults may emerge to continue feeding on warm days throughout the winter. The greatest adult feeding occurs, however, in April and May.

Pachylobius picivorus (Germar), sometimes called the pitch-eating weevil, is similar to the pales weevil in markings and habitat. In the more southern areas *Pachylobius* may be the most common. Both species are widely distributed east of the Great Plains.

Hylobius radicis Buchanan, known as the pine root collar weevil, looks much like the pales weevil. It attacks both young and old pines, especially those growing on poor sites from Minnesota east to the Atlantic Ocean. Scots, jack, red, Austrian, Corsican, and mugho are attacked in the range of the insect. Pitch pine is more resistant and white pine is rarely attacked.

The larvae of the root collar weevil feed in the phloem tissue around the root collar, killing the cambium in the process. A swollen trunk at the ground line and darkened pitch-infiltrated soil around the root collar indicate advanced infestation. Larvae complete development in June and July and adults emerge from August through September. The adults overwinter in the soil or in bark crevices. Eggs are laid mostly in the spring, but this weevil, like its relatives, is long-lived and may continue to feed and lay eggs throughout the summer. In fact some females may overwinter a second time and continue to lay eggs the second summer.

The weevil *Pissodes approximatus* Hopkins, which is very closely related to the white pine weevil (some people don't believe it is really different), sometimes attacks small transplanted pines and dead and dying trees. Occasionally, the adults feed on branches of healthy trees (A,B).

Another species, *Pissodes nemorensis* Germ., feeds both on stems and twigs. See page 54.

References: 50, 129, 273, 320

A. Douglas fir twig killed by *Pissodes approximatus*.
B. Close-up of a twig showing adult *Pissodes approximatus* feeding injury.
C. Sections of bark showing larval galleries of *Pissodes approximatus*.
D. A pupal chamber in bark. Close-up of section G.
E. Larva of *Pissodes approximatus*. It is difficult to distinguish between this larva and the larvae of other species mentioned in the text.
F. Adult *Pissodes approximatus*. Note how it blends into the background.
G,H. Root collar showing pupal chambers of *Pissodes approximatus*.
I. Adult pales weevil, *Hylobius pales*, and typical damage caused by it.

PLATE 21

Cypress Bark Moth (Plate 22)

Several members of the plant families Cupressaceae and Taxodiaceae are attacked by the cypress bark moth, *Laspeyresia cupressana* (Kearf.). This moth has a limited distribution and is known only in coastal California from Mendocino to San Diego counties. Monterey cypress, *Cupressus macrocarpa*, is a favored host and its cones, branch nodes, trunks, and damaged areas of trees are subject to infestation by the larvae.

Laspeyresia passes through two complete generations each year, one in spring-summer and the other in fall-winter. The adults, which have gray and white mottled wings with a spread of about 18 mm, lay eggs on suitable plant parts. The larvae tunnel in. Large quantities of reddish frass (C,D) are expelled during feeding beneath the bark or within cones. Extensive resin flow (A) often accompanies attacks on the trunk and may persist over several years. The larvae tend to feed only locally, seldom moving far from the initial site of invasion. The death of plant parts—excepting some loss in germination of seeds from *Laspeyresia*-infested cones—seldom, if ever, results directly from the feeding of this insect. Following the completion of feeding, the mature larva, which is 13 mm long and creamy white with a brown head, pupates within the plant and later emerges as a moth. The cast skins of the pupae frequently protrude from the infested site after the moths have escaped (B).

Laspeyresia commonly attacks sites on trees already infested by the fungus *Coryneum cardinale*, a known killer of trees. *Laspeyresia* moths are capable of serving as carriers of the fungus spores and may aid in the spread of the disease. Therefore, while it is no coincidence that the cypress bark moth and *Coryneum* commonly attack the same tree, it is the disease which frequently results in the death of branches and sometimes entire trees.

References: 36, 108, 109

A. Site of a fungus canker, caused by *Coryneum cardinale*, on trunk of a young Monterey cypress. Such sites are commonly infested by larvae of the cypress bark moth.
B. Site of infestation by a cypress bark moth, *Laspeyresia cupressana*. Note extruded larval skin of moth which has already emerged.
C. Trunk of Monterey cypress showing frass expelled by larvae of the cypress bark moth.
D. Monterey cypress cones infested by cypress bark moth larvae, showing copious quantities of frass (see circle) expelled by larvae during feeding.

PLATE 22

Pitch Moths (Plate 23)

Several *Vespamima* moths attack pines and certain other ornamental conifers in many parts of the United States. The adults are clear winged moths which resemble yellow jacket wasps.

V. sequoiae (H. Edwards) is a common pest in the West of Monterey pine, *Pinus radiata;* ponderosa pine, *Pinus ponderosa;* dwarf beach pine, *Pinus contorta* var. *bolanderi;* and sugar pine, *Pinus lambertiana.* Eggs are laid in wounds or on the bark of the trunk or limbs. The larvae tunnel into the inner bark, where a cavity is excavated, and feed there on exudations of resin (G). Large accumulations of pitch and frass form on the outside of the tree at the point of attack. New attacks often occur at the site of old ones. As the years go by, these masses may reach four to six inches in diameter. Pupation takes place within the pitch mass. The larval stage of *V. sequoiae* in California commonly lasts two years.

V. pini (Kellicott) causes injury similar to that caused by *V. sequoiae.* Its coniferous hosts can be found along the Atlantic coast, in New England, the Midwest, the Appalachian regions and southward, and in eastern Canada. Hosts include Austrian pine, *Pinus nigra;* eastern white pine, *Pinus strobus;* Scots pine, *Pinus sylvestris;* jack pine, *Pinus banksiana;* white spruce, *Picea glauca;* Norway spruce, *Picea abies;* and Colorado blue spruce, *Picea pungens. V. pini* is reported to require two to three years to complete its life cycle. Adult moths appear only during the summer months.

V. novaroensis (H. Edwards) attacks spruce, pine and Douglas fir in the western states and causes a pitch mass indistinguishable from that of *V. sequoiae.*

Although apparently healthy pines have been attacked by *V. sequoiae* it is believed that trees in a state of decline (due to an excess or deficiency of water, for example) are especially attractive to this insect. Trees which have been mechanically injured, even by pruning, also appear to be susceptible to the attack of these moths, for their attack sites often are located where the tree has been injured (D).

Vespamima by itself is not considered a serious pest, since the damage caused by it is local. However, when repeated attacks occur year after year in many places on the same tree the welfare of the tree may be a cause for concern.

Petrova albicapitana (Busck), known as the northern pitch twig moth, is widely distributed on young jack pine, *Pinus banksiana,* and lodgepole pine, *Pinus murrayana,* throughout the natural ranges of these trees in North America. The young larva forms a blister-like nodule on one of the growing terminals of the host. After spending one winter under a nodule, the larva moves to a new site, usually a crotch on the tree, and forms a second nodule. Here the larva completes its feeding stage and undergoes the pupal stage. The insect requires two years to complete its life cycle, and adult moths appear only during the early summer months. A number of other *Petrova* species cause similar damage to pine (C), spruce, and firs in widely scattered regions of North America.

References: 19, 36, 93, 153, 287

A. The bark of a Monterey pine showing numerous pitch masses mixed with "sawdust" at the opening made by *Dendroctonus valens.* The symptom is complicated by young larvae of *Vespamima sequoiae,* also present.

B. A mechanical scar on Monterey pine makes an ideal location for *Vespamima sequoiae* larvae. Note the accumulations of pitch.

C. The larva of the pitch twig moth, *Petrova comstockiana,* and pitch mass on Scots pine.

D,E. Pitch masses on the trunk of blue spruce caused by *Vespamima pini.*

F,G. Pitch masses opened to show the larvae. Section F is of *Vespamima pini;* Section G is of *Vespamima sequoiae.*

PLATE 23

Balsam Twig Aphid (Plate 24)

The balsam twig aphid, *Mindarus abietinus* Koch, has a complex life history. A single generation occurs each year, but three distinct forms are produced. In the spring, the overwintering eggs (E,F) hatch. After three molts, the mature, wingless stem mother (fundatrix) is ready to begin producing young. Her offspring gather in a colony around the bluish-gray mother (A) where they feed on old needles as well as the newly developing bud.

The progeny of the stem mother is the intermediate form called sexuparae. This form also undergoes three molts. After each molt, it produces a white, waxy covering over its body (C). It feeds primarily on new shoots. Of all the forms it is most injurious to the tree. The mature aphids of this form have wings and produce the final form called sexuales.

The sexuales are either males or egg-laying females, and they, too, feed on needles. After mating, the mature females produce several large eggs that are laid in bark crevices (E,F). The presence of brown eggs, covered with tiny rods of white wax, are conspicuous and are a useful index of the amount of injury that may occur during the next year.

Balsam twig aphids produce copious amounts of honeydew. Droplets are often found scattered over the surface of needles (G). If the aphid population is heavy, shoots may become saturated and needles may ahere to one another and be very sticky to touch. Eventually, rain will wash off the honeydew, often before black sooty mold fungi have a chance to grow.

Aphid feeding curls and twists the needles, killing some and leaving roughened twigs. Curled and twisted needles seem by far to be the most important type of injury. Such needles remain deformed as long as they remain on the tree although injury occurs primarily during the month of May. The major hosts of this insect are fir and spruce, both of which can tolerate large aphid populations. Over a period of years, however, even the healthiest of trees may lose vigor and become subject to the ravages of pathogenic organisms. Heavy infestations on specimen ornamental trees mar their appearance. In Christmas tree plantations, curled, twisted needles reduce sales value.

Balsam twig aphids are likely to be found wherever balsam fir, white fir and spruce are grown. They are known from Maine to Washington, in the Rocky Mountain region and in the higher elevations of the Appalachian Mountains. (See also Plate 127.)

References: 1, 50, 249

A. Three stem mother aphids, bluish-gray, with their offspring feeding on balsam fir buds.
B. New twigs that appear wet with honeydew.
C. Immature second-stage aphids. A large quantity of a white waxy substance adheres to their bodies and to needles.
D. A cluster of very young second-stage aphids at the tip of an opening bud.
E,F. Overwintering eggs, laid in late June, covered with tiny rods of white wax.
G. Several immature third-stage sexual forms that will later produce eggs. Note droplets of honeydew.
H. Typical needle injury versus healthy needles of balsam fir.
I. A mature second-stage winged form.
J. A young stem mother just hatched from the overwintering egg.

PLATE 24

Balsam Woolly Aphid (Plate 25)

The balsam woolly aphid, *Adelges piceae* (Ratzeburg), is not a true aphid, but is a member of a family closely related to aphids, Phylloxeridae. This pest of true firs (*Abies* spp.) was introduced into the United States from Europe or Asia around the turn of the century. From that time it has spread throughout the United States and Canada and has killed billions of feet of the finest fir timber on the continent. In some areas it has become a pest of yard trees and other ornamental firs. It does not attack Douglas fir, *Pseudotsuga menziesii*, a tree that is not a true fir, and it does minimal damage to Noble fir, *Abies piceae*.

The balsam woolly aphid has a strange life history. In the United States the entire population consists of females. The adults are less than 1 mm long, and are purplish to black when the straw-colored wax is removed. They are wingless and the legs are visible only under high magnification. They remain attached to the tree, by means of deeply penetrating mouthparts, throughout their adult lives.

The eggs hatch into active crawlers that move around on the host tree until they find a suitable place to settle, or until blown by the wind to another host. Because the crawlers are so small, they are capable of being carried great distances by the wind. A very small percent of windblown crawlers reach suitable hosts; however, this is thought to be the principal means of dispersion from one host tree to another. Once the crawler has found a suitable site it inserts its long sucking mouthparts, which are several times longer than its body, into the outer bark and sucks juices from the tree. White wax ribbons are secreted from glands along the sides and back of the crawler after it has been feeding for a while. Soon the entire body becomes covered with a white woolly material (see Figure 7).

An early sign of damage on some trees is a swelling or "gouting" (C) of the ends of twigs. The swelling is apparently caused by a growth-promoting substance which the aphid injects into the tree. When the infestation is heavy, the whole trunk of the tree becomes covered by the white "wool" of the aphids (D). New growth virtually ceases on heavily infested firs. More susceptible firs such as balsam, *Abies balsamea*, or subalpine fir, *A. lasiocarpa*, may be killed before the terminal swelling occurs.

There are two generations per year in the Northeast, occasionally three in the southern Applachians, and up to four in the West.

References: 13, 95, 153, 201

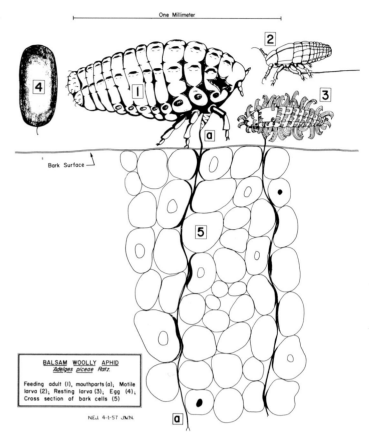

One Millimeter

Bark Surface

BALSAM WOOLLY APHID
Adelges piceae Ratz.

Feeding adult (1), mouthparts (a), Motile larva (2), Resting larva (3), Egg (4), Cross section of bark cells (5)

NEJ 4-1-57 JWN.

Figure 7.

A. An uninfested silver fir on the right and one whose height growth has virtually ceased due to infestation by the balsam woolly aphid.
B. Aphids on twig of Pacific silver fir.
C. "Gout" produced by feeding of woolly aphids.
D. Woolly secretions on the trunk of infested tree.
E. Adult (at arrow) and eggs. Highly magnified.
F. Close-up of woolly secretions on fir stem.
G. Newly settled crawlers (at arrows) on twig of silver fir.

PLATE 25

Woolly "Aphids" of Pine, Spruce, and Larch (Plate 26)

The insects illustrated in this plate and commonly called aphids are not true aphids, though they are closely related. They belong to the family Phylloxeridae (=Chermidae = Adelgidae) and occur primarily on conifers (see Plate 191). Fourteen species of adelgids (the correct term) are currently known. Most of these are found on spruce and other conifers.

Two species of the so-called woolly "aphids" commonly feed on larch in the Northeast. *Adelges lariciatus* Patch attacks the needles of larch and causes galls on Norway, black, Colorado and white spruces. Distribution is limited to the northern states and, in Canada, to Manitoba, Saskatchewan and Alberta. The woolly larch aphid, *Adelges laricis* Vallot (=*Adelges strobilobius*), feeds on the needles of *Larix decidua* (A,C,F). In the summer, when the infestation is at its height, the tree will appear to be covered with snow. Injury is negligible unless heavy infestations occur over several consecutive years. *A. laricis* may be found from New England west to Wisconsin and south to Maryland. It, like *A. lariciatus*, produces galls on spruce. These galls have very short needles (less than one-third the normal length) protruding from them and are much more pineapple-shaped than those made by the common eastern spruce gall aphid (Plate 41).

Trunks of white pine trees often have a whitewashed appearance when infested with the pine bark aphid, *Pineus strobi* (Hartig) (D,E). The pine bark aphid, accidentally introduced from Europe, attacks white, Scots and Austrian pines. It may be found in the United States and Canada nearly everywhere the hosts grow. Light infestations cause little damage, but persistent and heavy infestations will cause reduced growth of the tree and may eventually lead to its death. The pine bark aphid has no alternate host.

Like other "aphids" of this group the pine leaf chermid (adelgid), *Pineus pinifoliae* (Fitch), has a complex and only partially known life cycle of two years. It can be found in both eastern and western United States and Canada. Typically, its hosts are spruce and white pine. It has five distinct forms. The overwintering form is found on spruce at the base of the buds. These buds become galled, from adelgid feeding activity, and when fully developed look somewhat like small hairy cones. The hairs are sometimes described as thin scales. The gall is a symptom which occurs in the spring although it remains on the twig indefinitely. There are many chambers inside each gall. The gall turns brown by mid-June and the chambers crack open, allowing the insect inside to emerge. The gall insect form, which has wings, flies to the needles of white pine, where it sucks out sap, causing the needles to turn yellow. At this stage these adelgids look much like those shown in section F. They then lay eggs under their bodies and upon hatching crawl down the needles to the new shoots. As this new form develops, white wax appears over the individual bodies of the mass of insects making them clearly visible.

The feeding activities cause the new pine shoots to droop—an early summer symptom. By mid-summer the drooped portion may turn red and die. When heavy infestations of the chermid occur, most of the new shoots die and assume a striking appearance suggestive of late frost injury.

It should be remembered that on white pine the pine leaf chermid has leaf forms and twig or shoot forms and that their physical appearance is different.

Several other species of adelgids, distinguishable only by entomology specialists, attack and on occasion cause significant injury to both western and eastern pines.

References: 14, 50, 57, 153, 167, 169

A. A heavy infestation of *Adelges laricis* on larch, *Larix decidua*. Photograph was taken in early June in central New York.
B. Adelgid nymph on the needle of a white pine. Nymph is possibly *Pineus pinifoliae*.
C,F. The white cottony objects on the larch needles are woolly larch aphids, *Adelges laricis*.
D,E. A heavy infestation of pine bark aphids, *Pineus strobi*.

PLATE 26

Aphids on Conifers (Plate 27)

A number of aphids feed on conifers and cause various types of damage, including discoloration and deformation of needles, premature needle fall, reduction of shoot growth, sticky excretions and even death of the tree. Only a few of these aphids are illustrated here.

Several species of the genus *Cinara* attack conifers throughout the United States. These aphids, many of which are quite large, long-legged and almost spider-like in appearance, feed on the bark of the smaller twigs and the main stems of small trees. A complex of three species causes serious damage to young Douglas fir. One of these, *Cinara pseudotsugae* (Williams), is illustrated in section A. *Cinara sabinae* G. & P., an important pest of juniper in the Rocky Mountain region, causes the foliage of the infested junipers to turn brown prematurely and to fall. A closely related species, *Cinara tujafilina* (Del Guercio), a brown aphid with a touch of white bloom, causes foliage to turn brown and often kills branches of red cedar, arborvitae (*Thuja* sp.) and cypress in both the West and the East. On the East Coast this aphid is found from Maine to Florida. A complex of five or more species, the most important of which is probably *Cinara atlantica* (Wilson), attacks southern pines. *Cinara strobi* (Fitch), the white pine aphid, has been known to severely reduce growth and at times kill young eastern white pine.

These *Cinara* species occur in large colonies on the stems of conifers. They are sometimes accompanied by ants (A) which feed on honeydew produced by the aphids. Often, affected trees are blackened by a sooty mold that grows on honeydew. A primary problem around the home, city or park is the dripping of the honeydew onto cars, picnic tables and sidewalks.

The green spruce aphid, *Elatobium* (=*Neomyzaphis*) *abietinum* (Walker), a most ruinous pest of blue and other spruces in the West has also been reported in North Carolina. It kills all but the new needles, leaving the tree looking bare and sickly. It sometimes takes five or more years for an affected blue spruce to recover its normal complement of luxurious foliage. This aphid attacks early in the spring and completes its development before the damage is evident. The aphid tends to settle on a single needle and remain in the same position for long periods, frequently until the injured needle is about ready to drop. By the time the homeowner notices the damage, there is little evidence of the insect itself.

Eulachnus rileyi (Williams), feeds on the needles of Scots, Virginia, Austrian, mugho, red, eastern white and other pines. It is gray in color and accounts for its occasionally used common name, powdery pine needle aphid. Like the spruce aphid, it causes premature needle fall. Unlike the spruce aphid, *E. rileyi* may be found throughout the growing season. Christmas tree plantations often suffer severe damage. This aphid is widely distributed in the East.

Eulachnus agilis (Kaltenbach), often called the spotted pine aphid (G) because of numerous black spots on its back, feeds on second and third year needles of Scots and red pine. It is particularly damaging under plantation conditions. The initial symptom is chlorosis, followed by browning and premature needle drop. The aphid is very active and difficult to capture. There are two peaks in its population cycle, the first occurring in May and the second in late summer. *E. agilis* is common in the Appalachian region as far north as central New York and in Ohio.

The balsam twig aphid, because of its importance in the Northeast, is treated separately in Plate 24.

References: 33, 36, 50, 140, 146, 153

A. *Cinara pseudotsugae* aphids on Douglas fir bark being tended by ants.
B. Adult *Cinara* sp. on Douglas fir.
C. Parasitized *Cinara* sp. The larva of small wasps are inside the aphid skeleton as shown at arrow points. (See also Figure 23 on page 266)
D. *Mindarus* species on Pacific silver fir, *Abies amabilis*. See Plate 24.
E. Eggs of the white pine aphid on needles of *Pinus resinosa*.
F. A cluster of *Cinara curvipes* on the bark of *Abies concolor*.
G. *Eulachnus agilis*, sometimes called the spotted pine aphid. (Photo courtesy Department of Entomology, Penn. State University)

PLATE 27

69

Conifer Spittlebugs (Plate 28)

A number of species of spittlebugs feed on both broad-leaved and coniferous ornamental plants throughout the United States. Certainly the most striking characteristic of these insects is the frothy mass of "spittle" which clings to foliage produced by the immature spittlebug to keep it moist and protect it from many natural enemies. Spittle masses vary in size according to the species of spittlebug, stage of nymphal development and the number of nymphs contributing to its formation. Sometime the frothy material completely encompasses a cluster of pine cones.

The most significant spittlebugs found on ornamentals overwinter in the egg stage on the host plant or on weeds or other vegetation close by. In the spring the eggs hatch and the tiny nymphs insert their sucking mouthparts into living vegetation to feed on plant sap. While feeding, the insect produces a droplet of clear fluid which completely surrounds its body. Bubbles of air are incorporated into the fluid by the nymph, giving rise to the characteristic spittle mass. The size of the mass depends upon the size of the nymph or the number of nymphs congregating at the same feeding site. Rains, if heavy, wash away the fluid, but it quickly reappears when dry weather returns.

Some spittlebug species complete their development on the host on which the eggs were laid. Others feed initially on weeds or other low-growing vegetation, crawl to taller plants, and then on to ornamentals.

Most adult spittlebugs are blunt, wedge-shaped insects. They are gray to brown in color, and measure 6 to 12 mm in length, depending on the species. The adult is active; it can either hop or fly. Many spittlebugs undergo a single generation each year. Two generations of some spittlebugs occur annually, which ex-plains the appearance of new nymphs as late as October in some areas.

The Saratoga spittlebug, *Aphrophora saratogensis* (Fitch), is considered to be the most destructive of the spittlebugs that attack ornamental trees. This species is a pest of pines and certain other conifers growing in the northeastern and north-central states. Damage to the host can result from the withdrawal of sap by the adults, the blockage of conducting tissue by pitch that infiltrates the feeding punctures and/or the entrance of a fungus into the tree through the punctures. Symptoms of attack are dieback of plant tips, tiny punctures on twigs, most abundant on one-year-old growth, and brownish flecks on the surface of the wood at puncture sites—visible when the bark is removed. Nymphs feed on several herbaceous plant species, and, as they develop, many individuals migrate to sweet fern and brambles. Destruction of the nymphal host plants will control the pest. The peak of adult activity occurs from mid-July to mid-August.

A few spittlebug species cause a shortening of internodes or deformation of foliage on ornamental plants. Most of them, however, do not cause any noticeable injury to plants although their spittle masses are considered unsightly by some people.

Spittlebug adults look somewhat like large leafhoppers. Most of the economic species are brown and not easily seen. A colorful spittlebug, *Prosapia bicinata* (Say), occasionally injures holly (F,G). The young holly leaves become stunted or distorted, and older foliage becomes discolored. This spittlebug occurs from Massachusetts to Florida and west to Kansas and Texas.

References: 83, 304, 312

A. Spittle masses produced by *Philaenus spumarius* on ponderosa pine.
B. Spittle removed to disclose nymphs of the pine spittlebug, *Aphrophora parallela*, on Scots pine.
C,D. A western spittlebug, *Clastoptera juniperina*, on *Juniperus chinensis*. Note nymph at arrow.
E. Spittle masses of *Clastoptera arizonana* on *Acacia cardiophylla*.
F,G. An adult spittlebug, *Prosapia bicinata*. It occasionally feeds on holly. The immature spittlebugs are found on grasses.

PLATE 28

Mealybugs of Taxus and Pine, and the Woolly Pine Scale (Plate 29)

There are several species of mealybugs that feed on *Taxus* (Yew).

The taxus mealybug, *Dysmicoccus wistariae* (Green) (=*Pseudococcus cuspidatae* Rau), is known to occur in Massachusetts, New York, Connecticut, New Jersey, Ohio, and is believed to occur in other northeastern and central states. Severely infested plants may be sparsely foliated and the remaining needles and twigs caked with honeydew and black sooty mold. The taxus mealybugs feed on the bark tissue of the trunk and branches (B). When present in moderate numbers, they cluster in the crotches of twigs and branches. Adult females are present from June to August and begin giving birth to living young in early summer. In New Jersey, the taxus mealybug spends the winter as a first-stage nymph. Probably two or more generations occur each year in New Jersey and further south. Schread (253) reported a single generation in Connecticut. This species has been collected from other woody plants such as rhododendron, dogwood and maple, but large populations have not been reported.

The grape mealybug, *Pseudococcus maritimus* (Ehrhorn), feeds on woody as well as other perennial plants including tubers and corms. It has been a troublesome and persistent pest of *Taxus* in Ohio and other north-central states. Biological studies of this insect's association with grape have been done, mostly in central and western states where there are two generations per year. There are also two generations produced each year on *Taxus* in Ohio. The grape mealybug overwinters as an egg, or first instar crawler. The crawler ranges in color from yellow to brown. After the period of winter dormancy it is quite active. Adults are about 6 mm long, are dark purple in color, and are covered with a uniformly distributed white waxy powder. Filaments of wax extend from the margin of the body and from the posterior end. Except for size the adults look much like those shown in section B. Hosts for the grape mealybug include *Grevillea* sp., English ivy, ginkgo, laburnum, *Citrus*, pear, Japanese quince and Persian walnut. See Plates 131 and 132 for other mealybugs of deciduous trees.

The woolly pine scale, *Pseudophillippia quaintancii* Cockerell, is one of the soft scales (see page 296) but, in appearance, may be confused with mealybugs. It is covered with a white fleecy-looking secretion (C). The body of the mature female is greenish-brown, hemispherical and 2 to 2.5 mm in length (D-1). The biology and habits of this scale are unknown. First instar nymphs or crawlers (E-2) have been found in mid-June near Richmond, Virginia. Much honeydew is produced and colonized by sooty mold fungi. The sooty mold may blacken the pine needles as well as clusters of scales.

Hosts are limited to pine species, including mugho, loblolly, longleaf, pitch, Scots and table mountain pines. The woolly pine scale is known to occur from New York to Florida and Louisiana, and may occur in mixed populations with the mealybug *Oracella acuta* (Lobdell). *O. acuta* is presumed to be a North American species first described from pine in Mississippi and known to occur in the southeastern states from the Atlantic Coast west to Texas. It has also been reported on shortleaf pine from Pennsylvania. Other hosts recorded for *O. acuta* include loblolly and longleaf pines.

The mealybug is 2–3 mm long and is found enclosed in a whitish resinous cell, open at one end, from which the abdomen protrudes. Cells are attached to twigs near the bases of needles. Both young and old trees sustain direct injury resulting from insect feeding as well as indirect injury resulting from the interference of sooty mold. Photosynthesis, hence growth, is reduced when anything interrupts or reduces the quality of light reaching the needles.

The mealybug is distinguished from the cottony pine scale by its crystalline, resinous covering.

References: 184, 211, 253, 305

A. Typical appearance of mealybug-infested taxus.
B. Female taxus mealybugs, *Dysmicoccus wistariae*, feeding on a twig. Fully grown mealybugs are about 8 mm long.
C. Fleecy appearance of woolly pine scale. *Pseudophillippia quaintancii* attached to the twig.
D,E. Enlarged view of fleece-covered adult females of woolly pine scale: (1) adult female with fleece removed, (2) crawlers or first-instar nymphs, (3) eggs, (4) a coccid insect of uncertain identity—possibly the mealybug *Oracella acuta*.

PLATE 29

Golden Mealybug (Plate 30)

Plants of the genus *Araucaria* come from South America, New Zealand and Australia. They are tropical or subtropical evergreen trees, popular because of their unusual form. When *Araucaria bidwellii* was brought from New Zealand to North America it brought with it the golden mealybug, *Nipaecoccus aurilanatus* (Maskell). This species has now become a serious pest in California. It causes needle discoloration and reduces the growth rate of *Agathis* sp., *Araucaria bidwellii*, *A. heterophylla*, and *Diplacus longiflorus*.

Eggs are laid in a round spherical mass enclosed in a thin white cottony web (B). The young nymphs are dark with white furry patches (C). The adult has a characteristic longitudinal band of gold-colored "felt" on its upper surface with small patches around its edges. Adult females range up to 3 mm in length. Several generations occur each year.

Nipaecoccus nipae (Maskell) attacks palms (particularly queen palm, *Arecastrum romanzoffianum*), *Morus* sp., and *Persea* sp., in Florida, Louisiana and California. An introduced predator—the lady beetle, *Cryptolaemus montrouzieri* Mulsant—is an effective natural enemy of *N. aurilanatus* and other species of mealybugs. Larvae of the lady beetle are shown in sections A and F. These are clothed in white fluffy wax. The adult beetle (H) is about 4 mm long. It is a predator in both adult and larval stages. The beetles have been reared in large numbers and introduced into several states. They have become established in California, Florida and perhaps other states along the Gulf Coast, but since they cannot tolerate cold weather they must be reintroduced each growing season into regions which experience cold weather.

Eriococcus araucariae Maskell is a scale that resembles a mealybug. It was originally described in New Zealand and is now believed to occur wherever its hosts, *Araucaria* spp. are grown. The specimens illustrated in this plate came from California.

So far as is known they feed exclusively in the axils of leaflets (E). Several generations occur every year, depending upon temperature and other climatic conditions. The adult female makes an egg sac in which hundreds of yellow eggs are deposited (G).

References: 36, 182

A. Adult mealybugs, *Nipaecoccus aurilanatus*, and their eggs. At arrow: the larva of a lady beetle, *Cryptolaemus montrouzieri*.
B. Adult mealybugs and an egg mass (at arrow). Recently hatched young (shown in circle) are black with white spots on their backs.
C. Mealybug nymphs.
D. Heavy infestation of mealybugs on *Araucaria* twig.
E. A scale insect *Eriococcus araucariae*, on *Araucaria excelsa*.
F. A magnified view of the lady beetle, *Cryptolaemus montrouzieri*, larva.
G. Egg sac of *Eriococcus araucariae* opened to show yellow eggs.
H. An adult *Cryptolaemus montrouzieri*, a lady beetle.

PLATE 30

Irregular Pine Scale and Monterey Pine Scale (Plate 31)

The irregular pine scale, *Toumeyella pinicola* Ferris, is one of the most common and probably the most destructive scale insects attacking pine in California. It infests Monterey pine, *Pinus radiata;* Bishop pine, *Pinus muricata;* Canary Island pine, *Pinus canariensis;* dwarf mugho pine; *Pinus mugho* var. *mughus;* Aleppo pine, *Pinus halepensis;* Italian stone pine, *Pinus pinea;* and knobcone pine, *Pinus attenuata.* Monterey pine is attacked far more frequently than the others.

Scale insects reduce the vigor of trees by sucking plant juices; severely infested trees suffer retarded growth. Old needles turn yellow and die (B). Young trees may die if exceptionally heavy scale infestations are left uncontrolled for a period of years.

As the scales feed they produce vast quantities of sticky honeydew, which collects on the needles, branches and trunk. Sooty mold fungi colonize the honeydew and blacken the tree (C). Ants and yellow jackets seek the honeydew as food and create a nuisance by their presence.

The insect overwinters on the twigs of the pine tree. All the scale insects present during the winter are females. They are approximately 6 mm in diameter, robust and dimpled, and more or less circular in outline when viewed from above. They are mottled and resemble chips of marble (E). Immature male scales (H), which resemble grains of rice, may occur in large numbers on the needles.

The irregular pine scale may occasionally be found on the same tree with the Monterey pine scale, *Physokermes insignicola* (Craw.), although the latter species is not a common one. The mature female insects (F) are about the same size as the irregular pine scale, but they are dark, shiny, and bead-like in appearance. Males are found on the needles.

In southern California, the young crawlers of irregular pine scale begin to emerge from beneath the body of the adult females as early as mid-February. In the San Francisco Bay area crawler emergence begins in late April. During its life each adult female produces up to 2000 young. These crawlers are orange-yellow, oval, and distinctly flattened (G). They are easily visible as they crawl over, and settle on, the shoots and needles.

After settling, the young scales enlarge as they suck juices from the tree. In late summer tiny winged adult males emerge, mate with the still immature females, and then die. The females remain fixed on the shoots and continue to enlarge until spring, when they produce crawlers. Only one generation of the insect occurs each year.

References: 36, 152, 205

A. A young Monterey pine tree severely infested by the irregular pine scale, *Toumeyella pinicola.* This tree subsequently died.

B. The reduced needle length and the yellowing and browning of needles was caused by the irregular pine scale.

C. Blackened foliage results from sooty mold fungi; the fungus feeds on honeydew produced by the irregular pine scale.

D. Irregular pine scale females encrusted on a twig; this is their typical late winter appearance.

E. A single female irregular pine scale.

F. Monterey pine scale, *Physokermes insignicola,* females on twig of Monterey pine.

G. Newly hatched crawlers of the irregular pine scale on a needle.

H. Male pupal cases of the irregular pine scale on needles.

I. Settled crawlers of male irregular pine scales on needle.

J,K. Encrustations of irregular pine scale females on twigs of Monterey pine, showing typical appearance in the spring.

PLATE 31

Pine Tortoise Scale and Spruce Bud Scale (Plate 32)

Toumeyella parvicornis (Cockerell) (=*numismaticum*), known as the pine tortoise scale, is a common and sometimes serious pest of several species of pine. Its known range extends from the Dakotas and Nebraska eastward to New York and New Jersey and southward into Florida. The preferred hosts are Scots pine, *Pinus sylvestris,* and jack pine, *Pinus banksiana.* Also susceptible to infestation, but to a lesser degree than Scots or jack pine, are Austrian pine, *Pinus nigra;* red pine, *Pinus resinosa;* and several of the southern pines.

The immature female scales, which are brown in color, wrinkled, and more or less circular in outline when viewed from above, overwinter on the twigs of the tree. In the spring, development resumes. The females reach maturity in June in the more northerly parts of this scale's range. When mature, they are about 6 mm in diameter (C). Eggs are laid beneath the body of the adult female and the young scales, or crawlers, begin to appear in late June and early July. The young scales crawl away from the body of the parent, insert their long, slender mouthparts into the plant tissue, and begin to feed. Very soon thereafter the young scale's legs become functionless and the insect remains fixed at the feeding site. Crawlers are often dispersed from the tree on which they were borne by the wind, or are carried away by birds upon whose feet they happen sometimes to crawl. A high proportion of crawlers never reach suitable host plants. Yet because the parent scale is able to produce about 500 young, it is not necessary for more than a few of these to survive to maintain high populations.

The male scales develop differently than the females. After feeding for about one month, the males enter a brief pupal, or resting, stage. They then emerge as tiny winged insects, which fly about in search of females. The adult male has nonfunctional mouthparts and hence cannot feed; after mating, which must occur within a day or two, the male dies. The mated, but still immature, female remains immobile on a twig of the host pine and enters a state of hibernation with the onset of cool weather in the fall. There is never more than a single generation each year.

Young trees are more heavily attacked by the pine tortoise scale than are older trees. Generally, the lower foliage supports greater numbers of these insects than foliage higher in the tree. Needle yellowing, short needle growth, branch mortality, or the death of the entire tree can result from infestations of the pine tortoise scale. The degree of injury is related to the intensity of the infestation. The scales excrete large quantities of honeydew, which is colonized by sooty mold fungi. The infested tree, or parts of it, appears as though it has been dusted by coal soot.

The spruce bud scale, *Physokermes piceae* (Schrank), is a pest of various species of spruce, especially Norway spruce, *Picea abies.* It occurs throughout the northeastern states and Ontario, Canada, west to Minnesota and south to Maryland. On the Pacific coast, it is known in Oregon and California.

The mature scales are globular, reddish brown, 3 mm in diameter, and are typically found in clusters of three to eight at the base of the new twig growth (G). Because they so closely resemble the buds on the twig their presence is often overlooked upon casual inspection of the host (F). The lower limbs of the spruce are far more likely to be infested, and in greater numbers, than the upper branches. When infestations are great, low branches are often killed. Weakened trees are said to support higher numbers of bud scales than are healthy trees.

One generation of this insect occurs annually. According to Fenton (100) the young overwinter on the undersides of spruce needles, remaining dormant until late March. At that time, in Wisconsin, when temperatures are high enough they move about and in April the females move to the twigs and complete their development. Eggs are retained within the body cavity. The young crawlers begin to appear about June 1. Upon settling on the new growth, the scales begin to feed and to excrete honeydew, which supports the growth of sooty mold fungi. The mold is black and gives the tree an unthrifty appearance. Tree growth is reportedly suppressed under conditions of severe attack.

References: 50, 100, 171, 180, 239

A. A row of Scots pine attacked by the pine tortoise scale. The tree at right of center has been killed by the scale infestation.

B,C. Close-up photographs of scale insect clusters. Section C illustrates why the insect is described as a tortoise scale.

D. Twig on right shows the sooty appearance of pine foliage resulting from sooty mold fungi growing on the honeydew.

E. Mature female tortoise scale insects on the bark of Scots pine.

F,G. Spruce bud scales at different perspectives. Bark flakes partially cover the scale insect making it appear as part of the plant.

PLATE 32

Fletcher Scale (Plate 33)

The Fletcher scale, *Lecanium fletcheri* Cockerell, is also sometimes known as the arborvitae soft scale. In contrast to armored scale insects, no separate wax cover is produced. Wax secretions occur as a thin transparent film which does not conceal the insect itself. Dead, dried up females often appear as scale covers, enclosing the mass of eggs beneath (A,B). Prior to egg production females are hemispherical and distended with body fluid (D).

L. fletcheri is a common pest in the more northern parts of the eastern and midwestern United States, and in Canada. It occurs on arborvitae (*Thuja* spp.) and yew (*Taxus* spp.). There have also been reports of its occurrence on *Pachysandra* and on *Juniperus*. Infestations seldom cause visible injury to arborvitae. *L. fletcheri* is found primarily on the foliage of arborvitae. A serious pest of yew, it weakens the plants, causes foliage drop, and results in a heavy crust of sooty mold on twigs and needles. Twigs and stems are the predominant sites of infestation on yews and large populations of *L. fletcheri,* can frequently be seen on them.

There is great similarity between the various species of lecanium scales. The European fruit lecanium, *L. corni* Bouche, is much like Fletcher scale but has a very wide host range. However, host preference can be a general guide to identification, particularly with *L. fletcheri* which is restricted in common occurrence to *Thuja* and *Taxus*.

One generation of Fletcher scale occurs per growing season. Eggs begin hatching as early as June 11 in Connecticut and as late as the first week of July in Minnesota. Oval, flat, yellowish crawlers migrate short distances on a branch or frond in search of a feeding site. Since they do not crawl very far, populations tend to become dense on certain branches of a particular plant. During the rest of the season very little growth or development occurs in the scale insect. Small, slightly convex nymphs, amber to reddish-brown in color, remain on the plants throughout the fall and winter (E).

In the spring the juvenile scale grows quickly, and plant damage becomes obvious. Copious amounts of honeydew are produced, especially on yew, resulting in a dense black growth of the sooty mold fungi. Eggs are laid in May and hatching begins in June. Population increases often are abrupt because adult females are prolific. An average of 500–600 eggs are produced by a single female; the maximum is over 1000. All of the eggs hatch within a short period, thus making the motile crawlers easy to control with one application of an insecticide.

Reference: 211

A. Dead female Fletcher scales on taxus. Each contains hundreds of viable eggs.
B. Dead females and developing settled crawlers (at arrows) on arborvitae. Stippling of foliage is caused by feeding of the spruce mite. See Plate 43.
C. Close-up of dead Fletcher scales. Two scales have been turned over to show eggs and crawlers. Both eggs and crawlers are inside circle.
D. An adult female just prior to laying eggs.
E. Second-instar nymphs shortly after the crawler stage. Chlorotic areas are caused by the spruce mite.

PLATE 33

Black Pineleaf Scale (Plate 34)

Known in virtually all areas of the United States and Canada where susceptible hosts occur, the black pineleaf scale, *Nuculaspis californica* (Coleman), has in the past only occasionally inflicted sufficient damage to be considered an important pest, and even then, it was primarily in western North America. Its hosts include the following trees: *Pinus cembriodes*—three-needle pine; *Pinus contorta*—shore pine; *Pinus echinata*—short-leaf pine; *Pinus jeffreyi*—Jeffrey pine; *Pinus lambertiana*—sugar pine; *Pinus ponderosa*—ponderosa pine; *Pinus radiata*—Monterey pine; *Pinus rigida*—pitch pine; *Pinus sabiniana*—Digger pine; *Pseudotsuga menziesii*—Douglas fir.

This insect is commonly found in association with the pine needle scale, *Phenacaspis pinifoliae* (Fitch) (see Plate 38). Since it is gray to black, it is easily distinugished from the snow white *Phenacaspis*.

Infestations of the black pineleaf scale occur only on the needles. Injury is caused by the withdrawal of plant juices from the tree, and possibly by the introduction of toxic substances into the needles as the scale insects feed. Sites on needles infested by the insect tend to become spotted or blotched with yellow patches. Heavy infestations may cause premature needle drop and in extreme cases death of the tree.

The sequence of symptom expression begins with thin crowns, followed by reddish discoloration, chlorosis and finally necrosis of needles. Severely infested trees exhibit extreme shortening of needles, the degree of shortening being a function of the degree of scale infestation and number of years of continuous infestation. Scale infestation seriously reduces the number of years of needle retention.

Trees under stress from soil moisture deficit, soil compaction, root damage, smog, or other causes tend to be especially susceptible to black pineleaf scale attack. Trees along dusty roads often sustain higher infestations than those farther from such roads. This phenomenon may be due to the deleterious effect of dust on the natural enemies of the scale, or upon reduced photosynthesis (which may favor scale survival), or both.

One to three generations of this scale insect occur each year, depending on geographic location. Overwintering usually occurs in an immature stage. Eggs or live crawlers are deposited singly over an extended period of time. The crawlers disperse to other parts of the same needle, or to new nearby spring needles where they settle, insert their slender mouthparts, and begin to feed. Many crawlers are dispersed by the wind, and are carried for considerable distances. The male scale insects emerge as tiny winged individuals and mate with immature females by mid-June. About a month later the females reach maturity and begin laying their eggs.

A wasp parasitoid, *Prospaltella* sp. normally keeps scale populations at low densities in the northwest.

References: 84a, 153, 279

A. Infestation of black pineleaf scale on needles of red pine.
B. Yellowing of foliage of pinyon pine resulting from earlier attack by pineleaf scale.
C. Close-up of section A, showing degree of infestation.
D. Close-up of the scale cover of a mature black pineleaf scale. (1.5mm)
E. Mature and immature black pineleaf scales.

PLATE 34

Hemlock Scale (Plate 35)

The hemlock scale, *Abgrallaspis ithacae* (Ferris (=*Aspidiotus ithacae* = *Aspidiotus abietis*), is a native armored scale insect found on eastern hemlock *Tsuga canadensis*. It has also been reported on spruce, *Picea* sp. It feeds on the needles by piercing the tissue and sucking out the fluid. A small yellow spot seen from the upper side of the needle is the intitial symptom. If four to six hemlock scales take up residence on a single needle, the needle will turn yellow and fall from the tree. Mature scales are always found on the undersides of needles. Like all armored scales their protective cover is not physically attached to the insect. The cover, technically called a "test," is made of wax, secreted by the insect, and of its old molt "skins." The test of the female hemlock scale is dark brownish gray, round and about 2 mm in diameter.

There have been few detailed studies on the life history, biology and control of the hemlock scale. Stoetzel and Davidson (277) found that two generations occur each year in Maryland. Eggs produced by the first generation females hatch in June, mature in late July, and produce second generation eggs in August and September. The second generation crawlers settle on the needles and spend the winter in the second instar stage. (See seasonal history chart below.)

Wasp parasites are important means of natural control. These parasites emerge, in Maryland, at four times during the growing season: in early April, early June, mid-July and early August. Insecticides for control of scales should not be used when parasites are emerging.

The hemlock scale is known to occur in Connecticut, New York, Ohio, Indiana, Pennsylvania, and Maryland. It is probably present in the other eastern states where hemlock grows.

References: 59, 253, 277

Seasonal history of the hemlock scale in Maryland (after Stoetzel and Davidson)

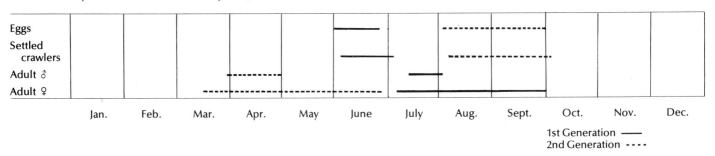

A. Typical injury to hemlock caused by the hemlock scale. View is of the upper surface of the needles.
B. Severe infestation by partially grown female scale insects, which locate themselves on the undersides of the needles.
C. Light to moderately infested needles; nearly mature females.
D. Three adult female scale covers and one immature female cover.

PLATE 35

Fiorinia Hemlock Scale (Plate 36)

The fiorinia hemlock scale, *Fiorinia externa* (Ferris), is an armored scale insect. It is primarily a pest of hemlocks, including Canada hemlock, *Tsuga canadensis;* Carolina hemlock, *T. carolinana;* and Japanese hemlock, *T. diversifolia.* Although it also occurs on yew, spruce, and fir, its populations on these trees do not reach damaging proportions. Such secondary hosts, if infested, are to be found near heavily infested hemlocks.

The fiorinia hemlock scale was first found in Queens, New York, in 1908. It was described as a new species in 1942. Since the 1950's, severe infestations have been reported in Massachusetts, Connecticut, Pennsylvania, New Jersey, Ohio, and Maryland. A species closely related to the fiorinia hemlock scale has been found in the Richmond, Virginia area. It is called *Fiorinia japonica* Kuwana. *F. japonica* is also known as a pest of pine and *Podocarpus* in California. The fiorinia hemlock scale is found chiefly in northeastern United States. Very few native stands of hemlocks have been found to be infested.

The fiorinia scale is a destructive pest of established landscape trees and hedges. Section A depicts the yellowing of the needles. Plant growth is slowed and needles drop prematurely resulting in thin, weakened plants. The fiorinia hemlock scale feeds by inserting its threadlike mouthparts into the needles. The flexible stylets then bend and are pushed extensively through the leaf tissue parallel to the surface. These mouthparts are up to three to four times the length of the body.

Mature females, which may live for a year or longer, deposit eggs under a waxy cover. Egg-laying is done over an extended period of time and is interrupted only by cold weather. Eggs hatch in about a month. First-instar nymphs (crawlers) emerge and migrate to the new needles on the same plant. There they settle on the undersides of needles, insert their mouthparts and begin to feed. After three to four weeks, the crawlers molt. About one month later females are mature and males emerge as extremely small, delicate winged insects. Eggs are produced one and one-half to two months after mating.

The seasonal history is complicated by the great overlap of various developmental stages. There is a preponderance of crawlers during late May. However, all stages may be present during the entire growing season, making control of this pest very difficult. Systemic insecticides that translocate to the part of the plant where the crawlers have settled have been effective in control.

Parasites and predators provide some measure of natural control of fiorinia hemlock scale populations. A small wasp, *Aspidiotiphagus citrinus* (Craw.), is most common in New York and is believed to be an effective parasite of the fiorinia scale. Other hymenopterous parasites along with the lady beetle, *Chilocorus stigma* (Say), feed on this scale (see Figure 28 on page 304) but apparently have little effect in controlling populations. Overpopulation can itself be a controlling factor. Drastic reductions in tree growth and in the amount of healthy needle tissue will sometimes reduce the nutritive level of the host to the point where the scales die of starvation and yet the tree recovers.

References: 60, 299

A. Chlorotic appearance of upper needle surfaces where fiorinia hemlock scale populations are high.
B. Undersides of yellowed needles showing typical damage caused by female and immature scales.
C. Immature females developing on a new cone.
D. Old adult females, near the end of their egg production period.
E. Scale covers of males (seen at arrow 1) are white and small compared to the newly mature females (at arrow 2), which are ready to begin producing eggs.

PLATE 36

Juniper Scale (Plate 37)

It can be safely guessed that juniper trees with leaves that have turned yellow or brown are hosts of either the spider mite (Plate 43) or the juniper scale, *Carulaspis juniperi* Bouche =*Diaspis carueli*), particularly if the tree is located in the eastern United States. However, it takes close and preferably microscopic examination to detect these pests. The first indication of damage to the host is loss of the normal lustrous color of a healthy plant. The infested foliage fails to develop new growth and the tree or shrub looks off-color. As the infestation progresses the foliage of individual branches will yellow and then die (C,D). Entire plants are known to succumb as a result of scale infestation.

The juniper scale, of European origin, is now distributed from coast to coast, and is known to attack various junipers and cypresses (*Cupressus*, but not *Taxodium*), and incense cedar. Of the ornamental junipers, red cedar, Irish, Savin and Pfitzer are most commonly attacked.

Carulaspis minima (Targ.), a scale insect closely related to the juniper scale, attacks arborvitae (E). Close observation of infested foliage will reveal many white to brownish scale covers, each of which are formed by the scales living underneath. Female scale covers are 1.5 mm in diameter and have a dark center (A). Males are elongated and are whiter than the females (B).

The scale overwinters as a mature female. The female then lays up to 40 eggs, starting in May in the Northeast but as early as March in parts of the South and West. The eggs hatch in

Figure 8. A wasp parasite, *Comperiella bifasciata* Howard, ovipositing on an armored scale. Arrow indicates ovipositor, the egg-laying organ. (Drawing courtesy Harold Compere, Div. of Bio. Control, Dept. of Entomology, Univ. of Calif., Riverside)

about two weeks and the yellowish crawlers seek a new site on the same host plant. They, like other scale and adelgid crawlers, are light enough to be blown by the wind to other hosts. After settling, the crawlers develop rapidly. The females molt three times and the males five. The tiny winged males are active in late summer or early fall when they seek out, and mate with, females. They then disappear. In most parts of the United States a single generation occurs annually, but at least one authority suggests that two generations may occur in California.

References: 36, 129, 211

A. Mature female scales on juniper foliage.
B. Male juniper scales on juniper foliage.
C,D. Dying foliage on *Juniperus communis* caused by a moderate juniper scale infestation.
E. *Carulaspis minima* on arborvitae found on the West Coast.

PLATE 37

Pine Needle Scale (Plate 38)

The pine needle scale, *Phenacaspis pinifoliae* (Fitch), is one of the most serious pests of ornamental pines in the United States. It was once referred to as the "white malady" because of the manner in which heavy infestations whitened the foliage of pines and some spruces.

In eastern United States the most frequently damaged hosts are mugho and Scots pine. Austrian and red pines are also attacked at times. In the prairie provinces of Canada, spruces and pines are seriously infested. Mugho, Monterey and ponderosa pines are favored hosts in the West. Douglas fir and cedar are also hosts in the West. In general, infestations in the West are far less severe than in the East.

Ornamental nurseries, Christmas tree plantations, ornamental plantings, and trees planted along dusty roads are more likely to be attacked than forest trees. Light attacks generally go unnoticed and cause little damage. As the populations increase, the needles become covered with the white scale insects (B) which suck juices from the needle mesophyll and cause the needles to turn yellowish and then brown (D). Whole branchlets or branches may be killed. Continued infestations can transform beautiful ornamentals into sickly looking trees with sparse, off-color foliage. Heavy infestations can lead to the death of the tree.

Ornamental pines should be inspected at least twice a year for evidence of infestation. The adult scales (E) are easily recognized even when only a few are present. The insects overwinter as reddish eggs beneath the female scale cover. Each female lays up to a hundred eggs. The eggs hatch in May or June. The reddish nymphs (C) crawl from beneath the scale covering and migrate to a new site on the same host, or they may be blown by the wind to more distant hosts. One or two generations occur annually, depending upon geographic location. Where two generations occur, the second lot of crawlers begins to appear in late July. Whereas the female scales are wingless, the male scale has wings and is capable of flight.

The black pineleaf scale, *Nuculaspis californica*, often attacks the same tree as the pine needle scale. The dark, more circular scale covering easily distinguishes the black pineleaf scale. See Plate 34.

References: 36, 54, 153, 229

A,D. A heavy infestation of pine needle scales, *Phenacaspis pinifoliae*, on mugho pine. Note the color of the infested twigs compared to the uninfested ones.
B. Moderate to heavy scale infestation on mugho pine.
C. Female scales (about 3 mm long) and newly hatched reddish crawlers.
E. Close-up of needles. The left one is covered mostly with the narrower male scale coverings, and the right one mostly with females. The circular holes indicate the places at which the tiny parasitic wasps emerged after killing the female scale insects.

PLATE 38

Armored Scales of Conifers (Plate 39)

The scale insects shown on the facing plate are poorly known but serious pests of numerous ornamental trees and shrubs.

The Asiatic red scale, *Aonidiella taxus* Leonardi, is a tropical species (C). In the United States it is known only in Florida and Louisiana, although it sometimes is found in greenhouses elsewhere. A severe pest of *Podocarpus macrophylla* and *Taxus baccata,* it feeds primarily on the undersides of leaves and causes yellow spots (A) to appear on the upper surfaces of the leaves. Angular blotches (B) and pits may develop in the newly formed leaves. The adult female is about 2 mm in diameter. Its biology has not been studied.

Parlatoria pittospori Maskell is another introduced scale, possibly from Australia (E). In the United States its distribution is now believed to be limited to California. Its hosts include *Cedrus deodara, Callistemon* sp., *Cotoneaster microphylla,* mimosa, olive, *Pinus halepensis, Pinus radiata, Pittosporum tobira, Podocarpus elongatus,* rose and *Viburnum tinus.* This scale insect occurs only on leaves and young stems. The females are about 1.5 mm long. Its biology has not been studied.

References: 67, 181

A. A *Podocarpus macrophylla* terminal twig showing the yellow spots and notched leaves caused by the Asiatic red scale, *Aonidiella taxus.*
B. Upper and lower sides of *Podocarpus* leaves showing symptoms and scales.
C. Both mature and immature (at arrow) female Asiatic red scales.
D. *Parlatoria pittospori* on needles of *Cedrus deodara* collected in October.
E. A close-up of the female scale covers of *Parlatoria pittospori.*

PLATE 39

Cooley Spruce Gall Aphid (Plate 40)

The Cooley spruce gall aphid, *Adelges cooleyi* (Gillette), has a complicated life cycle. Its common name is a misnomer, for although it is closely related to aphids it is not one. It has at least five different morphological forms and requires two years and two hosts to complete its normal life cycle. This adelgid also has the capability of reproducing continuous generations on spruce or Douglas fir.

In the normal cycle of development, the Cooley adelgid overwinters as an immature female on spruce. The female matures early in the spring to become a "stem mother," and then lays several hundred eggs on lateral terminals. When the eggs hatch, the nymphs migrate to the new spring growth where they feed at the base of the growing needles. Their feeding induces a unique gall (A) that soon envelopes the young insects. The gall may be up to 63 mm long. By midsummer an opening develops at the base of each needle on the gall (G). The adelgids inside migrate to the tips of the needles and transform into females with wings. These winged females then migrate to Douglas fir or another spruce. On Douglas fir they lay eggs on the needles and a generation of "woolly aphids" (D) is produced.

Douglas fir is sometimes so heavily attacked that the foliage appears to have been sprinkled with snow. No gall is produced on Douglas fir but feeding of the insect produces prominent yellowish spots (E,H) and bent or distorted needles. This insect produces galls on Engelmann, Sitka, Oriental and Colorado blue spruces; and causes needle injury to Douglas fir. These plant species may be attacked throughout the northern part of the United States and southern Canada.

A similar "woolly aphid," *Adelges tsugae*, occurs on the bark and needles of mountain hemlock, *Tsuga mertensiana*, and more recently it has been found on Canada hemlock, *T. canadensis*, in Virginia and Pennsylvania.

There are other adelgid species in the genus *Pineus* and *Adelges* that also cause galls on spruce (see "Key to Adelgid Galls on Spruce" below). Some of the galls are mistaken for those caused by the Cooley spruce gall aphid (see Plate 26).

Key to Adelgid Galls on Spruce*

1. Gall pineapple-shaped with gall needles often short and thick but never modified to thin scales 2
   Gall elongate, cone-like, or appearing as a scraggly deformed twig   4
2. Gall terminal on twig, small, pinkish or pale green; usually on *Picea mariana* .... *Adelges laricis* Vallot
   Gall rarely terminal, foliage green except closed mouths of cells red-brown to purple 3
3. Gall-needles variable but usually not less than ⅓ normal length; nymphs pale yellow with fine white pulverulency .... *Adelges abietis* Linn.
   Gall-needles less than ⅓ normal length, nymphs reddish with abundant flocculance .... *Adelges lariciatus* (Patch)
4. Gall cone-like, needles modified to thin scales .... *Pineus pinifoliae* Fitch
   Gall elongate or appearing as a scraggly twig, gall-needles not scale-like 5
5. Gall-needles radiating to expose gall-surface with lateral joining of tissue between swollen needle bases; gall terminal on twig 6
   Gall-needles more or less obscuring gall-surface and with no lateral joining of tissue between swollen bases of needles; mature galls often elongate and appearing as scraggly twigs .... *Pineus similis* Gill
6. On *Picea mariana*, rarely others .... *Pineus floccus* (Patch)
   On *Picea pungens* .... *Adelges cooleyi* Gill

* This key appeared in Volume 102 (1971) of the Proceedings of the Entomological Society of Ontario, in a paper entitled "The Adelgidae (Homoptera) on Forest Trees in Ontario with a Key to Galls on Spruce." Permission to reprint has been granted by the author, O. H. Lindquist, and the Great Lakes Forest Research Centre, Sault Ste. Marie, Ontario.

References: 50, 55, 56, 57, 153, 167, 256

A. Fully formed but unopened galls on Colorado blue spruce. Note that the galls are at the tips of twigs.
B. A gall after the "aphids" have left and at the time when most homeowners notice the damage.
C. A gall sliced open to show the small cells in which the adelgids develop.
D,E,H. Wool-covered "aphids" and damage to Douglas fir needles.
F. A third-instar nymph on a Douglas fir needle.
G. Recently opened cells in the gall. A winged adelgid may be seen at the arrow point.

PLATE 40

Eastern Spruce Gall Aphid (Plate 41)

The eastern spruce gall aphid, *Adelges abietis* (Linnaeus), is a primary pest of Norway spruce. Occasionally it damages Colorado blue, white and red spruce. Introduced from Europe before 1900, it has spread throughout northeastern United States and southern Canada. This insect causes galls to develop at the basal portion of shoots (A), thereby weakening the stems so that they will more readily break from weight of snow or other physical stresses. Galls detract from the beauty and symmetry of trees. If abundant, they will decrease a tree's vitality.

The eastern spruce gall aphid is not really an aphid but a closely related insect, an adelgid. It overwinters as a partially grown female, sometimes called a stem mother, and matures in early spring. The female lays her eggs about the time new buds are ready to break. From 100 to 200 eggs are surrounded by a coat of woolly wax (C,D). They hatch within ten days and the nymphs begin feeding on new needles. In a few days they move to the bases of the needles. The continued feeding of the nymphs causes abnormal twig growth and the subsequent development of the gall. The gall tissue grows around the young insects, and until the galls crack open, during mid- to late-summer, the nymphs remain entirely protected from parasites, predators and unfavorable weather conditions. As sections of the gall open (D), the nearly mature nymphs crawl out, settle on a needle, cast their nymphal skins and transform to winged, egg-laying females. They lay their eggs in unprotected masses, usually near the tips of needles. The eggs hatch and the young nymphs attach themselves to a terminal twig near or at a dormant bud to spend the winter.

Other adelgids cause galls on Norway and white spruce (see *Adelges lariciatus*, Plate 26). Some produce galls that may be mistaken for those caused by the eastern spruce gall aphid (see "Key to Adelgid Galls on Spruce").

References: 50, 130, 167

A. An old eastern spruce gall and a mass of eggs at the base of a bud (note arrow).
B. Eastern spruce gall aphid egg masses at the base of an expanding Norway spruce bud.
C. The "cotton" pulled apart to show the black eggs, now about ready to hatch.
D. A Norway spruce twig. Note the several newly formed pineapple-shaped galls at the bases of the new twigs; these were caused by the eastern spruce gall aphid, *Adelges abietis*.
E. An eastern spruce gall on Norway spruce. Gall is about ready to open and release the young adelgids.
F. A new gall cut open to show the cells and the young adelgids inside.

PLATE 41

Monterey Pine Midge (Plate 42)

Shortened needles, usually with greatly swollen bases, are characteristic of attack by the Monterey pine midge, *Thecodiplosis pini-radiatae* (Snow and Mills). Among the pines occasionally infested by this pest, which has a rather restricted distribution in coastal central California, are the bigcone, *Pinus coulteri;* digger, *P. sabiniana;* Bishop, *P. muricata;* and knobcone, *P. attenuata.* As the common name of this pest suggests, the favored host of the midge is Monterey pine, *Pinus radiata.*

The adult insects are very tiny, mosquito-like flies which deposit their eggs on the terminal buds of the pine tree during January, February, and March. The larvae, upon hatching, migrate to the bases of the newly forming needles. Here they burrow into the needle tissue and their feeding causes a clam-like swelling to develop. If, during the spring and summer months, the basal portion of an infested needle is carefully dissected, tiny white larvae may be found (E). The mature larvae are reported to leave the gall in November and December, and to drop to the soil, where the pupal stage is spent. A single generation occurs each year.

The midge attacks only the current season's needles. The following year such needles turn yellow and then brown, and drop prematurely from the tree. Severe infestations have been reported. Trees may be nearly denuded by the premature loss of older infested needles, and the current season's needles may be greatly reduced in length. Typically—and for reasons yet unknown—single, widely scattered trees are attacked by the Monterey pine midge year after year (also see Plate 9).

The Monterey pine midge is related to *Thecodiplosis liriodendri* O.S., a leaf miner of tulip poplar. The damage symptom looks much like a fungus leaf spot. The boxwood leaf miner, illustrated on Plate 78, is also related.

References: 93, 153

Figure 9. A tulip poplar leaf with leaf spot symptoms caused by *Thecodiplosis liriodendri,* a midge related to the Monterey pine midge.

A,B. Shortened needles with bulbous bases are characteristic of Monterey pine midge attack.

C,D. Close-up of needles affected by Monterey pine midge. Stippling of needles was caused by spider mites.

E. Swollen base of a needle cut open to expose larvae of the Monterey pine midge. The midge is about 1.5 mm long.

PLATE 42

99

Spider Mites of Conifers (Plates 43, 44)

Spider mites attack conifers as readily as they do the broad-leaved plants. Many conifer-feeding mites build up to damaging numbers in the spring and early summer and sometimes again in the fall. Hot dry summer weather often causes a marked cessation in their activities.

As they feed, spider mites destroy the chlorophyll-bearing cells at the surface of the needle or scale of the conifer. This results in a flecking, stippling (D) or bleaching of the affected foliage; some of the leaves often turn brown and later drop as a result of the mite injury. These symptoms may be confused with certain kinds of air pollution injury. Webbing may or may not be found, depending on the mite species involved.

To determine whether a plant is infested with spider mites, hold a sheet of white paper beneath some foliage, and jar the foliage sharply. If the tree is infested, mites will soon begin to crawl around on the paper. Although very small, less than the size of a pepper grain, the crawling mite can be easily seen against the white background. The presence of a few mites is of no concern. However, if dozens are seen running about on the paper, some measures should be taken to reduce the mite population before serious damage occurs to the plant.

Large and destructive populations of mites sometimes result from improper usage of insecticides on conifers. Some pesticides kill the natural enemies of the spider mites without eliminating the mites themselves. The insecticides BHC, carbaryl (Sevin) and lindane should not be used on conifers unless a specific mite-controlling chemical, known as an acaricide, is added to the spray tank and applied simultaneously.

Probably the most destructive conifer-feeding spider mite in the United States is the spruce mite, *Oligonychus ununguis* (Jacobi) (Plate 44, section F). This species attacks spruce, arborvitae, juniper, hemlock, pine, Douglas fir and sometimes other conifers. Tiny strands of webbing are often found among the needles upon which this mite feeds (Plate 44).

In the western states several other species of *Oligonychus* are destructive to conifers. *O. subnudus* (McGregor) is a serious pest of young Monterey pine, *Pinus radiata,* and especially of those grown for Christmas trees (D). Populations of *O. subnudus* tend to be highest in the spring.

Another species, *O. milleri* (McGregor), makes its appearance in the summer and fall on the same trees. Neither *O. subnudus* nor *O. milleri* is a web-forming mite.

For additional information on spider mites, see Plate 202.

References: 113, 211, 234

A. Unaffected foliage (at top of photograph) in contrast to the bleached, bronzed foliage of a pine infested with *Oligonychus* spider mites.
B. Stippling of pine foliage, the result of feeding by *Oligonychus subnudus.*
C. Infestation of *Oligonychus subnudus* on needles of Monterey pine. The tiny reddish objects are the mites.
D. Close-up of *Oligonychus subnudus.*

PLATE 43

102

PLATE 44

Eriophyid Mite of Hemlock (Plate 45)

Ornamental hemlocks in the northeastern states are sometimes seriously damaged by an almost invisible mite of a group called eriophyids. The eriophyids are different from other mites that affect ornamental trees in that they are very minute, elongated, are sometimes worm-like and move very slowly.

The hemlock rust mite, *Nalepella tsugifoliae,* feeds openly on the needles whereas those mites affecting pine are usually found between the needles within the needle sheath. The hemlock mite sucks juices from the hemlock needle. When mite populations are high, the normally dark green foliage of the hemlock turns "blue" and later a yellowish color before dropping (A). This mite has been a pest of hemlock in nurseries on Long Island, New York, and in Virginia. It causes most of its damage in the spring. By mid-summer, when the damage is most evident, the mite population diminishes to a very low level.

Because mites are not visible without magnification they often are not detected before it is too late to prevent damage to the tree.

This mite has been collected from a number of other conifers including firs, spruces, *Taxus, Pseudolarix* and *Torreya.* Another species of *Nalepella* causes distinct galls to form on the tips of Douglas fir branches.

A. An uninfested hemlock twig at left. At right, one that has been heavily fed upon by *Nalepella tsugifoliae* Keifer.
B. A highly magnified section of one needle showing a number of mites and eggs.
C. Magnified section with a single female mite and a group of three eggs which are about the same color as the body of the mite.

PLATE 45

INSECTS THAT FEED ON BROAD-LEAVED EVERGREENS AND DECIDUOUS PLANTS

Dogwood Sawfly (Plate 46)

All of the insects shown in Plate 46 are the larvae of *Macremphytus tarsatus* (Say), a sawfly. Shown are three larvae, each with a different color pattern from the other. In fact, if the growth of these larvae were not followed one might think that they were of different species.

M. tarsatus is found in the Northeast and in the Great Lakes states. It is a common defoliator of dogwood, primarily the gray dogwood, *Cornus racemosa*. One generation occurs each year. The larvae overwinter inside cells prepared in soft or decaying wood. Adult sawflies emerge over a rather long period from late May through July. Eggs are laid on the undersides of leaves. Well over 100 eggs may be deposited on a single leaf. When the eggs hatch the larvae feed together and skeletonize the leaf (G). As the larvae get older they eat all of the leaf except the midvein. After the second molt the bodies of the larvae become covered with a white powder-like material (B) that can be rubbed off. At their final molt they completely change their color pattern (E). At this stage they wander about, apparently in search of an ideal location for hibernation. Fully grown larvae are about 25 mm long. They become quite a nuisance at this stage and may cause some damage. They prefer to build their overwintering home in rotting wood found lying on the ground. They will burrow into composition wood fiber wallboard used for construction of modern homes and will also burrow into clapboard siding. Redwood siding and furniture is just as acceptable to them.

The color changes of the larva have given the entomologist reason to speculate that the white color of the feeding stage mimics bird droppings and thus helps to avoid enemies. Likewise the spotted last-instar larva is well camouflaged as it crawls over duff and litter beneath the bushes.

A closely related species, *M. varianus* (Nort.), which also feeds on dogwood, lays its eggs in an interesting manner. The female cuts a slit in the epidermis and inserts her egg in the soft parenchyma. This causes a slight flattened bulge easily visible from the underside of the leaf.

Reference: 50

A. Several *Macremphytus tarsatus* larvae feeding on *Cornus stolonifera*.
B. Typical posture of a resting dogwood sawfly larva, *Macremphytus tarsatus* larva.
C. *Macremphytus tarsatus* larvae feeding on the edge of a leaf. Note that the legs are not covered by the white powdery material.
D. A fully grown *Macremphytus tarsatus* larva in its final color form. Note the number of abdominal prolegs.
E. A larva in the act of molting.
F. Recently hatched *Macremphytus tarsatus* larvae on the underside of a leaf. The leaf shows the feeding injury typical at this stage of the larva's development.
G. Dogwood leaves: (left to right) lower leaf surface with a young colony of caterpillars; upper leaf surface showing injury; a leaf completely skeletonized.

PLATE 46

Mountain Ash Sawfly and Dusky Birch Sawfly (Plate 47)

The mountain ash sawfly, *Pristiphora geniculata* (Hartig) is found throughout northeastern United States and Canada. It survives only on the foliage of *Sorbus americana* or *S. aucuparia,* the American and European mountain ash. This insect occurs in both the Old and New World, but authorities differ in their opinions as to whether it is of European origin. The adults emerge during late May and early June to mate. The female lays eggs in slits she has cut near the leaf edge. Larvae hatch in early June; feeding and growing continues until mid-August.

The head and legs of fully grown larvae are yellow-orange. All body segments except the last are marked with black spots of uneven size and shape (D). The young larva is greenish with a black head and black legs. It skeletonizes leaves. As the larvae grow, they feed from the edge of the leaf inward until all but the mid-rib has been consumed. The larvae feed in colonies, devouring foliage on one small branch before moving to another. The feeding period lasts from two to three weeks. The mature larvae drop to the soil where they spin cocoons, similar to that shown in section C, in the duff and top soil beneath the host tree. A partial second generation is reported to occur in eastern Canada during late August. The insect spends the winter as a pre-pupa, then changes to a pupa and finally an adult in the spring.

The dusky birch sawfly, *Croesus latitarsus* Nort., is generally distributed through New England and the Great Lakes states. Its preferred host is gray birch, but black, red, paper and yellow birch are also sometimes attacked. One to two generations occur annually. The winter is spent as a pre-pupa in a cocoon in the soil. The pre-pupa transforms to a pupa in the spring and the adults emerge during May. Adults of the second generation may emerge from the middle of July to the middle of September.

The fully grown larva has a shiny black head and yellowish-green body (F). In the earlier stages its markings are not as distinct (E). Each mature larva assumes a curious S-shaped posture around the edge of the leaf when alarmed or not feeding.

References: 50, 82

A. Young sawfly larvae, *Pristiphora geniculata,* on leaves of mountain ash.
B. Sawfly larvae on a single leaflet.
C. Typical sawfly cocoons.
D. Mature mountain ash sawfly larva, about 18 mm long.
E. Mature larva (top) and younger larvae of *Croesus latitarsus* on birch leaf.
F. Mature larva of *Croesus latitarsus* on birch leaf. The brown spots on the leaves in sections E and F are caused by the birch leaf miner, *Fenusa pusilla* (Lep.) (see also Plate 73).

PLATE 47

Sawflies (Plate 48)

Certain sawfly larvae are borers and feed in stems or tender shoots of trees and shrubs. Some of these are closely related to the pigeon tremex (Plate 210), as is the case of *Hartigia trimaculata* Say. There is little biological data about *H. trimaculata* but it is assumed to produce one generation each year. The adult appears in early June and lays its eggs in punctures made in current-season rose or blackberry canes. Upon hatching, the larva may girdle the twig (D), causing the tip to wilt (A). As the larva matures it enters the pith and feeds downward. There is usually one borer per cane. *H. trimaculata* may be found along the Atlantic coast from Florida to Quebec and west to Louisiana and the Rocky Mountains.

A species related to *Hartigia trimaculata* and called *Hartigia cressoni* (Kirby) occurs in California and Nevada. The adult horn-tailed wasp appears in April and May. The female inserts a single white egg into canes of rose or bramble fruits. Eggs hatch into very small larvae which then spirally girdle the tips causing them to wilt and die. Individuals of this species attain a length of 22 to 25 mm. *H. cressoni* also bores into the pith of the canes and sometimes gets into the larger roots.

The other sawflies shown in this plate are free-living leaf feeders, capable of moving over comparatively long distances. Oak foliage supports several species of sawflies in the genus *Periclista*. The sawfly illustrated in photo E is believed to be *P. purpuridorsum* Dyar. The larvae are solitary feeders on white or red oak. They devour all or portions of the leaves. They are rarely, if ever, found in large numbers and thus are not of major economic importance. One generation occurs each year. Larvae are found in May in the vicinity of Washington, D.C., and in June in central New York. Fully grown larvae are about 26 mm long. Little is known about the biology or distribution of *P. purpuridorsum*.

The butternut woolly worm, *Eriocampa juglandis* (Fitch) (= *Blennocampa caryae* Norton), is 18 mm long when fully grown (F). Larvae feed gregariously on the foliage of butternut, black walnut or hickory. They may be found in July and August and are potentially destructive defoliators. Under the white cottony tufts is a larva with a smooth green body and white head. The white tufts rub off easily. This species occurs in the northeastern states, in Ontario and in eastern Canada. One generation is presumed to occur each year.

The larva of the black-headed ash sawfly, *Tethida cordigera* (Beauv.), is an occasional defoliator of red and white ash (G), particularly of shade trees. It is distributed throughout much of New England, and south to Maryland, and west to Kentucky and Michigan. Larvae are without wax or hair. In central New York they are found in late June. Fully grown larvae are about 18 mm long.

A related species, the brown-headed ash sawfly, *Tomostethus multicinctus* (Rohwer), is found in the same geographical area and causes the same kind of injury. It looks much like the black-headed ash sawfly but has a brown head.

References: 44a, 50, 93

A. A wilted rose shoot that has been girdled by the sawfly, *Hartigia trimaculata*.
B. A young *Hartigia trimaculata* larva dislocated from a rose stem.
C. A nearly mature *Hartigia trimaculata* larva. About 21 mm when fully grown.
D. A rose shoot dissected to show the girdling tunnel caused by a *Hartigia trimaculata* larva.
E. A fully grown sawfly larva, probably of the genus *Periclista*, on white oak. Note the way the tail wraps around the leaf. This is a typical position for many free-living sawfly larvae.
F. The butternut woolly worm on walnut. This specimen was collected in July on Long Island, New York.
G. A nearly grown blackheaded ash sawfly larva, *Tethida cordigera*.

PLATE 48

Gypsy Moth (Plates 49, 50)

Gypsy moth, *Lymantria dispar* (Linnaeus), is a familiar name, especially to Northeasterners. Probably no pest of trees has received more publicity or cost more to control.

In 1870, this announcement was made by a well-known entomologist: "Only a year ago the larvae of a certain owlet moth, *Porthetria dispar*, were accidentally introduced by a Massachusetts entomologist into New England, where it is spreading with great rapidity. It happened this way. Mr. Trouvelot, then living at 27 Myrtle Street in Medford, Massachusetts was in search of a silk moth that would survive in America. He brought eggs of the gypsy moth to his home where some larvae or possibly adult moths escaped" (Forbush and Fernald, 107). The gypsy moth was known to be a serious pest of forest and shade trees in Europe, and Mr. Trouvelot apparently knew this because he informed local authorities of the moths' escape.

Nothing was done and within 12 years it became a serious nuisance to those living on Myrtle Street. The local residents assumed it to be a native pest. The personal testimonies of residents of Myrtle Street in the early 1880's were a preview of things to come. One woman stated: "I went to the front door and sure enough the street was black with them [caterpillars]." Another resident who was out of town for three days in June of 1889 relates: "When I went away the trees in our yard were in splendid condition and there was not a sign of insect devastation on them. When I returned there was scarcely a leaf upon the trees". Another resident testified to having collected four quarts of caterpillars from one branch of his apple tree. Another said that the caterpillars covered one side of his house so thickly that it was impossible to tell the color of the house. Many people disliked going outdoors because the caterpillars dropped from the trees onto them. Streets and sidewalks were slippery in places because of the crushed caterpillars.

Placed in an environment devoid of its natural enemies, the gypsy moth multiplied and spread so rapidly that today it is a pest of trees in over two hundred thousand square miles of northeastern forestland. Despite strict quarantine regulations and chemical eradication and control programs, which have undoubtedly helped control the gypsy moth's activities, it continues to occupy new territory. (Automobiles and camping trailers are often transporters of the gypsy moth's eggs, and sometimes of other stages of the insect.) With the present ban on the use of persistent insecticides such as DDT, the insect appears to be spreading at an even more rapid rate. It has been found with increasing frequency in the Carolinas, Kentucky and California. Whether it will spread throughout all of the United States remains to be seen.

Adult gypsy moths are rather large. The wingspan of the female is about two inches (5 cm). The male is dark brown (Plate 50, section E) and the female nearly white, with wavy, blackish bands across the fore wings (Plate 50; sections D and E). Eggs are deposited on branches, fences, buildings or other suitable places in masses of 100–600 or more, and are covered with a dense mass of tan or buff-colored hairs (D). The individual eggs are pellet-like and range in color from brown to black.

The larvae hatch from early April to late May, the peak hatching period coinciding with the flowering of shadbush. The tiny larva often remains on the egg mass for several days before climbing the tree to commence feeding. It then spins a silken thread, suspends itself from a leaf, and is swayed back and forth by light breezes. If the wind velocity is great enough, it may become airborne. In a wooded area, the wind may carry a larva several hundred yards. In open terrain, larvae are reported to be transported several miles. The larva at this stage (Plate 50, section G) is hairy and basically dark in color. When fully grown it may be up to 2½ inches (5.5 cm) long.

As the caterpillar (larva) matures, its feeding habits change. It feeds at night and descends from the tree to take refuge in shady places. On a heavily infested tree it may continue to feed throughout the daylight hours.

Larvae feed on a number of hosts. Preferred are leaves of apple, alder, basswood, hawthorn, oaks, some poplars, and willows. Less preferred hosts include elm, black gum, hickories, maples and sassafras. A few larvae from a massive population may occasionally feed on beech, hemlock, white cedar, pines and spruces. Ignored or only rarely fed upon are ash, balsam fir, butternut, black walnut, catalpa, red cedar, dogwood, holly, locust, sycamore and yellow poplar.

Oaks suffer from the gypsy moth's attack more than other species. Most deciduous trees can withstand one or two consecutive years of defoliation before severe decline or death occurs. Conifers will die after one complete defoliation.

The larval stage lasts about seven weeks. After completing its feeding period, the larva finds a sheltered place and pupates in a brownish-black pupal case. Pupal cases are often found in clusters accompanied by molted skins of the last caterpillar instar.

Moths begin to emerge about the middle of July, males appearing several days earlier than the females. The female does not fly; she crawls to an elevated place and emits a liquid substance called a sex attractant, which volatilizes, and is carried in the air. With the proper wind conditions, the odor will be detectable and attractive to a male moth for a distance of about one mile. The sex attractant has been synthesized and is used as a means to survey an area to determine the presence of male moths. The synthetic sex attractant has control possibilities. After mating and deposition of eggs, the adults soon die without feeding.

Control has been effected by man's manipulations as well as through a number of natural factors. A bacterial pathogen called *Bacillus thuringiensis* kills larvae. Now prepared commercially, it is effective against *L. dispar* and certain other caterpillar species. Important parasites and predators from Europe and Asia have been reared and released with some success. The major parasites are *Ooencyrtus kuwanae* How., an egg parasite; *Sturmia scutellata* R. D., a fly parasite of the caterpillar; and *Calosoma sycophanta* L., a predatory beetle. The wasp shown in Figure 12 on page 156 is a parasite of the gypsy moth.

References: 50, 107, 212

A. A hillside in the Hudson Valley of New York. The trees at top of photograph were defoliated by the gypsy moth, *Lymantria dispar*.
B. Egg masses on the underside of an oak limb.
C. Gypsy moth larvae on partly devoured oak leaves.
D. Close-up of egg masses. The small pin holes mark exit holes of egg parasites.
E. A pupa, an empty pupal case, and an egg mass.

PLATE 49

A. Pupae and egg masses of the gypsy moth webbed together on a hemlock twig.
B. A mass of pupae. One dead larva hangs alone, killed by a virus disease called wilt.
C. Twig showing several larvae killed by the wilt disease.
D. Female gypsy moths laying eggs.
E. Male (dark) and female gypsy moth.
F. Roadway lined with oak trees completely defoliated by gypsy moth larvae.
G. Fully grown gypsy moth larva.
H. Front view of a gypsy moth larva.

PLATE 50

Cankerworms (Plate 51)

The fall cankerworm, *Alsophila pometaria* (Harr.), and the spring cankerworm, *Paleacrita vernata* (Peck), are two of the more common and injurious of the many species of loopers, spanworms and inchworms that attack ornamental trees. The common names of these two insects indicate respective seasons during which their eggs are laid. The fall cankerworm lays its eggs in late November and early December, and the spring cankerworm in late February and early March. The females of both species are wingless. Both are indigenous to North America and occur from Nova Scotia and southern Canada to the Carolinas, Texas, Colorado, New Mexico, California, Montana, and Manitoba. They have a wide host range, but are major pests primarily of elm, apple, oak, linden, and beech.

Both species hatch as soon as buds begin to open in the spring and occur together in mixed populations. Young larvae feed on buds and unfolding leaves. There are both green and dark larvae of each species. The larvae drop from the leaves on silk strands of their own making, from which they are often detached by the wind and blown considerable distances. Larvae devour all but the midrib of the leaf and often defoliate entire trees (B). Four to five weeks after hatching they enter the soil to pupate, usually in early June.

The fall cankerworm larva can be distinguished from the spring cankerworm larva by its three pairs of prolegs (including a small pair on the fifth abdominal segment) in contrast to the spring cankerworm's two pairs.

The eggs of the fall cankerworm are laid in carefully aligned masses of about 100 on small twigs (F). The spring cankerworm lays its spindle-shaped eggs in clusters of about 100 in the crevices of rough bark on larger limbs and trunk.

Since the wingless females (E) must crawl from the ground into the trees to lay their eggs, attempts have been made to control their populations by banding tree trunks with a sticky material such as tanglefoot. The surest control is achieved by spraying the tree with a residual contact insecticide soon after the larvae first become active and after the leaves have expanded. Chemicals sprayed on rapidly growing leaves will not provide sufficient coverage and adequate control. Bacterial and virus diseases help to regulate infestations naturally. *Bacillus thuringiensis* is a naturally occurring spore-forming bacterium which causes a fatal disease in cankerworms. Commercial formulations available from garden stores have been effective in the control of cankerworms.

References: 12, 50, 129, 150

A,C,D. Color variations of the fall cankerworm, *Alsophila pometaria*.

B. The fall cankerworms seen here have nearly defoliated a hickory twig.

E. Adult female cankerworm; note absence of wings.

F,G. Fall cankerworm eggs; in section F some have hatched.

PLATE 51

California Oakworm (Plate 52)

The California oakworm (or oak moth), *Phryganidia californica* Packard, is not known to occur outside California. It is, however, the most important insect affecting oak in that state. The cyclic nature of its population levels causes it to be extremely common in some years and virtually absent in others. Trees are seldom, if ever, killed as a result of defoliation by the oakworm, but the landscape and shade-producing value of affected trees is markedly reduced. Falling excrement, or frass, produced by the feeding larvae, and by the young larvae as they hang on silken threads are additional nuisances where pools and patios are situated beneath oaks. Nearly all species of western oaks are subject to attack by this insect.

The insect passes through two complete generations each year in all but the southernly parts of its range where a third annual generation is reported. In the San Francisco Bay area it overwinters as an egg or young larva. Larval development proceeds rapidly with the coming of warm temperatures in the spring. When young, the larvae feed by removing only one surface from the leaf (C). The injured parts of these leaves then turn brown. When the larvae are about half grown, they begin to feed completely through the leaves, excising large sections from them and collectively defoliating the tree.

At maturity the larva is about 31 mm in length. Pupation occurs on leaves, limbs or trunks of oak trees, other trees nearby, or on other objects such as fences and houses. Moth emergence from pupae occurs in May, June, or July. Adults fly in greatest numbers at dusk. The cycle is then repeated and the subsequent generation of moths occurs in October and November. These moths lay eggs on leaves, branches and limbs.

When infestations are heavy, either of the two generations is capable of severely defoliating oaks over a wide area. Because most of the eggs are deposited on leaves and because the foliage of deciduous oaks drops late in the fall, carrying the eggs or newly hatched larvae away with them, the deciduous oaks normally are spared spring infestations.

Evergreen oaks, on the other hand, commonly are infested by both generations of the insect.

The California oakworm is attacked by a number of parasites and predators. Also, disease-causing microorganisms sometimes result in the death of large numbers of the feeding caterpillars. The bacterium *Bacillus thuringiensis* Berliner has been demonstrated to be an effective control agent when sprayed to coincide with the early third instar larvae.

References: 34, 38, 93, 124

A. Adult female moth of the California oakworm.
B. Eggs on underside of an oak leaf. When newly laid, eggs do not have the reddened areas shown here.
C. Young larva at rest on underside of live oak leaf. Typical feeding on only one leaf surface is shown beneath larva.
D. Pupa of oakworm attached to underside of leaf.
E. Young larvae of *Phryganidia californica*. Note what appears to be an oversized head; this is typical of young larvae.
F. Mature larvae of California oakworm. Note that large larvae feed completely through the leaf tissue.
G. A valley oak, *Quercus lobata*, defoliated by *Phryganidia californica*.

PLATE 52

Satin Moth, Dagger Moth, and Silverspotted Skipper (Plate 53)

The satin moth, *Stilpnotia salicis* Linnaeus, was given its common name because of the white satin sheen of the adult moth (D). It is another of our imported pests, native to Europe and Asia. In 1920 it was found almost simultaneously in Massachusetts and British Columbia. In the intervening years it has spread throughout New England, New York and the Canadian maritime provinces as well as Washington and Oregon.

This insect overwinters as a small larva in a silken cocoon-like bag attached to the trunk or branch of a host tree. On the West Coast the cocoons may be camouflaged with moss and lichens. The larva comes out of hibernation after the leaves have formed and proceeds to devour them. Fully grown caterpillars (A) may reach 50 mm. The pupa (C) is glossy black. After about ten days as a pupa, the adult emerges. Moths are on the wing through much of July. They are strong flyers and are attracted to lights. Egg-laying takes place during July. The female often lays her eggs on leaves but they may be found anywhere on the tree. They are deposited in masses of one to 400. Upon hatching, the young larvae feed upon the epidermis of leaves. After feeding for five or six days, the larva encloses itself in a small, flat web where it molts. After molting, it continues to feed as a skeletonizer until early fall or the first frost, when it prepares for hibernation. Shade and ornamental poplars and willows are most severely attacked. Occasionally the larvae feed on oak and aspen.

Many of the native and imported parasites of gypsy moth attack the satin moth. The two most important parasites in the East are *Compsilura concinnata* Meig. and *Eupteromalus nidulans* (Thomson). On the West Coast serious outbreaks of the satin moth do occur but parasites such as the native tachinid fly, *Tachinomyia similis*, keep it in check.

Dagger moth is the common name given to the larva of *Acronicta americana* Harr. The photograph in section E indicates this insect is appropriately named. The fully grown larva is about 50 mm long. The head is shiny black. It occurs throughout the eastern part of the United States and Canada. Although the dagger moth is quite common it rarely occurs in large or damaging numbers. Its foodplants include apple, basswood, box elder, maple, oak, and willow.

The silverspotted skipper, *Epargyreus clarus* (Cramer), is a butterfly valued by collectors. Adults are strong daylight fliers and feed upon nectar. Larvae feed on black locust and wisteria and occasionally cause severe defoliation. A narrow constricted neck is a characteristic of skipper caterpillars. This species has a large, dull red head and pale green body. When fully grown it is 50 mm long. The larvae are solitary and feed at night. They have a curious habit of drawing leaves together and fastening them with silk. Two generations may occur each year in the southern part of its range. It is widely distributed throughout the United States and southern Canada.

References: 20, 50

A,B. Larvae of the satin moth, *Stilpnotia salicis*, on *Populus deltoides*. The arrow in section B points out its nearly invisible black head.
C. Pupa of the satin moth.
D. Adult satin moth.
E. The dagger moth, *Acronicta americana*, as found on *Acer platanoides*.
F. Larva of a sawfly sometimes confused with the silverspotted skipper.
G. A pinned adult silverspotted skipper showing wing pattern on the dorsal side.
H. A silverspotted skipper. The silver spots on the undersurface give it its name.

PLATE 53

Walnut Caterpillar and Other *Datana* Caterpillars (Plate 54)

The walnut caterpillar, *Datana integerrima* Grote and Robinson, feeds on the foliage of black walnut, butternut, Japanese walnut, Persian walnut, pecan and several species of hickory. Other reported hosts include birch, oak, willow, honeylocust and apple. Walnut caterpillars always feed in clusters. They devour all the leaves on one branch before they move to another. Isolated trees usually suffer more than forest or orchard trees. Defoliation leads to sunscald, which further weakens the trees and leaves them vulnerable to wood boring insects.

The pupa overwinters just beneath the surface of the ground, usually under the host tree. The adult, a heavy-bodied moth with a wingspan of 40 mm, emerges from its pupal case late in the spring. The fore wings are buff-colored with narrow, dark lines across them. Eggs are laid on the undersides of leaves (A), in masses of 300 or more. First-stage larvae (B) are skeletonizers. During the second stage the larvae devour all of the leaf except for the midvein. As they near full size they devour the entire leaf including the petiole. Third- and fourth-stage larvae are brick red (C,F). They feed a month or more before reaching maturity. The mature larvae are about 50 mm long with grayish-black bodies clothed with long, grayish-white hairs (F).

The larvae have several interesting habits. When disturbed, they arch their heads and tails as though to fight off a predator. When molting, they crowd together on a branch or trunk and all molt at the same time, leaving an ugly patch of fur-like hair and skin.

The walnut caterpillar is distributed throughout most of the eastern United States and as far west as Minnesota, Kansas, and Texas. In the northeastern states and west to Michigan one generation occurs each year. Two generations are common from North Carolina to Arkansas and south.

Eggs are subject to attack by several wasp parasites. Larvae are often heavily parasitized by the fly *Phorocera claripennis* Macq.

Other common caterpillar pests of walnut are *Schizura concinna*, the redhumped caterpillar (Plate 57) and *Datana angusii* G & R. Fully grown *Datana angusii* larvae are black with pale lines and clothed with white hairs. Their feeding behavior and life cycle are similar to that of the walnut caterpillar. In and south of Maryland the azalea caterpillar, *Datana major* G. & R., is frequently a problem. It, like other *Datana* caterpillars, is a gregarious feeder. First-stage larvae are skeletonizers. Later, the larvae devour the entire leaf. The fully grown caterpillar, 50 mm in length, has a red head and legs and a black body with longitudinal rows of yellow spots and sparse white hairs. Moths lay their eggs on the undersides of azalea leaves.

Datana major can be a serious pest of azaleas in the Southeast. It has been reported on blueberry in Delaware and red oak in Maryland. Occasionally it is found on andromeda.

References: 133, 161

A. Egg masses on the undersides of leaflets.
B. Eggs and newly hatched larvae.
C. A cluster of walnut caterpillars in their red stage.
D. Second-stage walnut caterpillar larvae feeding on leaves of *Juglans cinerea*. The brown leaves have been skeletonized by the first-stage larvae.
E. Walnut caterpillars massed on the trunk, about ready to molt.
F. The upper specimen is a fully grown walnut caterpillar. The lower specimen will molt again.

PLATE 54

Orangestriped Oakworm and Yellownecked Caterpillar (Plate 55)

The orangestriped oakworm, *Anisota senatoria* (J. E. Smith), is one of four closely related moths that are often abundant in the eastern part of the United States. The other three species are *Anisota stigma* (F), *A. virginiensis* (Drury) and *Dryocampa* (= Anisota) *rubicunda* (F), also known as the greenstriped mapleworm. These four species have many habits and physical features in common. *A. senatoria* and *A. virginiensis* moths both have a single white dot on their respective forewing. The larva of each has two recurved horns on the second thoracic segment, and the anal plate has three to four short terminal spines; all the above mentioned larvae are marked with conspicuous stripes and all have either short or long spines along the abdomen.

The fully grown orangestriped oakworm (B), about 55 mm long, crawls from trees and burrows from one to four inches into the soil. There it builds an earthen cell to pupate and pass the winter. The moths first appear in early summer and are attracted to artificial light at night. Over the period of a month the female will deposit from one to 500 or more eggs in a single cluster on the underside of an oak leaf, usually on lower branches. The newly hatched larvae are greenish-yellow but have the same characteristic horn-like projection as the mature larvae. The early instars are gregarious and skeletonize the leaf, consuming all except a network of veins. Older caterpillars eat all but the main vein; they usually defoliate one branch before going on to another. One generation occurs each year in its more northerly range.

The orangestriped oakworm moth has a rather wide distribution. It has been reported in a range extending from Wisconsin and Michigan east to New England and eastern Canada. It is also known in Georgia and Kansas, although it is more abundant in the northern part of the United States than in the southern areas. Herrick (129) says that the orangestriped oakworm moth seems to prefer white and scrub oak. It definitely prefers oak foliage but also feeds upon maple, hickory, birch and hazelnut. Destructive outbreaks of this insect have been reported in New York, Michigan, New Jersey and other states. Usually forest trees suffer most, but trees in parks and along city streets are, on occasion, severely attacked.

The yellownecked caterpillar moth, *Datana ministra* (Drury), is difficult to distinguish from the walnut caterpillar moth. The yellownecked caterpillar (E,F,G) has a rather broad range of host plants including crabapple, flowering peach, cherry, almond, quince, maple, elm, butternut, walnut, oak, hickory, chestnut, beech, linden, witch-hazel, birch, locust, sumac, azalea and boxwood. It is widely distributed throughout the United States, but it is not common in the southwest portion of the United States. It is known in British Columbia and probably occurs in other Canadian provinces.

As with other *Datana* caterpillars, it spends its winters as a pupa in an oblong cell an inch or so underground. Moths appear in June and July and lay their eggs in clusters of 25 to 100 or more on the undersides of leaves. The eggs of a single cluster usually hatch about the same time and the larvae feed gregariously throughout their four- to six-week larval period. Newly hatched caterpillars skeletonize the lower leaf surface; older ones devour all but the petiole. When disturbed, the larvae lift their head and tail portions high above the rest of their bodies as though to strike at a potential enemy. The yellownecked caterpillar gets its name because of the bright orange-yellow segment behind its head. When fully grown it crawls down the trunk and burrows into the soil. Male moths are attracted in moderate numbers to lights.

A number of natural enemies attack this species. Birds such as robins and bluejays feed on the yellownecked caterpillar, and it is often attacked by predaceous sucking bugs. Tachinid flies (D) are active parasites of it. They are common in the Appalachian Mountains and foothills.

References: 20, 129

A. The orangestriped oakworm, *Anisota senatoria*, on the remains of oak leaves.
B. A fully grown orangestriped oakworm larva. Note the short, terminal spines at the end of the abdomen.
C. Orangestriped oakworm on oak leaves.
D. A Tachinid fly, a parasite of the yellownecked caterpillar. Approximately 10 mm long.
E. A cluster of yellownecked caterpillars, *Datana ministra*.
F. The black color phase of the yellownecked caterpillar. Note the typical alarm posture of the insects.
G. A yellownecked caterpillar in the yellow-red color phase.

PLATE 55

Mourningcloak Butterfly (Plate 56)

Many insects are endowed with beautiful color and form; and so is the butterfly *Nymphalis antiopa* (Linnaeus). Even the caterpillar is attractively colored, but it can be a serious defoliator of shade trees such as elm, willow, poplar, birch, hackberry and linden. Elm and willow (A) are the preferred foodplants.

In the latitude of New York City, two generations occur each year. The adult butterflies hibernate during the winter in secluded places where they can avoid rain and wind. As a result they are one of the first butterflies to fly in the spring after the buds of food trees open. Eggs are laid in masses of 300 to 450 on twigs of newly burgeoning trees. The eggs are ribbed and are yellow at first, but later turn black. The caterpillars, commonly called spiny elm caterpillars, are gregarious. They devour the leaves of one branch at a time. When fully grown, they are 50 mm long. Their spines, while formidable in appearance, are practically harmless. Note that the abdominal legs as well as the single row of spots on the back are red. The black areas are abundantly sprinkled with small white dots. After the larva has completed its growth, it suspends itself from a twig and hangs downward to form a chrysalis (B). The butterfly emerges within a week and a second generation begins in early August in the southern part of its range (C). This beautiful butterfly is found throughout the United States and in Canada as far north as the Arctic Circle. It is both a woodland and city dwelling species and at times is abundant enough in an area to be classified a serious pest.

It is attacked by numerous wasp parasites. Black-and yellow-billed cuckoos, among other birds, sometimes devour the larvae.

References: 20

A. Caterpillars of the mourningcloak butterfly feeding on the leaves of a willow.
B. Chrysalises hanging from a defoliated willow.
C. The butterfly stage. Color patterns vary somewhat with individual butterflies. The center portions of the wings may range from dark maroon to nearly black. The wingspan ranges up to 63 mm.

PLATE 56

Redhumped Caterpillar and *Orgyia* Tussock Moths (Plate 57)

The redhumped caterpillar, *Schizura concinna* (J. E. Smith), is a pest of many ornamental, fruit, and nut trees throughout continental United States.

The moth stage is grayish brown with a wing expanse of slightly over 25 mm. Its spherical, white eggs are laid in groups of from 25 to 100 on the undersides of leaves of susceptible hosts. Newly hatched larvae, which feed gregariously at first, tend to disperse as the caterpillars mature. The mature larva is about 38 mm in length. It is yellow with a red head and is lined longitudinally with reddish, black, and white stripes (B). A number of very prominent black tubercles arise from the back and there is a large reddish hump on top of the first abdominal segment. It is this red hump that gives it its name. After completing its growth the caterpillar migrates down the tree trunk and pupates inside a silken cocoon constructed in the soil or among plant refuse on the soil surface. Here it spends the winter. One to five generations occur each year, depending on climatic conditions.

Larvae consume all the leaf tissue except the major veins. Damage is generally confined to scattered branches in the tree, though periodically defoliation of entire trees takes place over a widespread area. This happens periodically in California. There, the late summer and early fall generations of *Schizura* are more important on fruit trees such as walnut, than are those generations which occur earlier. Reduced foliage results in sunburned fruit.

The following are woody plants on which the redhumped caterpillar is known to feed: *Betula*—birch; *Caryae*—hickory; *Cornus*—dogwood; *Crataegus*—hawthorn; *Juglans*—walnut, butternut; *Liquidambar*—sweetgum; *Malus*—apple; *Populus*—poplar, aspen, cottonwood; *Prunus*—apricot, plum, prune, cherry; *Pyrus*—pear; *Rosa*—rose; *Salix*—willow; *Ulmus*—elm; and *Vaccinium*—huckleberry (blueberry).

Several related species of *Schizura* which may be noticed from time to time include the unicorn caterpillar, *S. unicornis* (Smith), and *S. ipomaeae* Doubleday. The latter species has been reported from the eastern states and from Idaho, Utah, and California. It feeds on maple, birch, *Ceanothus*, honeylocust (*Gleditsia triacanthos*), apple, plum, oak, rubus, elm, and *Vaccinium*. Neither *S. unicornis* nor *S. ipomaeae* look similar to *S. concinna* while in the larval stage. Instead of distinctive coloration, larva of both species are protectively colored in greens and browns so that their appearance is much like that of bits of leaves with brown or reddish edges. Both species have a prominent dorsal projection.

Several members of the genus *Orgyia*, known as tussock moths because of the characteristic tufts of hair on the larvae, are important pests of ornamental and forest trees throughout North America. (See Plate 58 for other tussock moths.)

Orgyia leucostigma (Smith), the white-marked tussock moth, occurs throughout the eastern states and as far west as Colorado and British Columbia. This insect spends the winter in the egg stage. Eggs are deposited in masses on the spent cocoons of the insect (C). Between April and June, depending on location, the eggs hatch and the larvae migrate to the leaves. Young larvae skeletonize the leaves, but older larvae chew the entire leaf except for the main veins and petiole. The fully grown larva is about 31 mm long. It has a red head and yellowish body tufted with distinctive hair. The mature larva pupates in a grayish cocoon, which contains many body hairs and is constructed on twigs or branches. One to three generations of the whitemarked tussock moth occur each year.

The male moth is ash gray and has a wingspan of about 31 mm. The female moth is dirty white, hairy and wingless.

O. leucostigma is a general feeder. It attacks the foliage of a wide variety of deciduous plants. The more common hosts are: *Abies*—(balsam) fir; *Acer*—maple; *Aesculus*—horse chestnut; *Betula*—birch; *Larix*—larch; *Malus*—apple; *Platanus*—sycamore; *Populus*—poplar; *Rosa*—rose; *Salix*—willow; *Tilia*—linden; *Ulmus*—elm; *Wisteria*.

The Douglas fir tussock moth, *Orgyia pseudotsugata* McDonnough, is sporadically a serious pest in northwestern United States and southwestern Canada, where it defoliates Douglas fir (*Pseudotsuga menziesii*) and true fir (*Abies*) (see Plate 5.)

Many other species of tussock moths occur on various ornamental plants in different parts of the United States. All seem to be sporadic in their appearance. They are quite numerous one year and virtually absent the next. A large number of parasites and predators have been collected from the tussock moths. These, together with microorganisms which cause disease and subsequent death of larvae, are believed to be responsible for the irregular appearance of these insects as pests.

References: 1, 93, 143, 183, 198

A. Larvae of redhumped caterpillars defoliating walnut.
B. Close-up of red humped caterpillars on poplar.
C. A cluster of tussock moth eggs on a juniper twig. Eggs were laid on the female's old cocoon.
D. A fully grown tussock moth larva on *Cotoneaster horizontalis*.

PLATE 57

Tussock Moths (Plate 58)

Orygia vetusta Boisduval is a tussock moth commonly found on the Pacific coast from British Columbia to southern California. It feeds on willow, hawthorn, manzanita, oak, walnut, crabapple, pyracantha, California holly, coffeeberry, and other plants. In southern California two generations may occur each year. In other areas there is but one. In northern California eggs are laid in late summer in felt-like masses upon old cocoons. Eggs overwinter and hatch early in the spring. The young larvae skeletonize the leaves (C); mature larvae devour the entire leaf. Mature larvae, 13 to 22 mm in length, are a nuisance when they wander about to find suitable places for pupation (A). They pupate on the leaves, bark, and twigs of shrubs and trees, and on fences, eaves of buildings and other man-made objects (D). The larva is attractively colored with spots of bright red and yellow. It has four round brush-like tufts of hair on its back, and horn-like tufts of black hair both posteriorly and anteriorly. It has a number of parasites, mainly parasitic wasps and tachinid flies, but these are usually inadequate for control.

The hickory tussock moth, *Halisidota caryae* Harris, is also known as the hickory tiger moth. This name comes from the markings on its wings (J). It is found from Missouri and Minnesota east to the Atlantic Ocean. It also occurs in southern Canada.

This insect produces one generation each year and over-winters as a pupa inside a densely hairy oval cocoon (F). Moths emerge in June and lay their eggs in clusters of a hundred or more on the undersides of leaves. The hickory tussock moth females have functional wings but because of their comparatively heavy bodies they are weak fliers. Young larvae feed gregariously; later they scatter to feed. The caterpillars require about three months to complete their development. During this time color patterns change (G,H) but the caterpillar is basically white, with a black head. When fully grown it is about 37 mm long. The caterpillars build their cocoons on or near the ground; in New York State this occurs in late September. Host trees include hickory, walnut, butternut, linden, apple, basswood, and aspen.

Several wasps parasitize the hickory tussock moth, but rarely hold it in check.

Halisidota harrisii (Walsh) attacks American sycamore and London plane tree. Outbreaks of this insect have occurred in New York City. Half or more of the foliage of street and park trees have been removed due to its feeding. On Long Island larvae are found in early July. Feeding is most active at dusk. The larva chews from the edge of the leaf. Its life cycle parallels that of other East Coast tussock moths (see pages 24 and 130).

References: 34, 50, 61, 93, 153, 256, 293

A. A fully grown larva of the western tussock moth.
B,D. Cocoons of the western tussock moth on a leaf and fence.
C. Young western tussock moth larvae on a skeletonized willow leaf.
E. An adult male moth.
F. A cocoon of the hickory tussock moth, *Halisidota caryae*.
G,H. Color forms of the larvae of the hickory tussock moth.
I. A fully grown sycamore tussock moth larva, *Halisidota harrisii*.
J. A hickory tussock moth.

PLATE 58

133

Several Subtropical Caterpillars (Plate 59)

Two subtropical caterpillars are very common in Florida and some areas of the Gulf Coast.

One species, *Syntomeida epilais jucundissima* (Dyar), feeds on oleander, a plant that is poisonous to most animals. Oleander is its only known host. Three generations occur each year. Larvae are known to be present in March, December and July. It is likely that generations overlap because the young larvae (B), the fully grown larvae (C), and the adults have been observed together in early December.

The moth is purplish with white dots on greenish black wings. Female moths lay oval, light yellow eggs in clusters of 25 to 75 on the undersides of oleander leaves. The eggs are laid close together but never touch. Upon hatching the young larvae first eat their own egg shells, then begin feeding gregariously on the underside of the leaf (B). Leaves are first skeletonized and later devoured completely (A). The fully grown larva is about 30 mm long. Cocoons are loosely woven from hair and silk threads. The life cycle requires about 60 days for completion. Adults live about 9 days.

The second subtropical species, *Homaledra sabalella* (Chambers), is the major pest of palms in Florida. The fronds are skeletonized, usually on the lower side, leaving the leaf folds packed with frass. Although palms are seldom killed, the upper surfaces of their leaves turn brown, destroying their ornamental value (D).

Up to 70 eggs may be deposited by a single female on the underside of a young leaf. After the eggs hatch, larvae feed under the egg shells for a few days and collectively spin a tent-like mat or web which protects the colony as it feeds. The frass is mixed with the continuously growing web (E). The larvae live in colonies of 35 to 100 individuals. When fully grown the larva is about 15 mm long. It pupates under cover of the web. Generations occur continuously throughout the year and moths may be collected at almost any time. The moths are attracted to light at night. Moths do not feed and live only three to ten days. *H. sabalella* has been found on the following palms and palmettos: butia, coconut, latania and date palms; and dwarf, cabbage and saw palmetto.

There is one very active predator of *H. sabalella*. A carabid beetle, *Plochinous amandus* Newman, helps keep the moth in check. The beetle larvae live under the web within the colony of caterpillars.

References: 29, 53

A. The larvae of *Syntomeida epilais jucundissima* feeding on oleander leaves.
B. A colony of young oleander caterpillars skeletonizing the underside of a leaf.
C. Fully grown oleander caterpillars.
D. A palm frond showing dead areas of leaves. Damage was caused by *Homaledra sabalella*.
E. Frass moved aside to expose a larva.
F. A close-up of a palmetto palm showing the webbing filled with frass under which is a colony of *Homaledra sabalella*.

PLATE 59

Leaf-eating Caterpillars (Plate 60)

Mahonia has a tough prickly leaf which would seem to be unpalatable to any animal; but for the moth, *Coryphista meadii* (Packard), which in its larva stage feeds exclusively on *Mahonia* and *Berberis* cultivars, tough fibrous leaves apparently are no obstacle. Where larvae are abundant the cultivars of these genera are defoliated by mid-summer.

There are two races of *C. meadii*. The dark form is dull brownish gray, and has several narrow wavy black bands across its wings. The other form is lighter in color.

Both have a wingspan of about 38 mm, and both overwinter as pupae. Adults emerge in the spring—about mid-May in New York. Eggs are usually laid singly on either side of the leaf. The female produces an average of 125 eggs; these she lays at night. Eggs hatch in three to four days and the larvae immediately start to feed on the leaves. At first they are skeletonizers, and leave behind a network of veins (B). Later they devour entire leaves. These caterpillars move in a looping motion and have a double pair of prolegs (E). When fully grown, about 24 mm in length, they crawl to the soil and burrow in a short distance. There, they pupate. Three generations occur each year in New York State as well as in Idaho. In Ohio the caterpillars are active until October. The *C. meadii* larvae are sometimes referred to by the name "barberry looper."

C. meadii occurs sporadically throughout much of the United States.

Several fly and wasp parasites undoubtedly are major factors in holding *C. meadii* in check. Birds devour many of the pupae by digging them from the ground.

The linden looper (C), *Erannis tiliaria* (Harris), periodically defoliates many deciduous trees, including linden, apple, birch, elm, hickory, maple and oak. It is a native insect found in the northern half of the United States from the Atlantic coast to the Rocky Mountains and in Quebec, Ontario and the Northwest Territories of Canada. The linden looper has been found to occupy the same kinds of trees as the cankerworm (see page 118).

Its eggs are laid three or four to a cluster under loose bark on the trunk and larger limbs. They hatch at about the time buds open in the spring. The caterpillars feed on the foliage for about one month. Although the color patterns of the individual linden loopers are essentially the same, the intensity of their coloring varies. They possess two pairs of prolegs and move with a looping motion. When fully grown they measure about 37 mm in length and are quite active. They crawl to the ground where they tunnel an inch or more into the soil to pupate. All this activity occurs before the first of July. Moths emerge from the ground from October to December. Eggs are laid at this time. The female is wingless, and can be identified by the two rows of large black spots on the back. Females measure about 13 mm in length. They must crawl up the tree to lay eggs. One generation occurs each year.

Ennomos subsignarius Hübn., a looper related to *Erannis tiliaria*, and variously named elm spanworm and snow-white linden moth, does not appear in damaging numbers every year. It is generally distributed from Nova Scotia to Georgia and westward to the Mississippi valley. It is also known in Colorado.

The larvae when fully grown are about 40 mm long. They are brownish black with yellowish markings, and have a remarkable resemblance to a stubby twig. They are found in trees in late May and through much of June. The moths are pure white and attracted to lights. When abundant they migrate in swarms over long distances. The caterpillars feed upon elm, linden, red maple, birch, beech, *Aesculus* and others. An egg parasite in the genus *Ooencyrtus*, a wasp, is important in controlling the populations of elm spanworm.

The caterpillar of *Pyramidobela angelarum* Keifer is described as a leaftier (F). This insect was first recorded in southern California in 1934 and is known to now live in the northern part of the state as well. It probably respresents an introduction from a more tropical region. Breeding apparently occurs the year round on its host, *Buddleia*, on which this insect is a specific feeder. *Pyramidobela* webs and skeletonizes leaves and feeds on the terminal buds. The larva is yellow to green and measures 12 to 14 mm when fully grown. The adult moth is ashen in color with a wingspan of 16 to 21 mm.

References: 32, 154, 210, 235

A. Ragged leaves on a *Mahonia* bush. Damage was caused by *Coryphista meadii*, sometimes called barberry looper.

B. Two larval stages of *Coryphista meadii*.

C. Two color forms of the linden looper, *Erannis tiliaria*.

D,E. Fully grown larvae of *Coryphista meadii*. Note the caterpillar in a looping posture and the double pair of prolegs.

F,G. Damaged *Buddleia calbillea* leaves caused by the webbing and feeding of *Pyramidobela angelarum*.

PLATE 60

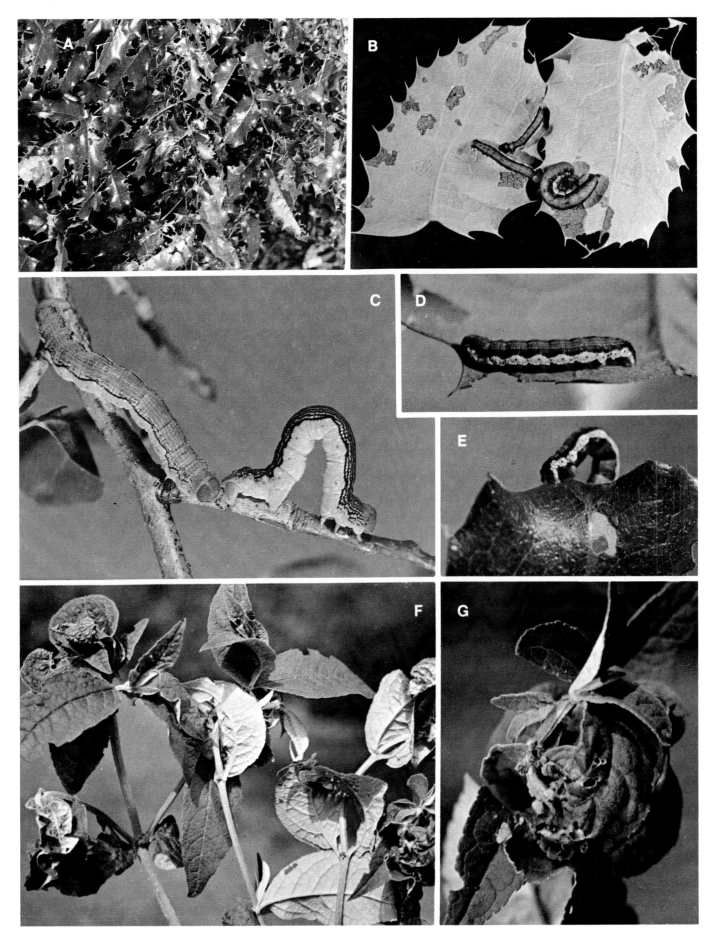

Leaf-eating Caterpillars (Plate 61)

The caterpillars shown in Plate 61 have major differences in external appearance such as transverse rows of hairs, beautiful tubercles and poisonous spines. All are unusually colorful.

Harrisina americana (Guerin), shown in sections A, B and C, is commonly known as the grapeleaf skeletonizer. It is found from New England to Florida and west to Missouri.

This species becomes abundant periodically. It devours the leaves of Virginia creeper, *Parthenocissus quinquefolia,* as well as the leaves of wild and cultivated grapes. These destructive caterpillars can be found in central Florida in early September, and in Connecticut in late June to mid-August. When fully grown the larva measures about 11 mm. In Florida adults are on the wing in March and September, and lay their eggs on the undersides of host leaves. Each year, two generations occur in the South and one in the North.

The eggs hatch at about the same time on any given leaf and the larvae line up side by side, sometimes two rows deep, and skeletonize the leaf (A). As they approach maturity, they become less and less gregarious and finally live separately. Fully grown larvae attach themselves to the woody stems and spin thin white cocoons (C). The moth is black (E) and has a wingspan of 25 mm.

In California and the Southwest, *Harrisina brillians* B. & McD., sometimes called the western grapeleaf skeletonizer, is at times a serious pest of grape. It has been brought under control largely by the use of insect parasites, one of the most effective of which is *Apanteles harrisinae* Mues., a wasp.

Automeris io (Fabricius), commonly called the io moth, is one of the favorites of moth collectors, partly because of the large eye-like spots on the hind wings. The larva (H) should be recognized if for no other reason than to avoid touching or handling it. It is covered with spines, each of which is connected to a poison gland. People who have come into contact with these spines react as if stung. The itching after effect may be mild or severe depending upon one's sensitivity to allergens.

The larvae feed on various trees and shrubs such as rose, willow, oak, sycamore, elm, beech, poplar, maple, birch, ash and linden. They are common in the East but are rarely found in large numbers. One generation occurs each year. The moths are attracted to lights.

The cecropia moth, *Hyalophora cecropia* L., is the largest of our native silk moths. Its wing expanse varies from 140 to 165 mm and is common in the insect collections of both amateur and professional entomologists. The larva (F) feeds on at least 50 species of plants including linden, maple, boxelder, elm, birch, willow, hawthorn and poplar. When fully grown it measures from 75 to 100 mm. It forms a large double-walled overwintering cocoon which is often attached to a twig of its host plant. Artificial control is often not necessary because the larvae are usually heavily parasitized by the tachinid fly, *Lespesia ciliata* (Mac.). One generation occurs each year.

Reference: 93

A. A grape leaf partly skeletonized by the larvae of *Harrisina americana*. Note the larva at the juncture of the leaf blade and petiole.
B. A fully grown larva of *Harrisina americana,* about 11 mm long.
C. Cocoons of *Harrisina americana*.
D. A fourth stage larva of *Harrisina americana*.
E. An adult female moth of *Harrisina americana*.
F. A fully grown cecropia moth larva, *Hyalophora cecropia*.
G. The anterior end of a cecropia caterpillar with white eggs of a parasite attached to its exo-skeleton.
H. The fully grown io moth caterpillar, *Automeris io*.

PLATE 61

Fall Webworm (Plate 62)

The fall webworm, *Hyphantria cunea* (Drury), is a native of North America and Mexico. In 1940, it was recorded in Hungary and since has become a major pest of trees throughout Europe and parts of Asia. Many of the important forest and shade tree pests of the United States were accidentally introduced from Europe and Asia; the fall webworm is one of a much smaller number of insect pests that went the other way.

It feeds on almost all shade, fruit and ornamental trees except conifers. In the United States, the fall webworm attacks at least 88 species of trees, and in Europe, 230 species of trees, shrubs, ornamentals and annual plants. In Japan, its diet includes 317 plant hosts.

In the United States, its feeding habits vary from region to region. Its preferences range from pecan or black walnut in some areas to persimmon or sweetgum in others. In Western Appalachia and the Ohio valley, American elm, maples, or hickory is preferred; in the western United States the fall webworm is common on alder, willow, cottonwood, madrone and fruit trees.

The fall webworm is distributed throughout most of the United States and Canada. At one time it was thought that there were two species, *H. cunea* and *H. textor*. Now there are known to be two races of a single species—one blackheaded (E) and the other, redheaded. These races differ in the markings of both the larvae and adults as well as in their food habits and biology. For example, in the southern United States, adults of the blackheaded race appear one month earlier than those of the redheaded race. The females of the blackheaded race deposit their eggs as single-layer masses in mid-March, whereas the redheaded form deposits most of its eggs in double layers in mid-April. When the larvae hatch, the blackheaded form is yellowish green to pale yellow with two rows of dark tubercles along the back. Its head is black, and its body covered with fine hair. When fully grown, the blackheaded form is yellowish or greenish with a broad, dark stripe along the back. The redheaded race is tawny or yellowish tan with orange to reddish tubercles.

The larvae of the fall webworm pass through as many as 11 stages of development. In each stage, feeding occurs within a distinct web made of silk produced by the larvae. The blackheaded race forms a flimsy web; that of the redheaded race is larger and more compact. When alarmed all the larvae in a "nest," whether of the black- or red-headed race, make jerky movements in perfect rhythm, possibly as a defensive mechanism. Depending upon climate, one to four generations of the fall webworm occur per year; in Louisiana, four are common.

More than 50 species of parasites and 36 species of predators of the fall webworm are known in America. A similar number of natural enemies is reported in Europe.

On small trees, nests of the fall webworm may be cut out and destroyed. The insect is mainly detrimental to the beauty of the host, and is thus more a nuisance than a threat to the health of the tree. Nests always occur terminally on the branches of the host.

References: 50, 198, 203, 217, 302

A. A nest of young fall webworms, *Hyphantria cunea*.
B,C,E. The color of the fall webworm caterpillar varies; the black dots are always distinctive.
D. A large web on a black cherry tree.

PLATE 62

Eastern Tent Caterpillar (Plate 63)

The eastern tent caterpillar, *Malacosoma americana* Fabricius, is apparently a native insect. Its existence was reported as early as 1646. It has been noted for many years that the eastern tent caterpillar occurs in great numbers at intervals of approximately ten years.

Some authorities consider this tent caterpillar to be the most widespread defoliator of deciduous shade trees in the eastern part of the United States. At times, the entire countryside seems to be enveloped in the silken tents this caterpillar makes.

Although it is called the eastern tent caterpillar it does occur as far west as the Rocky Mountains. Its favorite hosts are wild cherry, apple and crabapple, though occasionally it feeds upon deciduous forest and ornamentals such as ash, birch, black gum, red gum, willow, witch-hazel, maple, oak, poplar, cherry, peach and plum.

This insect overwinters (for nine months) as an egg. Eggs are laid in distinctive masses encircling the smaller twigs of the host plant (D). These masses are up to 19 mm long and contain 150–350 eggs. The masses have a varnished appearance.

The larvae hatch from the eggs in the spring at about the time the wild cherry leaves start to unfold (E). The newly hatched caterpillars gather at a branch fork or crotch and begin to build a web from which they go forth to feed on newly opened leaves. The larvae spin a fine strand of silk wherever they go. As the caterpillars grow so does their web. When the populations are large, whole trees become covered with webbing and all leaves are devoured.

The fully grown caterpillars are generally black and about two inches (5 cm) long. There is a white stripe down the back and a series of very blue spots between longitudinal yellowish lines (A). When the larvae reach this stage they leave the host tree and search for a place to spin white cocoons on fences, tree trunks or other natural or man-made objects. They transform within the cocoon into reddish brown moths with two whitish stripes running obliquely across each forewing. The adults emerge in late June or early July and after mating the females deposit their eggs on the twigs. One generation occurs each year.

Damage can be reduced on small trees by getting rid of the egg masses during the winter or by clipping and destroying the tents and their occupants at night while they are still small.

The forest tent caterpillar, *Malacosoma disstria* Hbn., doesn't really form a tent in the usual sense. The larvae gather on a silken mat (of their own construction) which is in turn located on a branch of the tree. From there on they forage in all directions. The egg masses encircle twigs and are squared off at the end in contrast to the spindle-shaped masses of *M. americana*. The fully grown larva of *M. disstria* (C) is easily distinguished from that of *M. americana* by the series of keyhole-shaped spots along its back (*M. americana* has a single solid stripe).

The forest tent caterpillar is distributed throughout much of the United States and Canada. A number of deciduous trees are fed upon but the foliage of ash, birch, black gum, red gum, sugar maple, oak and poplar are preferred. The life history is similar to that of *M. americana*.

See Plate 64 for tent caterpillars in western United States.

Reference: 20

A. Mature larva of the eastern tent caterpillar, *Malacosoma americana*.
B. *Prunus serotina* defoliated by *Malacosoma americana*. Note tent in center of photograph.
C. Mature larva of the forest tent caterpillar, *Malacosoma disstria*.
D. Egg mass of *Malacosoma americana*.
E. Young larvae recently hatched from egg mass, *Malacosoma americana*.

PLATE 63

Western Tent Caterpillars (Plate 64)

Several species of tent caterpillars of the genus *Malacosoma* are important enemies of western ornamental plants. These include: the forest tent caterpillar, *M. disstria* Hubner; the California tent caterpillar, *M. californicum* (Packard); the Great Basin tent caterpillar, *M. fragile* (Stretch); and the western tent caterpillar, *M. pluviale* (Dyar). Because the life cycles and activities of the various tent caterpillars are similar, only a few will be described here.

Probably the best known of the tent caterpillars is the forest tent caterpillar (see Plate 63). The wings of the adult are light buff-brown, and measure 25 to 37 mm across. The forewings have two dark, oblique bands near the center.

The female moths lay their eggs in the summer. They are laid on twigs in such a way that the twig is encircled by the eggs in a dark cementing substance. The new larvae appear soon after the first leaves begin to expand in the spring.

The forest tent caterpillar larvae feed on the foliage for about six weeks. Unlike other *Malacosoma* species, they do not construct tents of webbing. Instead, they build mats of webbing on the larger branches. The larvae are found at these sites when they are not feeding. The larvae are heavily clothed with hair and measure about 50 mm in length when mature.

Pupation of the forest tent caterpillar larva takes place inside a cocoon of its own construction; the cocoon attached to a tree trunk limb, or other object. When the moth emerges from the cocoon it mates and lays eggs which overwinter. A single generation occurs each year. Its range covers nearly all of Canada and the United States east of Minnesota.

Hosts of the forest tent caterpillar include: *Acer negundo*— boxelder; *Betula*—birch; *Chaenomeles*—quince; *Crataegus*— hawthorn; *Malus*—apple; *Populus*—poplar; *Prunus*—cherry, peach, plum, prune; *Pyrus*—pear; *Rosa*—rose; *Salix*—willow.

The California tent caterpillar is a common web-forming species (B). Oak, particularly the coast live oak, *Quercus agrifolia*, is a favored host and is attacked very early in the spring. The life cycle of the California tent caterpillar is similar to that of the forest tent caterpillar. Its host plants include: *Arbutus menziesi*—madrone; *Ceanothus*; *Cercis*—redbud; *Corylus*—hazel; *Fraxinus*—ash; *Heteromeles arbutifolia*—California holly; *Malus*—apple; *Populus*—poplar; *Prunus*—almond, apricot, cherry, prune, plum; *Quercus*—oak; *Rhamnus californica*—California coffeeberry; *Ribes*—currant; *Salix*—willow.

Tent caterpillars commonly found in the East are shown in Plate 63.

References: 1, 61, 93

A. Eggs of the western tent caterpillar, *Malacosoma pluviale*, on birch seed pods.
B. Tent formed by early instar larvae of the California tent caterpillar on coast live oak. Note droppings of caterpillars within tent.
C. Aggregation of larvae of California tent caterpillar on coast live oak.
D. Mature larvae of California tent caterpillar.
E. Tent of California tent caterpillar, with larvae crawling over surface. Tents are enlarged as larvae grow.
F. Defoliation of coast live oak by a colony of the California tent caterpillar.

PLATE 64

Ugly Nest Caterpillar, Oak Webworm, and Oak Leaf Rollers (Plate 65)

Some insects do a tidy job of chewing up their host trees, but not the ugly nest caterpillar, *Archips cerasivoranus* Fitch, nor its near relative, the oak webworm, *Archips fervidanus* Clem. These caterpillars spin a dense web around the feeding site that becomes filled with their excrement and bits and pieces of leaves. The larvae are gregarious and nearly 20 mm long when fully grown. They are yellowish-green with shiny black heads. The larvae pupate in the mess they create. The moth of the ugly nest caterpillar is dull orange with a wingspan of 18–25 mm. Emergence of the adult occurs from July to September depending upon climatic conditions. The eggs which are laid in late summer and early fall remain attached to the host plant all winter. They hatch in May and June and the larvae begin building a web nest where they remain until they emerge as moths.

The ugly nest caterpillar is generally distributed through the northern states and Canada where its favorite hosts are roses, hawthorn and cherry, although they are found on other species. It seldom does any lasting damage to its host, but its ugly nests are detrimental to the beauty of high-value ornamental plants.

The adult oak webworm is a brownish moth with a slightly shorter wingspan than the adult ugly nest caterpillar. The hind wing is gray while that of its close relative is orange. The larvae (C) are generally greener than the ugly nest caterpillar (D). The oak webworm feeds on scrub, red, black and scarlet oaks. Its life cycle and habits are similar to that of the ugly nest caterpillar.

Archips semiferanus Wlk., an oak leaf roller, may be a severe pest of native oaks in the eastern half of the United States and Canada. One generation occurs each year. Eggs are laid in masses of 40–50 at the base of large branches and depressed areas on both trunk and limbs. The keg-shaped eggs are covered with scales from the female moth's body. These eggs overwinter (for nearly ten months) and hatch early in the spring. Fully grown larvae (E) are about 20 mm long. The larvae are defoliators and may completely strip foliage from several oak species. They occasionally feed on witch-hazel and apple, although oak is undoubtedly their preferred host. In Pennsylvania, massive outbreaks occurred in 1970, 1971 and 1972. During these epidemics it became apparent that the larvae were carried from one place to another by the wind. Two tiny wasps, *Itoplectis con-*quisitor (Say) and *Phaeogenes gilvilabris* Allen, are important pupal parasites of the oak leaf roller.

The oak leaftiers, *Croesia albicomana* (Clem.) and *C. semipurpurana* (Kearfott) are often associated with *A. semiferanus*. Their larvae are about 12 mm when fully grown, and are a dirty-white to light green color. They have a pale brown head and brown to black thoracic legs. Newly hatched larvae are found in Connecticut from mid-April to early May. Larvae that hatch early enter unopened buds and feed on the newly forming leaves. Large populations can destroy nearly all the buds on a tree. Those buds that survive frequently produce leaves with a series of round holes, symptoms of earlier injury. Older larvae feed more openly since they are somewhat protected by their webbing and folded leaves. Mature larvae drop by means of silken threads to the ground, where they pupate. Adult moths emerge in June and July and lay eggs on twigs with rough bark. One generation occurs each year but damaging populations usually appear in several year cycles.

The oak leaftiers are found from Ontario and Quebec south to Texas. Injury occurs in late April and early May in Connecticut and Pennsylvania. Both *C. albicomana* and *C. semipurpurana* have a preference for red and scarlet oaks in the Northeast, and both cause spring defoliation, which results in greater injury than mid-summer defoliation.

The fruit-tree leaf roller, *Archips argyrospilus* Walker, is also a pest of oak, hawthorn, white birch, elm, maple, hickory, black and Persian walnut, California buckeye, poplar, cherry, pear and rose. It is a common pest of apple and crabapple. Its larvae feed on leaves and fruit in the spring. One generation occurs each year. It may be found wherever their host plants grow.

Archips negundanus (Dyar) occurs in widely scattered locations—from Florida to Washington, and in Canada. Its principal host is boxelder, although it has also been observed on honeysuckle, American elm, alder and paper birch.

The behavior of the larvae is much like that of other solitary *Archips* species. The larvae roll the leaves and feed from the inside. Larvae reach 20 mm in length. Damage occurs in the spring. One generation occurs each year.

References: 21, 50, 173, 213, 221

A. Black cherry twigs, webbed together by the ugly nest caterpillar, *Archips cerasivoranus*.
B. Nest of the ugly nest caterpillar, opened up to show the young larvae.
C. Larva of *Archips fervidanus* on an oak leaf.
D. Larva of the ugly nest caterpillar on cherry.
E. The anterior half of a larva of *Archips semiferanus*. (Drawn by Joseph A. Keplinger; from Chapman & Lienk, *Tortricid Fauna of Apple in New York*)
F. A nest of ugly nest caterpillars on rose.
G. A nest of ugly nest caterpillars on *Ilex glabra*.
H. Web and injury of the oak webworm, *Archips fervidanus*. Note larva at arrow.

PLATE 65

Euonymus Caterpillar and Green Fruitworm (Plate 66)

The deciduous species of *Euonymus* are remarkably free of insect pests. Occasionally, however, *Euonymus alatus* may be defoliated or badly mutilated by one of the ermine moth caterpillars named *Yponomeuta multipunctella* Clemens.

The eggs of the specimens shown in Plate 66 were collected in Guelph, Ontario; after the eggs hatched (in captivity), the larvae were observed.

Larvae of *Y. multipunctella* live in colonies within a web. If the web is disturbed, each larva in the web jerks and wiggles about like a tiny acrobat. The web becomes cluttered with black pepper-like frass. Fully grown larvae are about 20 mm long.

When the larvae are ready to pupate (about mid-June) they build cylindrical cocoons which are open at one end. The cocoons are constructed side by side and hang with the longer axis in a vertical position. The open end is up. Before pupating the larva positions itself within the cocoon so that its head faces toward the opening of the cocoon. The adult emerges in late June in Ontario. The moth is white and has rows of black spots on its fore wing. Its wingspan is about 22 mm. It may be found in eastern Canada, in New York and in the Appalachian region.

The green fruitworm, *Lithophane antennata* (Walker), sometimes called the green mapleworm, is an occasional pest of trees in the eastern quadrant of the United States and in southern Canada. It feeds on leaves, flowers and, occasionally, fruits of ash, maple, oak, hickory, redbud, elm, beech, crabapple, dogwood, apple, willow and many species and cultivars of *Prunus*. It also feeds on shrubs such as rhododendron, azalea, rose, *Forsythia*, and mountain laurel.

The caterpillars are bright to pale green and when fully grown are about 26 mm long. A lateral white stripe (see Figure 10) is a

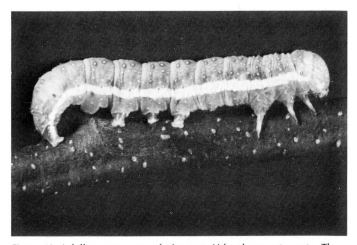

Figure 10. A fully grown green fruitworm, *Lithophane antennata*. There are several related species. Most are various shades of green and are marked with yellowish or whitish longitudinal stripes. (Photo courtesy R. W. Rings, Ohio Agricultural Research and Development Center)

distinguishing characteristic. In the spring, injury is done by the tiny larvae that enter flower or leaf buds. Later in the year, older larvae feed on foliage and fruit. In Ohio, the larvae complete their development by mid-June and burrow into the soil to pupate. One generation occurs each year.

Reference: 242

A. A nest of *Yponomeuta multipunctella* caterpillars feeding on the leaves of *Euonymus alatus*.
B. A group of cocoons. Note vertical orientation.
C. A close-up of cocoons. Some of larvae have not pupated. The cocoon is open at the top.
D. Mature caterpillars.
E. A close-up of a cocoon being constructed by the larva.

PLATE 66

Bagworms (Plates 67, 68)

There are twenty species of bagworms in the United States but only two or three cause enough damage to plants to be of economic importance. The sections in Plates 67 and 68 show the bagworm, *Thyridopteryx ephemeraeformis* (Haworth). It is indigenous to America, and has a wide range of host plants as well as an extensive geographical distribution (see Figure 11). According to Davis (61a) the bagworm feeds on a total of 128 plants. It is a common pest east of the Rocky Mountains, but is less common in latitudes north of Massachusetts. It can be devastating in the South as a pest of woody ornamentals.

The female bagworm never looks like a moth. She is eyeless; without wings, legs and antennae or functional mouthparts. Her body is soft, yellowish-white and almost devoid of hairs; she never leaves the bag she made while a larva. The male moth emerges from his bag and flies to the female, mates and dies in a few days. Males are black and have almost clear wings that span about 25 mm.

From the pairing, the female produces 500–1000 eggs in a single mass and all lie within the bag. The egg is the overwintering stage. In Florida, however, there is no dormant period. Eggs hatch in the mid-Atlantic states in late May and early June and larvae begin, immediately, to feed and construct their protective cases.

The bag is made of silk and bits of twigs or leaves interwoven to disguise and strengthen the case. When the larva is small it feeds on the epidermis on the upper side of the leaf with the bag pointed upward (Plate 68, section B). Epidermal feeding results in a brown spot on the leaf. Later, if feeding on a broad-leaved host, the larva moves to the lower surface and eats all the leaf except for the larger veins. As the larva grows it enlarges its bag. When fully grown the bag may be 30–50 mm long. Pupation takes place inside the bag, a structure homologous to a cocoon. The change from pupa to adult requires 7 to 10 days depending upon temperature.

Distribution of this insect from one plant to another is primarily dependent upon movement of the caterpillar. Because of the bagworm's feeding behavior and limitations in movement, a lone host plant may harbor a huge population in a single season.

The principal harm done by this insect is the destruction of foliage by the caterpillars. In some parts of the country, bagworms are predominantly found on arborvitae and juniper. In Ohio and Pennsylvania they are commonly found on hardwoods such as black locust, maple and sycamore. Other hosts include elm, buckeye, and boxelder. In Maryland and Virginia, the bagworm can be found on arborvitae, 13 types of juniper, eastern red cedar, Chinese elm, honeylocust, and eastern white pine, hemlock, Norway maple, deodar cedar, and spruce. In Texas it flourishes on cedar, cypress and willow.

In northern Florida, fully grown larvae, as well as first-stage larvae, may be seen during the winter months. This indicates

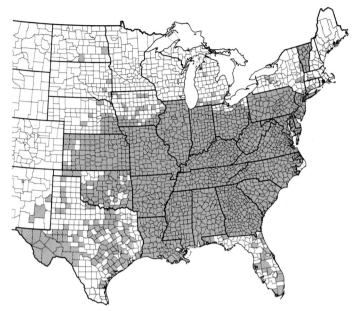

Figure 11. Distribution of the bagworm, *Thyridopteryx ephemeraeformis*, in the United States as of 1970. (Courtesy Pest Survey, Animal and Plant Health Inspection Service, USDA)

that continuous generations probably occur each year (no hibernation or overwintering period). In southern California, another species, *Oiketus townsendi* Cockrell, commonly feeds on ash, pear, sycamore, willow and locust. In Florida and the Gulf Coast states another bagworm species, *Oiketus abbotii* Grt., feeds on several subtropical trees and shrubs, including citrus.

Researchers working under the auspices of the United States Department of Agriculture have isolated a pheromone (sex attractant) produced by the female. If the research trials are successful, a synthetic attractant will be produced to lure the males into traps and reduce or prevent mating. Unfertilized eggs do not hatch.

There are a number of parasitic insects that are important in reducing numbers of bagworms. The ichneumon wasp parasites, *Pimpla inquisitor* Say, *P. conquisitor* and *Allocota thridopterigis* Riley are perhaps the most important. Unfortunately, populations of the bagworm usually increase to seriously damaging proportions before parasites are effective. *Bacillus thuringiensis* is a bacterial insecticide, shown to be effective in controlling bagworms.

References: 50, 61a, 96, 139

A. Black locust, *Robinia pseudoacacia*, partially defoliated by *Thyridopteryx ephemeraeformis*.
B. A bag with larva partially exposed. Larva is feeding on a leaf stem.
C. Bagworms on red cedar, *Juniperus virginiana*.

PLATE 67

A,B,C. *Feijoa sellowiana* foliage showing feeding injury by first-
and second-stage larvae of the bagworm *Thyridopteryx ephemeraeformis*. Note the first-stage larva on the upper surface
of the leaf in section B.
D. This bag contains a pupa.
E. A fully grown larva removed from its bag.
F. A bag opened to show a pupa.

PLATE 68

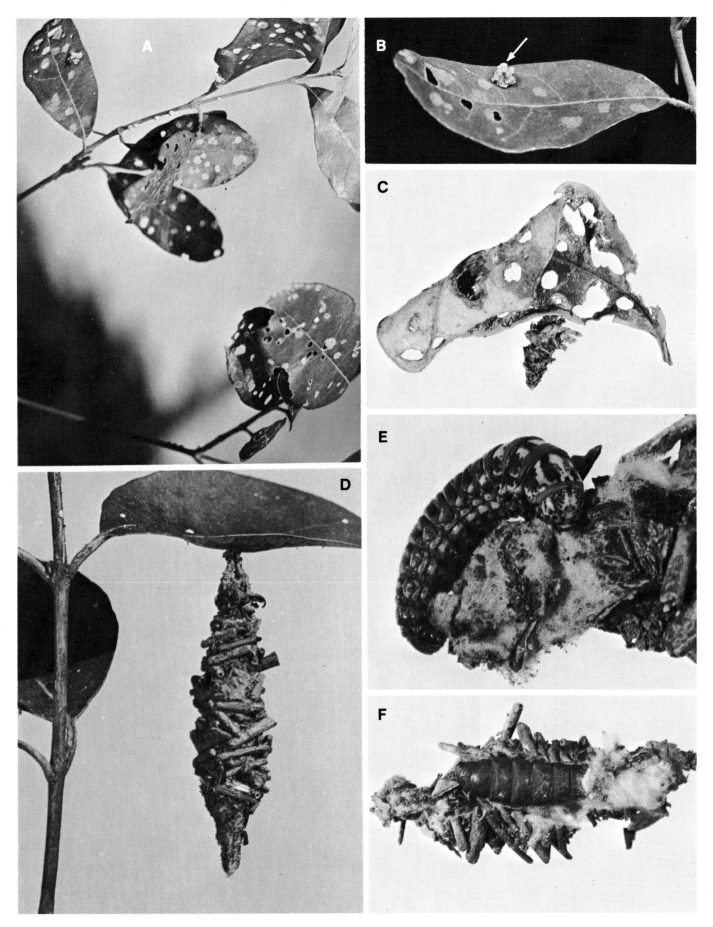

Mimosa Webworm (Plate 69)

The mimosa webworm, *Homadaula anisocentra* Meyrick (=albizziae Clarke), came to the United States from China. It was first detected in the United States in 1940 on mimosa, *Albizia* (=Albizzia) *julibrissin*. It is from this plant that it gets its common name. In the United States, however, the honeylocust, *Gleditsia triacanthos*, including the thornless cultivars, is a more important host than mimosa for the mimosa webworm.

Although the mimosa webworm is primarily an eastern and midwestern pest, several serious infestations were detected in California in the 1960's. In the south, mimosa is heavily attacked by the webworm. It is reasonable to believe that eventually the insect will be found wherever its host plants are grown in the United States.

Observations made in Indiana indicate that the thornless honeylocust (cultivar Sunburst) was found to be highly susceptible to attack by the mimosa webworm, whereas the cultivars Moraine, Shademaster, and Imperial were less susceptible. Since all were subject to attack, however, it was suggested that none of the thornless cultivars be planted without provision for annual inspection and control where necessary.

The adult is a silvery gray moth. It has wings which are stippled with black dots. The wingspan is about 13 mm. When fully grown, the larvae are about 16 mm in length and vary in color from gray to brown. On the body of the larva are five longitudinal white stripes.

The insect overwinters in the pupal stage in cocoons. The cocoons are located under scales of bark on the trunk of the host tree, or among plant refuse underneath the tree. In the Midwest the moths appear in early- to mid-June and lay their pearly gray eggs on tree leaves. The larvae web together several leaflets and feed on the foliage within the protection of the web. Commonly, a number of larvae feed together, and construct a large, unsightly nest of webbing (E). When alarmed, the larvae can move rapidly and may drop from the nest on a thread of silk. Upon reaching maturity, the larvae pupate, a new generation of moths appears in August, and the cycle is repeated. It is the pupa of this second generation that overwinters. In western New York this second generation emerges in early September, but offspring generally don't survive the winter. In Florida, Southern Georgia, and Alabama three or more broods emerge each year between May and September.

Often, an entire tree may appear covered by an unsightly tent of webbing (A). Although foliage is lost as a result of larval feeding, it is difficult to assess the actual damage to the leaves, since this injury is often hidden by the webbing.

References: 1, 6, 86, 211

A. Field view of mimosa damaged by the mimosa webworm.
B. Brown foliage and tents of webbing are characteristic of attack by mimosa webworm.
C. Close-up of webbing and brown leaflets caused by the feeding of young larvae.
D. Several mature larvae and their protective tent.
E. Webbing made by larvae of intermediate size. Note larva in circle.

PLATE 69

A Bougainvillea Caterpillar (Plate 70)

Bougainvillea is a popular subtropical flowering shrub. It can be found in Florida, in the Gulf Coast area and in California. Damage caused by the feeding of the caterpillar of a pyralid moth, *Asciodes gordalis* Guenee, limits its use as an ornamental shrub and destroys its beauty. Although the insect's biology has not been studied, it has been observed in Florida every month of the year except June, an indication that there are several generations each year. The larva is a leaf folder. After folding the leaf, it feeds on it from inside the fold. When the partially devoured leaf ceases to afford some protection, the larva moves on to another leaf, folds it, and continues to feed. By this process, the foliage of the infested plant generally appears ragged.

The larvae are about 24 mm when fully grown and are about the same green color as the foliage (C).

Figure 12. A wasp parasite, *Meteorus pulchricornis* (Wesm.), laying an egg on a caterpillar. (Photo courtesy Ronald Weseloh, Connecticut Agricultural Experiment Station)

A,B,D,F,G. These photographs show the extent and kind of damage caused by *Asciodes gordalis.*

C. A caterpillar of *Asciodes gordalis.* Note protective coloration.

E. An adult female *Asciodes gordalis.* Wingspan is approximately 22 mm.

PLATE 70

Birch Leaf Miner (Plate 71)

A sawfly named *Fenusa pusilla* (Lepeletier) is a common leaf miner pest of gray birch *Betula populifolia*, paper birch *B. papyrifera* and white birch *B. alba*. It rarely feeds upon black, yellow, European white, or river birch. Entomologists in Connecticut first recorded the sawfly's appearance in the United States in 1923. It came to the United States from Europe and has rapidly spread throughout northeastern North America.

The adult sawfly is black, and is about 3 mm long. It appears in the spring when the first birch leaves are half grown (E). The adults may be seen hovering about birch trees or crawling over the surface of leaves. Eggs are laid singly in the new leaves and may be seen easily if the leaf is held up to the light. Eggs soon hatch and the larvae begin to mine the leaf, feeding on the tissue between the leaf surfaces. At first, the mines are separate and small but soon several of them coalesce to form a single large, hollowed-out blotch on the leaf (C).

The larva is flat. When fully grown it is about 6 mm long. The period of larval development varies from 10 to 15 days. When mature, the larva cuts a hole through the leaf and drops to the ground. There, it builds a cell in which pupation takes place.

Two to three weeks are required for transformation into the adult stage.

The female sawfly deposits her eggs only on newly developing leaves, never on older leaves. In the spring, every leaf of a tree may be mined, giving it a brown color. A new crop of leaves soon develops, but by this time a second generation of egg-laying sawflies are again in the trees. Two to four generations of this sawfly occur per year depending upon the length of the growing season. In the Catskill Region of New York, three generations commonly occur.

Vigorous, growing trees are the most attractive to ovipositing adults. Such trees are able to withstand the attack of these insects for several years before showing symptoms of decline.

Investigations on the biological control of this insect in the United States have produced very little practical information. Studies in Eastern Canada indicate few if any host specific parasites attack the leafmining species, a circumstance that has contributed to their successful spread and high populations.

Reference: 20

A. Leaves of *Betula populifolia* showing an early stage of damage caused by the birch leaf miner, *Fenusa pusilla*.
B. Birch leaves after the first brood of leaf miners have completed their development.
C. Birch leaf miner larvae inside a leaf.
D. A severely infested birch tree with completely brown leaves, the result of damage done by birch leaf miners.
E. Adult sawflies, *Fenusa pusilla*.

PLATE 71

Leaf Miners *Fenusa ulmi* and *Coleophora ulmifoliella* (Plate 72)

A small, legless larva—that of the elm leaf miner, *Fenusa ulmi* Sund.—is responsible for the injury shown in sections A and B. *F. ulmi* is a European species that entered this country prior to 1898. In the United States and Canada, it attacks Scotch and Camperdown elms (cultivars of *Ulmus glabra*); English elm, *U. procera*; and American elm.

The adult insect is a black sawfly. It is about 3 mm in length. In New England, it may be found flying about its food-plant in May. Eggs are laid in the leaf tissues through slits the insect cuts with its saw-like ovipositer in the leaf's upper epidermis. In about one week the eggs hatch and the young larvae begin to make their blotch-like mines in the leaves. The mines appear first as tiny, whitish spots. The larvae confine their feeding to the area between the leaf's lateral veins, and eat the green tissue between the two layers of epidermis. Several mines may coalesce to form large blotches.

The larva completes its development in late spring, cuts a hole through the epidermis, drops to the ground and burrows into the soil to a depth of nearly 25 mm. It then prepares a papery cocoon where it remains as a pupa through the summer, fall and winter. One generation occurs each year.

Damaged leaves may remain on the tree throughout the growing season (A). Injured areas in the leaves turn brown and eventually drop out, leaving irregular holes. Such injury spoils the appearance of ornamental trees and reduces the tree's vigor and growth.

The insect is well established in the Northeast and in the Great Lakes region, including southeastern Canada. It has been observed as far west as North Dakota, Minnesota and Wisconsin.

The elm casebearer, *Coleophora ulmifoliella* McDunnough, is a native North American moth. It is buff-colored with gray markings and has a wingspan of about 13 mm. It occurs throughout the Northeast and as far west as Michigan. Older literature erroneously identifies it as *C. limnosipennella*, a European species.

After mating in late July, its eggs are laid on the leaves of elm. Upon hatching, the larva enters a leaf and makes a small mine between the epidermal layers. Soon the larva emerges from the mine and makes a case, which is enlarged as the larva grows. This tube-iike case, which the insect carries throughout the balance of the larval stage, serves as a protective covering. The cases are characteristic of the genus *Coleophora*.

Mines made by the elm casebearer take the form of small rectangular spots. When cool weather approaches in the autumn, the insect migrates to twigs where it fastens down its case and spends the winter in an immature larval stage. In the spring, migration to the new leaves takes place, and the insect resumes feeding as a miner, but never does it allow its entire body to leave the case. The case rarely exceeds 6 mm in length. Pupation occurs within the case and the adult moths emerge in July. A single generation occurs each year.

The amount of damage caused by a single caterpillar is small, but considerable injury can result from heavy infestations.

There are several related species of *Coleophora*. Each makes a case and causes similar injury on other trees and shrubs. They include the birch casebearer, *Coleophora fuscedinella* Zeller, which is limited to the northeastern North America. The larch casebearer (see Plate 8), feeds on all larch species. *Coleophora sacramenta* (Heinrich), sometimes called the California casebearer, feeds primarily on willow, but also on almond, cherry and peach. The pecan cigar casebearer, *Coleophora laticornella* Clemens, is a minor pest of pecan, hickory and black walnut. Its range extends from northern Florida and Texas to New Hampshire.

References: 32, 48, 129, 209

A,B. Leaves of *Ulmus glabra* injured by the larva of *Fenusa ulmi*. Note larva inside the mines in section B.

C,E. Elm casebearer, *Coleophora ulmifoliella*. Larvae are inside the brown cases. Note the leaf injury as seen from the underside of the leaf.

D. Leaf injury done by elm casebearer as seen on upper leaf surface.

PLATE 72

Leaf Miners (Plate 73)

The larva of a sawfly known as the European alder leaf miner, *Fenusa dohrnii* (Tischbein), mines the leaves of many species of alder. Blotches develop on the leaves due to the larval mining (A). These blotches turn brown and serve as a means of identifying the presence of the larvae.

Originally a European insect, the European alder leaf miner came to the United States sometime prior to 1891. It can probably be found wherever alders grow, but mainly in the eastern quadrant of the United States, and in southern Canada.

The eggs of the European alder leaf miner are laid in the leaves. Several larvae often develop in a single leaf. (See Plate 71, section C for an example of the larval form.) After completing their development, the larvae drop to the ground to pupate. The larva overwinters in a cocoon on the ground. The adult generally emerges sometime in May. It is a dark-bodied, wasp-like insect and is about 6 mm in length.

As many as three generations of this insect occur per year. This, of course, means that it may be found throughout the growing season. Little is known about its parasites and predators, since complete biological studies have not yet been made.

The various cultivars of the European alder, *Alnus cordata*, are most susceptible to attack by this insect. Some investigators have found that *Alnus rugosa*, *A. macrophylla* and *A. viridis* are immune.

Section D shows *Crataegus crus-galli* with mine injury caused by *Profenusa collaris* MacGillivray. *P. collaris* is a wasp-like sawfly and was first described by entomologists as a pest of sour cherries, *Prunus cerasus*. The insect, however, is a primary pest of *C. crus-galli*. At the beginning of the growing season it is in the ground in its pupal stage. Adults appear when the host tree's first leaf clusters begin to unfold and the blossom buds begin to open. Eggs are laid singly in the upper epidermis at the base of the leaf. Upon hatching, the larva feeds on the parenchyma between the leaf surfaces. Several larvae may feed on a single leaf. They mine toward the distal end, generally keeping close to the margin until large blotches, which often cover half the leaf, become apparent. The larvae have flattened bodies with three pairs of legs; they average about 7 mm in length when fully grown. They abandon the foliage about the middle of June by dropping to the ground. There, they make earthen cells in preparation for the winter.

This insect can be a serious pest of certain species and cultivars of *Crataegus*. *Crataegus persimillis* and *C. erecta* may be severely damaged while the leaves of *C. mollis* are rarely mined. From a distance, heavily infested trees have a brownish cast as though they've been singed by fire. Injury to the tree is not long-lasting, especially in the years that new leaves develop rapidly.

P. collaris is believed to be a species indigenous to North America. Its distribution is limited to the Northeast. Two wasp parasites, *Pezoporus tenthridinarum* Rohwer and *Trichogramma minutum* Riley, often control its populations.

Many of the members of the moth family Gracillaridae feed on foliage as leaf miners (see Plate 76). Each species consistently makes its own characteristic blotch or serpentine mine (see section C). Host plants include poplar, aspen, willow, oak, maple, cherry, birch and lilac.

References: 20, 223, 311

A. Typical leaf mines caused by the European alder leaf miner on *Alnus glutinosa*.
B,C. Leaf mines of the sawfly, *Profenusa collaris;* note the larva at arrowpoint in section C.
D. *Profenusa collaris* mines on *Crataegus crus-galli*.

PLATE 73

Leaf Mining Beetles (Plate 74)

One of the serious insect pests of the black locust, *Robinia pseudoacacia*, is *Odontota dorsalis* (Thunberg), which is commonly known as the locust leaf miner. In its adult stage this insect is a beetle that is 6 mm long (A). The beetle hibernates wherever winter protection can be found, often in litter under its host tree. In the spring, the beetles emerge and begin feeding on the black locust's developing foliage. After a short time, flat, oval eggs are deposited on the undersides of leaves. They soon hatch and the larvae eat into the inner layer of leaf tissue, forming a mine. As the larvae feed and grow, the mines enlarge. The terminal portion of the leaflet is the preferred feeding site. The mine, from its beginning, takes the form of an irregular blotch. When fully grown, the larvae are flattened and yellowish-white, with black legs, and a black head and anal shield. Pupation occurs in the mine. Upon emerging from their pupal cases, the beetles skeletonize the undersurface of leaves. A second annual brood occurs in southern Ohio and adjacent areas.

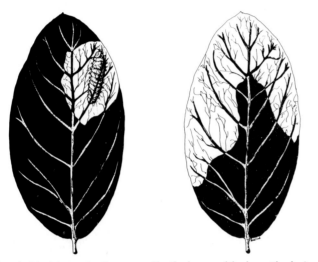

Mines in black locust leaflets caused by the larvae of the locust leaf miner. Redrawn after Weaver.

If a tree grows two sets of leaves in one growing season, the combined feeding of larvae and adults may destroy both sets. When this happens in successive years, the tree will die. In early summer, affected black locusts may look as though they have been swept by fire. Although larvae feed only on black locust, adult beetles feed on dogwood, elm, oak, beech, cherry, wisteria and hawthorn as well. They also feed on several herbaceous plants.

The locust leaf miner occurs with regularity in Pennsylvania, West Virginia and Ohio and all along the highland areas near the Ohio River. The species is also reported with frequency in Alabama, and in the area along the eastern seaboard extending north into Canada. It is known as far west as Missouri and south to Mississippi.

There are several wasp parasites of the locust leaf miner, including *Trichogramma odontotae* How. and *Spilochalcis odontotae* How. The wheel bug, *Arilus cristatus* (L.), is a common predator in southern states and feeds on leaf miners while they are still inside the leaf tissue.

The willow flea weevil, *Rhynchaenus rufipes* (LeConte), is a small snout beetle found in the cooler regions of North America including the Rocky Mountain states, Canada and Alaska. It is also known in Massachusetts, California and Oregon.

The adult flea weevil is quite small, about 2 mm in length, and is black (D). Its larva appears early in the spring and eats circular holes in leaves and in the tips of tender new shoots. When the willow flea weevil is abundant, even twigs may be killed. The larvae make small, regular blotch mines in leaves (C) which soon turn brown. By September, the leaves may be filled with tiny pits caused by adults. These pits turn brown or become holes when the injured tissue falls out. However, greater damage is done by the larvae.

In section C, the dark spot is a pupa between the epidermal layers. The host plant in this case is *Salix nigra*. Willows may be injured throughout the growing season although only a single generation occurs each year. Several species of willow are affected but *Salix pentandra* is most seriously injured.

Brachys aeruginosus Gory is a buprestid beetle which, as a larva, mines the leaves of *Fagus* species. The insect might well be called a beech leaf miner. Very little is known about its biology and life history, perhaps because it is of little economic importance. Its eggs are deposited on the lower surface of the leaf, then covered with a transparent secretion which glistens conspicuously long after the larvae have matured and left the leaf. The larvae, when fully grown, are 6 mm long and whitish with a slight tint of green. They are legless and flat with deep-cut abdominal segmentation. The adult is shown in section F.

Related species include *Brachys ovatus* Weber, which mines in oak leaves, and *B. aerosus* Melsh., which mines the leaves of elm and oak. These three species occur throughout much of the eastern quadrant of the United States.

References: 20, 50, 112, 209

A. Adult locust leaf miner.
B. A digitate mine always associated with the midrib vein on black locust leaves; it is believed to be caused by the caterpillar of *Parectopa robiniella*, a moth.
C,D. *Rhynchaenus rufipes* adult and mine on *Salix nigra*. Length about 2 mm.
E. A broad serpentine leaf mine found on *Populus trichocarpa* in southern California; the insect that made the mine is probably one of the leaf-mining caterpillars.
F. *Brachys aeruginosus* adult beetle. It mines beech leaves as a larva.
G. Leaf mines caused by *Brachys aeruginosus*.

PLATE 74

Oak Leaf Miners (Plate 75)

Leaf miners must accommodate to cramped living quarters. The thinner the leaf, the flatter or tinier the larva. The larval form may change as the leaf miner develops and as space is provided in the mined-out area. The head and mouthparts must, however, remain flattened if they are to continue to feed on the mesophyll layer within the leaf.

Across the United States larvae of numerous species of moths mine oak leaves. There are several common species in the eastern states. One of these is known as the solitary oak leaf miner (B), *Lithocolletis* (=*Cameraria*) *hamadryadella* Clemens. It attacks both red and white oaks. As the common name suggests, there is only one larva per mine, but there may be many miners per leaf. Fully grown larvae are about 4 mm long. The other common species is the gregarious oak leaf miner, *Cameraria cincinnatiella* (Chambers), which attacks primarily white oaks. As many as a dozen larvae of this leaf miner may occur in a single large mine.

Light to moderate attacks of either species on oaks leave spotted foliage. Heavy attacks may completely kill the leaves. In 1971, a heavy attack on white oak in Arkansas killed from 80 to 100 percent of the foliage by August, making the landscape look as if autumn had already arrived. Although normally leaf miners cause no serious injury to their hosts, the ornamental value of a yard tree may be reduced because of the mined foliage.

Depending on the location and species of the leaf miners, there can be from two to five generations per year. Both species pupate and overwinter inside dried leaves on the ground. They can be controlled by raking and destroying the leaves in the fall. However, if the trees in need of protection are near other oaks or near a wood lot, additional measures must be taken. Fortunately, the populations of leaf miners vary greatly from year to year, and seldom reach such high numbers that they need to be controlled by insecticides.

References: 50, 209, 254

A,B. Splotches on leaves of white oak were caused by *Lithocolletis hamadryadella*.
C. Damage caused by *Lithocolletis* sp. to *Quercus virginiana*.
D. Blotch mines on leaves of *Quercus robinia*, collected at Long Island, New York caused by *Lithocolletis hamadryadella*.

PLATE 75

Leaf Miners (Plate 76)

Lilac and privet are closely related plants. Both are subject to injury by the lilac leaf miner, *Caloptilia syringella* (Fabricius), which, in its caterpillar stage, causes a blotch-type leaf mine. The species, which originated in Europe, is now found throughout the northeastern states, in parts of eastern Canada and in the Pacific Northwest. It has been reported to occur occasionally on *Fraxinus, Deutzia* and *Euonymus.*

Eggs are laid along the midrib and other veins on the undersides of the leaves. The newly hatched larva enters the leaf directly under the shell and forms a linear mine which cannot be seen from the topside of the leaf. The second instar larva enlarges the mine to form a blotch (G). The last instar larva usually crawls out of the mine, folds the leaf and makes a thin white cocoon. The lilac leaf miner is capable of spending the winter in either its larval or its pupal stage. (In the Northwest, it is common to see young larvae hibernating in the mine.) Several generations occur each year. Moths may be found throughout the summer months.

A related moth, *Caloptilia cuculipennella* (Hubner), feeds on privet as a leaf miner. The whitish caterpillars are about 23 mm long when fully grown. Their mines are similar to those of the lilac leaf miner.

There are five species of leaf miners which feed on holly. One of them, *Phytomyza ilicicola* Loew, a fly, has been given the common name "native holly leaf miner." It may mine leaves of other hollies but can complete its development only in *Ilex opaca.*

This miner is found throughout the native range of its host. Adult flies begin to emerge in the spring after a few new leaves have formed. Emergence continues over a period of several weeks. Females must be about ten days old before they begin to lay eggs in the leaf. After hatching from the egg, the larvae make slender narrow mines in the leaves. These mines are not more than 12 mm long (D). Later the mine broadens into a long blotch (A). In heavy infestations, every leaf of a tree can be mined. When this happens, the tree drops most of its leaves and is practically bare until new growth begins the next spring.

Injury to the host tree is caused not only by the mining activities of the larva but also by feeding adults. In the case of the native holly leaf miner, this activity is limited to the females. The female obtains food by jabbing the leaf with her sharp ovipositor. From this minute wound flow a few drops of sap which she, and nearby males, imbibe. These wounds leave tiny round scars (D,E) and leaf distortion results from the numerous feeding punctures. Although the adults lay eggs only on American holly, they feed on cultivars of Japanese holly as well as American holly, and leave the same characteristic scars. One generation occurs each year. The native holly leaf miner overwinters as a larva or pupa in the leaf mine.

Phytomyza ilicis Curtis is commonly called the holly leaf miner. It is an introduction from Europe and feeds only on *Ilex aquifolium.* This leaf miner is found on both the east and west coasts. In the Pacific Northwest it is a pest in the commercial orchards of "Christmas" holly. The biology and damage caused by this species is similar to that of *P. ilicicola.*

Phytomyza opacae Kulp is a pest of *Ilex opaca.* The mines of this species are quite linear and may traverse the length of the leaf two or three times. Mines have a yellowish-orange color.

Phytomyza verticillatae Kulp mines the leaves of *Ilex verticillata.* Infested leaves fall to the ground where the pupae remain to overwinter. Two generations of this leaf miner are thought to occur each year.

Phytomyza vomitoriae Kulp mines the leaves of *Ilex vomitoria.* It forms linear-irregular mines. Little is known about its biology.

Phytomyza glabricola Kulp mines the leaves of inkberry, *Ilex glabra,* forming blotch mines. It is common in New England and occurs south to Virginia and west to Ohio. Two generations occur each year.

References: 163, 256, 307, 312

A. American holly infested by the native holly leaf miner, *Phytomyza ilicicola.*

B. American holly leaves (see section D).

C,E. Japanese holly, *Ilex crenata,* leaves showing feeding punctures caused by one of the holly leaf miners.

D. American holly leaf showing early mines, and the feeding punctures made by the native holly leaf miner's ovipositor.

F,H. Lilac twig with leaves injured by the lilac leaf miner, *Caloptilia syringella.*

G. Privet twig with leaves injured by the lilac leaf miner.

PLATE 76

Cherry Leaf Miner and Cambium Miners (Plate 77)

Hollyleaf cherry, *Prunus ilicifolia*, is a popular ornamental tree on the West Coast. The leaf-mining larva of a moth, *Paraleucoptera heinrichi* Jones, is perhaps its most severe pest. Little is known about its biology or distribution. The mine occurs on young leaves and the injury becomes noticeable by mid-July (A,C). The mine ordinarily follows the edge of the leaf. When fully grown, the larva, about 4 mm in length, leaves the mine and crawls to the upper surface of the leaf to pupate. Before it makes its cocoon, it constructs an H-shaped web tent (B,E). Under the tent it makes a disk-shaped cocoon. In the vicinity of Oakland, California, the adults (D) begin to emerge about mid-August. One generation is believed to occur each year. Hollyleaf cherry is also attacked by whiteflies. (See Plate 129.)

Cambium miners make linear or serpentine mines in the thin bark of saplings, twigs and small branches. Their name is a misnomer because the mining actually occurs in the cortex and phloem, immediately under the epidermis. The mines are readily visible and may be alarming to the gardener who has never seen them before. Young, thin barked trees like maple, shadbush, cherry, ash, birch, holly, white pine (Figure 13), Douglas

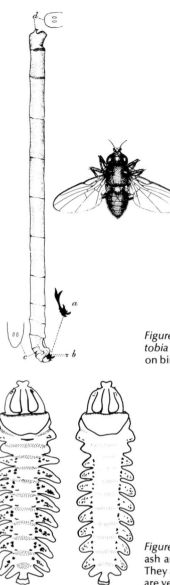

Figure 14. The larva and adult of *Phytobia pruinosa*, a cambium borer found on birch. (From Greene, 116)

Figure 13. A cambium mine on eastern white pine caused by the caterpillar of *Marmara fasciella*.

Figure 15. These larvae mine the bark of ash and belong to the genus *Marmara*. They are approximately 5 mm long, and are very flat. (From Fitzgerald, 104)

fir, white fir and shrubs like rose are most susceptible. *Phytobia amelanchieris* (Greene), a fly, mines the cambium of *Amelanchier canadensis*. The mine may begin on a twig and continue down to the root. The larval stage of a few tiny beetles and moths also produce cambium mines. These mines cause little damage to shade trees and shrubs.

Cambium borers feed primarily on the cork cambium of a tree. *Phytobia pruinosa* (Coq.), a fly, is a cambium borer on birch in its larval stage. When fully grown the larva may reach 30 mm in length and a little over 1 mm in diameter (see Figure 14). One generation occurs each year. *P. setosa* (Loew) mines the

bark of red (*Acer rubrum*) and sugar maples. Cambium borers do not, measurably, interfere with the growth and vigor of the tree. If a host tree is cut into lumber, and the boards have dark flecks, such marks are old mines that were produced years before.

Other cambium borers in the genus *Marmara* are illustrated in Figure 15.

References: 104, 274

A,C. Leaves of hollyleaf cherry, *Prunus ilicifolia*, mined by the caterpillar of *Paraleucoptera heinrichi*.
B. Larva in the process of making its "tent" and cocoon.
D. Adult moth of *Paraleucoptera heinrichi*. Wingspan is about 14 mm.
E. Close-up of the "tent." x 5.
F. Several cocoons and tents may occur on a single leaf.

PLATE 77

171

Boxwood Leaf Miner (Plate 78)

Boxwood has been used for hundreds of years in England and Europe in both public and private formal gardens. Hundreds of these plants were brought into the United States in the 1800's. Many of them found their way to the large estates of Long Island, New Jersey, Rhode Island, Delaware, eastern Pennsylvania, Virginia and the Chesapeake Bay area. Many of these old original plantings of *Buxus sempervirens suffrutiosa* still exist today.

With the introduction of other cultivars of the boxwood came the boxwood leaf miner, *Monarthropalpus buxi* Labou, but it was not reported from the United States until 1910. It is now considered by many to be the most serious insect enemy of boxwood and is found from the Atlantic to the Pacific wherever boxwood grows.

The boxwood leaf miner has a single generation each year. It passes the winter as a partly grown larva in the leaves. During the first warm days of spring it becomes active and grows rapidly. It pupates late in April and emerges as a fly when weigelia begins to bloom. When it is time for emergence, the pupa forces its way partly out of the mine, where the pupal case may cling for several days after the fly has emerged. The adults are tiny (2–3 mm in length), fragile, gnat-like flies. Females soon begin laying eggs in the underside of the young leaves, inserting each egg deep into the tissues. The female lays an average of 29 eggs and dies hours after her last eggs are laid. Eggs begin to hatch about three weeks after being laid.

Injury is caused by the larvae feeding in the soft parenchyma tissue. Mined or blistered leaves are evident from midsummer until the following spring. After new growth develops, mines are not evident for several weeks. Egg punctures are conspicuous, however, on the undersides of the leaves. Infested leaves are spotted yellow (B) and may drop prematurely. Infested plants grow poorly and lack the dense foliage characteristic of the healthy plant. Continuous infestations result in dead twigs and a weakened plant subject to disease, and winterkill in the colder areas.

Eleven cultivars of *Buxus sempervirens*, together with *Buxus microphylla* and *B. harlandii*, are subject to heavy infestations. However, English boxwood, *Buxus sempervirens suffrutiosa*, is seldom damaged. There are few known natural enemies of the boxwood leaf miner.

Reference: 266

A,C. *Buxus microphylla* var. Japonica with leaf miner symptoms as seen from both upper and lower leaf surfaces.
B. *Buxus harlandii* with leaf miner symptoms.
D,F. Upper and lower surfaces of infested *Buxus harlandii* leaves.
E. The lower epidermis of *Buxus harlandii* removed to show the young larvae.
G. A pupa of the boxwood leaf miner.

PLATE 78

Madrone and Other Shield Bearers (Plate 79)

The madrone shield bearer, *Coptodisca arbutiella* Busck, attacks the leaves of madrone, *Arbutus menziesii*. Damaged leaves appear as though they've been perforated by a paper punch. This insect species is also believed to be responsible for identical injury to the foliage of manzanita, *Arctostaphylos* spp., and the strawberry tree, *Arbutus unedo*. The madrone shield bearer is found only on the Pacific coast from California to British Columbia.

The adult of this species is a tiny, silvery-gray moth with a wingspan of only 5 mm. The females lay eggs in the spring on leaves that are about two-thirds expanded. It is not clear whether the eggs hatch after a normal incubation period, or are delayed in hatching until fall, but there is no evidence of mining by the larvae for about six months after the eggs are deposited. It is possible that after normal hatching occurs, the young larvae undergo a long period of inactivity at the site of egg deposition. Where eggs have been deposited, a tiny discolored dot appears.

The first evidence of leaf mining by the larva is visible in the autumn. Sinuous mines evident on the leaves soon become blotch mines. In late winter, the larva completes its development and cuts out an elliptical section of leaf from both the upper and lower leaf surfaces. The insect later pupates within this section. This elliptical section, also called a case or a "shield", drop from the foliage or is carried off and fastened to the bark by the mature larva inside. One or more perforations may appear in each affected leaf, depending on the intensity of attack. Adult moths appear in March and April in the San Francisco area.

Other shield bearers belonging to the genus *Coptodisca* occur on a number of plants. They have been collected from such plants as oak, grape, poplar, apple, pecan, and cranberry. The biology of these species often departs appreciably from that of the madrone shield bearer. For example, the resplendent shield bearer, *C. splendoriferella* (Clemens), a species asso-

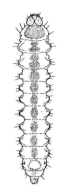

Tupelo leaf miner, 5 mm long. A dorsal view.

ciated with apple, is reported to have two generations each year. Several others do not have the long time lag between egg deposition and the appearance of the larval mine. All species, however, have the peculiar habit of cutting out elliptical leaf sections, and it is on this basis that the common name "shield bearers" was assigned to this insect family.

A common and sometimes devastating shield bearer, the tupelo leaf miner, *Antispila nyssaefoliella* Clem., is a pest of black tupelo, *Nyssa sylvatica*, also called sour-gum. The insect may be found wherever its host grows. Injury occurs first as a small linear mine, later as an oval blotch mine up to 25 mm in its widest dimension. When the larva is ready to pupate, it cuts a hole (10 mm) in the mined area of the leaf, attaching the 2 epidermal leaf disks to its body (similar to C). With the disks attached, it drops to the ground and pupates. There may be several generations each year. The fully grown larva is about 5 mm long, flattened, with distinct segments and a yellowish head. There are no legs.

References: 93, 224, 256

A. Manzanita twig with most of its leaves destroyed by the madrone shield bearer, *Coptodisca arbutiella*.
B. Close-up of an injured leaf.
C. Larvae and pupae inside the leaf disks. Some have dropped out, showing the characteristic elliptical holes.

PLATE 79

Yellow Poplar Weevil (Plate 80)

Odontopus (=*Prionomerus*) *calceatus* (Say), the yellow poplar weevil, is also known as the sassafras weevil, the magnolia leaf miner, and the tuliptree leaf miner (A). These common names were derived from names of its hosts. It also feeds upon *Laurus nobilis*. The yellow poplar weevil is found from Massachusetts to Florida and west to Louisiana, Iowa and Michigan. It is most abundant in the central Appalachian area.

Both larvae and adults cause injury to their hosts, the adult by feeding on buds and leaves and the larvae by mining the leaves. The adult beetles overwinter in duff and leaf litter found beneath their host trees. During warm days in early spring they fly to trees and feed on buds and new leaves. In May, they lay their eggs in the midrib of the leaves' underside. After the eggs hatch, the larvae mine the leaves and cause blotch-type mines. On tulip-poplar and *Magnolia grandiflora* leaves (C), the blotch starts near the leaf's apex. The larvae are white, legless, and less than 2 mm long. In tulip poplar there may be from one to nine larvae in a single blotch mine. Most of the larval activity occurs in late May and June. Larvae pupate in the mine. Adults of the new generation emerge and for a short time feed on leaves in the same manner as their parents. After July, adults greatly reduce their activities and are difficult to find. However, they have been found in magnolia trees as late as August in Mississippi. They may be found nearly every year on fence row sassafras on Long Island and occasionally on deciduous magnolias in the same area.

Damage done by this insect is not of great economic importance. In the deep south, some damage occurs on magnolia leaves, but the damage is rarely very serious. In 1967 and 1968 there was a severe infestation on tulip poplar in parts of West Virginia, Ohio and eastern Kentucky, where severe leaf injury occurred.

References: 40, 126, 161

A. Adult weevil, *Odontopus calceatus*. About 2 mm long.
B. *Sassafras albidium* leaves and buds injured largely by adult beetles. The injury by larvae usually occurs at or near the tip of the leaf.
C. Leaves of *Magnolia grandiflora* showing larval injury by *Odontopus calceatus*. Injury occurs at the tip of the leaf. (Photo courtesy Dr. L. C. Kuitert, University of Florida)
D,F. Deciduous *Magnolia soulangeana* leaf with adult injury.
E. *Magnolia grandiflora* leaf showing adult injury. (Photo courtesy Dr. L. C. Kuitert, University of Florida)

PLATE 80

Maple Trumpet Skeletonizer and Maple Leaf Cutter (Plate 81)

The maple trumpet skeletonizer, *Epinotia aceriella* (Clemens), feeds mainly on the foliage of sugar maple and red maple, *Acer rubrum*. Sugar maple is its principal host. There are also some records of it feeding on red, black, white and chestnut oaks as well as hawthorn and beech. This occurs most often where few maples are present. The moth is found from Ontario to New Brunswick, Canada, south to North Carolina and west to Michigan.

Adult moths appear in the spring as early as April. They are white, with a wingspan of about 15 mm and are attracted to lights at night.

Damage is caused by the larva. It eats the tissue between the larger veins on the underside of the leaf, leaving the leaf's thin, upper-epidermal layer intact. It spins a silken web on the leaf's underside and then folds the leaf. Inside this fold, it constructs a trumpet-shaped tube (B). The tube, made of frass and silk, is formed by a single larva. The length of the tube may exceed 5 cm. The larva feeds from within the protection of this tube and skeletonizes the area beneath the web. The remains of the web can be seen in section B on the green area of the leaf.

The larvae may be found on the leaves from early July through early October. The fully grown larva is 13 mm long, with a pale yellowish-green body and a yellowish head. It drops to the ground to construct its cocoon between two fallen leaves. Although its work attracts attention, injury is considered slight even if the insects are abundant, because the damage occurs late in the season. Minor infestations of maple trumpet skeletonizers can be found every year; occasionally larger defoliating outbreaks occur. Infestations can be reduced by raking the leaves from under infested trees, and composting or otherwise destroying them.

Other leaf-tying or leaf-folding insects are common on many trees and shrubs (Plates 65, 82). *Episimus tyrius* Heim., an olethreutid (moth) leaf tier is occasionally found in early summer on red and sugar maples. When fully grown, larvae are about 10 mm long.

The maple leaf cutter, *Paraclemensia acerifoliella* (Fitch), is widely distributed over the northeastern United States and southern Canada. Preferred host plants are the sugar and red maples. The insect has also been found on beech and birch that grow adjacent to maple trees.

The premature browning of leaves is a symptom of the damage caused by this species. Close observation of an infested tree will reveal numerous blotch mines made by the feeding of young larvae. This symptom occurs in June, and is often overlooked. The most characteristic signs of attack are circular holes in the leaves (D), which are usually not apparent until late July or August.

Ordinarily, the insect is unimportant; occasionally however, populations become abundant in limited areas and injury to foliage may be severe. If injury is severe for several consecutive years, older trees may be weakened or killed. Damage to scattered trees, as in landscape plantings, is seldom serious.

The adult moth is small, steel blue in color, and emerges in late May. Its eggs are laid in tiny slits on the undersides of the leaves. The newly hatched larva mines the leaves for about two weeks. After this, it cuts two oval pieces from the leaf, and sandwiches itself between them to form a case in which it lives (E). The larva reaches from its case to eat the surface of the leaf. This results in a circular skeletonized area around the case. When all of the leaf within its reach has been consumed, the larva drags the case away to another feeding site. An oval green area is left, surrounded by the circular dead area (D).

The larva is not more than 6 mm long. It is dull white, with a brownish head and thorax. The fully grown larva crawls or drops to the ground in September to pupate.

References: 49, 50, 127, 244

A. Folded maple leaves damaged by the maple trumpet skeletonizer, *Epinotia aceriella*.
B. One of the folded leaves opened to show the extent and type of injury. Note the "trumpet" tube of the larva and the white web (at arrow) used to fold the leaf together.
C. The work of two trumpet skeletonizers in a single sugar maple leaf.
D. The oval disks removed from this leaf have become the case in which a maple leaf cutter caterpillar resides. The round skeletonized areas with green centers (see arrow) are feeding sites of the nearly mature larva.
E. Left: an intact case of the maple leaf cutter. Right: the disk-shaped case opened to show the larva.
F. Close-up of a feeding site of the maple leaf cutter larva. Case of maple leaf cutter (at arrow) on leaf surface.

PLATE 81

Azalea Leaf Miner and Sawfly (Plate 82)

The azalea leaf miner, *Gracillaria azaleella* Brants, is a leaf miner for only the first half of its larval life. Later, it feeds externally as a leaf roller or tier, rolling a leaf or tying several together to form a self-protective canopy. The larvae rarely destroy entire leaves but disfigure them greatly. They feed singly, and, if disturbed, move rapidly either forward or backward. The azalea seems to be the only food-plant of this insect.

The eggs of the azalea leaf miner are white and are laid singly on the underside of a leaf along a midrib or vein. Upon hatching, the young larva enters the leaf directly beneath its eggshell, and feeds initially as a leaf miner (B). It then crawls to the upper surface of the leaf and by means of silk, pulls the leaf over its body and proceeds to feed by chewing holes. The larva also may tie the newly expanding leaves together at the tip of a shoot and feed there in the same manner. When mature, the larva often selects an undamaged leaf, rolls it up, and pupates inside. A small moth emerges after about one week, mates, and begins the cycle again.

The moth is about 10 mm long, is golden yellow in color, and has a wingspan of 12 mm. Adults are very secretive and spend most of this stage hidden among the leaves of their host. On Long Island, New York, there are at least two generations of the azalea leaf miner each year. In Georgia and Alabama three or four generations occur annually and in Florida, breeding is continuous. In Oregon the winter is spent as a last-instar larva or pupa in a rolled leaf, or occasionally as a tiny miner in a leaf.

This insect has become a destructive pest throughout the range of evergreen azaleas. It is found from Florida to Texas and north to Long Island, West Virginia and the Ohio Valley. It is also found in northern California and the Pacific Northwest. At one time it was considered primarily a pest of greenhouse-grown azaleas. Now, field-grown azalea nursery stock and plants in the landscape are commonly attacked. If controlled early, the plants will quickly outgrow the insect injury.

A sawfly of azalea, *Amauronematus azaleae* Marlatt, feeds on azalea leaves in the Northeast and parts of eastern Canada. Little is known about its biology. There appears to be one generation each year, with feeding activity occurring in late May and early June. The larvae feed from the edge of the leaf (D), devouring all but the midvein (F). When fully grown, they are about 10 mm long and are a shade of green similar to the coloring of the azalea leaf (D). They feed on both deciduous and evergreen azaleas.

References: 68, 256

A. Moderately damaged azalea plant. Tattered leaves were damaged by the azalea leaf miner.
B. Mined leaves have irregular brown blotches on them. An azalea twig showing rolled and chewed leaves.
C. *Gracillaria azaleella* larva, nearly fully grown. It is about 12 mm long.
D. Larva of the sawfly, *Amauronematus azaleae* Marlatt, an occasional pest of azalea in the Northeast.
E. Tattered leaves were damaged by the azalea leaf miner.
F. The green midveins of azalea leaves are positive symptoms of injury caused by the sawfly larva *Amauronematus azaleae*.
G. Leaf miner larva partially exposed; note the silk strands. The color of the larva blends with the color of the leaf.

PLATE 82

Maple Petiole Borer and Twig Borers (Plate 83)

The maple petiole borer, *Caulocampus acericaulis* MacGillivrary, a sawfly with peculiar habits, was introduced into the United States from Europe. The larvae mine in the petioles of maples, causing the petioles to break a short distance from the leaf blade (A,B,C,D). Damaged leaves fall from the tree in May and June causing considerable concern to the homeowner. However, seldom is the leaf drop serious enough to injure the tree. Several maple species are subject to attack by this insect.

A single generation is produced each year. The adults emerge in May and their eggs are laid near the base of the petioles of maple leaves (F). The newly hatched larva makes a tunnel and eats out practically all the inner tissues of the petiole. In about a month, the larva reaches maturity. The fully grown larva is only 8 mm long and resembles a weevil larva (E). The larva remains in the petiole stub attached to the twig; later dropping to the ground where it pupates 5–8 cm below the soil surface. Raking up and disposing of the fallen leaves will not reduce the insect population.

The full range of this insect is uncertain, but it has been seen in Connecticut, Massachusetts, New York and New Jersey.

The boxelder, *Acer negundo*, appears to be the only host of the boxelder twig borer, *Proteoteras willingana* (Kearfott). The boxelder twig borer, in its feeding, destroys the dormant buds of its host in the fall and early spring, kills the succulent new twigs during May and June, and causes swollen shoots and the subsequent development of adventitious growth. When the

Figure 17. A swollen boxelder twig, split open to show the tunnel and twig borer.

eggs hatch in mid-July, the tiny caterpillars feed by skeletonizing a small portion of the leaf. In autumn, the larva bores into the petiole and dormant leaf buds. There, it spends the winter. In the spring, the larva burrows into the new twig where it completes its development. The plant responds to this intrusion by producing what some authors term a gall, but it is little more than a swollen twig. Frass accumulates at the point of entrance and this serves as an excellent sign of the larva's presence (see Figures 16 and 17). The fully grown larva is whitish-yellow with a brown or nearly black head. In Canada, the female moth emerges in early July and shortly thereafter lays her eggs.

Affected trees become bushy after several years and undesirable as shade trees. The pest generally occurs wherever boxelder grows: from the east coast to North Dakota, and in Canada.

The cottonwood twig borer, *Gypsonoma haimbachiana* (Kft.), feeds in the pith and buds of rapidly growing twigs of several *Populus* species. The eastern cottonwood, *Populus deltoides*, seems to be a favorite host. The cottonwood twig borer, a caterpillar, is about 15 to 17 mm long when fully grown. The feeding injury stunts growth, kills twigs and repeated attacks result in a bushy tree. The twig borer is found throughout the natural range of eastern cottonwood.

References: 20, 230

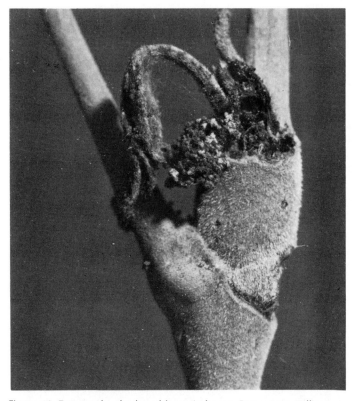

Figure 16. Damage by the boxelder twig borer, *Proteoteras willingana*. Note the accumulation of frass near the entrance hole.

A. Healthy leaves of *Acer saccharum* in contrast to one damaged by the feeding of the maple petiole borer. Note that some leaves have already broken off their stems.
B. Prior to dropping off, infested leaves shrivel and change color (see arrow).
C. Black and shrunken petioles resulting from larval feeding.
D. End of broken leaf stem.
E. Larva and borings.
F. Close-up of a puncture where the egg has been laid. The petiole becomes discolored from larval activity.

PLATE 83

Skeletonizers of Oak, Birch, and Apple (Plate 84)

The oak skeletonizer, *Bucculatrix ainsliella* Murt., is a native species that attacks both shade and forest trees. The moths initially appear in late May and lay eggs on the fully grown leaves. Upon hatching, the larvae begin to feed on the epidermis and soft parenchyma layers of the leaves, causing one side of the epidermis to resemble a translucent matrix, with the veins intact (A). Fully grown larvae are about 7 mm in length (E) and are pale yellow, sometimes tinted with green. If larvae are disturbed, they drop a few feet on a silken thread, often seeming to hang in mid-air. These suspended larvae become a nuisance when the tree is located in a yard or over a sidewalk.

When preparing for its several molts, the larva spins small, flat webs (B) within which it transforms to the next instar. Before the final molt, it spins a characteristic white ribbed cocoon (E) on a leaf, branch, trunk or nearby object.

There is some uncertainty as to how this insect passes the winter. It most likely hibernates as a pupa in its cocoon. Just prior to emergence, the pupa, through the propelling action of its abdomen, protrudes through the cocoon (C). The moth's wingspread is about 7 mm.

In parts of New England and New York, two generations of the oak skeletonizer occur each year. In 1971, a heavy infestation occurred in a city park in Binghamton, New York. The leaves of the affected trees were badly damaged by July 8, at which time the insects were nearing the end of their first generation. The green leaf color was almost gone by early September near the end of the second generation. This kind of defoliation affects the growth of the tree in the following year, and tends to make the tree more vulnerable to attack by wood-boring insects. Defoliation has been reported as the primary cause of top dieback in oaks.

Populations of the oak skeletonizer fluctuate widely from year to year, indicating that natural factors such as parasites and predators affect their numbers in cycles. Little is known about these parasites and predators.

The birch skeletonizer, *Bucculatrix canadensisella* Chambers, is a pest of native as well as exotic birches. Like the oak skeletonizer, its larvae feed on the leaves producing the type of damage shown in section D. Its biology is similar to that of the oak skeletonizer except that there is only one generation each year. The birch skeletonizer seems to occur in outbreak numbers on a ten-year cycle. It is distributed throughout the eastern range of birch as far west as Minnesota and throughout southern Canada to the Pacific Ocean. This insect is also known in Colorado.

Bucculatrix pomifoliella Clemens may occasionally be a problem on apple, flowering crabapple, cherry, shadbush and hawthorn. It is about the same size as the oak skeletonizer and has two generations each year. The cocoons vary in color from white on crabapple to dark brown on hawthorn. Cocoons on apple and quince look like the oak skeletonizer cocoon (C). This species is distributed from the Rocky Mountains to the Atlantic coast and from Texas throughout much of Canada.

On the West Coast, the oak ribbed casemaker, *Bucculatrix albertiella* Busck, lives on *Quercus agrifolia* and *Q. lobata*. Its biology and injury to foliage is essentially the same as for *B. ainsliella* and its cocoons are identical.

References: 20, 50, 93

A. View of upper surface of *Quercus rubra* leaf. Injury was caused by the oak skeletonizer.
B. The underside of a red oak leaf. Larvae molt beneath the white webs.
C. Cocoons of the skeletonizer with empty pupal skins protruding toward the bottom of the photograph.
D. Birch skeletonizer injury as seen on the upper leaf surface. Note cocoons and molting webs.
E. Larva and cocoons of the oak skeletonizer.

PLATE 84

Sawfly Slugs (Plate 85)

There are a group of sawfly larvae that have been commonly called slugs because of their superficial resemblance to true slugs. With the exception of the bristly rose slug, they have a slimy, nonsegmented appearance. When observed carefully, however, the characteristics of sawfly larvae are discernible.

The pear sawfly, *Caliroa cerasi* (Linnaeus), is an insect that was introduced from Europe. It is now distributed from the North Atlantic states to California. In Canada it is known from Ontario to British Columbia. It feeds on the foliage of a wide variety of trees and shrubs including hawthorn, mountain ash, shadbush, crabapple, cotoneaster and all of the flowering fruit trees with the exception of the Bradford pear.

The pear sawfly passes the winter in the ground as a fully grown larva. It changes to a pupa in early spring, and adult sawflies emerge in late May and June. Eggs are deposited singly inside leaf tissue. Upon hatching, the larva feeds as a skeletonizer on the upper side of the leaf (A). The injured area quickly turns brown, and if enough leaf surface has been consumed, the leaf drops prematurely. It is not uncommon for unattended trees to be completely defoliated. The larvae feed on the leaves for about four weeks. In their early stages they are greenish-black and slimy (E). Fully grown larvae are yellow and about 13 mm long. They drop to the ground to form pupal cells in the soil, and transform to adults in time for a second generation by early August.

There are three injurious slug-like sawflies of rose: *Cladius isomerus* Norton, commonly known as the bristly rose slug; *Endelomyia aethiops* Fabricius, the European rose slug; and *Allantus cinctus* Linnaeus, the curled rose sawfly.

The European rose slug (B) can be found from the Rocky Mountains east to the Atlantic coast. *Rosa* species are their only food-plants. The female sawfly deposits her eggs singly in pockets along the edges of leaves; the saw-like ovipositor (see Figure 3 on page 16) cuts a slit in the leaf and gouges out a pocket between the leaf surfaces for the egg. After hatching, the larvae skeletonize the upper surface of the leaf. When fully grown, about 13 mm in length, the larva enters the ground and constructs its overwintering cell. In central New York, all larvae are in the soil by early July, and remain there until they pupate the following spring. There is but one generation each year.

The bristly rose slug is found over a large geographical range. However, it is not found in warm climates. When fully grown, the larva measures about 16 mm and is pale green with many bristle-like hairs over its body. The young larva begins feeding as a skeletonizer but later chews large holes from leaves. There may be five to six generations each year.

The curled rose sawfly larva is 19 mm long when mature and is the largest of the three species. While it rarely occurs in great numbers, even a few can seriously damage a rose garden. The larva injures plants by devouring leaves and boring into pruned twigs. It begins by skeletonizing leaves; later it devours the entire leaf except for the main vein. When ready to pupate, the larva bores into the pith of twigs. This kills a portion of the stem and opens it to fungus infections. The larva is metallic green dorsally and is marked on the thorax and abdomen with white dots. The head is yellowish-brown. In Maryland, Kentucky and Ohio two generations are believed to occur each year.

Little is known about the natural enemies of the various sawfly slugs. With the exception of the pear sawfly, they rarely occur in large numbers, a fact which leads to the assumption that natural forces hold them in check. Slugs can easily be washed from trees and shrubs with a strong jet of water from a garden hose. They are not capable of crawling back onto the tree or bush.

References: 50, 199, 312

A. Leaves of *Crataegus stricta* severely injured by the pear sawfly, *Caliroa cerasi*. Note slug at arrow.
B. Rose leaves damaged by the rose slug, *Endelomyia aethiops*.
C. Mountain ash leaves injured by the pear sawfly.
D. A rose slug near full development.
E. A pear sawfly.
F. A pear sawfly near full development.

PLATE 85

Elm Leaf Beetle (Plate 86)

The elm leaf beetle, *Pyrrhalta luteola* (Muller), was accidentally introduced into the eastern United States early in the nineteenth century. It now occurs throughout the country wherever the elm, *Ulmus*, is an important shade tree. Essentially all species of elm are attacked but local preferences for one kind of elm or another are noticeable where a number of species are available to the insect. The elm leaf beetle readily feeds on the leaves of Japanese Zelkova, *Zelkova serrata*.

The insect overwinters in the adult stage in houses, sheds and in protected places out-of-doors (under the loose bark of trees or house shingles, for example). Elm leaf beetles often become a nuisance inside homes during autumn when they begin to search for suitable overwintering quarters. In the spring, the adults fly back to elm trees and eat small, roughly circular holes in the expanding leaves. Eggs are laid by the female beetle in clusters on the leaves. A female may produce as many as 600–800 eggs during her lifetime. Upon hatching from the eggs, the tiny, black, grub-like larvae begin to feed on the undersurfaces of the leaves. As the larvae grow they become green to yellow with lateral black stripes (E). Larval feeding results in a skeletonization of the foliage. The upper surface of the leaves and the veins are left intact. Badly affected leaves soon turn brown and drop from the tree prematurely. Trees which lose their leaves as a result of elm leaf beetle damage commonly put out a new flush of growth which may be consumed by the resident insects as quickly as it appears. When conditions are severe and trees are without leaves for several consecutive years, limbs or the entire tree may die.

At the end of the feeding period, larvae migrate to the lower parts of the elm tree and pupate openly on the ground at the base of the tree, or in cracks, crevices or crotches on the trunk or larger limbs. Transformation to the adult stage requires a week or two. At this time the new adults return to the foliage of the same or adjacent elms and lay eggs. In the late summer and fall the adult beetles leave the host tree and seek a suitable site for overwintering.

Two generations occur each year throughout the United States, although a third and sometimes a fourth generation are reported to occur in the warmer parts of the West.

References: 5, 20, 119, 129

A. Elm tree damaged by the elm leaf beetle.
B. Branch of elm showing the nature of leaf injury by larvae of the elm leaf beetle.
C. Leaf of elm showing cluster of eggs (in circle) and larvae feeding in vicinity of midvein.
D. Adult beetle and two egg masses of *Pyrrhalta luteola*. Adult length; approximately 5 mm.
E. Close-up of a leaf section, showing two feeding larvae and the nature of feeding injury.
F. Mature larvae and pupae of the elm leaf beetle on soil surface beneath an elm tree.

PLATE 86

Leaf Beetles (Plate 87)

The beetles shown on this plate, collectively called leaf beetles, feed on the leaves of poplars, including aspen and willows. Each of them, while in the larval stage, feeds by skeletonizing the leaf (A,B).

The cottonwood leaf beetle (F), *Chrysomela scripta* Fabr., is found throughout the United States. It feeds on the leaves of cottonwood, *Populus deltoides,* other poplars and several willows. It also feeds on the succulent bark of seedling cottonwoods and willows, and kills the tree or retards its growth.

This species hibernates under bark, litter and forest debris. Beetles may be collected in large numbers under or near cottonwood or willow trees in the winter. In the spring, after leaf growth begins, they become active and fly to host trees to feed on the leaves and twigs. In a few days, the female beetles begin to lay their lemon-yellow eggs in clusters of 25 or more on the undersides of leaves. The eggs hatch in two weeks or less and the young larvae immediately begin to feed in groups on the underside of the foliage. After a few days of aggregated feeding they separate, and feed alone. The very young larva is black.

The larva reaches full size in less than two weeks (C) and then develops into a pupa. The pupa attaches itself to leaves and hangs head-downward. After a second two-week period, the adult emerges and repeats the cycle. Four or more generations occur annually in the South and West. In the North, two and, occasionally, a partial third generation occur.

These beetles are serious skeletonizers, particularly in the southern and western states. Under forest conditions, they are often held in check by lady beetles which feed on the eggs and pupae.

The species *Chrysomela interrupta* (E,G) is closely related to *C. scripta,* and the two are often confused. They have a similar geographical distribution, although *C. interrupta* is believed to be more northern. Most collection records tend to substantiate this, although in April 1972 *C. interrupta* was recorded as far south as Gainesville, Florida. Records show it to be present all through the mountainous regions of the West and also in Alaska. *C. interrupta* prefers willow, but is frequently found on poplar and alder. Both *C. interrupta* and *C. scripta* have great variation in color markings within their species. The insects shown in sections E and G are *C. interrupta,* even though the wing markings shown in section E are subdued black spots and those shown in section G are jet black.

The larvae of both species have a remarkable protective mechanism. In the black tubercles along the thorax are glands that produce a foul-smelling milky fluid. When the larva is disturbed, it emits a droplet of this fluid. Predators rarely attack these larvae, and it is assumed that they are repelled by the repugnant odor. When the danger ends or the disturbance ceases, the larva retracts this droplet, giving us another example of nature's conservancy. The larvae of both species, according to some writers, cannot be distinguished from one another.

Other leaf beetle species are commonly found in the West. *Chrysomela tremulae* Fabr. feeds on aspen and poplars in the Pacific Northwest, and *Chrysomela californica* (Rogers) feeds on willow in California. *Calligrapha bigsbyana* (Kby.) (D) is found in the northeastern and north central states and it, too, is a defoliator of willows. A similarly marked *Calligrapha* beetle feeds on alder in Maine and northeastern Canada.

The elm calligrapha, *Calligrapha scalaris* (LeConte), feeds on the leaves of elm, linden, alder and willow in both its larval and its adult stage. It is likely to occur in scattered locations in Canada, the Northeast and the Midwest. Severe infestations on elm have also occurred in Kansas and other plains states. The elm calligrapha looks somewhat like *C. bigsbyana* (D) both in color and size. The beetles hibernate during winter and begin to lay eggs in the spring when leaves are beginning to develop. A new generation of adults appears about midsummer and feeds on the leaves until autumn.

References: 20, 129, 178, 285

A,B. *Salix caprea,* the pussywillow, showing the typical skeletonized injury caused by leaf beetles. When the skeletonized leaf dries, it tatters in the wind, breaking off and leaving only the main vein.

C. Larva of *Chrysomela interrupta.* Under field conditions the larva of *Chrysomela interrupta* and *Chrysomela scripta* cannot be told apart.

D. Adult *Calligrapha bigsbyana* and the damage typically caused by its feeding. About 8 mm long.

E,G. Both beetles are *Chrysomela interrupta;* there is great variation in the color pattern.

F. *Chrysomela scripta,* the cottonwood leaf beetle.

PLATE 87

Imported Willow Leaf Beetle (Plate 88)

In this country's commerce with other nations, it is inevitable that some insects of foreign origin unintentionally find their way onto American soil. This is the case with *Plagiodera versicolora* Liach., commonly known as the imported willow leaf beetle. Since it was first found in the United States in 1915, this beetle has become an important pest of willows and poplars.

The adult beetles (B,D) vary in color from nearly black to greenish-blue. They hibernate under loose bark or in other protected places on the tree trunk. In the spring, shortly after the leaf buds open, they emerge to feed on foliage and lay eggs. Their glossy, pale yellow eggs (E) are laid in irregular masses on the undersides of leaves. These eggs hatch in a few days and the blackish larvae begin feeding on the undersides of leaves. Later they may be found on the leaf's upper or lower surface. In three to four weeks, the larvae transform into pupae which are about 10 mm long, yellowish-brown in color and have dark markings. They remain as pupae for a short while, then transform into adults.

The larva causes the major damage to the plant by chewing the leaf so as to expose a network of leaf veins. The adult chews holes or notches in the foliage as seen in (B). When abundant, this insect can turn a beautiful ornamental willow into a unsightly one.

There may be four generations of *Plagiodera* during a single growing season in Virginia or North Carolina but probably only two or three in other parts of its range. It is often abundant in New England, the Atlantic coast states and eastern Canada. Recent records show it to have been reported as far west as Michigan. Most species of willow are acceptable as food, although some are more frequently attacked than others. The most susceptible are *Salix nigra* and *S. lucida*. The Lombardy poplar, *Populus nigra,* has also been reported as a food-plant.

Schizonotus sieboldi, Ritz., a chalcidoid wasp, is considered by some to be a highly efficient parasite of the imported willow leaf beetle pupa.

References: 20, 129

A. Imported willow leaf beetle larvae. Note injury to the upper leaf surface of *Salix babylonica.*

B,D. Each photograph shows a willow leaf beetle. Note that the adult feeding injury is different from that of the larva.

C. A cluster of willow leaf beetle larvae on the underside of a leaf. Note the nature of injury.

E. Cluster of eggs on the underside of a willow leaf.

PLATE 88

Asiatic Weevils (Plate 89)

The Japanese weevil, *Callirhopalus bifasciatus* Roelofs, was first found in the United States in 1914. It occurs in New England, the mid-Atlantic States, Kentucky and Indiana. Host plants are numerous and include privet, rhododendron, azalea, mountain laurel, camellia, hemlock, mimosa, Japanese barberry, forsythia, dogwood, lilac, holly, ash, spiraea, rose, *Deutzia* and weigelia as well as many others. Hedges may be badly injured by the adult weevil, particularly new leaves and shoots. The Japanese weevil feeds in the daytime and is easily overlooked because of its size and color. If alarmed, it drops to the ground and feigns death. In the course of feeding, it eats notches in the leaves until eventually only the petiole is left. One investigator found 265 adults on a single spiraea bush. Symptoms of injury to plants done by the Japanese weevil may be confused with those of *Otiorhynchus* weevils (see Plate 94). Larvae of Japanese weevils are presumed to feed upon the small living roots of woody plants. In Virginia, the weevils appear in late June.

The adult weevil is 6 mm in length. Its color varies from light to dark brown, with striations and color bands on the wing covers (C). The wing covers are fused, and since the insect cannot fly, dissemination is relatively slow. Morphologists have found all dissected specimens to be females, indicating the probability that there are no males and that females can produce viable eggs without mating. One generation occurs each year.

Calomycterus setarius Roelofs is a weevil native to Japan which was first reported in the United States in New York in 1929. It has since spread to much of New England, south to Maryland and Virginia, and west to Iowa.

Eggs are laid in the ground in grassy areas and the developing larvae are presumed to feed on roots. Adult weevils begin to appear in late June, and may be found in abundance during July and early August. They are grayish in color, 4 mm long, and grow darker as they mature. Major injury to the plant results from the adult weevil chewing on the foliage, leaving the margins of the leaf blade scalloped. Lights at night attract the weevils and they often become nuisance pests inside the home.

The Asiatic oak weevil, *Cyrtepistomus castaneus* (Roelofs), is an insect native to northeastern Asia (D,E). It was first reported in this country in New Jersey in 1933, and has since spread into New York, the central Atlantic states and west to Missouri and the Ozark Mountains. The adult weevil is greenish gray and, with age, may become nearly black. They are about 6 mm long. Males of this species are unknown. It feeds on the foliage of susceptible hosts by eating the interveinal area. The lower leaves of a host plant are attacked first. *C. castaneus* feeds on 36 or more species of woody plants including oaks, Chinese chestnut, beech, hickory, black locust, red maple, dogwood, willow, tuliptree, spice bush, sweet gum, sycamore, apple, redbud, persimmon and viburnum. If *C. castaneus* occurs in large populations it may become a household pest. It and *Calomycterus setarius* have a similar life development.

References: 148, 264, 312

A. A cluster of rhododendron leaves notched along the margins by the Japanese weevil, *Callirhopalus bifasciatus*.
B. An adult Japanese weevil feeding on the edge of a leaf. The adult is about 6 mm long.
C. A pair of adult Japanese weevils.
D,E. An adult Asiatic oak weevil, *Cyrtepistomus castaneus*.

PLATE 89

Fuller Rose Beetle (Plate 90)

The Fuller rose beetle, *Pantomorus cervinus* (Boheman), is a common pest of outdoor ornamentals and fruit and vegetable crops in the southern United States, California, and southern Oregon. The adult is a brown snout beetle (E). All are females; males of this species are unkown.

The adult beetles lay their eggs in the spring. The eggs are laid mainly on the ground, or, at times, in tiny crevices on the trunk, branches or foliage of the host plant. The larvae, upon hatching, tunnel into the soil and feed on the roots of many different plants. When populations of the weevil are high, their intensive feeding may cause the death of the host.

Pupation takes place in the soil. The new adults emerge from the ground from mid-summer until late fall. During this stage, the Fuller rose beetle is long-lived, often remaining alive for many months. The insect overwinters in the soil under plant refuse or other debris. There is never more than one generation each year. The weevil is incapable of flying.

The adult weevils cause the greatest injury to ornamental plants. They devour leaves, buds and blossoms and leave behind them trails of dark fecal material on uneaten foliage (C). A wide variety of woody ornamental plants are susceptible to injury by adult weevils. Some of the more common hosts are: *Abutilon*—flowering maple; *Acacia*—acacia, wattle; *Acer negundo*—boxelder; *Azalea*; *Camellia*; *Cissus*; *Citrus*; *Deutzia*; *Diospyros*—persimmon; *Dracaena*; *Feijoa*—pineapple guava; *Fuchsia*; *Gardenia*; *Hibiscus*; *Lugunaria*—primrose; *Malus*—apple; Palm; *Pentstemon*; *Plumbago*; *Prunus*—peach; *Pyrus*—pear; *Quercus*—oak; *Rosa*—rose.

References: 74, 93, 256

A,B. Foliage of *Hibiscus* (A) and boxelder (B) tattered by adult Fuller rose beetles. Note adult beetles (circle in section B) on boxelder.

C. Close-up of boxelder foliage damaged by adult Fuller rose beetle. Fecal matter is deposited on the foliage and is an easily identifiable symptom of the Fuller rose beetle's presence.

D. Buds of *Hibiscus* destroyed by the Fuller rose beetle. Note beetles feeding.

E,F. Adult Fuller rose beetles. Length: 7–9 mm.

PLATE 90

Japanese Beetle, European Chafer, and Rose Chafer (Plate 91)

The Japanese beetle, *Popillia japonica* Newman, was first found in the United States in 1916. New Jersey was its point of entrance and from this state it has spread through much of the eastern United States. Local infestations have occurred in Illinois, Kentucky, Tennessee, Michigan, Iowa, Missouri and California. Some of these have been eradicated. Its southernmost limit is Georgia and its range extends north to Ontario and Nova Scotia in Canada. It continues to spread each year. Climatological studies have led to the prediction that it will reach all of the southern states along the Gulf of Mexico. Its spread to northern areas will be limited because of the cold. In New Hampshire, Vermont and Maine some of the grubs require two years to mature, though a normal cycle is completed in one year. Its spread west into the plains states may be inhibited by lack of adequate rainfall during the late summer months and by cold winter temperatures. The coastal areas of Washington and Oregon are believed favorable for Japanese beetle development.

The Japanese beetle overwinters in the northeastern states as a partially grown grub in the soil below the frost line. In the spring, the grub resumes feeding, primarily on the roots of grasses, and then pupates near the soil surface. Adults begin to emerge about the third week of May in North Carolina and the first week of July in upstate New York, in southern Vermont and in New Hampshire.

The adults fly to trees, shrubs or food crops plants to begin feeding. Their adult life lasts from 30 to 45 days. After mating, eggs are laid in small groups in the ground at a depth of 2.5 to 10 cm. Each female is capable of laying 40 to 60 eggs. These hatch in about two weeks and the young grubs feed on fine rootlets until cold weather drives them deep into the soil.

Both adult beetles and larvae seriously injure plants. Grub injury may be unnoticed until the plants are badly damaged, often beyond recovery. The roots of premium grasses seem to be the choice food for grubs but young roots of woody ornamental nursery stock may also be consumed. Vegetable seed beds are also choice grub feeding sites. The adult beetles feed on nearly 300 species of plants. Upon emergence, they usually feed on the foliage and flowers of low growing plants such as roses, grapes and shrubs; later they feed on tree foliage. On tree leaves, beetles devour the tissue between the veins, leaving a lace-like skeleton (A). At a distance severely injured trees appear to have been scorched by fire. The beetles completely consume rose petals and leaves with delicate veins. They are most active during the warmest parts of the day, and prefer to feed on plants which are fully exposed to the sun.

Of the woody ornamental plants attacked, the rose seems to be the favorite host. Other plants that receive extensive damage include crape myrtle, flowering crabapple, flowering cherry, Japanese maple, Norway maple, gray birch, sycamore, pussy willow, linden, elm, Virginia creeper, certain varieties of azalea, flowering quince, weigela, wisteria, California privet, bayberry, viburnum and others. Beetles have not been observed feeding on dogwood, forsythia, American holly, snowberry or lilac.

The United States Department of Agriculture and several state experiment stations along the Atlantic coast have done extensive work on the biological control of this insect. From this work, ways have been developed to produce and disseminate a disease-causing bacterium commonly called milky disease. The milky disease organism, *Bacillus popilliae*, is commercially available for application by home gardeners. Naturally-occuring microorganisms that reduce grub populations include fungus diseases, protozoans and nematodes. The important parasitic insects are *Tiphia vernalis* Rohwer and *T. popilliavora* Rohwer, both of which are wasps. Birds and toads eat large numbers of Japanese beetle adults as well as grubs. Moles, shrews and skunks also eat large quantities of grubs.

The European chafer (E), *Amphimallon majalis* (Razoumowski), is another accidentally introduced foreign insect. It has a life development similar to that of the Japanese beetle, and the grubs of both species look very much alike. The larva feeds almost exclusively on the roots of grasses. The adult does little feeding and causes no noticeable damage. Spectacular mating swarms, however, attract much attention. About the middle of June the adults begin to emerge from the soil, appearing only for brief mating flights. Around sunset, on warm days, thousands of these insects swarm like bees around trees or large shrubs. They fly for about one-half hour, mate, and then the females enter the soil to lay eggs. Mating flights may be repeated several times in a season. Beetles are most abundant from mid-June to mid-July.

The European chafer is presently found in New York State, Connecticut, New Jersey, western Pennsylvania and in limited localities in Ohio. In Canada it is known only in the Niagara Falls, Ontario, area. The United States Department of Agriculture quarantines are in effect on this insect and are slowing its westward movement.

The rose chafer (D), *Macrodactylus subspinosus* (Fab.), skeletonizes leaves in much the same way as the Japanese beetle. The rose chafer feeds on many kinds of plants; if deprived of one plant it will take another. It is strongly attracted to blossoms and particularly to rose and peony flowers. The leaves of trees and of shrubs are commonly fed on.

The rose chafer overwinters as a larva. The grub enters the pupal stage in the early spring and emerges as an adult beetle in June. The adult lives for about one month. The eggs are laid at this time, most commonly in grassland soil. Upon hatching, the larva feeds on the roots of grasses and weeds.

Rose chafer development requires light sandy soil. This factor greatly limits its distribution. The larva is a white grub with legs and when fully grown is 18 mm long. The rose chafer occurs in restricted localities throughout the Northeast, in eastern Canada, and also in Colorado.

Birds are often killed by eating the adult rose chafer. Its body contains a poison which affects the heart of small, warm-blooded animals.

The western rose chafer, *Macrodactylus uniformis* Horn, greatly resembles the eastern species and its habits are similar. It occurs primarily in Arizona and New Mexico.

References: 20, 93

A. Typical feeding injury to cherry caused by the adult Japanese beetle, *Popillia japonica*.
B. Severe Japanese beetle damage to a linden leaf.
C. An adult Japanese beetle. Length is about 10 mm.
D. An adult rose chafer, *Macrodactylus subspinosus*. Length is about 12 mm.
E. The European chafer, *Amphimallon majalis*, in all stages of development. Adult length is about 13 mm. (Courtesy G. A. Catlin, New York State Agricultural Experiment Station, Geneva, New York)

PLATE 91

Baccharis Leaf Beetle, and Rose Curculio (Plate 92)

The baccharis leaf beetle, *Trirhabda flabolimbata* (Mannerheim), is one of many related leaf beetles which feed on sagebrush (*Artemisia*) and other wild rangeland shrubs or goldenrod (*Solidago*) in many parts of North America. *T. flabolimbata* feeds on dwarf chaparral broom, or coyote bush (*Baccharis pilularis*) only in the San Francisco region of California. Another common western species is *Trirhabda pilosa* Blake, which feeds on sagebrush in Nevada, Wyoming, California and in the provinces of Alberta and British Columbia in Canada. While many more species of *Trirhabda* are known in the western United States, only six species are reported from the East, where goldenrod is the dominant host.

The life histories of most *Trirhabda* species are fairly similar. Instead of overwintering in the adult stage, which is usual for the leaf beetle family *Chrysomelidae*, this species spends the winter in the egg stage, on the ground. The eggs hatch in the spring and the young larva climbs a suitable host plant, where it feeds first on tender terminal foliage. The older larva is less discriminating in its choice of food, and feeds readily on all foliage (A). At maturity, the larva, which measures about 13 mm in length, returns to the ground where it forms pupal cases just below the surface of the soil. The adult baccharis leaf beetle appears in mid-summer and lays eggs soon thereafter. The adult beetle is commonly a metallic blue or green, although some species are somber in color. The beetle feigns death and drops to the ground quickly when its host plant is disturbed. There is only one generation each year. The larvae likewise are metallic blue-green.

Widespread serious damage to sagebrush has resulted from defoliation by *T. pilosa* in parts of western North America.

Where sagebrush is considered a pest plant on rangeland, interest has been expressed in the possibility of utilizing *T. pilosa* as a means of control of the plant.

The rose curculio, *Rhynchites bicolor* (Fabricius), is found in a number of black to red color phases. It is destructive to roses throughout the United States and is most common in the cooler northern regions. While roses—both cultivated and wild—are its principal host, the rose curculio also feeds on wild brambles. The greatest damage to roses is caused by the adults feeding on the flower buds. The adult punctures the floral parts contained inside buds. Later, if the flowers succeed in opening, these floral parts are riddled with holes, resulting in ragged, unsightly blossoms. If flower buds are not plentiful, the adult curculio may feed on the tips of new rose shoots, causing the death of the terminals. At other times, the stems of buds are gouged, causing the bud to wilt and die.

Eggs are laid in the flower buds by the female insects. After hatching, the white, legless larva completes its development by feeding on the reproductive parts of the blossom. Larval development may occur in blossoms which remain on the plant or in those which drop to the ground. The fully grown larva leaves the bud and enters the soil where it passes the winter. Pupation takes place in the soil in the spring. The new adult then emerges from the soil several weeks later, begins feeding on available host plants, and the cycle is repeated. The adult is about 6 mm long. Apparently, there is only one annual generation wherever this insect occurs.

References: 9, 15, 24, 93, 135, 187

A. Larvae of *Trirhabda flabolimbata* feeding on *Baccharis*.
B. A close-up of *Trirhabda flabolimbata* larva.
C. A rose flower damaged by the rose curculio.
D. An adult rose curculio.

PLATE 92

Root Weevils (Plates 93, 94)

Root weevils are insidious pests of ornamental shrubs. The adults feed on the leaves but the injury is often inconspicuous unless large numbers are present. The larva feeds unseen on roots in the ground, and, if undetected, may consume most of the feeder roots, causing the plant to die abruptly. Such plant losses often are attributed to other causes by those unaware of the presence of root weevils. Diagnosis of dead or declining plants should include examination of the roots. Early detection is possible through recognition of adult feeding symptoms (see Plate 94).

The most injurious weevils on broad-leaved evergreens and taxus are species of *Otiorhynchus* (= *Brachyrhinus*). Most common of the several species are the black vine weevil, *O. sulcatus* F., and the strawberry root weevil, *O. ovatus* L. The adult of *O. sulcatus* is 9-13 mm in length, while that of *O. ovatus* is slightly less than 6 mm long. *O. rugosostriatus* in the West and *O. rugifrons* in the East are intermediate in size. The relative size and appearance of the above species are illustrated in Plate 93. The strawberry root weevil is more prevalent as a garden pest and the black vine weevil is more important on woody ornamental plants. Both of these species, however, attack a wide variety of hosts.

The black vine weevil, also known as the taxus weevil, is a native of Europe and is the most destructive and widespread of the root weevils throughout the northern half of the United States and in Canada. It is destructive, primarily in its larval form, to taxus, hemlock, rhododendron, and several other broad-leaved evergreens, as well as to strawberry, and some greenhouse plants such as impatiens. As an adult it has a wide host range which includes both deciduous and herbaceous plants. It is a serious pest in nurseries as well as in landscape plantings.

The adult is black and is the largest of the *Otiorhynchus* species found on ornamentals. It is active at night. During the day the adult hides in dark places on the stems of very dense plants or in ground litter and mulch. When disturbed, it drops quickly to the ground. All adults are female and cannot fly. A period of two to three weeks of feeding occurs before the adult begins to lay eggs. During mid-summer, the adult alternately feeds and lays eggs for a month or more.

Injury caused by adult feeding on broad-leaved evergreens and other hosts consists of marginal notching of the leaves. The damage is indistinguishable from that caused by the Japanese weevil, Fuller rose beetle, and other weevils. However, since other weevils do not feed on taxus, notched and cut-off needles are positive diagnostic symptoms of black vine weevil. To detect weevil infestations early on taxus, it is necessary to look at needles at the center of the plant near the main stems. Excessive feeding on the foliage of host plants indicates a high larval population around the roots of favorite hosts in the vicinity.

The larva, or grub, is highly destructive to plants. Adult feeding rarely injures plants seriously, although it might be extensive. Larval feeding takes place from mid-summer, when the eggs hatch, into the fall, and then again in the spring. Feeder roots and bark on larger roots are consumed by the larger larvae in the spring, often resulting in the death of the plant. Root feeding injury may not cause noticeable injury to growing plants in the nursery, but plants may die after having been transplanted. Root weevil grub species cannot always be distinguished from one another in the field. All are legless, C-shaped, and white with brown heads (F). They may be found at a depth of from 2 to 40 cm in the soil around the roots. Pupation occurs in the soil near the surface. The pupa is milky white in color and has conspicuous developing appendages.

There is usually one generation each year. Partially grown larvae overwinter in the soil. Occasionally adults may survive by living in houses during the winter. Adult emergence from the soil usually starts about mid-June in the Northeast, and egg laying begins one to two weeks later. Each female lays up to 500 eggs in the soil near the base of the plant over a period of two to three weeks. The eggs hatch in ten days to two weeks and the larvae tunnel through the soil to feed on roots. The most extensive feeding occurs in late May and early June, just prior to pupation.

In the Northwest, the woods weevil (also known as the raspberry bud weevil), *Nemocestes incomptus* (Horn), and the obscure root weevil, *Sciopithes obscurus* Horn, are destructive to azalea (A), rhododendron, viburnum, camellia, rose, yew and others. The larva of *Nemocestes* chews the bark of stems beneath mulch, and also feeds on roots deep in the soil. Development of this weevil is reportedly continuous throughout the year although activity is less during the summer. The adult weevil is about 6 mm long.

Many other root weevils have been described and are pests of ornamentals: the arborvitae weevil, *Phyllobius intrusus* Kono., is a pest of arborvitae, retinospora, and juniper in New England; the asiatic oak weevil, *Cyrtepistomus castaneus* (Roelofs), of oak and chestnut in the East (Plate 89); the citrus root weevil, *Pachnaeus litus* (Germar), of citrus in Florida; the imported long-horned weevil, *Calomycterus setarius* Roelofs, of woody and herbaceous plants in the Northeast and west to Illinois; the Japanese weevil, *Callirhopalus bifasciatus* Roelofs, of a wide variety of hosts in the Northeast and south through Virginia; the pine root collar weevil, *Hylobius radicis* Buchanan, as well as *H. rhizophagus* M. B. & W. and *H. warreni* Wood, of Scots, Austrian, red, and jack pine in the Northeast; and the Fuller rose beetle, *Pantomorus cervinus* (Boheman) of ornamentals in the South.

Generally, many of these weevils are parthenogenetic; that is, no male is needed for successful reproduction. The adult cannot fly, since the hard, shell-like fore wings are fused together. The larva and the pupa of many species are very similar in appearance, making identification of the species difficult without adults. The larva of most species feeds throughout the root zone deep in the soil.

References: 93, 148, 196, 204, 264, 294

A. A larva of *Nemocestes incomptus*. Note damage done to an azalea cutting.

B,G. Girdling of a rhododendron stem by weevil larvae.

C. Adult of the strawberry root weevil, *Otiorhynchus ovatus*; 4–6mm long.

D. Adult of the rough strawberry root weevil, *Otiorhynchus rugosostriatus*; 7–9 mm long.

E. Adult of the black vine weevil, *Otiorhynchus sulcatus*; 10 mm long.

F. Typical appearance of root weevil larvae and pupae. Note that the larvae have no legs.

PLATE 93

A. Typical feeding injury by black vine weevils on leaves of privet.
B. Fatal injury to roots of taxus resulting from attack by black vine weevil grubs. Note that the tender bark has been chewed from most of the roots.
C. Adult feeding injury on severely infested azalea.
D. Adult black vine weevil.
E. Typical damage to taxus caused by weevils.
F. Injury on euonymus caused by feeding of adult weevils.

PLATE 94

Seagrape Borer and A Seagrape Gall Midge (Plate 95)

The seagrape borer, *Hexeris enhydris* Grote, is probably the most important pest of the seagrape, a small tree common to central and southern Florida. The larva of this pest bores into the stem, the leaf petiole, and occasionally the main vein of leaves. The stem is left weakened and subject to wind breakage. If the leaf petiole is attacked, the leaf dies and turns brown, providing a diagnostic symptom.

The fully grown larva is about 15 mm long, with a light brown head and a pale brown, partially translucent body. It chews one or more small holes in the stem from which it ejects small masses of dark frass. Pupation occurs in the stem. There are

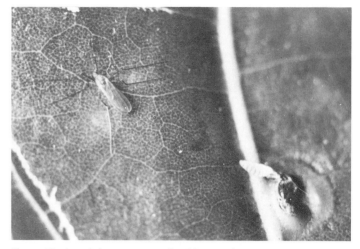

Figure 19. An adult seagrape gall midge, and empty pupal case on a seagrape leaf. (Photo courtesy Division of Plant Industry, Florida Department of Agriculture and Consumer Services)

probably three generations each year. Adults appear in December, from March to May, and from July to September. The moth has a wingspan of 34 mm. Its body is a pale brown color and its fore wings have numerous wavy rusty lines. The biology of this species has not been fully studied. Its only known host is the seagrape.

A minute gall midge *Ctenodactylomyia watsoni* Felt, can also substantially reduce the ornamental value of seagrape as a result of the numerous galls produced by this pest on the seagrape's leaves. Each gall is hemispherical in shape, is succulent, and has rather thick walls. The galls are visible from both surfaces of the leaf (see Figure 18). If one is cut open, a small maggot or larva will be found. If there is a hole in the gall, the adult midge has emerged (see Figure 19).

The flatid planthopper, *Metcalfa pruinosa*, may also be found on the leaves of seagrape (see Plate 178), as can the greedy scale (Plate 155), and black citrus aphid (Plate 121).

Reference: 192

Figure 18. The lower surface of a seagrape leaf showing galls of the midge *Ctenodactylomyia watsoni*. Two-thirds natural size. (Photo courtesy Division of Plant Industry, Florida Department of Agriculture and Consumer Services)

A,B. The seagrape, *Coccolobis uvifera*, with dead leaves, which are symptoms of the presence of *Hexeris enhydris*, the seagrape borer.
C. Leaf vein damage from borer feeding.
D. Exit hole with frass at the base of a leaf.
E. Hollowed out stem with borer inside.

PLATE 95

Walnut Insects (Plate 96)

The walnut tree is useful for both shade and food. Because it has a dual purpose, close observation and additional care are necessary to prevent insects from defoliating the tree or from ruining its fruit.

The butternut curculio, *Conotrachelus juglandis* Leconte, feeds on Siebold walnut, butternut, Persian (English) and black walnut. It is an eastern species found from Texas, Kansas and Wisconsin eastward to the Atlantic coast; it is also found in south-central Canada.

Injury to the tree is caused by both larvae (B) and adults (C). The adult feeds on nuts, tender twig terminals and leaf petioles; the larva burrows into the nuts, young shoots, leaf petioles and stems. Of greatest consequence to the health of the tree is the injury by the larva to stems and branches. New shoots are sometimes killed back to the wood of the previous season.

C. juglandis overwinters in its adult stage, probably in ground litter. The first eggs are laid in new twig growth. Later, as nutlets begin to form, the eggs are deposited in crescent-shaped excavations which are eaten into the nutlet's husk near the blossom end by the adult curculio.

The larvae become fully grown in four to five weeks. In West Virginia, they begin to leave the infested nuts and twigs about the middle of July. At this time, they enter the ground to pupate. The new adult emerges from the soil in late summer to feed on terminals, shoots and leaf petioles until cold weather causes it to hibernate.

The black walnut curculio, *Conotrachelus retentus* Say, closely resembles the butternut curculio in both behavior and appearance. The black walnut tree is the preferred host. This species may be found from Pennsylvania and New Jersey south to North Carolina and west to Mississippi, Arkansas, Kansas, Missouri and Illinois.

Two other major pests of walnut are the husk maggot of the genus *Rhagoletis* and the codling moth, *Laspeyresia pomonella* (Linnaeus). The codling moth is of European origin and is a fruit pest around the world wherever apples and walnuts are grown. In the western United States it is a serious pest of Persian walnuts; in the East there have been locally severe infestations, but it is not considered a major pest.

The female moth (E) lays her eggs on foliage, twigs and nuts. The location of her eggs is dependent upon the time of the year she is active. The young larva enters the nut from the calyx end, where two nuts come into contact (D). After this invasion it acts as a borer and expels frass, keeping its tunnels fairly clean. The frass collects on the outside of the nut and serves as a symptom of the larva's presence. The larva is creamy white in its early stages, but when fully grown it is pinkish-white, about 25 mm long, and has a brown head. In the south and in California there may be two to three generations each year.

Mites also cause damage to walnut. An eriophyid gall mite, possibly *Eriophyes brachytarsus* (Keifer), caused the formation of the excrescence shown in section F. The galls are formed in late spring, and persist through the life of the leaf. This mite causes galls only on the upper side of the leaf. The gall is hollow inside except for hundreds of tiny mites feeding upon the succulent tissue. They are invisible to the unaided eye. In addition to the eriophyid gall mite, a number of spider mites cause injury to walnuts, particularly in the western states.

References: 17, 143, 198

A. Black spots on the stem (see arrow) were made by the adult butternut curculio, *Conotrachelus juglandis*, on *Juglans* sp.
B. A new shoot split open to show larvae of *Conotrachelus juglandis*.
C. An adult curculio, *Conotrachelus juglandis*.
D. A persian (English) walnut infested with codling moth larvae. Note the accumulation of frass between the two nuts.
E. The codling moth, *Laspeyresia pomonella*.
F. Leaf galls on *Juglans hindsii* caused by an eriophyid gall mite.

PLATE 96

Oak Twig Girdler (Plate 97)

Patches of dead foliage scattered throughout canopies of oak trees (A) in California are characteristic symptoms of the activities of the oak twig girdler, *Agrilus angelicus* Horn. It is considered to be the major insect on oak in southern California. The California live oak, *Quercus agrifolia*, seems to be affected more than any other oak. Most complaints of damage caused by this insect arise from infestations in the California live oak. This is probably due to the dense human population in areas where this tree is a native species. The interior live oak, *Quercus wislizenii;* the Engelmann oak, *Q. engelmanni;* and several introduced oaks are reported to be susceptible to attack as well.

The adult insect is a brownish bronze beetle about 7 mm long (C). After mating, the female lays eggs singly on the twigs of the tree's most recent growth. The eggs hatch after two or three weeks and the larvae bore directly into the twig.

The larva is white in color, legless, and looks like a string of flattened links of sausage because of the definite constrictions between the body segments. When mature, it measures about 19 mm (E).

After hatching and boring into the twig, the larva tunnels just beneath the bark, making a slender gallery in the direction of the older twig growth. The larva then begins to girdle the twig, spiralling in the direction of older growth. At this time, the leaves behind the girdled area begin to die; additional leaves continue to die as the girdling advances. After nearly two full years within the twig, the larva reverses its course and tunnels back toward the tip of the twig for a distance of up to six inches. There, it pupates, and emerges as an adult several weeks later. Emergence of adults occurs any time between May and September. Along the southern California coast most of the adults appear in late June and early July. Inland, peak emergence takes place from late May to early June. The entire life cycle requires approximately two years.

The cause of dying patches of foliage on oak is best ascertained by pruning out several of these patches and removing the twig bark at the juncture between the living and dead foliage. If the oak twig girdler was the cause of the damage, a gallery filled with brown, powdery frass, and possibly a larva will be found (D). Other causes exist, of course, for the dieback of patches of foliage on oak. One of these is the activity of the larva of the roundheaded oak twig borer, *Styloxus fulleri* (Horn). Instead of a spiral gallery beneath the bark, this insect makes a linear tunnel directly through the central part of the twig. See Plate 98 for more twig girdling insects.

References: 34, 93

A. Patches of dead foliage on California live oak caused by the oak twig girdler.
B. Close-up of an oak twig showing dead foliage beyond point (see arrow) girdled by the oak twig girdler.
C. An adult oak twig girdler, *Agrilus angelicus.*
D. Twigs showing area of girdling.
E. Larva of *Agrilus angelicus* removed from its gallery, tail end out.
F. A hickory twig showing larval injury by *Elaphidionoides* sp. (see text accompanying Plate 98).

PLATE 97

Twig Pruners and Twig Girdlers (Plate 98)

There are a few wood-boring beetle species that tunnel in twigs during their larval development. The twigs are partially severed by the larva so that they break easily and drop to the ground. Twig pruning, whether it be done by insect or man, increases the density of a tree crown by encouraging latent buds to grow. Excessive pruning damages the tree and greatly alters its shape.

Small, cleanly cut twigs of oak, maple, hickory, pecan, locust, flowering fruit trees and a few other ornamentals found lying under a tree are symptoms of the injury caused by *Elaphidionoides villosus* (Fabricius), sometimes called the oak twig pruner (B). Twigs and small branches from 6 to 50 mm in diameter are subject to attack.

The adult is believed to deposit its eggs in midsummer, under the bark of small twigs. The developing larva feeds towards the base of the twig. By fall, the borer has eaten away most of the fibrous tissue, leaving only bark (see section F of Plate 97). It then backs up and packs the anterior of the hole with castings (C). High winds cause the nearly severed twig to break. The larva completes its development in the twig on the ground. In the Northeast one generation of oak twig pruners occurs each year.

The twig girdler, *Oncideres cingulata* (Say), causes damage to twigs while in the adult stage (G). Injury occurs in the fall of the year when the beetle chews a continuous notch around the twig, girdling it. This is done below the site of egg deposition, apparently because the larva is unable to develop successfully in wood containing large volumes of sap. Girdled twigs soon die and break off. The eggs hatch in the fall and the larvae remain dormant inside twigs on the ground. The fully grown larva is cylindrical and between 18 and 25 mm in length when mature. It completes its development during the latter part of August when it emerges as an adult beetle to repeat the cycle. One generation usually occurs each year although some individuals do not complete their development until the second season. Hosts of the twig girdler include elm, oak, linden, hackberry, apple, hickory, pecan, persimmon, poplar, basswood, honeylocust, dogwood, some flowering fruit trees and others. It is known to be generally distributed throughout the eastern United States from New England to Florida and west to Kansas, Texas and Arizona.

The insects shown in sections A, D and E have been identified only as members of the genus *Agrilus*. They are twig pruners of red oak and other shade trees in the Northeast. The injury caused by this species is particularly noticeable in early September. See Plate 97 for a description of the oak twig girdler, *Agrilus angelicus*, in California.

References: 96, 179

A. Red oak tree with dead twigs—symptom of attack by *Agrilus* sp.
B. Drawing of the oak twig pruner by Joutel in 1900. Following his legend: (7) A larvae in its tunnel; (7a) A thin shell of bark, the wood being nearly all eaten; (8) A pupa in its burrow; (9) An adult beetle.
C. A fully grown twig pruner larva *Elaphidionoides villosus*, exposed in its tunnel. Its head is to the right.
D. Egg of *Agrilus* species laid near a leaf scar.
E. An *Agrilus* larva in a red oak twig (see arrow).
F. A broken red oak twig where an Agrilus larva has been feeding.
G. The twig girdler, *Oncideres cingulata*. (From author's collection; photographer unknown)

PLATE 98

213

Dogwood Borers (Plate 99)

The flowering dogwood, *Cornus florida*, is one of our most beautiful flowering trees. Boring insects greatly limit its success in home and park plantings. Artificial control of these pests is frequently necessary. The most serious is *Synanthedon scitula* Harris, commonly known as the dogwood borer (E). In the South, this clearwing moth has been called the pecan borer. The adult's appearance is similar to that of a wasp. It is a swift flyer and is on the wing during the daylight hours. Although only one generation occurs annually, moths may emerge throughout the summer months. In the vicinity of New York City, the first moths of the season appear after mid-May; farther south, they appear earlier. The eggs are laid on both smooth and rough bark, but the female moth is particularly attracted to injured bark. After hatching, the light brown larva wanders about until it finds a satisfactory point of entrance to the tree's cambium. The larva cannot chew through the rough, corky bark but finds ready access to the cambium through wounds or scars. The crotches of limbs are also likely places of invasion. These borers are cambium feeders and remain in or just under the bark throughout their developmental period. The fully grown larva is 17 mm long, and is white, with a pale brown head.

Cultivated trees are usually more heavily infested than those which grow in woodlots. Sloughing of loose bark is an early symptom of attack. Dieback (F) and adventitious growth are advanced symptoms. Since dogwood borers commonly live in the bark, their presence may be indicated by small, wet areas on the bark. Later in the summer, fine, white, dustlike borings that have been pushed from the burrows may be seen. Old trees that are infested annually may persist in an unhealthy condition for years.

The dogwood borer is generally distributed throughout the eastern half of the United States. Its numerous hosts include flowering cherry, apple, mountain ash, hickory, pecan, willow, birch, bayberry, oak and others. The insect is often found in twig galls caused by other insects or fungi.

The dogwood twig borer (D), *Oberea tripunctata* (Swederus), completes its larval development in the twigs of dogwood, viburnum, elm and fruit trees of the genus *Malus* and *Prunus*. The insect is found primarily within the climatic range suitable for dogwood. The adult beetle emerges from infested twigs in early summer to lay its eggs in healthy twigs. Upon hatching, the developing larva tunnels into the pith, and makes frequent holes (B) to the surface. Frass is expelled through these holes. At intervals, the larva cuts off parts of the twig from within. This is the major form of injury caused by this insect. One generation occurs each year.

Oberea ulmicola Chitt is a closely related species. Its larva has been found in branches of hickory, dogwood and black cherry. Adults are active in June and July.

References: 85, 289, 297

A. Twig of dogwood, *Cornus florida*, showing typical injury caused by the dogwood twig borer. The larva normally feeds downward, or towards the trunk.
B. Small holes in the bark where the dogwood twig borer larva expels dry frass.
C. The dogwood twig borer excised from its channel in the pith.
D. An adult dogwood twig borer, *Oberea tripunctata*.
E. An adult dogwood borer, *Synanthedon scitula;* a clearwing moth.
F. A flowering dogwood showing typical crown dieback caused by severe dogwood borer injury.
G. Scars on the trunk and limbs, along with adventitious growth, are symptoms of dogwood borer injury.

PLATE 99

Shothole Borer (Plate 100)

Trees that have been attacked by *Scolytus rugulosus* Ratz. appear as though they have been blasted with a shotgun; hence this insect's common name, "shothole borer" (C). The shothole borer and the peach bark beetle, *Phloeotribus liminaris* (Harris), attack fruit and ornamental trees that are unhealthy due to other causes. Trees in neglected orchards are particularly susceptible. The shothole borer attacks our common fruit trees, wild plums, cherries, serviceberry and, occasionally, declining shade trees such as the elm. The peach bark beetle attacks the stone fruits, mountain ash, elm and mulberry. Both insects have similar habits and life histories. Only the shothole borer will be discussed in detail.

The adult beetle is attracted to weakened and dying trees. It bores through the bark, making a hole about the diameter of pencil lead and leaving reddish dust-like borings in the bark crevices. The parent gallery of the shothole borer parallels the grain of the wood, whereas that of the peach bark beetle normally runs across the grain. As with other bark beetles, eggs of the shothole borer are laid in small niches along the sides of the parent galleries. The larvae that hatch from these eggs feed out from these galleries, generally at right angles, gradually enlarging their side galleries as they develop. Pupation occurs under the bark, and the new adult bores out through the bark, leaving a shot-hole effect. Two generations occur annually in the northern part of the United States and three further south.

The shothole borer was introduced into this country from Europe and now occurs throughout the United States. The peach bark beetle occurs from New York westward to Michigan, south to Tennessee and eastward to Maryland.

Attacks by either insect can be minimized by keeping trees in good health. Proper cultivation, fertilization and irrigation all help to prevent attacks. All dead and dying trees and prunings should be promptly removed from the orchard or home grounds and burned, chipped or taken to the dump to destroy existing beetle populations and prevent reproduction.

References: 93, 196, 256

A. A twig of *Prunus laurocerasus* killed by the shothole borer.
B. An adult shothole borer, *Scolytus rugulosus* Ratz. About 2 mm long.
C. Emergence holes made by adult shothole borer.
D. Healed over bark, evidence of unsuccessful attack by adult shothole borers.
E. A shothole borer larva. About 2 mm long.
F. An adult (at arrow) constructing egg gallery.
G. An adult (at arrow) boring into dying twig.
H. Bark removed to reveal larval galleries.

PLATE 100

Elm Bark Beetles (Plates 101, 102)

Elm bark beetles were of little concern until Dutch elm disease arrived in America. It is through these insects that the fungus responsible for the disease is able to enter the tree and produce its devastating effect. The native elm bark beetle, *Hylurgopinus rufipes* (Eichhoff), and the smaller European elm bark beetle, *Scolytus multistriatus* (Marsham), are the insects involved in disease transmission. Of the two species, the European elm bark beetle is the major vector of the disease in most areas, because of its breeding dominance over the native species. The adult *S. multistriatus* is shiny, reddish brown and about 3 mm long. *H. rufipes* is slightly smaller, is dull brown and has a rough body surface. The adults of the two species are easy to distinguish from one another. However, their eggs, larvae and pupae are so similar in appearance that, in the field, they cannot be told apart unless their galleries (under the tree bark) are well developed and can be examined.

The native elm bark beetle (C) occurs in the eastern and central states from Maine to Virginia and west to Mississippi, Kansas and Minnesota. It has also been found in Ontario, Canada. It overwinters either as a fully grown larva in dying trees or as an adult in the bark of the trunk or of large limbs of living elms. Adults begin to appear in May and make their egg-laying galleries in dying or recently killed trees. These galleries extend across the grain of the wood (A). Two or more generations occur each year.

The European elm bark beetle (D-2), as its name implies, is a native of Europe. In the United States, it was first discovered in 1904 near Boston, Massachusetts. Since that time it has spread to most of the states which lie east of the Rocky Mountains and to Utah, Nevada, Oregon, California and Ontario, Canada (see Figure 20).

This species overwinters as a fully grown larva in the bark.

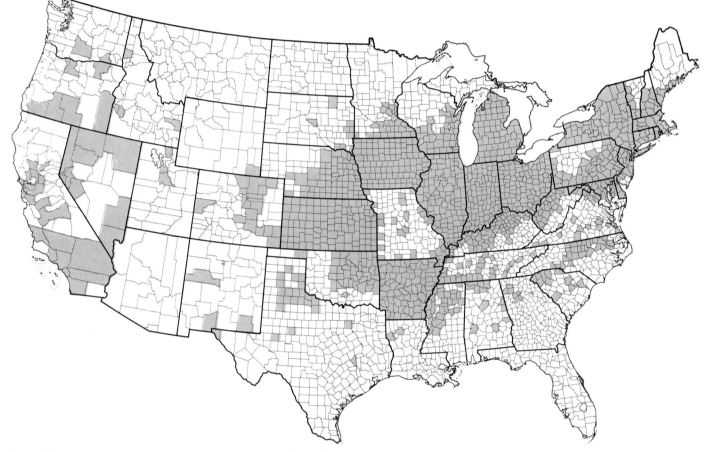

Figure 20. Distribution of the smaller European elm bark beetle *(Scolytus multistriatus)* in the United States as of 1974. (Courtesy Pest Survey, Animal and Plant Health Inspection Service, USDA)

A. Brood galleries of the native elm bark beetle. Note the horizontal alignment of the central egg gallery.
B. Adult European elm bark beetle feeding injuries in the crotches of American elm twigs.
C. An adult native elm bark beetle, *Hylurgopinus rufipes;* 2.5 mm long.
D. (1) A newly emerged native elm bark beetle. (2) The European elm bark beetle *Scolytus multistriatus;* 3 mm long.
E. Elm bark cut away to expose bark beetle larvae.
F. Brood galleries of the European elm bark beetle. Note the vertical alignment of the central egg gallery.
G. Bark beetle larvae as they appear from the inside of the bark.

PLATE 101

Larval and pupal development is completed in the spring and the adult begins to emerge about the middle of May. The emergence period extends over several weeks. The adult feeds on young bark. It selects the crotches of elm twigs (B) as its major feeding site. When the female is ready to lay eggs, she chooses an unhealthy elm tree and bores into the bark of the trunk or larger branches to prepare the egg-laying gallery which is oriented parallel to the grain of the wood. The gallery shown in section F was produced by one female. She laid 62 viable eggs.

Each tunnel radiating from the central egg-laying gallery is the work of one larva. When the larval stage is completed, the insect pupates at the end of its feeding gallery. Upon emerging from the pupa the adult chews a hole through the bark and becomes free to migrate to other elm trees. Two or more generations occur each year.

Reference: 32

A. Early symptoms of phloem necrosis, a disease vectored by a leafhopper.
B. Fruiting bodies of the Dutch elm disease fungus at the end of stalks. Highly magnified.
C. Streaking symptom seen in the summer wood after bark removal.
D. American elm with characteristic Dutch elm disease symptoms (see crown of tree).
E,F. Sapwood discoloration in elm twigs caused by Dutch elm disease.

PLATE 102

American Plum Borer (Plate 103)

The American plum borer, *Euzophera semifuneralis* (Walker), is a minor pest of fruit trees, mainly apple and peach. In the late 1950's and 1960's many London plane trees, *Platanus acerifolia*, were planted as street trees in eastern cities. They received considerable abuse, and many developed weakened conditions or suffered bark damage. Consequently, they were subject to infestation by the American plum borer.

In the larval stage the American plum borer injures weakened trees by feeding on the inner bark and cambium.

It overwinters as a mature larva inside a thin, but tough cocoon. The cocoon is generally located in the crevices of, or under, loose bark (B). In Virginia, the insect pupates in early April. Moths begin to appear in late April. They mate, and soon lay eggs. The moth shown in section D, a female, has a wingspan of about 25 mm. Her eggs are deposited singly or in small groups, usually in cracks under loose bark. The female lays about 26 eggs and lives only about 8 days. The eggs hatch after a few days and the larva crawls about until it finds a broken place in the outer bark. When it has found such a place it invades the tree. Larval tunnels or galleries are shallow and are filled with frass. They have frequent openings to the outer bark, where red frass accumulates (E). In young trees, early season infestations may be recognized by wet spots on the bark where sap oozes from the cambium in response to the presence of the feeding insect. The fully grown larva is about 25 millimeters long (F).

The American plum borer has been recorded as being injurious to mountain ash, mulberry, flowering apple, peach and cherry, persimmon, walnut, pecan, olive, linden, poplar, sweet gum, ginkgo and, only recently, sycamore. It occurs from New York to Florida and west to Arizona and Colorado.

A number of parasites and predators of the American plum borer have been recorded. They include the wasp parasites *Idechthis* sp. and *Mesostenus thoracicus* Cress., and the larva of the predatory beetle *Tenebroides corticalis* Melsheimer. Woodpeckers also help keep the American plum borer in check.

Reference: 25

A. A London plane tree damaged by the feeding activities of the American plum borer, *Euzophera semifuneralis*.
B. Large sections of bark can be easily stripped from trees heavily infested by the American plum borer. Note the white cocoons.
C. A young London plane tree. Note the numerous scars and cut places in the bark resulting from willful abuse. Larvae are active in the vicinity of the larger scars.
D. Pinned specimen of *Euzophera semifuneralis*.
E. An older tree trunk with much loose bark and red frass accumulations, the result of feeding by the American plum borer. Fully grown larva is 25 mm.
F. The inner surface of some loose bark with two cocoons. Note larva at the arrow.
G. A sycamore with plum borer infestation starting where a guy wire was located.

PLATE 103

Lilac Borer and Ash Borer (Plate 104)

The lilac borer, *Podosesia syringae syringae* (Harris), is a clear-winged moth in its adult stage. It resembles a wasp, a fact which undoubtedly contributes to its survival. The pest is found east of the Rockies.

In Ohio, adults emerge from infested hosts during late May and June. The eggs are deposited on the rough bark of lilac and on scarred or broken bark caused by insect or mechanical injury. After the eggs hatch, the larvae tunnel through the bark and feed for a time on the sapwood. As they mature they bore into the heartwood. They maintain contact with the outside and expel much "sawdust" or frass which accumulates around the exit hole (B).

Ugly scars (A), accompanied by enlarged or swollen areas, are associated with repeated infestations. Branches may be severely weakened at the feeding sites. During dry periods in late summer, terminal shoots of infested plants wilt. The infestation is often found near the root crown and up to a height of one meter. The borer is creamy white with a light brown head and is about 25 mm long when fully grown. One generation occurs each year.

The ash borer, *Podosesia syringae fraxini* Lugger, is similar to the lilac borer, and injures its host in much the same way. It has been found in Kansas, Colorado and other Rocky Mountain regions north to Montana and Manitoba, Canada. Seriously injured ash trees have been observed in city parks and along city streets in Texas, Colorado, South Dakota, Montana, and Manitoba. In severe cases, a tree may contain 50 or more borers. Woodland trees are less prone to infestation. The date of emergence of moths from ash trees varies from March and April in the South to July and August farther north. Privet is also a host of the ash borer. Neither the ash borer nor the lilac borer is found west of the Rocky Mountain states.

An ichneumonid wasp, *Phaeogenes ater* Cress, is occasionally found as a parasite of the lilac borer. Little is known about its effectiveness as an agent of biological control.

References: 85, 255, 312

A. An old lilac showing several deep scars of past lilac borer infestations.
B. A young lilac with fresh sawdust-like frass produced by an active borer. The infestation was at ground level.
C. An excised lilac borer, *Podosesia syringae syringae*.
D. An adult female lilac borer. Although this insect is a moth it looks at first glance like a wasp.

PLATE 104

Wood-boring Caterpillars (Plate 105)

In the caterpillar stage this group of moths has strong well-developed mandibles for chewing wood. The adult moths are of varied sizes and shapes. *Paranthrene simulans* (Grote) is of interest, not only because of the injury it does to trees, but because it looks so much like a wasp that few people would try to capture it without a net. It does not have a sting as do the wasps it mimics. This species is found in the northeastern quadrant of the United States and in eastern Canada. Oak seems to be its major host but elm becomes infested also. *P. simulans* may be readily found on farm woodlot, park or street trees.

Young shoots or saplings are particularly attractive to the egg-laying female. The eggs are laid on thin bark. The young larva makes tunnels under the bark. By late spring, it bores into the solid wood. It maintains contact with the outside to expel frass and wood cuttings; dark frass held together by a light web is noticeable on infested trunks or limbs. (A) The mature larva pupates in the galleries and the adult emerges in the spring. Heavy infestations can kill trees, and even a single larva can open up the tree to decay fungi. The woodpecker is one of the chief natural enemies of the wood-boring caterpillar.

Some authors have called *Zeuzera pyrina* Linnaeus the leopard moth because of the dark, sometimes greenish spots, on its white wings (E). It came to the United States from Europe, northern Africa and Asia Minor, and was first found in the United States in New Jersey in 1879. Since that time, it has continued to spread westward and southward. The moth may appear throughout the growing season from May to September.

It is a heavy-bodied, weak flyer, with a wingspan of from 30 to 40 mm. The male moth is strongly attracted to light. Eggs (H) are laid in masses, or, more commonly, in small clusters in bark crevices. A single female may lay as many as 800 eggs. Upon hatching, the larva often crawls some distance before boring into the bark. The larva is a wood feeder, and tunnels into the heartwood, where it does most of its feeding. Should a larva bore into a branch too small for it to complete its development, it chews its way out and finds a bigger branch. It then enters, and continues to feed. A single larva may kill a limb three inches in diameter. Larval development is usually completed in two years. The caterpillar is flesh-colored. It has a brownish-black head and thorax. When fully grown, it is about 50 mm long.

An infested tree may exhibit several symptoms. An accumulation of sawdust-like frass on the bark indicates the presence of borers; however, dead branches may be the first evidence of damage. Exit holes are often found in the tree limbs, sometimes with a portion of the old pupal case remaining in the hole.

The leopard moth larva feeds on more than 125 species of deciduous trees. Among these are maple, elm, beech, ash, oak, walnut, chestnut, poplar, willow, lilac and all the flowering *Malus* and *Prunus* species. Even though the moth is widespread, it is not a major pest because it is rarely found in large numbers. Control is difficult after the insect has become established in a tree.

References: 32, 85, 129

A. The trunk of a young oak, *Quercus palustris,* containing one or more *Paranthrene simulans* larvae. Note the frass and dark sap-stained area.
B. Old entrance hole exposed to show its relative size.
C. Larva of *Paranthrene simulans* exposed in its tunnel.
D. Vacated pupal case protruding from an elm branch.
E. Female leopard moth. Note the sharp ovipositor.
F. Male leopard moth. Note the form of the antennae. Wingspan is 38 mm.
G. Adult male *Paranthrene simulans.* Wingspan is 28 mm.
H. Eggs produced by the female in section E.

PLATE 105

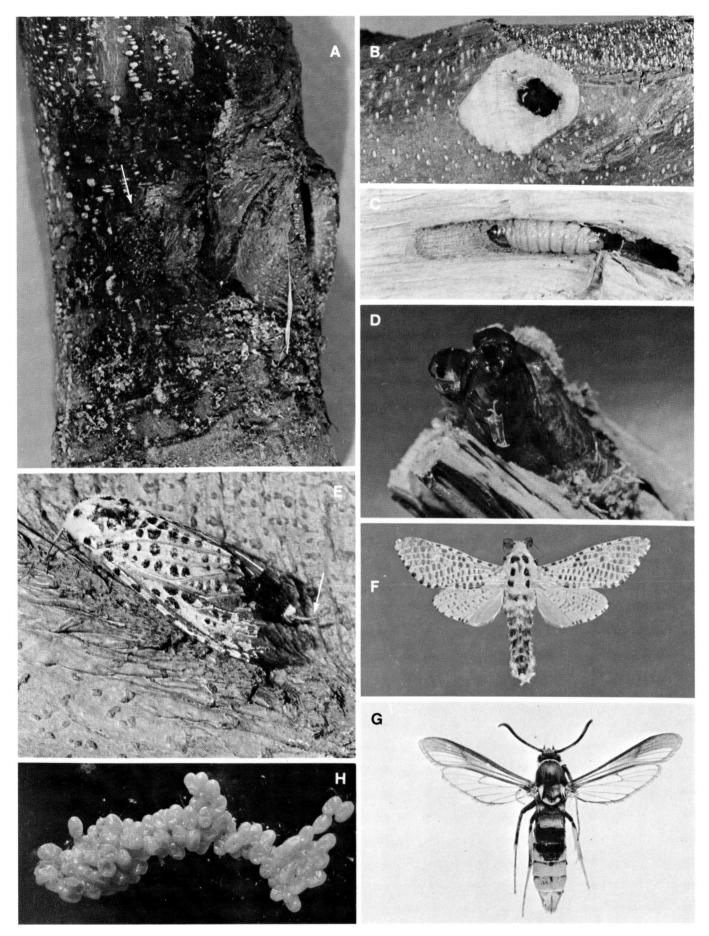

227

Wood-boring Caterpillars (Plate 106)

In central and southern California and in several other parts of the Southwest, a clearwing moth, *Ramosia resplendens* (Hy. Edwards), often becomes a pest of western sycamore, *Platanus racemosa*. The larvae are voracious feeders in the inner bark but rarely in the wood. They prefer to feed in the trunk of older trees, i.e., trees on which the bark has begun to exfoliate. Recurring attacks by the larvae cause the sycamore to lose all of its pleasing bark character; it becomes dry and acquires a checked appearance (A), like dried mud in the summer sun. Large sections of bark, some as thick as 20 mm, slough off, giving the trunk an unsightly appearance. When the loose bark is scraped away, numerous meandering tunnels are exposed. This insect causes similar damage to coast live oak, *Quercus agrifolia*.

The moths emerge over a long period, from May to early August. Eggs are laid singly in small cracks or depressions on the trunk. Upon hatching the larva bores into the inner bark and makes twisting tunnels over an area of about 100 square cm. The larva is pinkish-white with a brown head, and is 18 mm long when fully grown. In southern California, it feeds through most of the winter months and pupates in the early spring. One generation occurs each year.

The dogwood borer, *Synanthedon scitula* (Harris), attacks a large number of hardwood trees. Its biology and behavior is discussed on Plate 99. Section B shows the adult moth. Wounds on the tree trunk are attractive to ovipositing moths; such sites may in time become ugly knots. The moths also are attracted to *Prunus* trees that have been infected with the black knot fungus, *Apiosporina morbosa* (D), and to oak twig galls (Plate 189). The cherry branch (D) with black knot disease was held in a rearing cage for about three weeks and produced six moths (B).

The lesser peach tree borer, *Synanthedon pictipes* G & R, is well known to peach growers. It is also a pest of flowering cherry, and almond. *S. pictipes* is frequently found at or near a tree crotch, or at the site of an old trunk injury. Injury typical of that caused by this pest is shown in section F. Such damage often results in sucker and adventitious growth. This insect is concentrated primarily in southern and eastern regions, although it also occurs as far north as eastern Canada.

The rhododendron borer, *Synanthedon rhododendri* Beuten-müller, is the smallest of the native clearwing moths. Although its chief host is rhododendron, it also feeds occasionally upon mountain laurel, *Kalmia latifolia*. The larva is a serious pest of ornamental rhododendron in the Atlantic coast states. It rarely injures the wild rhododendron, which is abundant in the wooded areas of West Virginia and the central Appalachian Mountains.

Infestations may be recognized by wilted, off–color foliage, reduced annual growth and dead branches. Past infestations may be recognized by shallow, longitudinal scars in the bark (H).

The moths emerge in May and June. The eggs are laid on bark. The larva bores into the inner bark where it makes long tunnels which are filled with small reddish pellets. As the larva matures it bores into older wood. In time, the bark over the tunnel peels off, exposing a shallow groove or scar in the wood. The larva becomes fully grown before the arrival of cold weather. At maturity, it is about 12 mm long. After hibernating during the winter, the rhododendron borer pupates in one of its tunnels in early spring. The larva is white with a brown head. One generation occurs each year.

There are several other clearwing moths that damage ornamental trees and shrubs. Throughout the United States, the peach tree borer, *Synanthedon exitiosa* (Say), attacks trees in the genus *Prunus*. The larva of the peach tree borer is found near the root crown and behaves much like the larva of other clearwing moths. The adult has a body with a metallic purplish-black luster and a wingspan of about 28 mm.

The hornet moth, *Aegeria apiformis* (Clerck), resembles the European hornet, *Vespa crabro* (Plate 210), in size and color. The larva is primarily a pest of poplar. When abundant, this insect limits the use of poplar trees as shade or street trees. It is a European species, now found throughout much of the northern United States and parts of California.

Little is known about the natural enemies of any of these species. Woodpeckers may be important predators; because they are woods–inhabiting birds they are not commonly found in cities.

References: 85, 297

A. Western sycamore, *Platanus racemosa*, with bark injured by *Ramosia resplendens*.
B. Adult dogwood borer, *Synanthedon scitula*.
C. Close-up of sycamore bark showing the dry, caked appearance typical of a site under attack by *Ramosia resplendens*. Note the empty pupal case at the opening of a larval tunnel.
D. Black knot infection on a flowering cherry branch caused by *Apiosporina morbosa* fungus. From the fungus infection areas, six dogwood borers emerged.
E. Close-up of the pupal skin of *Ramosia resplendens*.
F. Typical injury caused by *Synanthedon pictipes* on flowering cherry. In the black hemispherical knot one or more larvae may be found.
G,H. Rhododendron branches showing scars resulting from earlier rhododendron borer infestations.

PLATE 106

Wood-boring Caterpillars (Plate 107)

Wood-boring insects often have a life cycle of two or more years. The carpenterworm, *Prionoxystus robiniae* (Peck), is believed to require from three to four years to complete its development in the northern states and in Canada. Certain broods in the south (Mississippi) emerge regularly on one year cycles. Except for two months of each year, the insect stays in the larval stage while feeding within the host. When fully grown, the larva measures from 50 to 75 mm, making it one of the largest known wood-boring caterpillars.

The adult female moth has a wingspan of about 75 mm; the male moth is considerably smaller. Both the male and the female have heavy bodies and are similarly marked. Their forewings are basically light gray and mottled with black. The hind wings of males are marked with orange. The carpenterworm moth is often a prize specimen of amateur insect collectors.

In southern California, the moths begin to emerge in early April. In the lower Mississippi valley, emergence coincides closely with the leafing out and flowering of pecan. Egg laying begins shortly after the moths emerge. The period of oviposition lasts about one month. Sticky egg masses may be found on the trunks or branches of susceptible hosts, often in crevices, wounds or in the scarred areas resulting from previous larval infestations. A single female may lay from 300 to 400 eggs. Upon hatching, the larva bores into the wood. It remains in the sapwood for only a short period of time, since it prefers the heartwood. All through its development, the larva maintains contact with the outside and expels large quantities of sawdust and frass that clings in masses to the bark (C). The larva is creamy white with a dark brown head. It has several short, stout hairs on each of its body segments.

Over a period of time, the activities of the carpenterworm larvae may prove disastrous to the host tree especially if the tree is located near a house or other building. The tunnels of the larva (D) are up to 13 mm in diameter. Thus, the strength of the infested wood may be greatly reduced, making the tree or its large branches subject to breakage by high winds. In addition, the bark may be severely scarred, ruining the wood for saw log purposes. A tree may be reinfested year after year. Such infestations open up the tree to wood-rotting fungi which over a number of years may hollow it out, making it more susceptible to wind damage.

Host trees include elm, ash, locust, oak, cottonwood, maple, willow and, occasionally, ornamental shrubs. In the eastern and southern states, red oaks show the heaviest damage. In the prairie states green ash, *Fraxinus pennsylvanica*, has been the chief host; in the Rocky Mountain region poplars are favored; and in California, American elm and live oak, *Quercus agrifolia*, are most commonly attacked. The carpenterworm is distributed over the entire United States from Maine to California and southward to the Gulf of Mexico. It is reportedly the most destructive borer of hardwoods in Missouri. Little is known about its natural enemies.

A related species, *Prionoxystus macmurtrei* (Guer.), sometimes called the little carpenterworm, is often confused with *P. robiniae* in all stages. It is primarily a pest of oaks in the eastern half of North America. A wet spot on the bark made by oozing sap is an early symptom of the borer's presence. No part of the tree is immune from attack. Small branches, one inch in diameter, often contain tunnels of this insect. Branches high in the crown are often killed, ruining the tree's symmetry. In Canada, three years are required to complete one generation. A fully grown larva is about 62 mm in length.

Parathrene robiniae (Hy. Edwards) is one of the colorful clearwing moths (E) that looks much like a vespid wasp. The larva feeds in the cambium and heartwood of *Populus trichocarpa*. The specimen shown in section E was collected in Claremont, California, in mid-August. Little is known about its biology. It is a western species found throughout the northern Rocky Mountains, Montana, Alberta, British Columbia, and along the Pacific coast to southern California. See Plates 104, 105, and 106 for photographs of other wood-boring caterpillars.

References: 50, 85, 125, 129, 141, 179, 272

A. American elm on a ranch in the foothills of the Sierra Nevada. It is heavily infested with the carpenterworm, *Prionoxystus robiniae*. This tree has probably been continuously infested for 25 years. Note size of the bark scars.
B. Scarred bark with large quantities of frass and "sawdust" expelled by carpenterworm larvae.
C. A close-up of frass at the opening of a carpenterworm's tunnel.
D. Tunnels chewed out by carpenterworm larvae.
E. An adult clearwing moth, *Parathrene robiniae*.
F. Injury to the trunk of *Populus trichocarpa* caused by the larva of *Parathrene robiniae*.

PLATE 107

Bronze Birch Borer (Plate 108)

Agrilus anxius Gory, known as the bronze birch borer, is a beetle native to North America. It occurs throughout the range of birch, from Newfoundland to British Columbia in Canada south to New Jersey, Ohio, Colorado and Idaho. It can be a serious pest of forest and shade trees.

In winter, the bronze birch borer larva is found hybernating in the xylem at the edge of the summer wood and the bark. All instars are represented in the overwintering population. In the spring, the immature larva completes its development and pupates. In southern Canada, adult emergence begins near the end of June and lasts for about six weeks. The flight and egg-laying period extends into August. Eggs are laid, singly or in groups, in crevices beneath the outer layers of bark. The preferred location for egg-laying is at the site of a recent mechanical injury. The eggs soon hatch, and the larva bores into the cambium where as it feeds, it makes tortuous engravings on the surface of the xylem (C). The larva in all instars is nearly white in color. The tail segment terminates in a pair of minute, brownish-black, forcep-like horns (for a larva similar in appearance see Plate 97 section E). The larva may remain in the cambium for either one or two years, depending on the time of egg laying and the condition of the host tree.

According to Barter (18), "The [bronze birch borer] larvae cannot survive in healthy trees. Successful larval development is dependent upon the host being in a weakened condition from repeated unsuccessful attack or other injury such as defoliation, adverse weather conditions or old age." The trees of most birch species are relatively short-lived; they seldom live longer than 50 or 60 years.

Injury is caused by the creation of feeding galleries by the larvae that, in effect, girdle the trunk or branch. Trees that survive borer attack have conspicuous swollen areas (B) caused by the healing process. Chlorotic leaves and sparse foliage are early symptoms of the presence of borers; these are most evident in the upper crown and are sometimes accompanied by increased adventitious growth in the lower crown. Should such adventitious growth develop, it is accompanied by twig dieback in the upper crown. The adult beetles feed on birch leaves but seem to have a preference for alder. Adult feeding injury is, however, insignificant.

Woodpeckers and parasites such as *Phasgonophora sulcata* Westw. (Hymenoptera) are major natural control agents of the bronze birch borer. These animals are not, however, generally effective in urban or suburban situations. Vigorously growing birch trees are less inclined to be damaged by the bronze birch borer than are trees in poor condition. The monarch birch, *Betula maximowieziana*, and Japanese white birch, *B. platyphylla japonica*, are said to be resistant to the borer.

References: 18, 50, 129, 262

A. A paper birch, *Betula papyrifera*, dying as a result of bronze birch borer attack.
B. Lumpy bark is an external indication of attack by the bronze birch borer.
C. Bark removed to show larval galleries.
D. Left: adult female bronze birch borer; right: the male.

PLATE 108

233

Locust Borer (Plate 109)

Figure 21. Black locust logs with bark removed to show sapwood damage. The dark scars are points of injury caused by young locust borer larvae. (Photo courtesy United States Department of Agriculture)

The locust borer, *Megacyllene robiniae* (Forster), is probably the most serious pest of black locust, *Robinia pseudoacacia*. The adult, a black and yellow beetle, is 13 to 20 mm long and is often seen feeding on the pollen of goldenrod. After a period of such feeding, the female deposits her eggs beneath the bark scales of the black locust. The larva hatches and overwinters in the corky bark. In the spring, it bores deeper into the bark, and then into the wood (see Figure 21). The first evidence of attack is pitch flowing from an entry gallery. The larva continues to mine throughout the heartwood until just before goldenrod blooms again, at which time it pupates in the trunk of the tree and emerges as an adult a short time later.

The borer prefers locust trees that are at least four years old, but once the trunk reaches 15 cm in diameter the attacks become less abundant. When heavily attacked, the trunk of the tree may become so weakened that it may break off in storms. Trees that do not break off show characteristic swellings and scars (B). Damage seems to be greatest on trees growing on poor rocky and thin soils.

The borer is found in most parts of North America where locust is grown. It is particularly damaging to host trees in central and northeastern United States.

References: 50, 129, 323

A. Scar caused by locust borer, and holes made by a woodpecker.
B. A swollen trunk is a symptom of locust borer injury.
C. Opened trunk showing locust borer galleries in the heartwood.
D. Adult beetle feeding on goldenrod.
E. Pupa in feeding gallery.

PLATE 109

Poplar and Willow Borer (Plate 110)

Willow trees are plagued by many insect pests. In 1882, a willow weevil native to Europe was discovered in the United States. Since that time this weevil, the poplar and willow borer *Cryptorhynchus lapathi* (Linnaeus) has spread from the east to the west coast and as far south as North Carolina. It is also established throughout southern Canada. Weevils, as a group, are known for the peculiar mouthparts which are attached to the tips of their long snouts (see section D).

During winter the poplar and willow borer is a partially grown, legless larva which can be found in the sapwood of infested willow trees (C). When plant growth resumes in the spring, the larva grows rapidly and expels much frass through openings of its own making to the outside of the tree. This frass clings to the bark and serves as an external symptom of the borer's presence. The oozing of sap from the bark may also signal infestation by this pest.

Pupation takes place in June. By midsummer, adults (D) begin to appear. They become abundant in August. In New York, they have been observed on or near their foodplant as late as mid–October, but these late individuals do not survive the winter.

The adult weevil feeds on young shoots by chewing small holes in the bark of twigs, but the injury caused is minor. White eggs are produced over a period of four to six weeks, and are laid singly or in groups of two to four in slits chewed by the adult weevil from corky bark or scar tissue on the trunk. Upon hatching, the young larva feeds on the inner bark. The larva has a C-shaped posture. When fully grown it is about 6 mm long. Typical injury caused by boring of larva is shown in sections B and C. When ready to pupate, the larva usually bores inward and upward and prepares a pupal cell in the center of the stem.

The poplar and willow borer feeds upon, and lays its eggs in, all *Salix* and most *Populus* species common in the United States, although *P. tremuloides* is not affected. It also feeds upon *Alnus*, *Betula pumila* and *B. nigra*.

Injury caused by the larva is greatest on nursery stock and on newly set trees in landscape plaintings. Infested trees may be killed or may lose their form and become bushy from coppice or adventitious growth. Young *Populus deltoides* respond to larval injury by producing bulbous swellings. After completion of insect development, these swollen areas exhibit emergence holes and much scar tissue.

References: 123, 188, 256

A. Severely scarred pussywillow stem with several adventitious sprouts. These grow as a reaction to severe injury by the poplar and willow borer.
B. Tunnels in the wood where larvae have prepared pupal chambers.
C. Larvae in what will become their pupal chambers.
D. An adult popler and willow borer, 8–10 mm long. Note the snout. The posterior part of the wing covers and abdomen is covered by pale yellow scales. On a dark background the adult is nearly invisible.
E. An old girdling tunnel caused by a larva.

PLATE 110

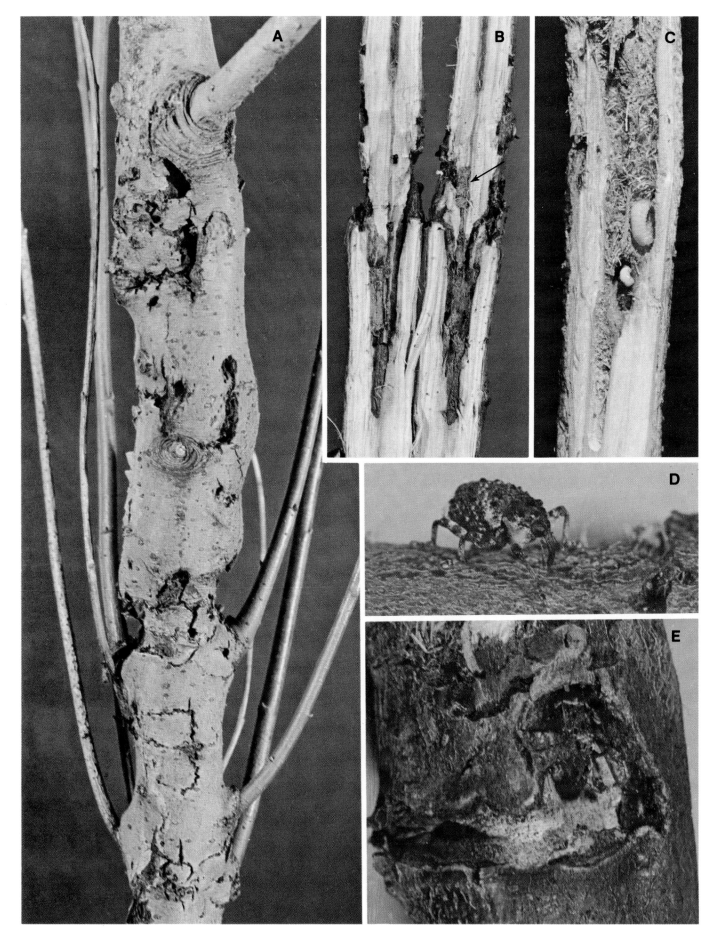

Wood-boring Beetle Larvae (Plate 111)

Many of the wood-boring beetles can be classified as either flatheaded or roundheaded borers. They damage shade trees by tunneling into the conducting tissue. More dangerous to the tree's health, however, may be the fungi that enter through the tunnels made by the insects.

The flatheaded apple tree borer, *Chrysobothris femorata* Olivier, (B), is a common species that feeds on many kinds of deciduous shade trees, fruit trees, and shrubs such as maple, oak, sycamore, tulip poplar, willow, rose and cotoneaster. The beetle is about 12 mm long, has a somewhat flattened appearance and is a dark metallic brown.

Some adult beetles emerge from their pupae late in the spring; others continue to emerge throughout the summer. The adult lays its eggs in bark crevices. The legless larva enters the bark at the place where the eggs were laid. If the tree is vigorous, the borer may be killed by heavy sap flow; if the tree or shrub is in a weakened condition, or the bark has been badly damaged, the larva enters and develops rapidly. It bores in the inner phloem, making irregular tunnels and partially filling them with powder-like frass. A single larva may girdle a young tree. Transplanted ornamental trees and shrubs are particularly susceptible to injury. When nearly mature, either in the spring or fall, the flatheaded apple tree borer bores deep into the heartwood (C) where it pupates. Adults feed at the bases of twigs, on partially defoliated young trees.

The flatheaded apple tree borer is found predominantly in the eastern and central states, but is known throughout the United States and southern Canada. One generation occurs each year. Regular fertilization and irrigation of most ornamental plants will promote vigorous growth, and reduce attacks by this insect. Newly transplanted trees are highly susceptible to attack.

A species on the west coast closely related to the flatheaded apple tree borer and called the Pacific flatheaded borer, *Chrysobothris mali* Horn, causes the same kind of injury, usually under similar conditions (E). It is considered one of the worst enemies of newly planted trees and shrubs in the Pacific coast states and in British Columbia, Canada. Seventy or more woody plants, including the rose, are attacked. In some of the higher elevations, more than a year is required for a complete generation. The borer has a number of natural enemies. The most common predator in Oregon is the mite, *Pediculoides ventricosus* (Newport), which attacks the larva in its tunnels.

The two-lined chestnut borer, *Agrilus bilineatus* Weber (D), is primarily a pest of oak, beech and chestnut, both in the forest and in the city. Like the flatheaded apple tree borer this pest attacks weakened trees. The beetles emerge from infested trees in May and June and feed on foliage for some time before laying eggs. Their eggs are laid on rough bark. The young larva bores into the tree's inner bark, where it makes meandering tunnels that may measure one meter long by the time the larva is fully grown. The larva is cream colored, and about 12 mm long. It has a flat head and an elongated body (A). Two years are required to complete its development in the northern United States. The first symptoms of an infestation are dead limbs in the upper crown of a tree. The species occurs throughout the central and eastern United States.

References: 39, 105, 129, 179, 198, 256

A. A two-lined chestnut borer larva, *Agrilus bilineatus*, in oak bark. (Photo courtesy Connecticut Agricultural Experiment Station).
B. A larva of *Chrysobothris femorata*, the flatheaded apple tree borer, in the crotch of a mountain ash tree. Note that the tree wrap did not prevent egg laying or injury.
C. Larvae of *Chrysobothris mali*, the Pacific flatheaded borer, in the heartwood of almond.
D. A two-lined chestnut borer adult *Agrilus bilineatus;* about 13 mm long.
E. Larvae of *Chrysobothris mali;* about 13 mm long when fully grown.
F. Larvae of *Chrysobothris femorata*—about 12 mm long.
G. An adult *Chrysobothris mali*—about 10 mm long.

238

PLATE 111

Wood-boring Beetles (Plate 112)

Many of the wood-boring beetles of importance to woody ornamentals belong to the family *Cerambycidae*. Commonly known as longhorned beetles, these insects bear antennae which are about as long as the body of the female and which are up to four or five times the length of the body of the male (A). The cerambycids are also known as roundheaded borers, because of their body structure and the characteristic feeding tunnels of their larvae. Most species in this family infest and feed upon dead or dying trees. There are, however, a number of important pests in this group which attack living healthy trees and shrubs.

The ponderosa pine bark borer, *Acanthocinus* (*Canonura*) *princeps* (Walker), is an example of a species that avoids healthy trees. This insect attacks only dying or dead pines, and feeds in their bark (A, B). *A. princeps* is a western species which occurs on the Pacific coast in British Columbia, Washington, Oregon, and California on *Pinus ponderosa* and *P. sabiniana*. *Acanthocinus spectabilis* occurs on *P. ponderosa* and *P. scopulorum* from Montana and South Dakota through the Rocky Mountain states into Mexico. Other similar species include: *A. nodosus* (F), which occurs from Pennsylvania south to Florida and west to Texas, and *A. obsoletus* (Oliv.), which occurs in eastern North America west to Minnesota and Texas.

The cerambycid *Saperda populnea* L. is an example of a borer which attacks healthy trees and which produces galls on poplar and willow (section D; and Plate 113, sections A,B,C and D). It was originally a European species, but is now found in the United States west of the Rockies, New York state and probably other eastern states. It causes twig galls on poplar (see Plate 113) and willow. Galls are often so numerous that on a given tree nearly all twigs with diameters of 15 mm or more may have one or more galls. The galls result in weakened twigs which break easily and litter the ground. An infestation in a young tree will greatly modify its normal growth characteristics. The fully grown larva is about 25 mm long and 8 mm in diameter. Very little has been written about the biology of this species.

The poplar twig borer, *S. moesta* Lec., causes galls on stems and branches of poplar across the northern parts of the United States. The poplar-gall saperda, *S. inornata* Say (=*concolor*), is another common and destructive species. It inhabits the living stems and twigs of willow and poplar.

The habits and development of gall-making saperdas on poplar and willow are basically similar. In Michigan, adults of the poplar-gall saperda appear from late May to early July, and lay eggs in small holes gnawed through the bark. One to five horseshoe or shield-shaped egg niches are made by the female in the outer bark, usually in a ring around the stem. The young larva tunnels in the cambium before boring into the wood. Callus tissue accumulates around the wound area resulting in a swollen, spindle–shaped gall. One and sometimes two adults complete development in each gall. The life cycle of an individual may be completed in one year, but may require two years, depending on when eggs were laid. Adults feed on the leaves of the host tree.

In the genus *Saperda* the following species attack living trees and are very similar except for color patterns: *S. vestita* attacks linden; *S. obliqua*, alder; *S. mutica*, willow; *S. hornii*, willow; *S populnea*, poplar and willow; *S. moesta*, balsam poplar; *S. tulari*, willow; *S. inornata* (=*concolor*), poplar and willow; and *S. fayi*, hawthorn.

The following species of *Saperda* attack only weakened, dying, or recently killed trees: *Eutetrapha* (=*Saperda*) *tridentata* attacks elm; *S. discoidea*, hickory; *S. lateralis*, hickory; and *S. puncticollis*, Virginia creeper.

The sugar maple borer (E), *Glycobius speciosus* Say, has a deceiving beauty. It is native to North America and is probably the most serious pest of sugar maples in the northeast. This insect also occurs throughout the Appalachian Mountains region. The injury is largely the work of the larva which infests the trunk and larger branches. It feeds on the inner bark and sapwood. Its feeding activity in one season may produce a tunnel nearly one meter long. The bark over the tunnel dies and, in the healing process, is pushed outward, causing the old bark to crack. When it sloughs off, an ugly scar becomes visible. As few as two or three borers strategically located in the tree, can kill it.

The life cycle of the sugar maple borer requires two years for completion. In the spring, new adults emerge from their pupal cells in the tree trunk. The eggs are probably laid in mid-summer in bark crevices usually at or near the base of the larger limbs. The young larva bores into the bark and makes a shallow tunnel which is sometimes noticeable from "bleeding" symptoms. There seems to be no larval activity during the winter months. Pupation of the sugar maple borer occurs after it has been in the larval stage about 16 months. The fully grown larva is about 50 mm long. The adult beetle looks somewhat like the locust borer (Plate 109).

References: 93, 97, 129, 179, 215

A. An adult male of the ponderosa pine bark borer—about 30 mm long.
B. Larva and typical tunnel of *Acanthocinus princeps* in pine.
C. Adult female of *Saperda populnea;* an old specimen with most of its scales rubbed off. See Plate 113.
D. Swollen stem or gall of poplar with larvae of *S. populnea* and tunnels. Also see Plate 113, section A.
E. Pinned specimen of the sugar maple borer.
F. Drawings by Joutel of the life stages of the sugar maple borer, *Glycobius speciosus* (Say). (1) Place where egg was laid; (1a) another with more larval activity showing borings thrown out by the larva; (2) borer as it would appear in September from an egg laid in the same season; (3) nearly fully grown borers; (4) female beetle; (5) hole through which the beetle emerged; (6) sawdust or borings packed in a burrow.

PLATE 112

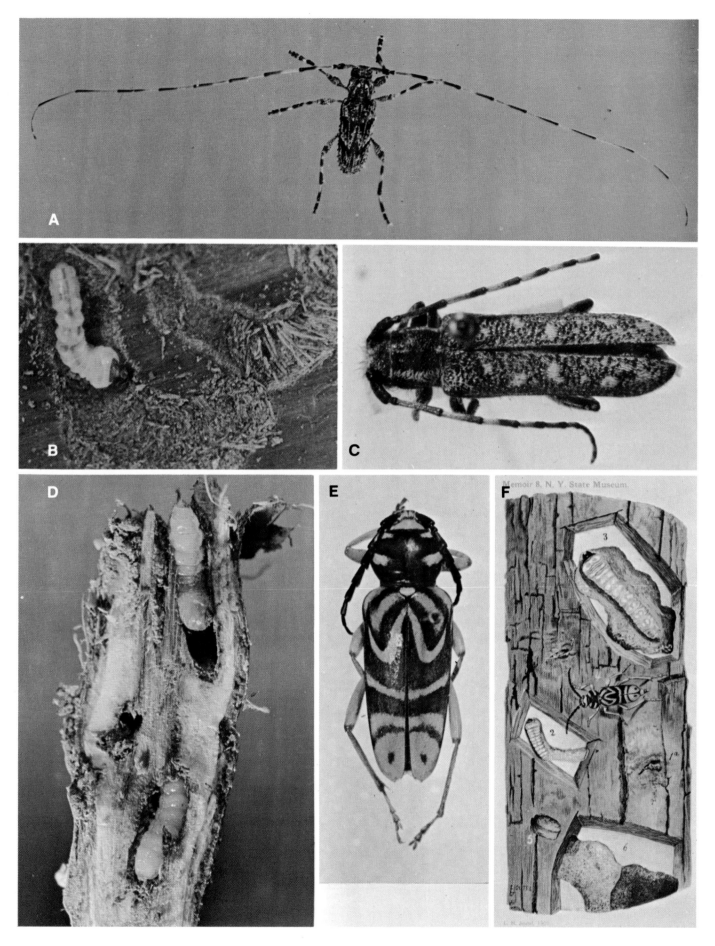

Wood-boring Beetles (Plate 113)

A pair of long antennae is the major characteristic for the field identification of the beetles illustrated in this and the preceding plate. Several galled poplar twigs caused by the longhorned beetle, *Saperda populnea* (L.), are shown in sections A and B. An explanation and description of this insect is included in the discussion of Plate 112.

Of the species belonging to the genus *Saperda,* the roundheaded apple tree borer, *Saperda candida* Fabricius does the most damage to tree crops. In the mid-1880's it was a serious problem for apple producers in the northeastern United States. Next to the codling moth, it was the worst enemy of the apple tree. With current pest management programs, however, it is now of little concern to fruit growers. Even so, the insect remains a major pest of several ornamental trees and shrubs, including hawthorn, mountain ash, shadbush, cotoneaster and flowering crabapple. The larva does the greatest damage but the adults do feed on the fruit, bark and foliage of host trees.

This insect is found throughout the northeastern quadrant of the United States as well as in the hilly areas of Georgia, Alabama, and South Carolina. It is also known from Texas north into southern Canada.

It takes about three years for a roundheaded apple tree borer (E,F) to complete its life cycle. The adults emerge from infested trees in May in the latitude of Washington, D.C., and in June in central New York State. The female beetle lives about 40 days. She devotes much of this 40-day period to egg laying. The female is secretive and deposits her eggs at night. A longitudinal slit, about 13 mm in length, is made in the bark of a tree trunk, usually near the ground, and a single egg is inserted. The egg soon hatches and the larva bores into the sapwood. It moves upward or downward in the trunk (depending upon the time of the year), all the while enlarging the tunnels and compounding the damage. In the early spring of the third year, it changes to a pupa and soon emerges as an adult.

The golden and downy woodpeckers are the only natural enemies that seem to have any effect on the population of the roundheaded apple tree borer. There are very few insect parasites of *S. candida.* One investigator wrote: "Possibly no other economic insect of equal importance has had so few natural enemies recorded definitely and specifically as have the roundheaded apple tree borer" (131).

The redheaded ash borer (G), *Neoclytus acuminatus* (Fabricius), is a pest of ash, elm, hickory, hackberry, oak, and linden. Forest entomologists consider it a pest of cut logs. However, the female lays her eggs on weakened or newly set trees. The larva works in the inner bark and summer wood, cutting off the flow of sap. In young trees, burrows may extend both horizontally and vertically through the trunk making it subject to breakage during high winds. This borer is a severe pest of young stock in the north central states.

The redheaded ash borer overwinters in the trunk. Adults begin to emerge in April about the time that red maple is in bloom. In Illinois, one generation occurs most years; occasionally, a partial second generation appears. This insect occurs in New England, the Appalachian mountain area, the north central states, the Ozark mountains and west from Missouri to Arizona.

References: 12, 93, 97, 101, 131

A,B. Galls in poplar twigs caused by the larvae of *Saperda populnea.*

C,D. Galls cut open to show the internal character of the gall and the developing larva.

E. Adult roundheaded apple tree borer, *Saperda candida.*

F. Larva of a roundheaded apple tree borer in cotoneaster.

G. Redheaded ash borer, *Neoclytus acuminatus.*

H. A newly emerged *Saperda populnea.* Note difference in color pattern, with specimen shown in Plate 112C.

PLATE 113

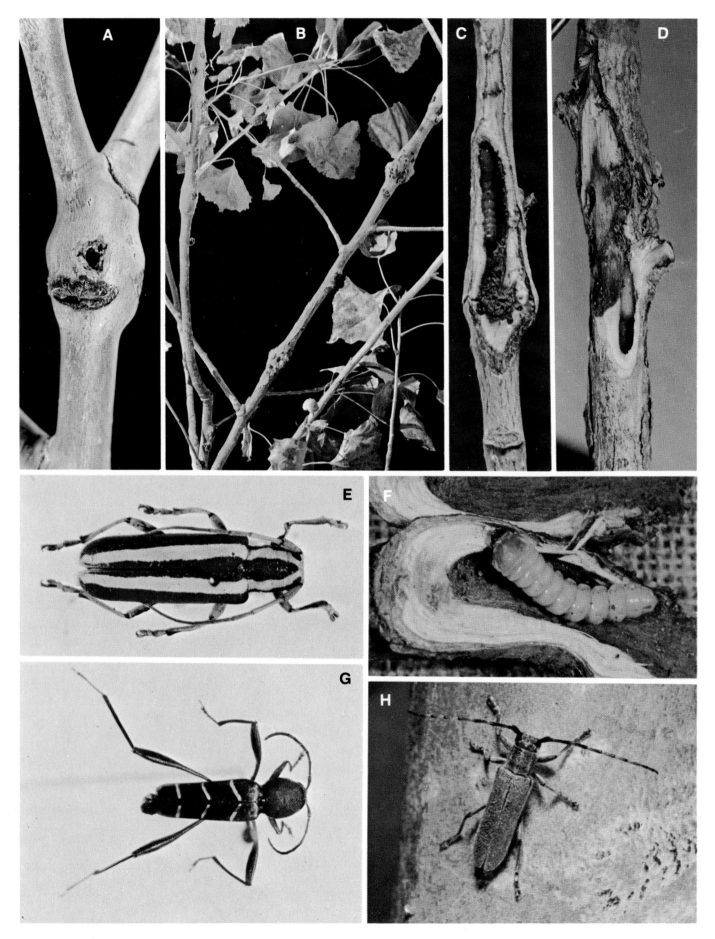

243

Albizia Psyllid (Plate 114)

Since the discovery of the Albizia psyllid, *Psylla uncatoides* (Ferris and Klyver), in the United States in 1954, this insect has become a major pest in California. The psyllid is also known in Hawaii and Arizona. The insect causes a yellowing effect and dieback on the tips of new growth. It is also a nuisance pest, for the adult insects are attracted to lights at night, and sometimes limit outdoor activities by their sheer numbers. On infested landscape trees which extend over patios, the white pellets of solidified honeydew produced by the immature psyllids create an additional problem as they "rain" down from the trees.

The adult psyllid (E) is a small, leafhopper-like insect which lays its yellow eggs in masses on the tips of *Albizia* and *Acacia* plants (D). The nymphs which hatch from the eggs feed by sucking plant juices. Sometimes thousands of nymphs, adults and eggs coexist on a single tip of a plant.

Reproduction occurs throughout the year, but populations are highest in the very early spring. At least eight generations of this insect occur each year in central coastal California.

Data from southern California show clearly the wide variation in susceptibility of *Acacia* and *Albizia* to attack by the psyllid. Reference to the list below may indicate which non-susceptible or lightly susceptible plants might be substituted for those known to be heavily attacked by the Albizia psyllid.

Occurrence of Albizia Psyllid on Acacia and Albizia

No occurrence	No occurrence
Acacia species	howittii
adansonii	karroo
albida	kempeana
aneura	latifolia*
arabica*	linearis
armata	lineata
aroma	linophylla
aspera	nealii
baileyana*	nerifolia
bonariensis	oswaldii
brachystachya	oxycedrus
caffra	pennata
calamifolia	plumosa
cambagii	podalyraefolia
congesta	salicina
crassiuscula	spirocarpa
cyanophylla	verticillata
dealbata	vestita
deanii	visco
dentifera	woodii
diffusa	Albizia species
drummondii	fastigiata
flexifolia	odoratissimi
giraffae	polyphylla
horrida	

Occurrence of Albizia Psyllid on Acacia and Albizia

Light occurrence	Light occurrence
Albizia species	sclerosperma
kalkora	scorpioides
thorelii	sophorae
Acacia species	sowdenii
abyssinica	spectabilis
adunca	stenophylla
auriculaeformis	stricta
burkittii	suaveolens
bynoeana	subulata
caesiella	trineura
cardiophylla	triptera
cavenia	undulaefolia
cyclops	visite
decurrens	
farinosa	*Moderate occurrence*
farnesiana	Acacia species
floribunda	acuminata
galpinii	argyrophylla
georginae	brachybotrya
glaniformis	cultriformis
glandulicarpa	cuthbertsonii
gnidium	elata
graffiana	elongata
implexa	estrophiolata
jonesii	euthycarpa
ligulata	extensa
longifolia*	koa
macradenia	obtusa
mearnsii	sentis
melanoxylon	strongylophylla
murrayana	subporosa
myrtifolia	unciniella
notabilis	Albizia species
pendula	julibrissin
penninervis	
pycnantha	*Heavy occurrence*
riceana	Acacia species
richii	falcinella
rupicola	maidenii
saligna	merrallii

*Includes cultivars

In 1971, eggs and developing nymphs of *P. uncatoides* were found on *Citrus* in Orange County, California. Although eggs have commonly been found on many different plants growing near infested *Acacia* or *Albizia*, the immature psyllids hatched from such eggs have invariably died, because of the unsuitability of the host.

References: 159, 208

A. Albizia psyllid infestation on leaves, stem, and flowers.
B. Infestation of the albizia psyllid on *Acacia longifolia*. Note dead tip killed by the psyllid (at arrow).
C. Very heavy nymphal infestation on stem of *Acacia longifolia*.
D. Clusters of eggs of *Psylla uncatoides*.
E. Adult psyllid.
F. Nymph of *Psylla uncatoides*.

PLATE 114

245

Psyllids (Plate 115)

Insects in the family Psyllidae, like other Homoptera, have piercing-sucking mouthparts and wings which are held in an inverted V-shape over the abdomen when the insect is at rest. In comparison to many other groups of insects, there are relatively few species that are pests of ornamentals. Some, such as the pear psylla, *Psylla pyricola* (Foerster), feed on leaves, while others, such as boxwood psyllid, *Psylla buxi* (L.), feed on developing buds and new leaves. The hackberry psyllids, as well as a number of other psyllids, cause galls on leaves and in buds (see Plate 194).

The boxwood psyllid is very common in the more temperate parts of the United States. It is highly conspicuous because of the leaf cupping effect it produces on host bushes, but it is not as destructive as some pests. The cupping of the leaves results from injury done to leaf tissue as it is formed in rapidly growing leaves.

Boxwood psyllids overwinter as very small, orange, spindle-shaped eggs. The eggs are inserted between the bud scales of the host bush by females during early summer. Only the tips of the eggs protrude past the edge of the bud scale. As soon as buds begin to open in early spring, the eggs hatch, and nymphs emerge to begin feeding. Studies have shown that embryonic development is complete before winter, and that nymphs overwinter inside the eggshell.

As nymphs develop on the expanding foliage, leaves become cupped, enclosing several nymphs in a pocket of leaves. The nymph produces a waxy filamentous secretion which provides it with additional protection. By late May and June, adults appear.

The adults are greenish jumping plant lice. They spring from the leaves to become airborne and sustain flight with their wings.

Adults may occasionally bite humans, but the bites are not serious. In severe infestations, thousands of adults may occur on relatively few plants at the time they lay their eggs in the buds. Only one generation occurs annually. The American boxwood is most frequently and severely infested. The English boxwood is less severely attacked.

There are a number of other psyllids which feed on ornamental trees and shrubs. *Calophya flavida* Schwarz occurs in the eastern United States on smooth sumac. *C. flavida* nymphs spend the winter on terminal twigs of this tree (C). The nymphs are small, flat and black, although they have a white fringe. *C nigripennis* Riley, another eastern species, may be found from Pennsylvania south to Alabama. *C. californica* Schwarz is known in California (H), and is also a pest of sumac, *Rhus ovata*. *C. triozomima* Schwarz occurs on *Rhus trilobata* in Arizona, Colorado, and California, and on *Rhus aromatica* in Missouri. This insect has a yellow abdomen.

D. L. Crawford (52) published a monograph on the Psyllidae in 1914, listing some 29 genera and about 161 species of psyllids in the Americas. Many, if not most, of these insects were known to feed on ornamental trees and shrubs, including pine, spruce, arborvitae, sumac, willow, mimosa, boxelder, false mastic, red bay, ceanothus, currant, raspberry, alder, birch, pear, hazel, laurel, maple, apple, and plum.

References: 52, 93, 256

A. Typical cupping of leaves resulting from feeding by the boxwood psyllid.
B. Boxwood psyllid nymphs and their waxy secretions in cupped leaves.
C. Overwintering nymphs of *Calophya flavida* on sumac.
D. Dark, flattened appearance of overwintering *Calophya flavida* nymphs.
E. Typical appearance of psyllid nymphs and their wax secretions.
F. Psyllid nymphs and their waxy deposits on dogwood.
G. Psyllid nymph on dogwood. The pest shown is color-adapted to the leaf surface.
H. The psyllid *Calophya californica* on *Rhus ovata*.
I. Psyllid nymph outside its protective waxy web.

PLATE 115

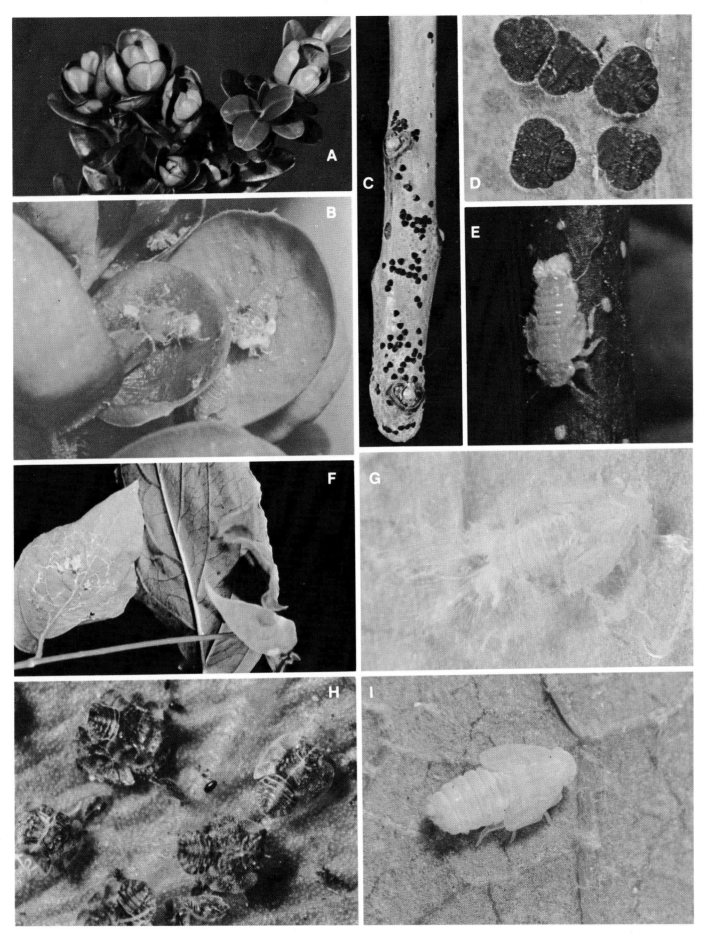

Aphids (Plate 116)

Free-living aphids which occur in colonies on the foliage of shade trees and other ornamental plants are common, persistent, and troublesome pests. They vary greatly in color from yellow, green, pink, or red to purple, brown, or black. There is also considerable variation in size between species. In small numbers their effect may be innocuous; in some cases, even large numbers may not be seriously injurious to plants. Some aphids are important not because of their direct feeding on the plant, but because they act as vectors, or carriers, of virus diseases. The winged adult aphid has considerable mobility and the highest reproductive potential of all insects. Its excreted honeydew droplets are annoying when found on cars and furniture in outdoor living areas. The resultant growth of sooty mold fungi on the honeydew is unsightly, and sometimes injurious, whether on leaves or on man-made objects.

Types and habits of various species of aphids differ widely. Some infest only one kind of host, others have alternate hosts, and still others have a wide variety of hosts. A list of aphid species that attack shade trees alone would be extensive, and would include at least one species for most of our common trees.

Aphids may occur throughout the growing season, although most tend to occur in specific seasonal periods. The tuliptree aphid, *Macrosiphum liriodendri* (Monell), occurs wherever the tulip-poplar *Liriodendron tulipifera*, grows (A). In Illinois, this aphid is found from mid-June through most of October. On flowering crabapple, the apple grain aphid, *Rhopalosiphum fitchii* (Sanderson), is present only in the very early spring. It then spends the remainder of the season on grain crops. The apple aphid, *Aphis pomi* DeGeer, does not migrate, but continues to feed on apple from early spring until new growth ceases in midsummer. The leaves of willow tend to be infested with aphids from spring to late summer.

In most cases, the piercing-sucking feeding activities of aphids produce inconspicuous signs of damage. Leaves may, however, be slowly depleted of plant food, and this gradually weakens the tree.

Injury to a host by the walnut aphid, *Chromaphis juglandicola* (Kaltenbach), is an example of the extent of conspicuous injury which aphids can cause. Like many free-living aphids, the walnut aphids overwinter as eggs on the twigs (E) and buds of the host. The eggs are black, and usually hatch in early spring when buds begin to open. Feeding occurs primarily on the undersides of leaves. This results in stunted leaves, nuts and twigs. This species is an occasional pest of Persian (English) walnuts in California where the wasp parasite *Trioxys* sp. usually keeps the population low. In the West, it is likely to occur wherever Persian walnuts are grown; in the East their damage is minimal.

The walnut aphid was introduced from Europe in 1909. It is a small yellow insect, about 1.5 mm long at maturity, and lives in colonies. Both males and females are produced as fall approaches. After mating, females lay eggs which overwinter. Egg-laying females are wingless, and can be distinguished from other aphids by two dark bands across their backs, one much broader than the other.

Injury by the black pecan aphid, *Tinocallis caryaefoliae* (Davis), is shown in sections C, D, and F. The adult aphids have a series of large black tubercles on the back and sides, and are not found in crowded colonies. This species is known to occur wherever hickory or pecan are grown. A related southern species, *T. kahawaluokalani* Kirkally, occurs in large colonies on the twigs and leaves of crape myrtle.

In the hickory woodlots of the North, as well as in the pecan orchards of the South it is common to see extensive patches of foliage marred by large, yellow, angular blotches (D). These are the first symptom of black pecan aphid injury. The yellow areas eventually turn brown as the season advances. As aphids increase in number, leaf damage increases, resulting in premature leaf drop. Some entomologists have speculated that discoloration of the leaf tissue is caused by the aphids' injection of toxic salivary fluids into the leaf at the feeding site. The aphids feed on both sides of the leaves, and seem to prefer the shaded inner parts of the tree. In the South, as many as fifteen generations are known to occur during the growing season. In the fall, adult females lay their eggs on twigs and bark, and the aphids overwinter as eggs.

References: 137, 143, 165, 166, 198, 265

A. Underside of a tuliptree leaf with a developing colony of *Macrosiphum liriodendri*, the tulip tree aphid.
B. Tulip tree aphid nymphs and wingless adult females.
C. Moderate injury to hickory leaves caused by the black pecan aphid.
D. Early stage of hickory leaf injury caused by the black pecan aphid.
E. Black aphid eggs matted on the bark of Persian walnut twigs.
F. Hickory leaflet that dropped prematurely from the tree because of injury caused by the black pecan aphid.

PLATE 116

California Laurel Aphid and Podocarpus Aphid (Plate 117)

The California laurel aphid (A), is sometimes mistaken for an immature whitefly. Careful examination is required to avoid this error. *Euthoracaphis umbellulariae* (Essig) is known only from California in the western hemisphere. It occurs primarily on California laurel, *Umbellularia californica*, but has been found in small colonies on common, or American sassafras, *Sassafras variifolium;* camphor tree, *Cinnamomum camphora,* and avocado, *Persea americana.*

In all its life forms, this insect is blunt and robust. The wingless (egg-laying form) females are covered with white waxy material. The winged aphids are jet black in color. This insect occurs in all its stages on the undersides of the older leaves of the host tree, often in neat rows (B).

The wingless female looks much like a juvenile whitefly. It is oval in form and appears to have a fringe of waxy filaments or plates (see Plate 129). Apparently, these females do not move once they have settled to feed. Individuals become fixed to the leaf surface and produce white cottony wax which envelops their bodies.

The California laurel aphid excretes large quantities of honeydew, from which black sooty mold grows. Often, the honeydew drops to leaves below and these are also blackened. No direct damage to the foliage of California laurel has been noticed as a result of the feeding of *E. umbellulariae.*

In central California migration from tree to tree by the winged form of this aphid occurs from spring to fall. Wingless forms may be found on the leaves throughout the year, evidence of numerous overlapping developmental stages. The number of generations that occur each year is unknown.

Podocarpus spp. are evergreen trees native to Australia and Asia. In the United States, one of the insects that feed upon *Podocarpus* is an aphid, *Neophyllaphis podocarpi* Takahashi. This aphid was probably introduced into the United States when the first podocarpus plants were imported. It is presently found in California, Florida, Mississippi, and Louisiana. In the future, the aphid will very likely be found wherever *Podocarpus* grows. There are at least twelve *Podocarpus* species grown as ornamentals in the United States; all of them are susceptible to this aphid.

The aphid causes a stunting and curling of the new terminal leaves. On older leaves a hard, resin-like substance may appear at feeding sites (E). The aphids feed primarily on the undersides of leaves, on young twigs and on fruit stems (D). They produce honeydew that gives the podocarpus fruit and leaves a bluish-white bloom. In time, sooty mold fungi grows in the honeydew and imparts a dusty bluish appearance to the affected plant parts.

The biology of this aphid under conditions in the United States is unknown. Several generations are produced each year.

References: 72, 91, 132

A. Light infestation of the California laurel aphid, *Euthoracaphis umbellulariae,* on the undersides of leaves of the California laurel.
B. Parasitized California laurel aphids. They are lined up in rows on either side of a vein in a characteristic manner.
C. California laurel aphids on a camphor tree leaf.
D. Clusters of podocarpus aphids, *Neophyllaphis podocarpi,* on twigs and fruit stems of *Podocarpus macrophylla.*
E. Resinous substance on leaves at the feeding sites of the *Podocarpus* aphid.

PLATE 117

Aphids of Beech, Birch, and Manzanita (Plate 118)

Phyllaphis fagi (Linnaeus) is an aphid that appears to have but a single host: beech. It has no generally accepted common name, although some authors have called it the woolly beech leaf aphid because of the quantity of wool-like filaments extruded from its body. These filaments are waxy in nature. The specimens shown in sections A and B are on *Fagus sylvatica* and were collected during the month of July. These aphids are gregarious and are found almost exclusively on the undersides of leaves. Large numbers of cast skins may be found attached to leaf hairs, adding to the whitish appearance of the leaf.

Phyllaphis fagi is widely distributed in the East and is also known in California. In general, it is able to survive wherever beech is grown. Beech trees in the United States seem capable of maintaining huge populations of this aphid year after year with little observable tree injury. In Europe, however, where this aphid originated, a great deal of harm to beech has been reported. On specimen shade trees a heavy infestation could probably not be tolerated because of the tremendous quantity of honeydew produced by the aphids. Clear droplets of fresh honeydew are shown in section B. The fluid is very sweet and sticky and is the same substance which, when dried, was called manna in the time of Moses. Honeydew is an attractive food for bees, wasps and ants, and also serves as food for certain fungi commonly called sooty molds. This "mold" is black and is unsightly when found on ornamental plants (see Plate 119).

Another woolly aphid common to beech is the beech blight aphid, *Prociphilus imbricator* (Fitch), which feeds primarily on the bark of twigs and small branches. The beech blight aphid looks much like the woolly alder aphid shown in Plate 122, although greater quantities of snow-white down are attached to *P. imbricator*.

Hamamelistes spinosus Shimer also has no accepted common name, but it might well be called the spiny witch-hazel gall aphid. This aphid has a complex and most interesting life history, the scenario of which alternates between two host plants of ornamental interest: witch-hazel (*Hamamelis*) and birch (*Betula*).

This species may survive the winter in two ways: as an egg, laid on witch hazel twigs, or as a "pupa" on a birch tree. In the spring, after winter dormancy, the egg hatches. The resulting aphid develops into what is called a stem mother. Its feeding results in the formation of a bud gall on the host (see Figure 22). Plant buds thus affected become green to reddish oblong galls that are about 18 mm in length and which are covered with long, sharp spines. Each gall is hollow and contains numerous reddish young aphids, the offspring of the stem mother. An exit hole at the base of the gall allows the mature aphids to emerge and fly to their secondary host, the birch.

While the spring development on witch-hazel is occurring, changes are taking place in the overwintering aphid on birch. The hibernating female, sometimes called a "pupa", becomes active at about the time birch leaf buds are opening. It moves from the bark to the new leaves and begins giving birth to young aphids. The insect's growth and reproduction is extremely rapid, and the leaves of an infested host soon acquire symptomatic corrugations. The undersides of leaves within the corrugated folds become filled to capacity with aphids and white granular material (E,F). Winged migrants develop on the leaves and seek witch-hazel on which to lay their eggs and complete the life cycle. All of these activities occur before the end of June. Photographs shown here were taken in south-central New York State in early June. The host is *Betula populifolia*.

Hamamelistes spinosus, is commonly found throughout New England though it occurs as far south as North Carolina and as far west as Colorado. A related species, *Hamamelistes agrifoliae* Ferris, feeds on coast live oak in California.

Injury by *H. spinosus* ranges from light to severe—from premature leaf drop to dead twigs and branches. There is keen competition in some areas between the birch leaf miner, *Fenusa pusilla* (Plate 71), and this aphid. Where both occur, the birch leaf miner dominates, and thereby reduces the aphid population.

Calaphis betulaecolens (Fitch)—a common, large green aphid—also occurs on birch. It feeds on the birch leaves, producing quantities of honeydew which smut much of the foliage. All common species of birch are hosts to this pest and hosts may be found throughout North America wherever birch is grown. This species spends its entire life on birch. It is not a serious pest of forest birch, but is frequently a problem on shade and specimen trees.

The birch aphid, *Euceraphis betulae* (Koch), injures leaves of birch and alder. They are large yellowish to green aphids which occur on the undersides of leaves and drop readily when disturbed. *E. betulae* is assumed to occur wherever birch trees normally grow.

Tamalia coweni (Cockerell) is believed to infest only manzanita, on which it forms green or reddish galls at the edges of leaves. For this reason some authors refer to it as the manzanita leafgall aphid. Its damage is shown in section D. Records show the aphid to have been present on Long Island, New York, Colorado and California. It is usually more disfiguring than damaging to its host.

References: 93, 96, 98, 129, 165

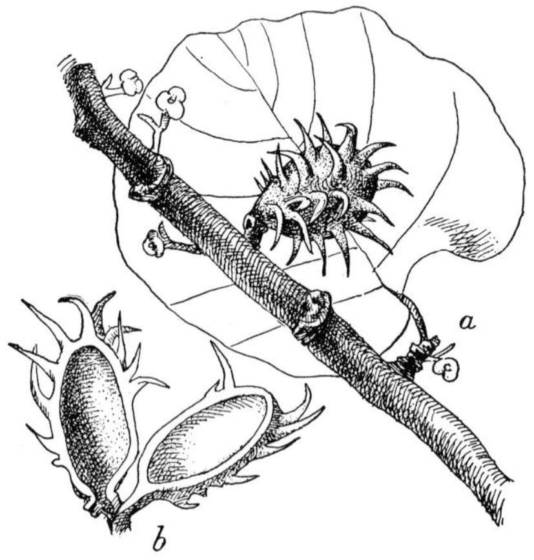

Figure 22. A bud gall on witch-hazel caused by the aphid *Hamamelistes spinosus*: (A) the mature gall; (B) section of the empty gall. (Drawing by Pergande)

A. Several beech leaves with *Phyllaphis fagi* aphids and cast skins.

B. Underside of a beech leaf showing aphids, cast skins and large droplets of honeydew.

C. *Betula populifolia* leaves showing the corrugation symptoms caused by *Hamamelistes spinosus*. Normal leaves are on the right.

D. Gall injury to manzanita caused by the aphid *Tamalia coweni*.

E. Birch leaf close-up showing the corrugations and the chlorotic secondary veins on the upper side caused by *Hamamelistes spinosus*.

F. Close-up of *Hamamelistes spinosus* aphids on the underside of a birch leaf.

PLATE 118

Aphids (Plate 119)

The plant injuries shown in Plate 119 were caused by at least five species of aphids. Sections A and D show injury caused by the snowball aphid, *Neoceruraphis* (= *Aphis*) *viburnicola* Gillette on two cultivars of viburnum. Although this aphid has secondary host plants, they are unknown. Viburnum is the host on which it overwinters, because it is on the twigs and buds of this plant that the aphid lays its eggs in the fall. The eggs hatch at the time the buds open in the spring. These buds serve as the feeding site for the developing aphids. At maturity, the insects are plump and about 2.5 mm in length. They are of a bluish-white color, and their bodies seem to be dusted with white powder. As "stem mothers," they produce large numbers of young aphids without mating.

Within three weeks after bud break the leaves of the viburnum are grossly misshapen; sometimes even the leaf stem is bent. Severe leaf curling damage to *Viburnum opulus* and *V. opulus sterilis* occurs, but other species of viburnum, such as *V. tomentosum,* are immune. On viburnum that has been infested, twisted foliage is a primary symptom. Two months after the eggs hatch, all the progeny leave the viburnum, but it is not clear just where they go. In September, migrant forms return to the viburnum and give birth to the sexual aphid forms that produce the overwintering eggs. *Neoceruraphis viburnicola* is found in the northern half of the United States as far west as Colorado, and in eastern Canada.

A second species of aphid, *Aphis viburniphila* Patch, known as the viburnum aphid, seems to have a year-round association with this plant. Unlike *N. viburnicola,* this species is not known to cause leaf deformation. In the Northwest the bean aphid *Aphis fabae* Scopoli causes foliage injury to viburnum. It has a black or dark olive-green body.

The aphid injury to mountain ash shown in section B was probably caused by the apple aphid, *Aphis pomi* DeGeer. This is a European species believed to have been introduced into this country prior to 1851. It is now considered to be worldwide in distribution.

The apple aphid is a very destructive insect and has been the subject of many intensive entomological investigations. Its life history is simple compared to many aphid species; it requires but a single host. Like most aphids, it spends the winter as a dormant egg. In winter, clusters of these black eggs may be seen on the previous summer's twigs (see Plate 116 section E). The eggs hatch while the new leaves are very young and the summer forms emerge. These may be winged or wingless. In Virginia, there may be as many as seventeen generations of summer aphids on apple. In the fall, when leaves begin to turn color, sexual forms are produced. These lay eggs to carry the species through the winter.

The apple aphid may take up residence on numerous host plants but apple seems to be its favorite. All the hosts of the apple aphid are in the rose family and include *Crataegus, Prunus, Pyrus, Malus* (flowering crabapple), *Chaenomeles* (flowering quince), and *Sorbus americana,* the plant shown in section B. On all host plants, the injury, caused by aphids appears to be essentially the same: the leaf blades and petioles become curled and stunted. Early in the year, new shoots may be so infested that all growth stops. Under ornamental nursery conditions, this aphid cannot be tolerated; likewise, if many leaves were curled on a specimen tree (as shown in section B), the tree would certainly not be accepted as ornamental. The common aphid predators such as lady beetles, lacewings, nabid bugs and syrphid fly larvae, as well as parasitic wasps, help keep this pest in check.

Section C shows a mixed colony of *Myzus persicae* (Sulzer), the green peach aphid, and *Macrosiphum euphorbiae* (Thomas) on daphne. The green peach aphid is described on page 256.

The potato aphid is the common name given to *Macrosiphum euphorbiae* (Thomas). It is about 3 mm in length and has green and pink color forms. Though not a major pest of woody ornamentals, it is a severe pest of many vegetable crops. The potato aphid overwinters in the colder regions of the United States as an egg on rose, *Cotoneaster,* and possibly other rosaceous plants. In the spring, the hatched migrant forms fly to other plants to produce the summer generations. As well as infesting vegetable crops, this species infests woody ornamental plants such as crabapple, *Citrus, Fuchsia, Cornus, Ribes, Lonicera* and *Euonymus alatus.* In warm regions, this species is found the year around, with the egg stage omitted altogether. The potato aphid is commonly found throughout the United States and Canada.

Section E shows severe smutting caused by aphids feeding on citrus. The honeydew becomes so thick that the leaf is completely covered. The black color comes from one of several fungi commonly called sooty molds, which grow on the honeydew. As the leaf continues to grow, and if the aphids do not persist, the thin coat of smut ruptures and peels away from the leaf. Injury is caused not only by the presence of the feeding aphids which reduces the amount of sap in the tree, but also by the presence of the sooty mold covering, which interferes with the photosynthetic process carried out by the leaves.

References: 114, 137, 165, 166

A,D. Two cultivars of viburnum with leaf injury caused by the snowball aphid, *Neoceruraphis viburnicola.*

B. The apple aphid, *Aphis pomi,* caused these leaves on *Sorbus americana* to become deformed.

C. The green peach aphid and the potato aphid in a mixed colony on daphne.

E. Black sooty mold mixed with honeydew on a citrus leaf. Pressure from the expanding leaf causes the black film to break and peel.

PLATE 119

255

Leaf-feeding Aphids (Plate 120)

Some of the symptoms of injury caused by four species of aphids are shown on the facing plate. *Wahlgreniella nervata* (Gillette) is a common, early season aphid in northern California and is a serious pest of manzanita (*Arctostaphylos*). It produces a large quantity of honeydew which makes the foliage of its host plant sticky. Cast skins (A) remain attached to leaves and twigs for a long period. Severe infestations kill leaves and twigs. Because of the absence of summer rainfall in most sections of northern California, infested shrubs appear dirty and unthrifty. Little is known about this aphid's biology or behavior.

Myzus persicae (Sulzer), also known as the green peach aphid (D; see also Plate 119, section C), is a universally distributed aphid. Its biology and behavior are well known. Leonard (165) called it "our commonest aphid" when describing the aphids of New York. Essig (93) describes it as one of the most common aphids in North America. In the northern two-thirds of the United States, the green peach aphid overwinters as a shining black egg attached to the bark of peach, plum, cherry and other trees of the genus *Prunus*, including the flowering cultivars.

The aphids' chronological development is not complicated. The overwintering hosts are considered to be primary hosts, for it is on them that the sexual forms are produced. Two or three generations of green peach aphids develop on *Prunus* in the spring. The aphids then migrate to any one of 100 or more plant species for continued summer development. Most of the aphids' summer hosts are herbaceous plants but some are woody. The woody ornamental summer hosts include *Clematis*, *Citrus*, *Juglans*, *Bougainvillaea*, *Vinca* (D), and *Hedera helix*. In the milder sections of the country, the green peach aphid is abundant on the summer hosts throughout the year. It apparently never goes through the egg stage to reproduce.

The summer form of this aphid, and the one most likely to be seen, is a pale yellowish-green. It has red eyes. Close observation, will reveal three rather distinct lines of green extending from the back of the head of the aphid to the end of the body.

In addition to injury by direct feeding, the green peach aphid is capable of transmitting more than 100 different plant viruses. These viruses are best known on vegetable crops. They seriously reduce vegetable production.

In addition to the common aphid predators which include lady beetles, lacewings, syrphid flies and nabid bugs, fungus diseases aid in natural control. A number of parasitic wasps also provide a degree of natural control of this species.

Aphis spiraecola Patch has been given the common name spirea aphid. It is believed to be native to North America, and is distributed throughout the United States. It is often found in large colonies. Spiraea seems to be its basic host plant. In Florida, it has been recorded on eleven ornamental plant species. Leaf curl (C) is the typical injury caused by this aphid. Feeding occurs on the undersides of leaves or on stems. The leaves of trees and shrubs which support large populations of this pest appear stunted.

Over most of the range of the spirea aphid, eggs are produced by the sexual form of the insect in the fall. These eggs apparently may be laid on any species of *Spiraea*. In central and southern Florida, however, as well as in southern California, this aphid appears to have no sexual stage.

All mature aphids are parthenogenic and give birth to living young. During the summers these adults produce both winged and wingless forms. The bodies of aphids in this stage are dark green. Winged forms seem to be produced because of population pressures and are regulated by the availability of food.

When food is scarce on one plant, winged females fly to more suitable or succulent plants to start another colony. Single parthenogenetic females may produce as many as 70 individuals. As many as 44 generations in a single year have been recorded in Florida.

Meteorological conditions have a tremendous effect on the spirea aphid as well as on other species. Heavy rain and strong winds knock them to the ground where they die. They have numerous parasites and predators. Occasionally, *Empusa fresenii* (a fungus) helps control aphid populations, especially in the South.

Aphis ceanothi Clarke is a reddish-brown and black species that can severely injure ceanothus (E). This species occurs primarily on the undersides of leaves, but heavy populations may force them to feed on the young tender stems as well. By August in northern California, a population may increase to the point where the leaves and twigs of the host plant die (B). Biological studies have not been conducted on this species.

References: 93, 137, 165

A. Manzanita hedge showing some of the symptoms associated with the aphid *Wahlgreniella nervata*.
B. Ceanothus severely injured by a heavy infestation of *Aphis ceanothi*.
C. Young twigs of citrus. Curling of leaves was caused by *Aphis spiraecola*.
D. Green peach aphid, *Myzus persicae*, colonized on *Vinca*.
E. Massive colony of *Aphis ceanothi* on the undersides of ceanothus leaves.

PLATE 120

Black Citrus Aphid and Other Leaf–feeding Aphids (Plate 121)

The black citrus aphid, *Toxoptera aurantii* (Fonscolombe), is an important and common pest of camellias in many parts of both the United States and Europe. As its common name implies, this species attacks citrus wherever it is grown. This aphid has been reported to occur on *Pelea, Straussia,* and *Coffea* in Hawaii, and *Ixora, Clusia,* seagrape, and *Ilex aquifolium* in the eastern United States.

The black citrus aphid is small, measuring only about 2 mm in length. Its color is usually a shiny black, but may vary from dull black to the color of mahogany. Although most abundant in the early spring, it persists all year in citrus orchards. Colonies are formed at the buds or on the leaves of the host. On camellias, the aphids often congregate in large numbers on the buds of the flowers (A). Leaf cupping, curling, or twisting are symptoms associated with the damage done by this aphid. Other symptoms include the inevitable blackening of plant parts resulting from the production of honeydew by the insects, and, on camellia, flower malformation.

The black citrus aphid has many natural enemies. These include lady beetle larvae and adults, lacewing larvae, and syrphid fly larvae. The most dramatic of these natural enemies are tiny parasitic wasps which develop inside the bodies of the aphids (see Figure 23 on page 266). At maturity, the parasite cuts a tiny hole in the back of the killed aphid through which it escapes, leaving a brown mummified shell as evidence of its activities. These mummies persist for some time on the leaves of the host plant.

Myzocallis tiliae (L.), sometimes called the linden aphid, probably occurs wherever basswood, littleleaf European linden, or other linden shade tree species are grown. Street trees are frequently found infested with them, and the honeydew from these aphids soils cars parked under the trees. These aphids are green with black lateralstripes. Winged forms have clouded wings. There is continuous development of new progeny throughout the host's growing season.

Maple trees are frequently attacked by several leaf-feeding species of aphids belonging to two genera: *Drepanaphis* and *Periphyllus*. Large populations frequently develop in the absence of natural control organisms. When trees are heavily infested, copious amounts of honeydew collect on objects beneath them. Summer leaf drop may occur and it is not uncommon for silver and Norway maple to nearly defoliate. Most of these aphids are greenish-yellow; one species is reddish.

Drepanaphis and *Periphyllus* species are found throughout the United States and in parts of Canada. They may also infest *Aesculus* and sycamore. All stages occur on a single host.

References: 84, 87, 149, 312.

A. Camellia bud infested with the black citrus aphid.
B. Close-up of black citrus aphids and cast skins on a camellia bud.
C. Black citrus aphids on a camellia leaf.
D. Skeletons of black citrus aphids (on a camellia leaf) that have been parasitized by a minute wasp. Note the exit hole of the wasp parasite.
E. Colony of black citrus aphids on leaves and stem of camellia.

PLATE 121

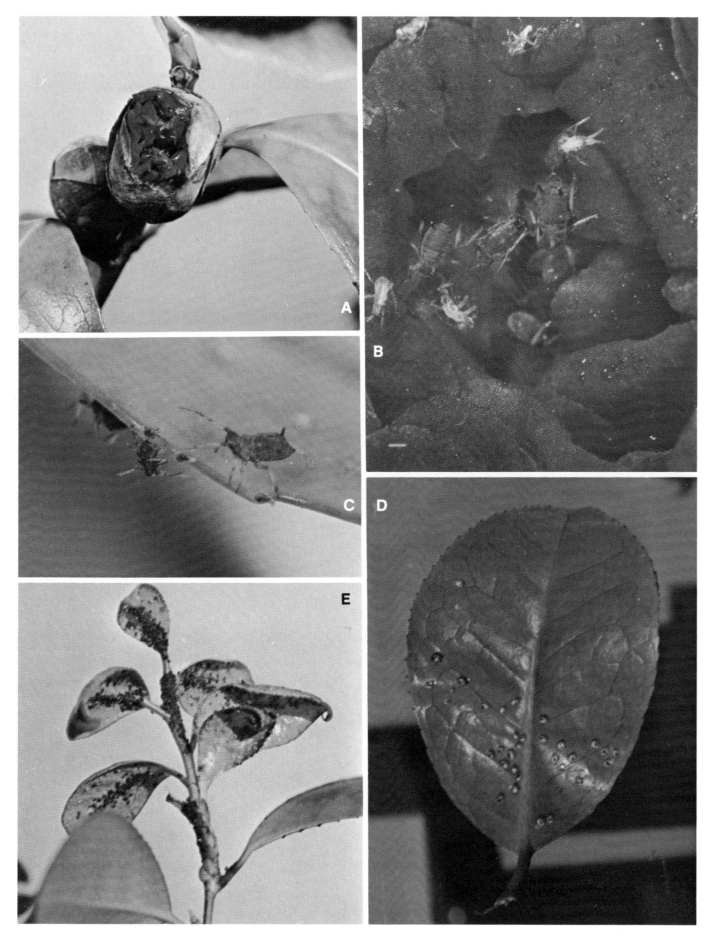

Woolly Aphids (Plate 122)

Those aphids shown in sections A and B of the facing plate are believed to be *Stegophylla quercicola* (Monell) on red oak, *Quercus rubra*. These aphids spend part of their lives in colonies on either side of oak leaves. Several aphid forms may be found concurrently in these colonies, including the parthenogenetic females, which appear as plump, milky-white individuals, and winged males.

A large colony of these aphids may cause the host leaf to curl; this is the only noticeable injury to the host. Heavily infested shade trees are conspicuous due to the white patches of flocculent wax strands, produced by the aphid colony. The colony becomes covered with the wax mixed with cast molt "skins." As the colony ages the white patches begin to look like dirty snow giving the tree an unsightly appearance. *Stegophylla* species have been recorded on five species of oak. *Stegophylla quercifolia* (Gillette) also occurs on native scrub oak in Colorado. *S. quercicola* (Baker) affects coast live oak in California by rolling the edges of leaves to form a pseudogall. These aphids may occur wherever deciduous or evergreen oak trees are native.

The woolly alder aphid is the common name given to *Prociphilus tesselatus* (Fitch). The prolific production of white waxy filaments is the most distinctive sign of its presence on an infested plant. Its biology is of special interest to the naturalist. Two hosts are required: alder (see Plate 123, sections A, B, C, and G) and silver maple.

Eggs are deposited in the fall on the bark of maple trees. The eggs hatch in the spring as soon as the new leaves appear. Immediately, the immature insect seeks out the underside of a new leaf and settles at the mid-vein (C). Young aphids are all females (stem mothers) capable of reproducing asexually. They produce large colonies which collectively withdraw great quantities of sap from the host, causing its leaves to curl inward, and thus making a protective cover for the enclosed insects. The young of the stem mothers develop into migrant forms which, by the end of July, fly to alder trees (E). This winged migrant is quite large, measuring 10 mm from wing tip to wing tip. Like the stem mother it reproduces asexually. The young aphids, now on alder, collect on the twigs to start a new life cycle for the species. A number of generations develop on alder (see Plate 123, sections A, B and C), and produce large amounts of white, fluffy wax. Honeydew is also produced and foliage on infested trees may appear wet from its abundance. Each aphid is covered with white down in a checkerboard-like pattern. A maturing colony may be completely concealed beneath a dense covering of the white waxy material. The aphids beneath are plump and gray and measure about 2 mm in length.

In the vicinity of Washington, D.C., migrants mature on alder and fly back to the trunk and branches of maple trees around the first of October. These are sexual forms, both male and female. After mating, the female produces but one egg which she deposits on loose bark and covers with white woolly down.

Not all the aphids on alder mature and fly back to maple; some remain throughout the winter in closely packed colonies which are so crowded that the aphids literally stand on their mouthparts, which are embedded in the bark. It would appear that the species can exist indefinitely on alder, by reproducing without fertilization. The aphids shown in Plate 123 were photographed in late August in south central New York State, indicating that late development of the leaf form may occur in the North. The alder forms have also been seen with some frequency in the Adirondack Mountains of New York State in early August.

Predators of the woolly alder aphid are numerous and include lacewings and lady beetles. Ants invariably tend woolly alder aphids particularly those on alder, to obtain honeydew.

The woolly alder aphid is not considered particularly injurious but may become quite annoying around homes because of the amount of white, woolly threads that accumulate on the ground under heavily infested trees.

The reported range of the woolly alder aphid is from Canada to Florida and west to the Mississippi River. There are several related species of *Prociphilus* on the West Coast. These include *P. alnifoliae* (Williams) which infests Christmas berry and shadberry, and *P. californicus* (Davidson) which feeds on Oregon ash.

References: 165, 166, 228

A. Red oak leaf with a colony of aphids believed to be *Stegophylla quercicola*.
B. Close–up of the colony showing the mature wingless form, the immature form, and the winged form of the aphid.
C. Colony of woolly alder aphids, *Prociphilus tesselatus*, on silver maple.
D. Close–up of two woolly alder aphids covered with wax strands.
E. Winged adult of the woolly alder aphid.

PLATE 122

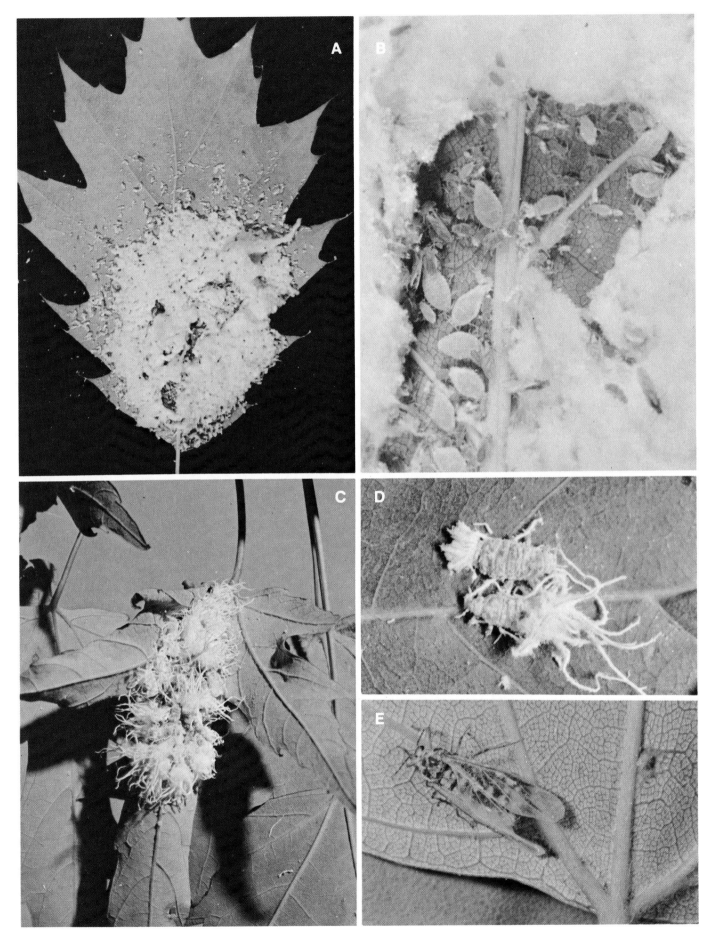

Woolly Aphids (Plate 123)

Under natural circumstances, neither animals nor plants cover themselves with clothing or a parasol of white unless it aids in protection or survival. White quickly catches the eye of friend and foe alike. The woolly aphids, the woolly adelgids and a number of closely related sucking insects clothe themselves in white waxy ribbons or threads. Apparently this habit is beneficial to the insect, but exactly how no one is quite sure. The white color certainly does not aid in camouflaging the aphid from its enemies.

Some of these woolly aphids are curiosities of nature rather than serious pests but sometimes they may become abundant enough to cause plant owners concern. The aphids shown in sections A, B, and C are the woolly alder aphid, *Prociphilus tasselatus* (Fitch), and are described in Plate 122.

It is claimed that all species of *Eriosoma* aphids feed at some point in their life history on elm, *Ulmus*. Firm evidence for this may not be available, but many are known to have some association with elm. All *Eriosoma* species have complicated and quite remarkable cycles of existence. Section H shows *Ulmus americana* leaves supporting a large population of *E. americana* (Riley), and the leaf curl or roll resulting from this infestation. *E. lanigerum* (Hausmann) causes a leaf cluster to develop into a rosette. *E. rileyi* (Thos.) is a bark-feeding species. *E. crataegi* (Oestlund) occurs primarily on hawthorn but also on pyracantha, flowering crab and other *Malus* species. All these *Eriosoma* aphid species commonly occur in the United States and Canada.

The most important species on elm are the woolly elm aphid, *Eriosoma americana*, and the woolly apple aphid, *E. lanigerum* (see Plate 127). Eggs are laid in the fall by females whose sole function is to produce a single egg; the female is not even endowed with functional mouthparts and when her egg is laid, she dies. The egg is placed in a bark crevice where it is able to withstand the rigors of winter. In the spring, when the elm leaves are unfolding, the egg hatches into a young, wingless female which seeks out the underside of a leaf and proceeds to feed on its sap. At maturity she is capable, without mating, of giving birth to young aphids. Within a few days she gives birth to nearly 200 young, all females. Soon, the leaf becomes curled and serves to protect the colony from wind, rain and other elements of nature. By the end of June, the colony has become so crowded and full of cast skins that individuals begin to spill over onto other leaves. About this time, a winged generation matures. These migrants, again all females, desert the elm leaves and instinctively seek the *Amelanchier* bush, which is variously known as shadbush or serviceberry. Upon finding a bush and establishing residence, they begin to give birth to young, again all females. The young crawl down the twigs and branches to the underground parts of the plant. This is the summer destination of the woolly elm aphid, *E. americana*. Several generations are produced underground and the roots of the *Amelanchier* bush are injured. In the fall, winged females are produced underground which migrate back to the elm to perpetuate the species and start the cycle again.

Eriosoma species are found throughout the United States and Canada and are presumably limited to areas where elm trees are grown. Elm leaves are severely damaged, both functionally and in appearance, when either *E. americana* or *E. lanigerum* are present in large numbers. There is little evidence of any mortal injury, but the pest cannot help but reduce tree vigor. The pest could not be tolerated under nursery conditions. Predators common to aphid species such as lacewings, lady beetles and syrphid fly larvae are often present. However, these predators can do little toward reducing leaf damage. By the time the predator population has reached an effective number, the migratory aphids have often vacated the curled elm leaves and have flown to their secondary host.

Two mirid (plantbug) predators are often found in the curled leaves of elm. *Deraeocoris aphidiphagus* Knight feeds on *Eriosoma americana* and *D. nitenatus* Knight feeds on *E. lanigerum*. The nymphs of both bugs are covered with a white wax-like material similar to that which covers aphids.

References: 165, 166, 202, 228

A,B,C. Mature woolly alder aphids on black alder, *Alnus glutinosa.*

D,E,F. Aphids believed to be woolly apple aphids, on hawthorn (*Crataegus*) species.

G. Woolly alder aphids under and beside long strands of waxy filaments.

H. Woolly elm aphid on elm, *Ulmus americana.*

I. Syrphid fly larva feeding on an aphid colony.

J. Woolly psyllid, *Psylla floccosa,* on *Alnus* sp. Insects other than aphids also produce flocculent masses of wax.

PLATE 123

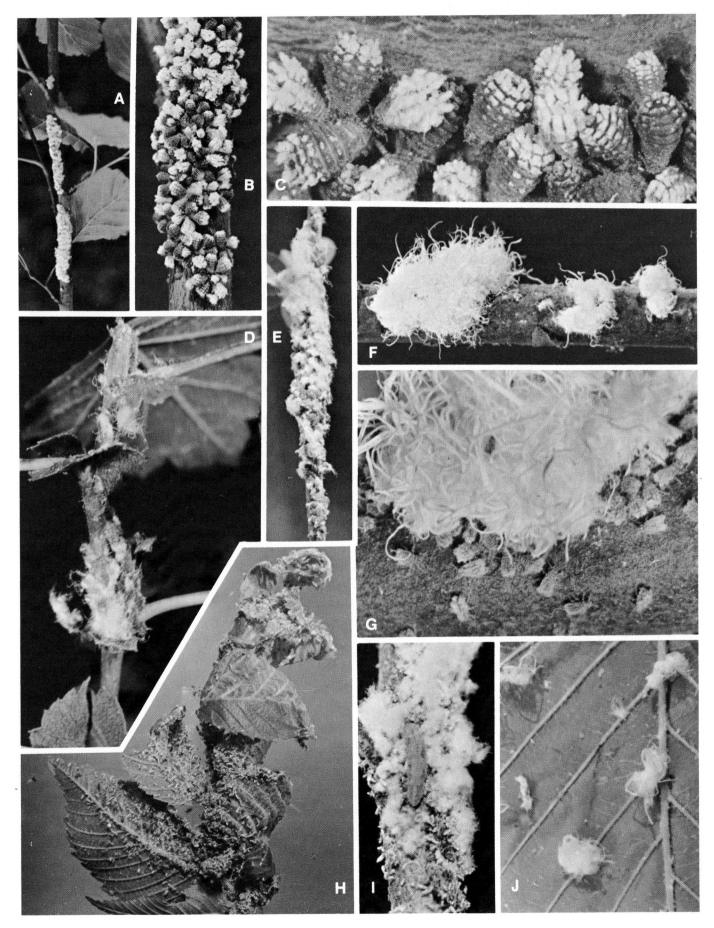

Leaf and Stem Aphids (Plate 124)

Aphids have so many and such varied ways of existence that no generalized account can adequately describe them. Their behavior is governed largely by food preference and feeding site. Some feed underground on roots, others on bark, twigs, leaves, flowers and fruit. The facing plate shows some examples of aphids that choose to feed on the stems, flowers, and leaves (blade and petiole) of their hosts. Section A shows all stages of the cotton or melon aphid, *Aphis gossypii* Glover, on leaf and flower of *Hibiscus*. The dark forms are mature females, which may vary in color from yellowish-green to dark mottled green in their wingless stage. In the Northeast, the cotton aphid overwinters as an egg on catalpa and rose of Sharon. During the growing season, it has been collected on at least 40 plants in New York State, but it is most frequently found on herbaceous plants. It is a cosmopolitan species occurring throughout the United States, and in parts of Mexico and Canada. Where its population is abundant, it frequently is heavily parasitized by tiny parasitic wasps. The arrow points to brown mummies that have resulted from aphids killed by such parasites.

Heavy aphid populations result in an unthrifty appearance of host plants, distorted leaves and flowers, and wilt symptoms during times of water stress. Several virus diseases, which are particularly severe on vegetable crops, are vectored by this aphid.

The rose aphid (B), *Macrosiphum rosae* (Linn.), has both pink and green forms, and feeds on the stem and developing bud of its host. It is presumed that its entire life history is confined to rose. Single plants can tolerate fairly high aphid populations; however, the quality and quantity of flowers are reduced. Rose connoisseurs, plant nursery owners and greenhouse producers of roses find high aphid populations particularly intolerable. The rose aphid is common throughout the United States and Canada wherever roses are grown.

Macrosiphum rhododendri Wilson looks much like the rose aphid but is found only in the Northwest on rhododendron. *Aphis hederae* Kaltenback is commonly called the ivy aphid and is shown in sections C and D. This species usually occurs in black clusters, which seem to stand one on top of the other. The primary host plant is English ivy, *Hedera helix*, of which there must be more than 15 commercial cultivars. Growing tips and young leaves are the preferred feeding sites. When the aphids are abundant, they may cause severe stunting of the growing tips and leaf malformation. The ivy aphid produces large quantities of honeydew. Ants are attracted to the honeydew and often tend these aphids in a symbiotic relationship.

In southern California, ivy aphids may be abundant the year round. Official collection records of this aphid indicate that this species is likely to be found wherever English ivy grows. The ivy aphid has also been reported on *Aralia*, euonymus and viburnum.

Aphis craccivora Koch (E) has been given the common name "cowpea aphid" because of its affinity for members of the legume family, which includes many ornamental trees and shrubs. The cowpea aphid's body is shiny and black. Its legs and the basal half of its antennae are either white or pale yellow. Immature forms vary in color from dark green to brown to black. The aphids shown in section E are feeding on leaf petioles and stem of *Wisteria floribunda*. Injury to this host was severe. Leaf blades were severely scorched because of the quantity of fluid extracted by the feeding aphids. Tree hosts include *Laburnum, Robinia, Gleditsia, Pyrus, Malus, Citrus* and *Eucalyptus*. Feeding occurs primarily on young twigs. No assessment of tree injury can be given.

Records of this aphid's geographic distribution show it to occur all along the Atlantic coast, in all the southwestern states (including Texas), and in Colorado.

References: 93, 137, 165, 166

A,F. *Aphis gossypii*, the cotton or melon aphid, on *Hibiscus* sp.
B. Rose aphid, *Macrosiphum rosae*, on *Rosa* sp. Note the two different color forms.
C. Badly deformed ivy leaf with aphids attached to the petiole.
D. Tightly packed aphid cluster (*Aphis hederae*) on stem, leaf petiole and blade of ivy.
E. *Aphis craccivora*, the cowpea aphid, on the petioles and stem of *Wisteria floribunda*.
G. Winged adults and wingless females of the cowpea aphid.

PLATE 124

Aphids of Oleander and Bamboo (Plate 125)

The aphid *Aphis nerii* Fonscolombe is common throughout the southwestern states where oleander, *Nerium oleander*, is widely grown. This aphid is a European species which gained access to this country some years ago. The species is commonly referred to as the oleander and milkweed aphid, for milkweed is a secondary host. The insect is bright yellow with black markings. It appears in the early spring and colonizes the young shoots and buds of oleander. Huge colonies often develop and persist into early summer, when warm temperatures and/or natural enemies contribute to their decline. Oleander is such a vigorous plant, however, that very little damage results from this pest.

Two aphid species, *Takecallis arundinariae* Essig, and *T. arundicolens* Clarke, both known as bamboo aphids, are common in California wherever bamboo is grown. In 1972, *T. arundinariae* was found in Maryland for the first time, on dwarf bamboo, *Shibataea kumasasa*. These aphids are pale yellow with black markings. The exact markings vary with the particular species. Both species infest the undersides of leaves. Here, large colonies are often formed causing the foliage to blacken as a result of the sooty mold fungi which colonize the insects' honeydew. Weakening of the plant may also occur. Virtually nothing is known of the biology and seasonal activities of the bamboo aphid.

References: 88, 93

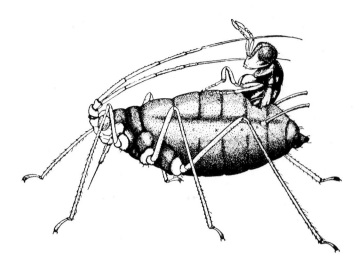

Figure 23. A wasp parasite emerging from an aphid. (Drawing by Grace H. Griswold, Cornell University Press)

A. Colony of oleander aphids, *Aphis nerii*, on the foliage of oleander.
B. Colony of oleander aphids (adults and nymphs) on an oleander stem.
C. Most of the oleander aphids shown here have been killed by a species of parasitic wasps.
D. Off-color foliage and dead leaves are symptoms of aphid injury to bamboo.
E. Colony of *Takecallis arudinariae* (adult females, nymphs and winged aphids) on bamboo.

PLATE 125

Leaf and Stem Aphids (Plate 126)

In California, *Aucuba japonica* is often injured by the foxglove aphid, *Acyrthosiphon solani* (Kaltenbach) (= *aucubae* Barth.). New leaf growth is stunted and curled, and if the infestation is severe, leaves may die (A). Much sticky honeydew is formed. Dust adheres to the honeydew and adds to the plant's unsightly appearance. Similar symptoms may occur from scale insect infestations.

Pterocomma (*Clavigerus*) *smithiae* (Monell) is a large aphid, about 3.5 mm in length, with bright orange cornicles (see arrow in section B). It feeds gregariously on the bark of willows and many species of poplar, and has been reported on silver maple. Periodically these aphids appear in damaging numbers. These aphids appear to have a rather simple life cycle and are content to remain on the same host through many generations. In the autumn, eggs are laid on twigs. These eggs are yellow at first and later turn black. Adults have been observed from May through October. Those illustrated in section B were collected in June in central New York State, although they are most abundant in August and September. Distribution records are sparse but this species is known to occur throughout Canada, in parts of the northeastern United States, in Illinois, and throughout the Rocky Mountain region.

Longistigma caryae (Harris) is commonly called "giant bark aphid." The length of its body is about 6 mm. Because of its long legs, however, it appears much larger. Winged migratory forms of this aphid are also produced (E). Their color pattern is distinctive, and their short, black cornicles make field identification easy. An egg-laying female is depicted in section D. In section C, the arrow points to one of many *Asterolecanium* scale insects (see Plate 145). Eggs that overwinter are deposited late in the growing season—in October in northern Illinois. These eggs are laid in bark crevices as well as on the smooth bark of smaller branches. The aphids shown in these pictures were on *Quercus rubra* and *Q. palustris*. Other hosts include beech, sycamore, linden, birch, chestnut, hickory, pecan, walnut and willow.

The giant bark aphid may be found throughout the growing season, but it becomes most numerous during the late summer. It is capable of causing severe injury to its host. Twigs or branches may die due to its activities. When the aphid population is large, a twig may be completely covered with eggs. The eggs are black, and look much like those shown in section E of Plate 116. The giant bark aphid is found throughout much of the eastern half of the country. It ranges from New England south to Florida and west to Arkansas and Minnesota but does not seem to be an important problem in the Great Lakes region.

Lachnus salignus (Gmelin), sometimes called the giant willow aphid, is a large (4–5 mm), gray to black, twig-feeding insect. Willow is its only host. The amount of damage inflicted by this insect is probably minor but its presence is likely to alarm any homeowner. It may be found wherever willow grows.

References: 137, 165, 241

A. Variegated *Aucuba japonica* injured by *Acyrthosiphon solani*, an aphid.
B. Cluster of black willow aphids, *Pterocomma smithiae*, on the bark of weeping willow.
C. Wingless female giant bark aphids, *Longistigma caryae*, on the bark of red oak. Note that the aphid color blends in with its background. Arrow points to a pit scale (*Asterolecanium* sp.).
D. Giant bark aphid on a contrasting background.
E. Winged form of the giant bark aphid together with three immature females.

PLATE 126

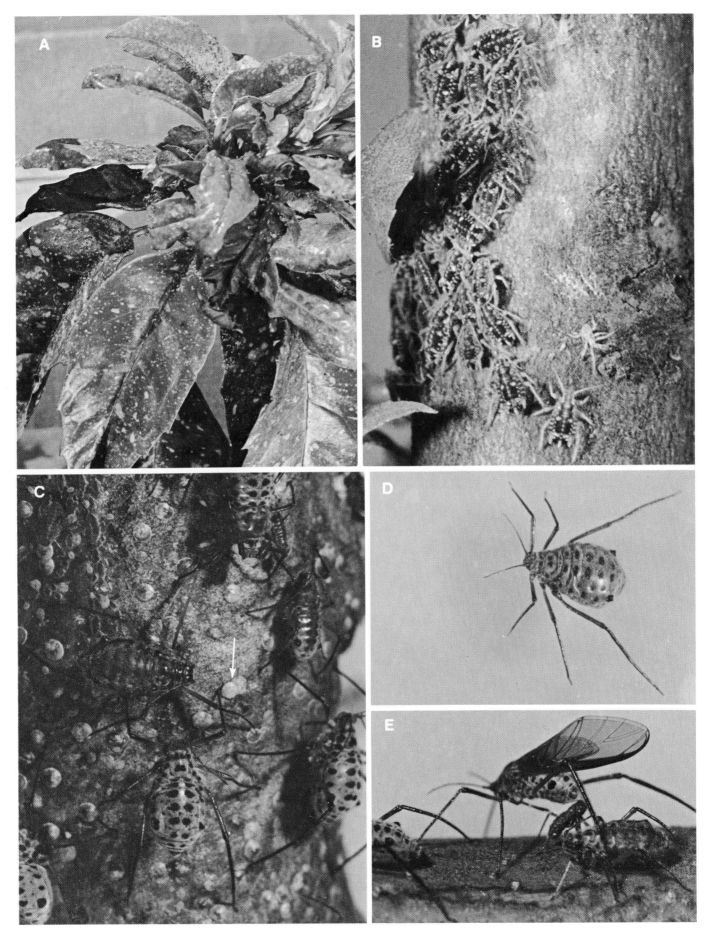

Stem Aphids (Plate 127)

The woolly apple aphid, *Eriosoma lanigerum* (Hausmann), causes severe galls to form on the twigs, branches, and roots of flowering fruit trees and pyracantha (A). Mountain ash and hawthorn are attacked as well. This aphid appears during the summer and colonizes stems and twig spurs. Old pruning wounds are also favored as colony sites. Colonies may develop that are so large that woolly patches easily show through dense foliage (B). In addition to the twig injury, affected plants often appear unthrifty. The aphids produce much sticky honeydew which traps dust and produces an unsightly appearance. In the fall, this aphid normally leaves its summer host for elm trees, where it lays its overwintering eggs. In most of the western states, however, its life cycle is spent on the summer host (see Plate 123, section H for a similar aphid).

Macrosiphum crataegi Monell is sometimes called the four-spotted hawthorn aphid. This common name is appropriate because of four dark green spots which are arranged on its back like the four points of a rectangle. The aphid's basic color is yellowish-green. Its entire life is spent on hawthorn, where it feeds on the undersides of leaves. The first symptom of infestation by this pest is leaf curl. The larger the colony, the more tightly the leaves are curled. Damage may be moderate to severe; under the latter conditions trees may be defoliated or killed outright.

The black eggs (E) are laid on twigs and small branches in the fall. The eggs hatch in May or June depending on their geographic location. The four-spotted hawthorn aphid is found throughout the Northeast, occasionally in Illinois, and in several of the Rocky Mountain states.

References: 93, 166

A. Woody galls on the stem of pyracantha are caused by the woolly apple aphid. The aphids are underneath the patches of "wool."
B. Colonies of woolly apple aphids as seen through dense pyracantha foliage.
C. Pyracantha twig showing severe galls caused by the woolly apple aphid. The aphids had vacated this host by the time the photograph was made.
D. Colony of black aphids feeding on the succulent stem of *Ribes sanguineum*. These aphids are thought to belong to the genus *Aphis*.
E. Mass of eggs of *Macrosiphum crataegi*.

PLATE 127

Whiteflies of Rhododendron and Azalea (Plate 128)

The rhododendron whitefly, *Dialeurodes chittendeni* Laing, is an important pest of rhododendron in the United States. It arrived in this country about 1932 on rhododendrons imported from England, where the pest had been known for many years. Entomologists believe, however, that the insect is native to the Himalayan region of Asia.

The rhododendron whitefly prefers to feed on the tender terminal leaves of its host plant. The eggs are laid by the adults on the undersides of leaves, and when the nymphs hatch, they affix themselves there to feed for the duration of their immature lives. Heavily infested foliage takes on a yellow, mottled appearance on its upper surface. On some varieties, a curling of the leaf margins occurs as a result of the whitefly's feeding. Honeydew produced by the nymphs drops to the leaves below, giving them a varnished appearance. Sooty mold fungi grows on the honeydew-covered leaves, changing the varnished appearance to that of a leaf dusted with coal soot. This type of injury is both harmful and ugly on a plant such as rhododendron, which retains its leaves for about three years.

So far as is known, the rhododendron whitefly attacks only rhododendron. Research has shown a great deal of difference between plant varieties in their susceptibility to the whitefly. Those plants which have a thick and leathery epidermis often escape infestation completely.

In the state of Washington, a single generation of the rhododendron whitefly occurs annually. The insect overwinters in the nymphal stage. During the growing season, there is a great deal of variation among the developmental stages found at a single location, and one or another of the immature stages may be found at any time. Adults, however, occur only from mid-May until early August.

The azalea whitefly, *Pealius azaleae* (Baker and Moles), is widespread in the eastern and southern United States and in California, wherever the hairy-leaved *Azalea ledifolia alba* (= mucronatum) is grown. This evergreen azalea is hardy as far north as Washington, D.C., and is widely grown in southern gardens. It evidently has been used as a parent by many hybridizers, since named varieties now on the market have hairy leaves and are susceptible to whitefly attack. In the immature stages, the azalea whitefly is pale yellow to orange and lacks the distinctive waxy fringe characteristic of many other juvenile whiteflies.

For additional information on whiteflies that are destructive to woody ornamental plants, see Plates 129, 130.

References: 93, 164, 312

A. Yellowing, cupping and rolling of terminal leaves of rhododendron are all characteristic symptoms of injury by the rhododendron whitefly.
B. Undersurface of rhododendron leaves showing numerous whitefly adults.
C. Adults and eggs of the rhododendron whitefly.
D. Immature azalea whiteflies. Note the black discoloration caused by sooty mold fungi.
E. Close-up of underside of azalea leaf showing immature whiteflies.

PLATE 128

Whiteflies (Plate 129)

In the United States, whiteflies are far more important economically on *Citrus* fruit crops and on greenhouse-grown ornamentals than on ornamental plants grown out-of-doors. By and large, where outdoor plants are concerned, whiteflies are much more abundant in the southern portions of the country than in northern regions.

The wings of the whitefly are generally covered with a powdery substance. Adults vary in size from 1 to 3 mm and are noticeable to the casual observer only when present in large numbers. Usually, eggs are laid by the adult females on the lower leaf surface (D,G). The eggs are initially light yellow, but those of many species turn gray as incubation proceeds. The eggs are oval and are attached to the plant by a stalk. They require one to three weeks to hatch, depending on the season. The young nymphs, or immature whiteflies, crawl about on the lower leaf surface for several hours and then settle to feed. After settling, the juveniles remain fixed in the same position until they grow to maturity. The nymph has a flattened, scaly form, and the nymphal period requires three to four weeks. A most distinctive feature of the nymph is the fringe of waxy material which projects radially outward from its body. This fringe may consist of fine strands, or thick, wavy plates, depending on the species of whitefly. Its characteristic appearance is extremely helpful in making field identification of species. At the end of the nymphal stage, the pupa appears. The insect spends this stage within a case which is fixed to the leaf. The case is somewhat more bulbous and segmented than the covering of the nymph. The adult whitefly emerges from this case through a T-shaped slit on the case's dorsal surface.

On any infested leaf, whiteflies may be found in all stages of development. There are several generations each year, exact numbers depending on the species and its location. The insect overwinters in either the nymphal or pupal stage. Damage to plants by whiteflies is primarily caused by the removal of sap by the nymphs. Heavy feeding results in yellowing and drying of the foliage. Fully as important as direct feeding injury is the honeydew produced by the nymphs. The honeydew covers the leaves and imparts a blackened appearance as a result of sooty mold fungi which colonize the honeydew.

The greenhouse whitefly, *Trialeurodes vaporariorum* (Westwood), is present throughout the United States on many greenhouse plants, but persists out-of-doors in the southern parts of the country. Some of its preferred woody ornamental hosts are *Berberis*, barberry; *Cercis*, redbud; *Fuchsia*; *Gleditsia triacanthos*, honeylocust; *Hibiscus*; *Lantana*; *Rhamnus*, coffeeberry; *Robinia pseudoacacia*, black locust; *Rosa*, rose; and *Solanum pseudo-capsicum*, Jerusalem cherry.

The wasp parasite, *Encarsia formosa* Gahan, has been shown to be an effective biological control agent of the greenhouse whitefly under greenhouse conditions.

The Stanford whitefly, *Tetraleurodes stanfordi* (Bemis), is well known in coastal California, where it attacks the coast live oak, *Quercus agrifolia,* and to a lesser extent, tanbark oak, *Lithocarpus,* and coffeeberry, *Rhamnus.*

The deer brush whitefly, *Aleurothrixus interrogatonis* (Bemis), commonly occurs on *Ceanothus* in California (B). The deer brush whitefly nymph has a pale yellow to tan coloring. The nymph is characteristically surrounded by a transparent jelly-like ring. Other forms of whitefly pupae are depicted in Plate 131.

References: 30, 43, 84, 93

A. Fuchsia leaves infested by the greenhouse whitefly.
B. Ceanothus leaves supporting a high population of *Aleurothrixus interrogatonis* whiteflies. These may be confused with ceanothus lacebugs (see Plate 181).
C. *Robinia pseudoacacia* leaflet with Stanford whitefly pupae, *Tetraleurodes stanfordi.* The pupa is about .8 mm long. The fringe of white wax filaments is characteristic of several whitefly species.
D. Eggs, presumably those of the Stanford whitefly.
E. Mahonia leaves heavily infested with *Aleurothrixus interrogatonis* whiteflies.
F. *Tetraleurodes* sp. infestation on the lower surface of leaves of the California bay.
G. Eggs of the greenhouse whitefly are about .5 mm long. They are laid on end, and are attached to the leaf by a short stalk.
H. Nymphs of the greenhouse whitefly measure about 1 mm. The number of hair-like wax filaments is less that that of the Stanford whitefly in section C.

See Plate 131, sections E and F, for photographs of other whitefly pupae.

PLATE 129

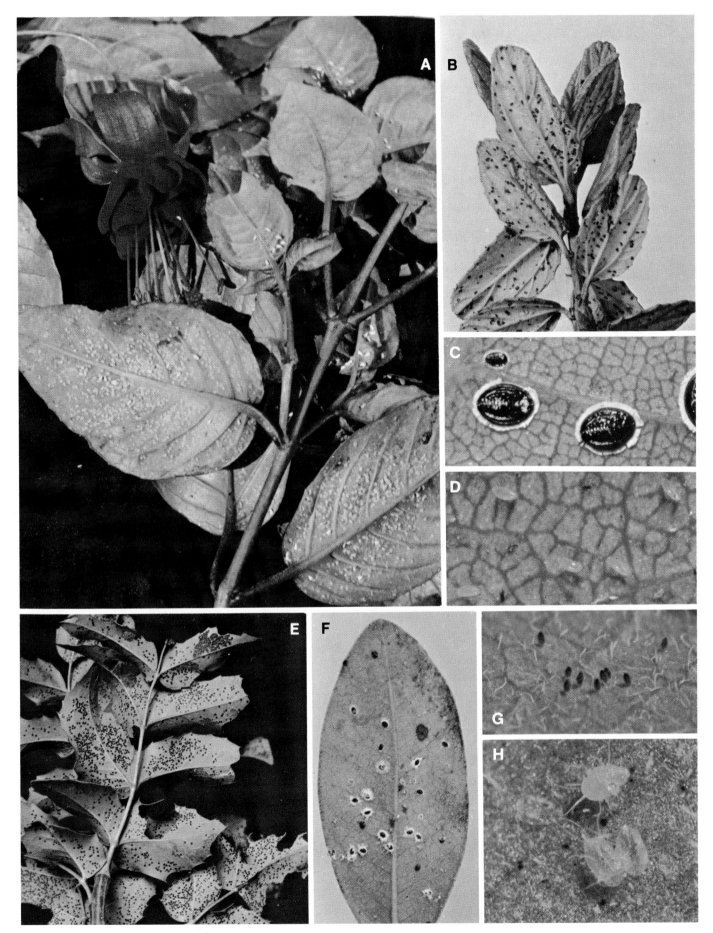

Whiteflies (Plate 130)

The woolly whitefly, *Aleurothrixus floccosus* (Maskell), was first observed in the United States in 1909, and is believed to have been accidentally brought into this country from Cuba. Its common name comes from the fluffy covering of long, curly, waxen filaments that cover the "pupae" (D).

In Florida, four generations occur each year. The adults are active during December and January, and again in May, July and October. They are much like other whitefly species in shape and size (A), but are distinctly more yellow. They differ from other whiteflies in their sluggish habits; they are so sluggish that the adult frequently lays its eggs on the leaf on which it developed.

Eggs are laid in circles on the undersides of leaves. The first-stage larva is light green. Soon after hatching, it inserts its sucking mouthpart and does not move again until it becomes an adult. The third-stage larva develops a woolly coat which remains on it throughout the pupal stage (E).

The injury caused by the woolly whitefly is threefold. It withdraws great quantities of sap from the trees; excretes copious amounts of honeydew on which sooty mold grows and subsequently interferes with the proper functioning of the leaves. Its presence creates conditions favorable for severe infestations by purple scale, *Lepidosaphes beckii*. The honeydew given off by this species is quite syrupy, and is eagerly sought by ants and wasps.

Its hosts seem limited to all species of citrus. The insect is kept in check with little help from man by the minute wasp parasite, *Eretmocerus haldemani*. This parasite also attacks other species of whiteflies.

A striking red-colored fungus, *Aschersonia aleyrodis* (F), is an effective natural control organism that attacks the nymphal stage of whiteflies. Spore solutions of the fungus have been prepared and sprayed on citrus orchards in Florida, resulting in successful control of the pest.

References: 117, 161

A. Young hibiscus leaves with many adult greenhouse whiteflies, *Trialeurodes vaporariorum*.
B. *Catalpa japonica* badly damaged by *Tetraleurodes* sp. in California. Leaves are not only mottled from feeding injury, but are disfigured by the growth of sooty mold.
C. A citrus leaf with a colony of woolly whiteflies.
D. A close-up view of the cottony filaments formed by the woolly whitefly. Note pupa at arrow.
E. A magnified view of woolly whitefly pupae. They are approximately 2 mm long.
F. A fungus, *Aschersonia aleyrodis*, which is pathogenic to immature whiteflies. The red fungus covers the juvenile whiteflies.

PLATE 130

Mealybugs and Whiteflies (Plate 131)

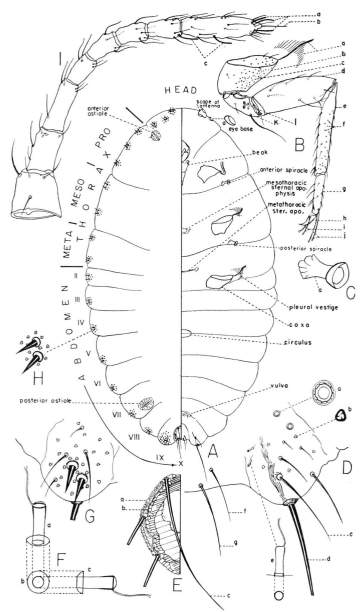

Figure 24. Diagramatic drawing of a mealybug. The dorsal side is shown to the left of the center line; the ventral side to the right. Enlarged at I is the antenna; B, a leg; C, the posterior spiracle; D and E, the last abdominal segment. All of the major identifying characters are illustrated. Many species of mealybugs must be mounted on a microscope slide and viewed through a high-power microscope to obtain a positive identification. (Illustration courtesy the University of Maryland Agricultural Experiment Station, College Park, Maryland)

Mealybugs derive their common name from the white, waxy, mealy secretions that cover their bodies. Mealybugs infest all plant parts: feeder roots, root crowns, stems, twigs, leaves, flowers and fruits. The long-tailed mealybug, *Pseudococcus longispinus* (Targoni), is a plant pest in Florida, Texas and California and occurs as a greenhouse pest in most states. This species feeds on new shoots and leaves and has a wide range of hosts including gardenia (A), pittosporum, *Pinus pinea, Cedrus deodora, Ceanothus,* citrus, persimmon, *Hedera helix,* hibiscus, *Ficus, Jasminum,* apple, oleander, avocado, taxus and rhododendron.

The major feature for field identification of the long-tailed mealybug is its long posterior wax filaments (D). These filaments may be as long as the insect's body. They break off readily, but in any large cluster of mealybugs there generally are several individuals that have retained their long tails. Adult females are about 3 mm long. They multiply rapidly, and all stages are usually in clusters on a host plant at the same time. It is believed that in warm climates they never produce eggs, but instead give birth to living young. Ants sometimes aid in distributing mealybugs from plant to plant. Ants are attracted to mealybugs by their honeydew excretions.

Injury to the host plant is caused by loss of sap, which results in discolored and wilted foliage, leaf deformation (A) and the eventual death of the affected parts. Mealybugs often share their host with other species of homopterous insects such as soft scales (C) or whiteflies (E). In Florida, the number of mealybugs is greatly reduced by *Entomophthora fumosa,* a parasitic fungus.

Aleurochiton forbesii Ashm. is one of the few species of whitefly found in the Northern United States (E). It occurs exclusively on maples and feeds on the undersides of leaves. It rarely causes measurable damage to its host trees. Little is known about its biology and behavior.

References: 84, 161, 182

A. Colony of the long-tailed mealybug, *Pseudococcus longispinus,* on leaf and stem of *Gardenia jasminoides.*
B. The stem colony. x 4
C. Mealybugs of the genus *Pseudococcus.* At arrow: a recently settled soft scale crawler. The insects are on *Viburnum opulus nanum.*
D. Long-tailed mealybugs on *Ficus nitida.*
E. A "pupa" of the whitefly *Aleurochiton forbesii* Ashm. on *Acer rubrum.* Length of the pupa is 1.5 mm.
F. Whitefly "pupa" (probably the greenhouse whitefly) belonging to the genus *Trialeurodes.* Length of the pupa is 0.7 mm (see also Plate 129).

PLATE 131

Comstock Mealybug (Plate 132)

The Comstock mealybug, *Pseudococcus comstocki* (Kuwana), is believed to have originated in Asia. It was first reported in the United States in 1918 at two distant points, California and New York. It has since spread to all the coastal states and into the Ohio and Mississippi River Valleys. Its hosts include mulberry, maple, pine, *Catalpa bungei*, peach, apple, pear, Boston ivy, holly, boxwood, avocado, California privet, regal privet, citrus, Dutchman's pipe, elm, *Elaeagnus*, *Euonymus alatus*, *Aesculus*, *Hibiscus*, olive, *Paulownia tomentosa*, persimmon, *Photinia villosa*, poplar, viburnum, wiegelia, wisteria and yew.

The biology of this insect was studied in Virginia on the umbrella catalpa, *Catalpa bungei*. The Comstock mealybug overwinters in the egg stage. The eggs hatch in May and the young mealybugs feed throughout the spring on the undersides of the host's leaves. Usually the young nymphs are unnoticed until their deposits of honeydew and the growth of sooty mold on these deposits make the plant unsightly. As the nymphs approach the adult stage, there is a tendency for them to migrate from the leaves, and to cluster on the older branches at a pruning scar, or a node, or at the base of a young branch. When a number of individuals begin to feed at the same location, a knot-like gall starts to form.

Oviposition occurs on the bark in early summer, and the generation hatched from these eggs in turn produces eggs in the fall. Eggs are deposited into a sac-like structure attached to the female's abdomen. The sac is covered with a grayish-white wax. When the female lays all of her eggs, she dies, and her dead body adheres to the ovisac.

Plant injury is caused by removal of sap, from formation of knots, and from adventitious growth (B). When leaves are covered with honeydew, dust and dirt collect. When sooty mold develops, the affected leaves may stop functioning and drop prematurely.

There are several wasp parasites of the Comstock mealybug. Among them are *Allotropa burrelli* Mues. and *Clausenia purpurea* Ishii. Predators of this pest include the lacewings *Chrysopa rufilabris* Burmeister and *Hemerobius stigmaterus* Fitch.

Reference: 138

A. Mulberry tree with many woolly egg sacs of the Comstock mealybug, *Pseudococcus comstocki*. Note the knots and swollen areas at the base of the small branches.
B. Mulberry tree heavily infested with Comstock mealybugs.
C,D,E. Mealybugs on the bark of flowering dogwood, believed to be an aberrant form of the taxus mealybug (see plate 29).

PLATE 132

Manzanita Mealybug (Plate 133)

Known only in California, the manzanita mealybug, *Puto arctostaphyli* Ferris, appears primarily on the leaves of its only recorded host plant, manzanita (*Arctostaphylos*). The adult female is large (over 5 mm in length) and extremely attractive. She is covered with long white filaments which radiate outward from her body. Like most mealybugs, this species is covered also with cottony white waxy material. The male of *Puto* is a tiny, winged individual with slender rod-like appendages which are three to four times as long as the body. These appendages protrude from his posterior end. Virtually nothing is known about the biology or seasonal history of the manzanita mealybug.

P. arctostaphyli may be confused with *P. albicans* McKenzie, another California mealybug which infests manzanita and which is commonly called the white mealybug. The white mealybug lacks the long body filaments possessed by the manzanita mealybug. Instead, it has short plate-like projections which radiate outward from the body of the female. Both species, however, may so cover the foliage of manzanita that the leaves appear to be lightly powdered with snow.

The manzanita mealybug reduces the vigor of the host plant by withdrawing plant fluids when it is in its developing stages. The honeydew which is deposited by the feeding insects, and the sooty mold fungi, which forms on the honeydew, detract from the appearance of the plant.

References: 102, 182

A. The spots of white on the upper leaf surfaces of this manzanita bush are mealybugs, *Puto arctostaphyli*.

B. Close-up of mealybug adults showing their long waxy filaments.

C,D,E. Adult female mealybugs and young nymphs.

PLATE 133

Noxious Bamboo Mealybug (Plate 134)

The noxious bamboo mealybug, *Antonina pretiosa* Ferris, is a subtropical insect commonly found in California and Florida. It is likely to be found in all of the Gulf states. Bamboo plants shipped north from these states may be infested with mealybugs. The mealybugs, however, are not likely to overwinter except in greenhouses.

The adult female mealybug and her eggs are entirely covered by a cottony white sac. She excretes honeydew which is colonized by sooty mold fungi, resulting in blackened plant parts and occasionally discolored egg sacs. When the eggs hatch, the young crawlers select nodes and the bases of leaves as feeding sites (B,C,D). Female crawlers lose their legs after the first molt and thus remain stationary for the balance of their lives. Bamboo is the only known host of the noxious bamboo mealybug.

References: 103, 182

A. Stems of bamboo showing dead leaf sheaths and blackened nodes. White woolly patches are present but difficult to see.

B,C,D. Mealybugs collect under sheaths and at the bases of leaves. They feed on the stalks.

E,F. Dark mealybugs with the cottony wax removed from their bodies.

PLATE 134

Beech Scale, and Bark Mealybug (Plate 135)

From 1850 until the early 1900's, a number of very important pests of trees were introduced into eastern America. These included the gypsy and satin moths, the European pine shoot moth, numerous sawflies, the balsam wooly aphid, chestnut blight, and Dutch elm disease. *Cryptococcus fagisuga* Lindinger (= *fagi* Baer), commonly called the beech scale, is another pest that came to America from abroad.

The beech scale population like that of the balsam woolly aphid (Plate 25), consists only of females that produce other females. The adult is pale yellow, less than 1 mm in diameter, wingless, and has a spherical body that is covered with white wool-like threads (D). The scales live only on the bark of native or introduced beeches (*Fagus*).

Eggs are laid in early July and hatch about four weeks later. The newly hatched nymphs, or crawlers, wander over the bark surface in search of a place to insert their long, tube-like mouthparts. The crawlers are spread from tree to tree by the wind. One generation of the beech scale is produced each year. Huge populations may develop on a tree in two to three years.

Heavily infested trees are covered with a white mass of "wool" (A). The beech scale itself seems to be of little consequence to the health of the tree, but in combination with the fungus *Nectria coccinea faginata* it has killed many forest and ornamental beeches. The fungus cannot be controlled once it has colonized on the tree. Both fungus and insect are found in eastern Canada and northeastern United States. The spread of this insect and concomitant disease seriously jeopardize shade tree and forest beech populations. The beech scale has spread much more slowly than the balsam woolly aphid, a species that has similar habits.

Ehrhornia cupressi (Ehrhorn) is sometimes called a scale insect but is in fact a mealybug. It is sessile and is about 1.5 mm long when fully grown. Those shown in section E are immature and therefore are just starting to cover themselves with a white, waxy secretion. The waxy secretion completely hides the adult insect, which is red. Adults are found beneath bark flakes and in cracks on the trunk and larger branches of the host tree. Dead twigs and small branches at the top of affected trees are the first visible symptoms of infestation. Such symptoms spread downward from limb to limb until the tree is completely dead. Yellow and red areas may appear on infested cypress hedges. These areas later die.

The insect overwinters as a mature female. Egg laying begins in the spring and continues through the summer.

In the United States, *E. cupressi* is found in California and Oregon on Monterey cypress, *Cupressus macrocarpa;* Arizona cypress, *C. glabra;* and other *Cupressus* species as well as on incense cedar, *Calocedrus decurrens.*

References: 50, 182, 259

A,B,C. Beech stems covered with the white wool-like material produced by the beech scale.

D. Close-up of individual patches of wool. Each patch covers a single female.

E. Young mealybugs, *Ehrhornia cupressi,* on the trunk of Monterey cypress. Loose bark was removed to reveal the insects.

F. Yellowish eggs and crawlers of beech scale are intertwined in the white woolly egg sac.

PLATE 135

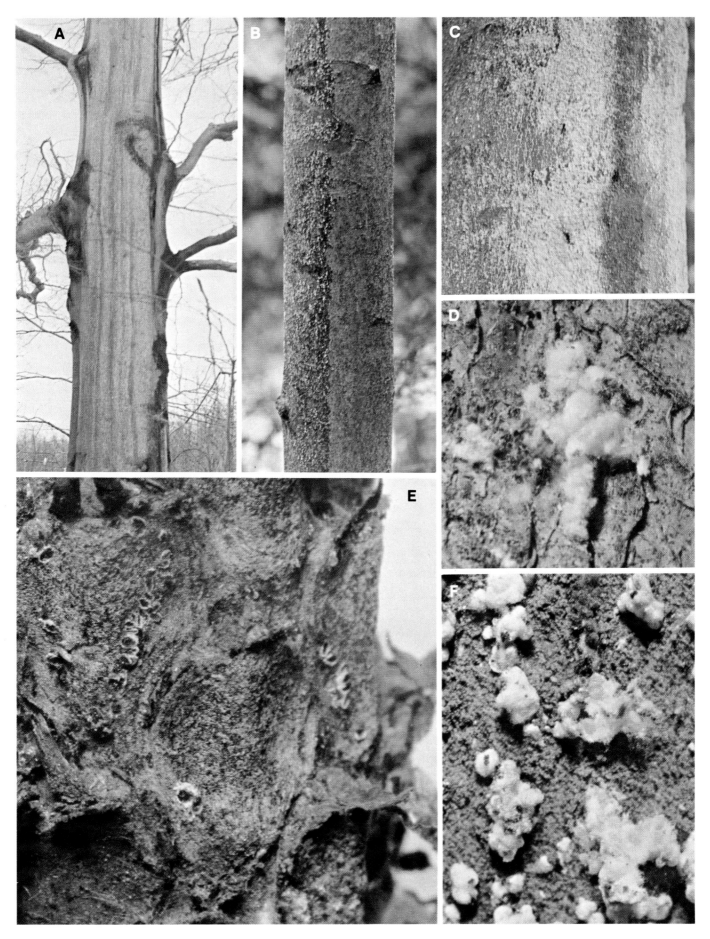

Sycamore Scale (Plate 136)

The sycamore scale, *Stomacoccus platani* Ferris, is the most important pest of both native and introduced sycamore (*Platanus*) in California. The insect also occurs in Arizona. Leaves infested by this pest become disfigured by yellow spots which develop at the feeding site of each scale. These spots gradually turn brown as the affected tissue dies (G). Young infested leaves are often smaller than uninfested ones, and often become distorted. Twig dieback may also result from the feeding of sycamore scales on the bark of branches and twigs. The sycamore scale can cause continual and premature leaf drop on sycamore. Leaf drop, however, may also be caused by other factors.

The scales overwinter on the tree beneath plates of bark on the trunk and limbs (C). In late winter, the scales mature, and the females begin to lay eggs in masses of cottony wax. In the early spring, the eggs hatch, and the tiny crawlers leave the woody parts of the tree and migrate to the new foliage. There, the mouthparts are inserted into the leaves and feeding begins. At maturity, the majority of the scales migrate again to the woody parts of the tree, and lay eggs to begin the cycle again. There may be three to five generations each year.

The sycamore scale is unusual among scale insects because it is mobile while in the adult stage. Female scales of most other species lose the use of their legs after feeding begins, and do not move again during the remainder of their lives. Male scales fly about during their brief two- or three-day adult life.

References: 35, 267, 268, 270

A. Twig of sycamore showing egg-laying sites of *Stomacoccus platani*. The cottony wax in the cracks of the bark indicates the presence of eggs.
B. Close-up of twig shown in section A. Note orange-yellow eggs barely visible within masses of cottony wax. See arrows in B and D.
C. Overwintering sites of sycamore scale beneath bark plates. Females lay the eggs in cottony wax.
D. Newly hatched crawlers of *Stomacoccus platani* leaving egg masses. Both eggs and crawlers appear as yellow spots within the white cottony material.
E. Developing sycamore scales on a leaf of sycamore. Note leaf discoloration beneath sites where scales are feeding.
F. Female sycamore scale in process of laying eggs. Sycamore scales are about 1.6 mm long. Note cluster of eggs at arrow.
G. Sycamore leaf with yellow spots which indicate scale feeding sites.
H. Distorted leaves (upper right) are characteristic of heavy sycamore scale attack.

PLATE 136

Azalea Bark Scale (Plate 137)

The azalea bark scale, *Eriococcus azaleae* Comstock, was described in 1881 from specimens found on azalea in a greenhouse in Washington, D.C. It was discovered in Connecticut in 1917, and since then has been reported from Florida, Alabama, Indiana, Ohio, Michigan, and New York. Eventually this species is likely to occur throughout the eastern United States. It feeds on the bark of twigs and stems and tends to settle in branch crotches. In addition to azalea, it has been found on rhododendron, andromeda, hawthorn, poplar, and willow.

The azalea bark scale is closely related to, and in some ways resembles, a mealybug. It does not, however, belong to the mealybug group. The female scale is dark purple, and is covered with a white waxy sac (D). She does not have the strands of wax characteristic of a mealybug. A mature female measures about 3 mm in length, including her egg sac. Males are similar but are less than half the size of females. This scale might be confused with *Eriococcus borealis* Cockerell (though some taxonomists say they are the same) which occurs in the western United States on *Salix, Populus, Ribes, Algama, Grossularia, Celtis,* and *Liquidambar.*

In Connecticut, one generation of *E. azaleae* occurs annually. Overwintering scales mature in the spring at which time they lay eggs. The eggs hatch in the latter part of June through mid-July. Crawlers tend to settle in bark crevices, in branch crotches, or on the axils of leaves. Two generations have been reported in the southern states. First-generation eggs are laid in March. The second brood of crawlers occurs in September.

The azalea bark scale is a potentially serious pest, but to date its infestations have been minor and occasional. About one-third of the population of the azalea bark scale dies before winter for as yet unexplained reasons. Comstock, in his original description of the scale, reported that the majority of the specimens he collected had been parasitized by the chalcid wasp *Coccophagus immaculatus* Howard.

References: 175, 253

A. Typical appearance of *Eriococcus azaleae* on azalea.
B. *Eriococcus azaleae* females in bark crevices.
C. The appearance of the waxy sac of the azalea bark scale is unlike that of the wax secretions of mealybugs.
D. Side view of the azalea bark scale with its wax removed. Note the eggs, the white waxy covering, and the color of the female scale, which is about 2 mm long.

PLATE 137

Cottony Cushion Scale (Plate 138)

The cottony cushion scale, *Icerya purchasi* Maskell, is one of the largest and most conspicuous of the scales that attack woody ornamental plants (A). It was accidentally introduced into California from Australia in 1868, and now also occurs in North Carolina, Arizona, Texas, Florida and all the Gulf states. The most striking feature of this scale is the large, elongated, cottony white and fluted egg sac which protrudes from the end of the adult female's body. Inside the sac are hundreds of bright red, oblong eggs.

Upon hatching, the scale crawlers (E) move to the leaves and twigs of the host plant and begin to feed. Later, the insects withdraw their mouthparts and migrate to the larger twigs and branches. Unlike most scales, the cottony cushion scale retains its legs and its mobility throughout life. Damage to the host plant results from the extraction of sap by the insect. The subsequent reduction in vigor of the plant sometimes leads to defoliation or twig dieback. Also, plant parts become blackened by the sooty mold fungi which colonize the honeydew produced by the scales as they feed. A wide variety of woody ornamental plants is attacked. These include: *Abies*—fir; *Acacia*—acacia, wattle; *Acer*—maple; *Aesculus californica*—California buckeye; *Aloysia*—verbena; *Buxus*—boxwood; *Carya*—pecan; *Casuarina*; *Cedrus libani*—cedar of Lebanon; *Celtis occidentalis*—hackberry; *Chaenomeles*—quince; *Citrus*; *Cupressus*—cypress; *Erythea edulis*—Guadaloupe palm; *Garrya*; *Juglans*—walnut; laurel; *Liquidambar*; locust; *Lyonothamnus*—ironwood; *Magnolia*; *Malus*—apple; *Parthenocissus tricuspidata*—Boston ivy; *Pinus*—pine; *Pittosporum*; *Prunus*—almond, apricot, peach; *Punica*—pomegranate; *Pyrus*—pear; *Quercus*—oak; *Rosa*—rose; *Salix*—willow; *Salvia*—sage; *Schinus*—pepper.

The cottony cushion scale is a classic example of an insect that has been brought under biological control by the introduction of a natural enemy from the native home of the pest. Soon after the scale was discovered to cause extremely serious losses to the California citrus industry, a small, red and black lady beetle, known as the vedalia, *Rodolia cardinalis* (Mulsant), was purposefully introduced into the California citrus groves from Australia. Within two years, the cottony cushion scale ceased to exist as an economic pest. This was the first recorded instance of the successful introduction of a beneficial insect into any nation for the purpose of destroying an insect pest. The vedalia was introduced into other areas where the cottony cushion scale was causing problems on citrus or other plants, and the results were similarly effective. Where there have been noticeable reinfestations of this pest, the cause has often been the destruction of large numbers of vedalia by the use of pesticides on host plants.

References: 84, 93

A. Adult female cottony cushion scales, *Icerya purchasi*, on branch of maple.
B. Orange crawlers leaving the egg sac of female scale (shown on right), in search of suitable feeding site.
C. Adult female cottony cushion scale (at circle) and immature scales on leaf of ivy.
D. Immature *Icerya purchasi* on underside of leaf.
E. Close-up of scales shown in section D.
F,G,H. Partly-grown cottony cushion scales. Notice in section H that functional legs persist.

PLATE 138

Cottony Maple Scale (Plate 139)

The cottony maple scale, *Pulvinaria innumerabilis* (Rathvon), is one of the largest and most conspicuous of the many scale insects that attack ornamental trees in the United States. It has been reported from virtually every state and from several Canadian provinces. As the common name implies, the favored host of this insect is maple—particularly soft maple—but it is also known to occur on a wide variety of woody ornamental plants. These include: *Acer*—maple, boxelder; *Alnus*—alder; *Celtis*—hackberry; *Cornus*—dogwood; *Crataegus*—hawthorn; *Euonymus*; *Fagus*—beech; *Maclura pomifera*—osage orange; *Malus*—apple; *Morus*—mulberry; *Parthenocissus quinquefolia*—Virginia creeper; *Platanus*—sycamore; *Populus*—poplar; *Prunus*—peach, plum; *Pyrus*—pear; *Quercus*—oak; *Robinia pseudoacacia*—black locust; *Rosa*—rose; *Rhus*— sumac; *Salix*—willow; *Syringa*—lilac; *Tilia*—linden; *Ulmus*—elm.

The cottony maple scale overwinters as an immature, flat, inconspicuous female on the twigs of its host. With the onset of warm spring temperatures, it grows rapidly. By late spring, the characteristic white egg sac of the female is evident (C). Each egg sac contains up to 1000 eggs.

In late June and July, tiny motile crawlers begin to appear. These young scales migrate to the leaves of the host plant, where they insert their slender mouthparts and feed by withdrawing sap from the plant (B).

The cottony maple scale spends the summer months on the leaves. Male scales reach maturity in late summer and emerge as tiny winged individuals, which mate with the immature females. The males die within a day or two of their appearance, for they have nonfunctional mouthparts and cannot feed.

Before the leaves begin dropping in the fall, the females migrate back to the twigs, where they attach themselves for overwintering. A single generation of the cottony maple scale occurs each year.

Damage to the host tree is caused in several ways. The withdrawal of plant sap by heavy populations causes the dieback of twigs and branches and, under extreme conditions, may kill the entire tree. During the time the scales are feeding on leaves and on twigs, a large quantity of honeydew is produced by the insects. This material is colonized by sooty mold fungi, which imparts a blackened appearance to leaves, twigs, and branches. Some premature loss of foliage results from scale attack.

A number of natural enemies of the cottony maple scale are quite important in regulating populations of this species. Many wasp and fly parasites of the females are known, and various lady beetles feed on the immature scale stages while they are feeding on the leaves (see Figure 28 on page 304). The English sparrow is believed to be an important factor in limiting the population of the fully grown cottony maple scale female.

Pulvinaria acericola Walsh and Riley, known as the cottony maple leaf scale (see Plate 140) infests the leaves of maple in many of the same areas in which the cottony maple scale is active.

References: 50, 147, 247

A. Adult cottony maple scale females on the underside of a branch of silver maple, *Acer saccharinum*. Mature females are about 5 mm long.

B,D. Close-up views of immature cottony maple scales on underside of a maple leaf.

C. Dead females of cottony maple scale with their white egg sacs.

E. The cottony maple scale egg sac has been pulled apart. The brownish spots inside the cottony mass are eggs. The brown part at the top of photograph is the dead female skeleton.

F. Mature females look like popcorn strung out along twigs of maple.

PLATE 139

Cottony Scales and Mealybugs (Plate 140)

Some species of scales, mealybugs, whiteflies and aphids produce white waxy secretions which cover their bodies, making field identification confusing. On eastern maples, it is common to find "cottony" mealybugs, scales and aphids. The cottony maple scale, *Pulvinaria innumerabilis,* is illustrated in Plate 139.

The cottony maple leaf scale, *Pulvinaria acericola* (Walsh & Riley), occurs primarily on maples throughout most of the eastern United States; as well as in Iowa. It has also been reported in some western states and in southern Canada. Hosts other than the maple include dogwood; the hollies, *Ilex cornuta, I. crenata,* and *I. opaca;* andromeda; and gum, *Nyssa sylvatica.* The cottony maple leaf scale may become numerous enough to cause premature leaf drop, and sometimes even the death of twigs and branches.

Before egg sacs begin to form, the adult female is maroon, with a mid-dorsal keel that is yellow-brown. The partially grown nymphs feed on twigs and branches of the host tree, and later overwinter at their feeding sites. In April, the males mature and mate with immature females. In May, the mature females migrate to the host's leaves where they lay their eggs in a white ovisac. On the average, their egg masses (ovisacs) contain over 2500 eggs. After hatching, usually by the end of June, the nymphs scatter over several leaves and settle along the leaves' midribs and larger veins. The young scales are pale green. Since they are about the same color as the leaf, and lay snugly against the vein, they are not easily seen by the unaided eye. They remain on the leaves until autumn, when they migrate to the bark. One brood occurs each year.

Several parasites and predators of *P. acericola* have been recorded, but their effectiveness in controlling pest populations has not been studied.

The maple mealybug or maple phenacoccus, *Phenacoccus acericola* King, is found from the northeastern United States west to Minnesota, and south to Tennessee. Throughout its life, this insect is covered with a flaky wax secretion (B,C). The maple mealybug may become abundant in an area but infestations are usually more injurious to the appearance than to the health of the host.

White nymphs overwinter in crevices in the bark of the host's trunk and branches. In early spring, the nymphs move to the leaves, where they feed until they become mature. In May, males crawl to the bark where they pupate. In June, the females migrate to the bark, and after mating, return to the leaves to lay eggs. During late June and early July, large white masses of 500 or more eggs are the most conspicuous symptom of the infestation. Eggs hatch in July and the young maple mealybugs crawl to the bark where they spend the winter. A report from Ohio indicates that two or three generations occur there annually.

The cottony azalea scale, *Pulvinaria ericicola* McConnell, was described in 1949, after being observed in Maryland, where a wild *Rhododendron nudiflora* was found to be infested at its base, below the ground cover of leaves. Other rhododendrons and azaleas in Maryland and New York have been found to be infested on their upper stems (D). This scale has also been reported in Florida on huckleberry.

The cottony azalea scale overwinters as a fertilized immature female. In Maryland, oviposition occurs annually in June.

References: 10, 129, 175, 315

A. Egg sacs (ovisacs) of the cottony maple leaf scale, *Pulvinaria acericola,* on sycamore maple. The egg sacs were collected on Long Island, New York in July.
B. Maple mealybugs, *Phenacoccus acericola,* on sugar maple.
C. Immature females of *Phenacoccus acericola.*
D,E. Egg sacs of the cottony azalea scale, *Pulvinaria ericicola,* collected in New York in July.

PLATE 140

Cottony Camellia Scale (Plates 141, 142)

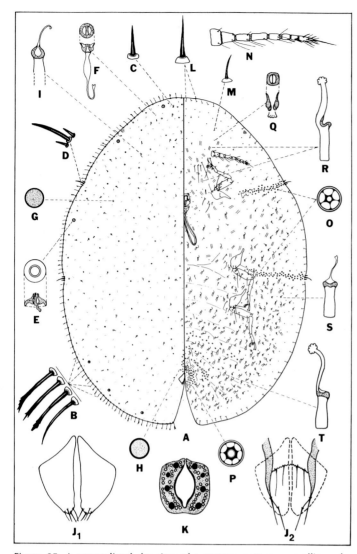

The *Pulvinaria* scales are classified as soft scales, and are characterized by their white cottony ovisacs (egg sacs). At least eight species are found in the United States. Three of these—the cottony maple scale, cottony maple leaf scale, and the cottony azalea scale—are shown in Plates 139 and 140.

Pulvinaria floccifera (Westwood) has two common names, the cottony camellia scale and the cottony taxus scale. One generation is produced each year throughout its range. Overwintering occurs in the second nymphal stage usually on twigs. When the female reaches maturity she is mottled tan to yellowish in color and shaped like a slightly convexed long oval, about 3 mm long (see Figure 25). She may migrate to the underside of a leaf where she lays her eggs in a white fluted egg sac. After all her eggs are laid she dies and in a short time the dried-up body falls away, leaving only the white egg sac attached to the leaf. The egg sacs are from 5 to 10 mm long and may contain over 1000 eggs. The eggs begin to hatch in June in Connecticut. The crawlers settle on the leaves by extracting sap through their piercing-sucking mouthparts. The settled crawlers shown in section B were photographed about mid-July on Long Island, New York. For comparison, see also Figures 26 and 27.

Damage to the host plant occurs primarily in late summer and early spring and takes the form of off-colored, light green foliage. The presence of the cottony camellia scale becomes obvious only after the ovisacs appear (see section A, and Plate 142, sections A and B).

Host plants include camellia, holly, taxus, *Jasminum* sp. rhododendron; maple, *Acer palmatum;* hydrangea, *Abutilon,* English ivy, and *Callicarpa americana.* The cottony camellia scale occurs along the Atlantic coast from Massachusetts south to Florida, in the Pacific coastal states, Texas and Indiana.

One parasite has been reported. It is a tiny wasp, *Coccophagus lycimnia.*

References: 253, 315

Figure 25. A generalized drawing of a mature cottony camellia scale, *Pulvinaria floccifera,* of the type used by an insect taxonomist to compare with slide-mounted scale specimens. The upper (dorsal) side of the scale is shown to the left of the center line; at right is the lower or ventral side. Note the tiny, but well-developed legs. The structures identified by letters around the border of the illustration are important characters for species identification: bristles, glands, pores, etc. (Illustration courtesy M. L. Williams)

A. The underside of a taxus branch showing numerous ovisacs of the cottony camellia scale, *Pulvinaria floccifera.*

B. A close-up view of two ovisacs and settled crawlers (at arrows) of *Pulvinaria floccifera.*

C. A single holly leaf showing several *Pulvinaria floccifera* egg sacs. Note the dead female scale at arrow 1. Lined up along the main vein are many tiny yellowish crawlers.

D. An egg sac of *Pulvinaria floccifera* on camellia.

E. Egg sacs of *Pulvinaria floccifera* on the undersides of holly leaves, *Ilex aquifolium.*

F. *Pulvinaria floccifera* in various stages of development on a camellia leaf. Arrow points to a female, whose egg sac is beginning to form (note the white fringe at the posterior end).

PLATE 141

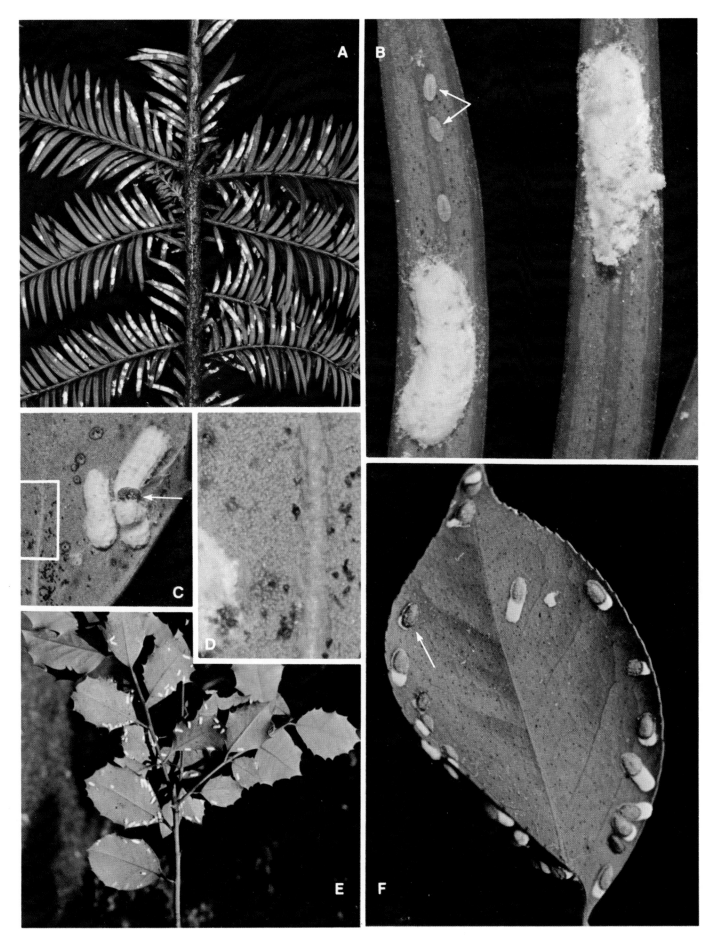

299

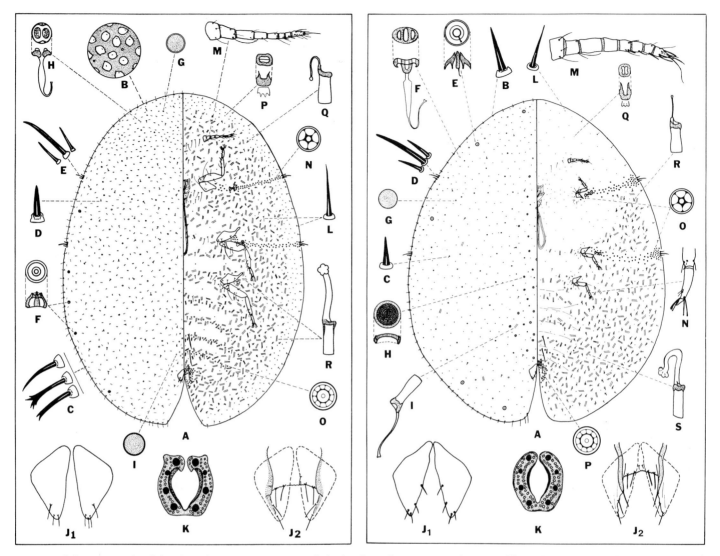

Figure 26 (left). A generalized drawing of a mature cottony maple leaf scale, *Pulvinaria acericola,* as used by an insect taxonomist to compare with slide-mounted scale specimens. See also Plate 140, section A. (Illustration courtesy M. L. Williams) *Figure 27 (right).* A generalized drawing of a mature cottony azalea scale, *Pulvinaria ericicola,* as used by an insect taxonomist to compare with slide-mounted specimens. See also Plate 140, sections D and E. (Illustration courtesy M. L. Williams) To be positively identified, many scale insects must first be killed and mounted on microscope slides then examined with the aid of a microscope. The prepared specimen is compared with drawings such as those shown here in order to identify the species. Compare the structures at F and K in Figure 27 with those at H and K in Figure 26. These characters differentiate the two species.

A. Viburnum leaves showing a heavy infestation of *Pulvinaria* scale egg masses. Eggs have begun to hatch; the rust-like spots near the arrow point are crawlers. These specimens were collected in mid-July in southeastern New York.
B. A *Pulvinaria* scale with protruding white egg sac.
C. A close-up of one of the scales shown in section A. Part of an egg sac has been opened to show the pale brownish-orange eggs. A number of crawlers are present on the leaf surface.
D. Young mealybugs, possibly *Phenacoccus acericola,* on viburnum.
E. Flowering dogwood leaves infested with *Pulvinaria innumerabilis.* The brown part at one end of the egg sac is the dead female. The white mass is the egg sac.
F. A female *Pulvinaria* scale and her protruding egg sac. The dead, shriveled female is at bottom of photograph.
G. An adult female *Pulvinaria* scale just beginning to produce her egg sac (note the white upper edge of the scale).
H. Egg sacs of a *Pulvinaria* sp. on flowering dogwood. Many tiny crawlers have settled along the leaf veins.

PLATE 142

Pit-making Pittosporum Scale (Plate 143)

The pit-making pittosporum scale, *Asterolecanium arabidis* (Signoret), is known in the eastern, north central, and Pacific coast states. The list of hosts subject to attack by this insect is quite extensive, including many woody and herbaceous plants. Its favored hosts, however, are mock orange, *Pittosporum tobira*, privet, green ash and *Ligustrum*.

In the adult stage, the scales are oval in shape when viewed from above and are about 3 to 4 mm long by 2 mm wide. The color of the insect's shell (D) ranges from white to brown, and this covering is strongly convex on its dorsal surface. Very little is known about the biology and seasonal history of *A. arabidis*.

The scales infest the stems, twigs, and leaf petioles of its host. Apparently a toxic substance is injected into the plant during feeding, which causes a retardation in normal plant growth as well as enlarged and distorted shoot development. The tips of branches may die as a result of attack. Depressions or pits are commonly formed beneath the feeding insects, which account for their common name.

The following are additional woody ornamental hosts of the pit-making pittosporum scale: *Aralia; Aractostaphylos* spp.—manzanita; *Berberis*—barberry; *Carpenteria californica*—bush anemone; *Ceanothus* spp; *Cestrum* sp.; *Chaenomeles japonica*—Japanese flowering quince; *Cistus* sp; *Correa harrisii*; *Cotoneaster horizontalis*—rock cotoneaster; *Daubentonia tripetii*—glory pea; *Deutzia scabra*—fuzzy deutzia; *Eriophyllum confertiflorum; Fraxinus americana*—white ash; *F. pennsylvanica*—green ash; *Fremontia* sp.; *Hedera helix*—English ivy; *Helianthemum nummularium; Jasminum* sp.—jasmine; *Ligustrum* spp—privet; *Lotus scoparius*—deerweed; *Pentstemon* spp.; *Philadelphus mexicanus*—evergreen mock orange; *Pittosporum tobira*—mock orange; *Pyracantha* sp.; *Rosa* spp.—rose; *Salvia* sp.—sage; *Spartium* sp.; *Syringa* spp.—lilac; *Veronica* spp.; *Vitex* sp.; *Weigelia florida*.

References: 8, 91, 245

A,B. Swollen twigs of *Pittosporum tobira* caused by the scale insect *Asterolecanium arabidis*.

C. A close-up of B section showing the scale insects.

D. *Asterolecanium arabidis* scales. x 14.

PLATE 143

Bamboo Scale (Plate 144)

The bamboo scale, *Asterolecanium bambusae* (Boisduval), is found only on bamboo. It is widely distributed throughout the tropical areas of the world but in the United States it is known outdoors only in Florida and California. It occurs on greenhouse plants in many states.

This insect has a soft body, typical of the scale family Asterolecaniidae to which it belongs. Its colors range from pale yellow to amber (B) to grayish black, and its form is gently oval, flattened, with a slightly convex shell surface. The posterior end of the body is slightly drawn out into a blunt point. The adult averages about 2 mm in length by 1.5 mm in width.

The bamboo scale infests both surfaces of the leaves as well as the stem of its host plants. It does not produce noticeable amounts of honeydew. Consequently, attacked plants are not blackened by sooty molds. There does not appear to be any dramatic loss of color or reduction in growth of infested plants, so this insect must be considered a pest of only minor importance. Lady beetles are its main predators in most of the tropical countries in which it occurs (see Figure 28).

References: 88, 194, 245

Figure 28. The adult of a scale-feeding lady beetle, *Chilocorus orbus* Casey. (Photo courtesy F. E. Skinner, University of California, Berkeley)

A. A bamboo stem heavily infested with bamboo scale, *Asterolecanium bambusae.* Scales usually collect at a node under a sheath.

B,C,D. Series of pictures of increasing magnification to show adult female bamboo scales. Note fringe of "hairs" outlining the body.

PLATE 144

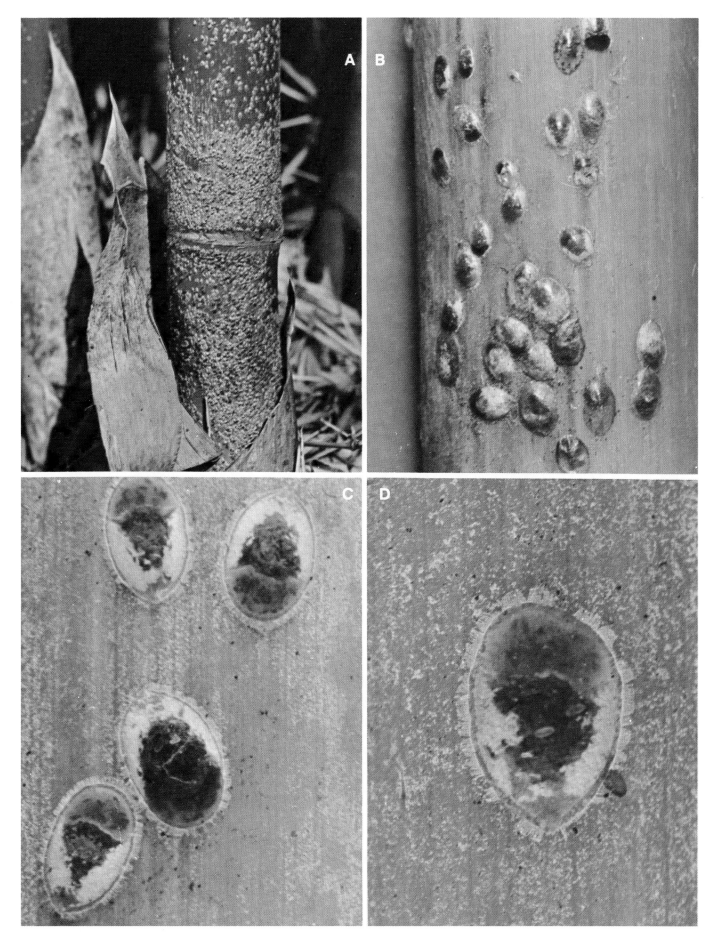

305

Pit-making Scales (Plate 145)

The pit scale, *Asterolecanium puteanum* Russell, is a pest of American, Chinese and Japanese hollies in the central and south Atlantic states (from Delaware to Florida). English hollies seem to be free of this pest.

Like the injury caused by many scales, injury to host plants of the pit scale develops slowly and subtly. A large-scale population may exist before the injury symptoms are observed. Twigs become roughened (A), pitted (C) and somewhat distorted. Growth is reduced and foliage becomes sparse. Adult scales as shown in section B may be more yellowish-green than those shown on this plant specimen. The adult female is about 1.5 mm in diameter. Scale crawlers appear in late June. Little is known about the biology of this insect.

Three species of *Asterolecanium* scales attack the twigs of oak in both the eastern and western United States. These are *A. variolosum* (Ratz.), known in the east as the golden oak scale (F), and the species *A. minus* Lindinger and *A. quercicola* (Bouche). All three are called pit scales in the western states. Their life history and food preferences are so similar that it is not necessary to distinguish between them for control purposes. A wide variety of both white and black oaks are affected.

The male of this scale is not known to occur in North America. The mature female, which varies in size from 1 to 2 mm in diameter depending on the species, are green, golden or brown. Usually the female is found in a depression, the result of inhibited growth at the site where the scale is attached; hence the common name, "pit scale." After overwintering on the twigs, the adults produce living young during the spring and summer months. Young crawlers do not move far from the parent and, for the most part, tend to colonize current-season and one-year-old wood. After settling, the young scales begin sucking juices from the tree and do not move from that place for the duration of their lives. Maturity is reached several months after settling. There is one generation each year.

Damage to the tree is caused by the removal of plant fluids, and the localized pits where the scale is, or was, attached. Poor growth and dieback of twigs is a common result of the infestation. Dieback first becomes noticeable during the summer and early fall. Affected trees retain the dead leaves on the killed twigs throughout the winter, which gives the tree an unusual appearance. A severe infestation can delay the leafing out of deciduous oaks as much as three weeks in the spring. Young trees may be killed by *Asterolecanium* scales when heavy attacks occur year after year. On the East Coast, the golden oak scale is often associated with anthracnose, a fungus disease of oak. White oaks are particularly susceptible. Together they can quickly bring about the demise of well-established trees.

References: 34, 245

A. Stem of a Japanese holly, *Ilex crenata*, with the pit-scale *Asterolecanium puteanum*.
B. Scales in typical pits on the bark of a holly.
C. *Asterolecanium puteanum* scale in an unusually deep pit.
D. A valley oak, *Quercus lobata*, with dead leaves and twigs resulting from attack by a west coast oak pit scale.
E. A heavy infestation of pit scale on an oak twig.
F. Golden oak scales, *Asterolecanium variolosum*. x 6.

PLATE 145

Wax Scales (Plate 146)

The so-called wax scales comprise a unique group which belongs to the genus *Ceroplastes*, found in warmer climates around the world. They are unique because of the thick, heavy covering of white wax over their bodies. Well over 100 species have been named, including over 20 from North America and 13 from the United States. While most of the United States species are common in the deep south, the Japanese wax scale, *C. ceriferus* (F.), occurs as far north as Maryland. One other species, thought to be the Chinese wax scale, *C. sinensis*, is established as far north as southern Virginia. In Florida, southern California and other southern states the following have become common, serious pests: the barnacle scale, *C. cirripediformis* Comst.; the Florida wax scale, *C. floridensis* Comst.; and the Japanese wax scale, *C. ceriferus* (F.).

There is some size variation between species of adult *Ceroplastes*. Size also varies within a species, depending on the host plant it infests. Both *C. ceriferus* and *C. cirripediformis* attack and remain on the stems and branches of their respective host plants. *C. floridensis* is commonly found on the leaves as well as the stems. In Virginia, crawlers of *C. sinensis* settle entirely on the foliage, but, beginning in August, females migrate from the leaves to the stems where they remain to lay eggs the following May.

Except in its most southern range, the Japanese wax scale has one generation each year. In Virginia mature females overwinter and begin laying eggs in late April; in Maryland they begin in May or June. Eggs begin hatching three to four weeks later, beginning as early as the first of June and as late as the third week of June. Soon after the crawlers settle, cones of wax begin to protrude from their bodies. By the time the second instar has developed, the wax secretions have increased to give a "cameo" appearance to the insect. During the third instar, a central cone of wax is produced rather rapidly, giving rise to the term "dunce-cap" stage (H). By August, scales become mature. Females begin laying eggs the following spring. A single female lays an average of about 2,000 eggs, which explains the population explosions that often occur on ornamental plants. In the greenhouse, one generation requires about three months from the time the eggs hatch to the time females lay their eggs.

The host range of *C. ceriferus* is very broad. Well over 50 species of plants are known to support the pest. Most commonly infested are the Japanese and Chinese hollies, particularly *Ilex burfordii*, euonymus, pyracantha, boxwood, hemlock, camellia, spiraea, flowering quince, barberry, and numerous others. Mature females have been observed on several species of shade trees and perennial weeds.

Parasites of the Japanese wax scales have been uncommon in the wax scale's northern range. The eulophid (a wasp), *Coccophagus fraternus* Howard, has been collected occasionally. More commonly, the predator *Laetilia coccidivora* (Comst.) has been found feeding on *C. ceriferus* and also on the magnolia scale, *Neolecanium cornuparvum* (Thro.). The caterpillar of this pyralid moth spins a web enveloping scales as it works its way along a twig (F). It tunnels through the wax, eating the scales as it increases the length of its nest. In 1956, Heinrich (125a) published a detailed description of this predator, listing over 15 species of soft scale insects that it attacks.

The barnacle scale, the Florida wax scale, and the Japanese wax scale have at least two or three generations in the most southern states. The host plants of all three are extensive and varied. There is no evidence that the barnacle and Florida wax scale have survived in Virginia.

References: 115, 125a, 315

A. Adult females of *Ceroplastes ceriferus* on pyracantha.
B. Typical appearance of *Ceroplastes ceriferus*. The adult female is about 5 mm in diameter.
C. Adult females of the barnacle scale *Ceroplastes cirripediformis*, on *Euonymus*.
D. Overturned *Ceroplastes ceriferus* female (at top of photograph) beginning to lay eggs; and dead female (at bottom).
E. Mature female barnacle scale.
F. Portion of stem with webbing occupied by the predator, *Laetilia coccidivora*, a caterpillar.
G. Early wax production in *Ceroplastes ceriferus* after crawlers settle.
H. An immature wax scale in the "dunce cap" stage.

PLATE 146

Black Scale (Plate 147)

The black scale, *Saissetia oleae* (Bernard), is one of the most common and most destructive of the soft scales in California. This species is known in the Southwest, Florida and the Gulf states. The black scale is a common pest of certain greenhouse-grown plants in many states.

The mature female scale insect is dark brown to black in color, is nearly hemispherical in form, and ranges from 3 to 5 mm in diameter. One of the most helpful features in distinguishing this species from others like it is the presence of ridges on the back of the insect (see section D). These ridges form the letter "H."

In coastal California, the black scale goes through two complete generations each year. Inland there is only one annual generation. In areas where more than one generation develops, overlapping of the generations occurs, and all developmental stages can be found during the growing season.

The black scale can overwinter in any stage of growth, although it usually overwinters as a partially grown female. In the spring, the females complete their development and deposit as many as 2000 eggs beneath their shells. The young crawlers issue from the body of their parent and migrate to twigs, leaves, and branches of the host, where they insert their mouthparts and settle to feed. In inland California, the adult stage is reached in eight to ten months. Although male black scales are known, they are far outnumbered on the plant by the females. Most reproduction, therefore, takes place parthenogenetically, that is, without mating.

Injury to the host plant is caused by the loss of sap through feeding by the scales. Severe infestations on leaves, twigs, or branches result in premature loss of foliage or dieback of the woody parts of the plant. Also injurious to the host plant is the fouling of foliage by vast quantities of honeydew which are excreted by the scales. This material collected on plant parts soon turns black as a result of the sooty mold fungi which colonize the honeydew.

The black scale is attacked by many parasites and predators. The most important parasites are tiny wasps. They insert their eggs into the bodies of the developing scales (see Figure 8 on page 88). The developing larva feeds internally on the scale. After killing the host insect and completing their development inside the scale, the adult wasps leave by way of tiny holes (H) chewed in the dorsum of the host scale's cover. An important predator of the black scale is the lady beetle, which feeds in both its larval and adult stage on young scales. Under certain conditions, these natural enemies are able to prevent the development of severe infestations of the black scale.

The host list of *Saissetia oleae* is extremely long, and includes the following plants: *Acer*—maple; *Aralia*; *Arbutus unedo*—strawberry tree; *Artemisia*; *Asparagus plumosus*—asparagus fern; *Camellia*; *Cedrus deodara*—deodar cedar; *Cestrum*; *Chaenomeles japonica*—Japanese flowering quince; *Choisya ternata*—Mexican orange; *Citrus*; *Codiaeum variegatum*—croton; *Duranta*; *Eucalyptus*; *Fagus*—beech; *Ficus*—fig; *Feijoa sellowiana*—pineapple guava; *Fraxinus dipetala*—mountain ash; *Fuchsia*; *Gleditsia triacanthos*—honeylocust; *Grevillea*; *Grewia*; guava; *Hibiscus syriacus*—rose of Sharon; *Ilex*—holly; jasmine; *Juglans regia*—Persian walnut; *Juniperus communis* 'Stricta'—Irish juniper, laurel; *Ligustrum*—privet; *Magnolia*; *Malus*—apple; *Myrtus*—myrtle; *Nerium*—oleander; *Olea*—olive; palms; *Pittosporum*; *Platanus*—sycamore; *Populus*—poplar; *Prunus*—almond, apricot, plum, prune; *Punica*—pomegranate; *Pyrus*—pear; *Rhamnus*—buckthorn; *Rhus*—sumac; *Robinia pseudoacacia*—black locust; *Rosa*—rose; *Schinus*—pepper tree; *Solanum jasminoides*—nightshade; *Torreya californica*—California nutmeg tree; *Umbellularia*—California bay; *Vitis*—grape.

References: 84, 93

A. Note damage to oleander leaves caused by black scale infestation.
B. Close-up of section A, showing scales on shoot and sooty mold on leaf.
C. Immature black scales on undersides of oleander leaves.
D. Maturing black scale female, showing raised ridges outlining letter "H" on dorsum.
E. Mature black scales on Mexican orange.
F. Black scales on twig of holly.
G. Close-up of scale shown in section F.
H. Encrustation of black scale on citrus. Some of these scales have been parasitized. Close observation will reveal holes where the parasite has emerged.
I. Mature black scales on citrus twig. They vary from 3 to 5 mm in diameter.
J. Young black scales on a California bay leaf.

PLATE 147

Nigra Scale and Hemispherical Scale (Plate 148)

The nigra scale, *Saissetia nigra* (Nietner), was a serious pest of ornamental plants during the early decades of this century, but subsequently has become relatively unimportant. First detected in Washington, D.C., in the early 1900's, this insect is now known to occur outdoors in Florida and California, and indoors in greenhouses in many states. It is believed that the nigra scale survives outdoors in all the Gulf states.

The dramatic decline of the population of the nigra scale in California in recent decades is attributed to its natural enemies. Some 24 or 25 species of parasitic wasps, many of which have been deliberately introduced into the United States for biological control purposes, are known to destroy large numbers of *S. nigra*. Other important natural enemies include the larvae of the lacewing and the larvae and adults of the lady beetle.

In California one generation of *S. nigra* occurs each year. Adults are found in the months of April, May and June. In the adult stage the insect is brown to deep black in color, usually elongated in shape, and is 3 to 5 mm in length (C). The shape of the adult scale is quite variable, depending on the substrate on which it develops. On leaves, for example, the insect is broad, whereas on slender twigs, it tends to be narrow and elongated. Eggs are laid beneath the body of the females from May until the February of the following year. The majority of eggs are deposited from May to September. After an incubation period of one to three weeks, the young crawlers migrate away from the body of the parent and settle on the leaves of woody parts of the host. Scales molt twice before the adult stage is reached. Unlike many scale insects, *S. nigra* is capable of movement at any time during the eight- or nine-month period of development from crawler to adult. In California, no males of the nigra scale have ever been recorded. Reproduction, therefore, takes place entirely without mating.

Damage to the host plant is caused by the withdrawal of plant juices by the developing scales. This may result in premature loss of foliage or twig or branch dieback. Blackening of foliage resulting from sooty mold development on honeydew, which is excreted by the scales, is another form of damage to plants caused by *S. nigra*.

The nigra scale has been known to attack 161 species of plants in California, many of which are important woody ornamentals. Its favored hosts are said to include Japanese aralia, *Fatsia japonica*; English ivy, *Hedera helix*; English holly, *Ilex aquifolium*; oleander, *Nerium oleander*; orange pittosporum, *Pittosporum undulatum*; and *Hibiscus*.

The hemispherical scale, *Saissetia coffeae* (Walker) is a brown scale about 3 mm in diameter when mature (H). In profile, it has a hemispherical shape; from above it appears to be gently oval. This species is far more important as a greenhouse pest than as one which affects outdoor-grown ornamental plants. Because it is a tropical species, it is found outdoors only in the more southern portions of the United States, such as Florida and California.

This insect, a soft scale, produces honeydew. The sooty mold fungi which feed upon the honeydew impart a blackened appearance to the foliage of infested plants. Additionally, damage to ornamentals is caused by the withdrawal of sap from the host, resulting in yellowing and premature loss of leaves, and in dieback of twigs and branches. The hemispherical scale has a life and seasonal history similar to that of the black scale, *S. oleae*.

Woody ornamentals attacked by *S. coffeae* include; bignonia; *Camellia*; *Citrus*; *Codiaeum variegatum*—croton; ferns; guava; *Myrtus*—myrtle; *Nerium*—oleander; palms; *Rhus*—sumac; *Schinus*—pepper tree; *Zamia*.

References: 84, 93, 269

A. Nigra scale on leaves and twigs of *Daphne*.
B. Nigra scale on stem of *Maytenus boaria*.
C. Close-up of scale shown in section B, showing crawlers and adult females.
D. Nigra scale on leaves of *Daphne*.
E. Hemispherical scale encrustation on twig.
F. Hemispherical scale on fern. This plant is a very susceptible host.
G,H. Close-ups of hemispherical scale adult and crawlers. Note blackening caused by sooty mold fungi in section G.

PLATE 148

Tuliptree Scale (Plate 149)

The tuliptree scale, *Toumeyella liriodendri* (Gmelin), is a serious pest of the tulip tree or yellow poplar, *Liriodendron tulipifera,* and the magnolia, *Magnolia soulangeana.* The insects are so prolific that they often completely cover all of the host's twigs and branches, resulting in a rapid decline of the infested tree. Additional hosts of this scale insect include linden, *Tilia* spp., and the magnolias, *M. grandiflora* and *M. stellata.* In Florida, the tuliptree scale has been observed on banana shrub, *Michelia fuscata;* cape jasmine, *Gardenia jasminoides;* loblolly bay, *Gordonia lasianthus;* buttonbush, *Cephalanthus* spp.; red bay, *Persea borbonia;* and walnut, *Juglans* spp. In the United States, tuliptree scale is found east of the Mississippi River Valley and in California.

The tuliptree scale is one of the largest of the soft-scale insects, and is easily mistaken for the magnolia scale, which is about the same size and has a similar life cycle, but attacks only magnolias (see Plate 151). A mature female is 6–12 mm in diameter and hemispherical in shape (C). Eggs develop within the body of the female and the young crawlers are born alive. A single female can produce as many as 3000 or more crawlers over a period of several weeks. Reproduction occurs in late August and September. Crawlers are of the size of a pinhead and settle on twigs in the fall. Young nymphs overwinter and actively feed from spring until late summer. The insects deplete the bark tissue of sap and nutrients with their piercing-sucking mouthparts. Severe dieback of branches and even death of the entire plant results from repeated, heavy infestations. Infestations are most conspicuous when many females are present. During the summer considerable honeydew excretions encourage the growth of sooty mold fungus and attract ants, wasps, and hornets.

Natural enemies are common among tuliptree scales, but these enemies are seldom able to control infestations until the host plant is so weakened that the scale is on the verge of starvation. The lady beetles, *Hyperaspis signata bipunctata* (Say), and *Chilocorus* spp., feed on nymphs. The caterpillars of a phycitid moth, *Laetilia coccidivora* (Comst.), spin silk webs 2.5 to 7.5 mm long on the twigs covering the scales, and consume the scales under the protection of their webs. This caterpillar is common in Virginia. Four species of wasps that parasitize them are *Aphycus flavus* (Howard), *Anicetus toumeyellae* (Miliron), *Coccophagus flavoscutellum* (Ashm.), and *Coccidoxenus mexicanus* (Girault). Certain fungi are also known to kill the tuliptree scale.

Reference: 76

A. Yellowing of tulip poplar foliage and the dieback of lower branches are caused by a heavy scale infestation. Note twig dieback at circle.
B. Typical encrustation of nearly grown female tuliptree scales on large twigs.
C. The shape and coloration of mature female tuliptree scales.

PLATE 149

315

Lecanium and Kermes Scales (Plate 150)

The genus *Lecanium* includes approximately a dozen species of closely related "soft" scale insects which are common pests in the United States and Canada. They are difficult to distinguish from one another. Positive identification requires microscopic study by an expert. In general, however, knowledge of their host preference and their relative size can be a helpful, though not entirely reliable, means of field identification of the species. After laying eggs, the body of the adult female turns brown, and becomes brittle, and hemispherical. The length of *Lecanium* species varies. *L. nigrofasciatum* Pergande, for example, measures less than 3 mm, while *L. caryae* is 12 mm long.

The *Lecanium* species have similar histories of growth and development. The period of greatest growth of all the species is in spring and early summer. This is also the time when the most damage is incurred by the host plant. The female deposits her eggs during June or early July. As she does so, her body becomes increasingly hemispherical and dry. The so-called "scale" is the dead, brittle body of the female which protects the eggs until they hatch (C,D). Crawlers emerge from beneath the female shell and migrate to the leaves, usually during June or July. In late summer, second-instar nymphs (see arrows in section C), except for *L. nigrofasciatum*, return to the twigs where they overwinter. Generally, one generation of *Lecanium* scale insects occurs each year.

The hickory lecanium, *L. caryae* Fitch, is huge by comparison to other species. It measures up to 12 mm in length. It is somewhat flattened when it occurs on large limbs but is quite convex and smaller when on twigs. It is brown and is characteristically covered with a dusty-looking coating of purplish-white wax. On infested elm trees in New York, the hickory lecanium occurred on limbs 4 to 12 cm in diameter while *L. corni*, the European fruit lecanium occurred chiefly on small twigs. Other host plants include *Carya* spp., *Castanea dentata*, *Platanus occidentalis*, *Pyrus* sp., *Quercus rubra* and certain species of *Betula*, *Fagus*, *Salix*, *Celtis*, *Juglans*, *Gleditsia*, *Malus*, *Morus* and *Prunus*. Adult females each lay 100 or more eggs which hatch in late June or early July.

The European fruit lecanium, *L. corni* Bouche (C), is the most abundant species of this genus. Its geographic range is wide and its list of hosts is virtually unlimited. It occurs on shade trees, fruit trees, shrubs, and other woody ornamental plants. It varies widely in shape and form from host to host making positive identification difficult for a non-entomologist. Williams (315) indicated that *L. corni* could not be consistently distinguished from *L. fletcheri* Cockerell and *L. quercifex* Fitch on the basis of structural characters. Yet, *L. fletcheri* is generally identified as the species found on *Taxus*, *Thuja*, and *Juniperus*. *L. quercifex* has been associated with *Quercus*, *Platanus*, *Diospyros*, *Carya*, *Castanea* and *Xanthoxylum*.

The terrapin scale, *L. nigrofasciatum* Pergande, (not illustrated) is a native species found chiefly on *Acer* species and *Prunus* (especially peach) as well as linden, *Mimosa*, *Platanus*, *Sassafras*, hawthorn, apple, birch, redbud, mulberry, poplar, live oak, *Vaccinium* and twelve other genera. The terrapin scale, also known as the black-banded scale, is an eastern species which occurrs in every state east of the Mississippi River except Maine, New Hampshire and Vermont. It also occurs in the Gulf States, New Mexico, parts of the Midwest and in Ontario, Canada. The terrapin scale does not lay eggs. Young are born as crawlers early in the spring. They migrate to the leaves and attach themselves to the larger veins on the leaves' undersurfaces. Before frost occurs in autumn, the young scale insects migrate back to the twigs and small branches where they remain for the rest of their lives. Unlike other *Lecanium* species, the adult female, rather than the second-instar nymph, overwinters. Partially grown females are easily identified in the field by their red-orange color which is intersected by black radiating lines. To some, its body shape and markings resemble those of a land terrapin. Females are globular insects and when fully grown measure about 3–4 mm in diameter. There is one generation each year. A chalcid wasp, *Coccophagus lecanii* Fitch, is the most abundant parasite recorded in Maryland.

The European peach scale, *L. persicae* (Fab.) attacks many hosts including *Albizia*, *Berberis*, *Elaeagnus*, *Euonymus*, *Lonicera*, *Ulmus* and *Vitis*. It has been reported on plum in Florida and was erroneously reported as *L. magnoliarum* in California. It can be a serious pest of ornamental plants and fruit crops.

The globose scale, *L. prunastri* (Fonscolombe) (Plate 152), is primarily a pest of stone fruits including the ornamental flowering cultivars. *L. pruinosum* (Coq) (section F, and Plate 151, section B), sometimes called the frosted scale, is common in the West on deciduous and flowering fruit trees, mountain ash, birch, hawthorn, laurel, locust, rose, sycamore and walnut trees. It has been reported on grape in New York State. Other *Lecanium* species have been described but are not known to be of significant economic importance.

Several related, similar species previously included under *Lecanium* are now classified separately in other genera: *Coccus hesperidum* L., the brown soft scale; *Toumeyella numismaticum* P. & M., the pine tortoise scale (Plate 32); *T. pini* (King); *Toumeyella liriodendri* (Gmelin), the tuliptree scale (Plate 149); *Saissetia coffeae* (Walker), the hemispherical scale (Plate 148); *Neolecanium cornuparvum* (Thro), the magnolia scale (Plate 151); and several other less common species in these genera. The soft scale insects (family Coccidae) have not been studied as thoroughly as the armored scales (family Diaspididae). The most comprehensive and recent publication about soft scales is that of M. L. Williams (315).

Lecanium scale populations are subject to rapid increase and decline. A great many parasites and predators have been reported to attack species of *Lecanium* and frequently account for the collapse of populations (sections B and F show parasitized specimens). However, the manipulation of parasites in achieving control of scale insects on ornamental plants has not been adequately developed. A number of the natural enemies have been observed to be efficient parasites in nature and should be explored as a means of scale control. A wasp, *Encyrtus californicus* Girault, is a common parasite in the West, and *Cordyceps clavulate* Ellis is an important fungal parasite in the northeastern and north-central states.

The genus *Kermes*, in the family Kermidae, represents a small group of scale insects which are known only on oak, *Quercus* spp. Although a number of species has been described, *K. pubescens* Bogue alone has been studied in detail in the United States. In Maryland, McConnell and Davidson found that adult females of this species (A) lay eggs over a month-long period beginning in late June. Eggs begin to hatch early in July. Crawlers migrate to cracks in the bark of the trunk to spend the winter. In the spring, after the first molt, the nymphs migrate to the new growth. They frequently settle or attach themselves near leaf axils. By early June, the females are mature and globular in shape, resembling small tan galls or buds. Adult males develop to maturity on the trunk without migrating to new growth.

References: 75, 100, 176, 177, 185, 261, 281, 315

A. Kermes scale on the bark of red oak.
B. Nearly mature female *Lecanium* (probably European fruit lecanium). The black specimen has been parasitized.
C. Dead adult females of the European fruit lecanium and overwintering second-instar nymphs (at arrows) on twigs of redbud, *Cercis canadensis*.
D. European fruit lecanium females full of eggs. Arrow indicates where dead female was removed to reveal eggs.
E. Scales of *Lecanium* sp. on the underside of a leaf of California holly, *Heteromeles arbutifolia*.
F. Parasitized *Lecanium pruinosum* scales on walnut. Note the parasite exit holes in "shell."
G. A species of *Lecanium* on elm showing the coloration and appearance of a female approaching maturity; possibly parasitized.
H. Same species as that shown in section G. Insect in this photograph is older than that shown in section G.

PLATE 150

Soft Scale Insects (Plate 151)

In evolutionary development, soft scales are related on one side to mealybugs and on the other to armored scales. The bodies of many soft scales, like those of mealybugs, are covered during part of their development with a white, waxy powder (B,H). Some soft scales produce a white egg sac. Like armored scales, soft scales remain immobile for most of their lives. Unlike armored scales soft scales do not have shell-like covers over their bodies. Instead, what appears to be a "shell" is an external skeleton and cannot be removed without killing the insect. Soft scales generally excrete large quantities of syrupy honeydew which becomes blackened when colonized by sooty mold fungi (see Plate 119 section E). Armored scales rarely, if ever, produce honeydew deposits.

The magnolia scale, *Neolecanium cornuparvum* (Thro), is the largest scale insect found in the United States. The adult female of this species sometimes measures up to 13 mm in length (D). It is a native insect and is distributed throughout the eastern United States. Its principal hosts are *Magnolia stellata, M. acuminata, M. liliflora* and *M. soulangeana.* Other species of magnolia may be attacked, but usually with less frequency. Severely infested plants can be seriously injured or killed by this insect. Great amounts of honeydew are produced, giving the affected plant an untidy, unthrifty appearance because of the sooty mold growing on the honeydew.

The insect overwinters as a bluish-black first instar nymph on one- or two-year-old twigs. In New York, the first molt occurs in late April or May and the second in early June, by which time the insects have turned a deep purple. Stems of the host plant that are normally light green appear enlarged and purple from a massive incrustation. The nymphs secrete a white powdery layer of wax over their bodies (external skeleton) (H). By late August, most of the females have produced nymphs that wander about for a short time before settling on the new growth of a twig where they start the cycle again. In the northeastern United States a single generation occurs each year.

The calico scale, *Lecanium cerasorum* (Cockerell), is a colorful, white-dark brown calico, from which it gets its name (A). The color is brightest when the scale reaches maturity, after which time it quickly darkens with age (E). It is globular in shape and is about 6 to 8 mm in diameter. At maturity, its color, size and shape characters are sufficient for positive field identification. In winter, immature females are oval, flattened and light to dark brown.

Like other lecanium scales, only one generation of the calico scale occurs each year. Calico scales overwinter on twigs as partially-grown nymphs. In California and the coastal areas of Virginia, the nymphs have matured and have begun to produce eggs by early May. Upon hatching, the crawlers move to the leaves where they settle and remain during the summer months. Before leaves drop in the fall, they move back to the twigs to spend the winter. A large amount of honeydew is produced in the spring. Injury at that time is not due to the sap loss, but to reduced photosynthesis caused by heavy sooty mold growth on the honeydew.

Calico scale is a pest of all stone fruits and their ornamental cultivars, as well as Persian walnut, elm, Zelkova, maple, *Pyracantha*, pear, *Liquidambar*, Boston ivy, Virginia creeper, dogwood, buckeye, and flowering crabapple. Entomologists in California first reported the calico scale. It is now known to occur in the Pacific coast states and several eastern states including Maryland, Virginia, Delaware and Long Island, New York.

On the Pacific coast, birds are important predators of the calico scale. Among the bird predators the audubon warbler, *Dendroica auduboni*, is the most notable. The wasp parasite, *Blastothrix longipennis* Howard, also a west coast species, is known to aid in calico scale population control.

Lecanium pruinosum Coquillett, frequently called the frosted scale, is presumably limited in geographical distribution to California and Arizona. The mature female is a large, convex, brown scale, 6 to 8 mm in diameter, and is covered with a white frost-like wax (B). After the insect reaches maturity, its wax covering tends to weather away, leaving a color and form much like that of the European fruit lecanium (Plate 150).

The frosted scale has one generation each year. Eggs are produced during April and May and hatch as brownish crawlers in June and sometimes July. The crawlers migrate to leaf blades and petioles as well as to the current season's twigs. Individuals that settle on leaves tend to move to twigs during the early autumn. Maturation of the frosted scale continues through winter and, by early spring, the young females become covered with a powdery white wax. When dense populations develop, the foliage of the host tree becomes covered with hundreds of small clear droplets of honeydew. The honeydew is syrupy and soon becomes overgrown with sooty mold fungi. Frosted scales may be found on crabapple, hawthorn, mountain ash, apricot, prune and other species of *Prunus*, birch, elm, laurel, locust, rose, sycamore and walnut.

In California, the wasp *Metaphycus californicus* (Howard) is the most important and abundant parasite of the frosted scale. With proper management, this parasite has the capability of reducing the scale to nondestructive levels.

References: 128, 184, 197, 198, 315

A. Mature female calico scales on walnut.
B. *Lecanium pruinosum*, the frosted scale, on Persian walnut.
C,D. Mature magnolia scales, about 13 mm long.
E,F. Dead female calico scales on *Pyracantha*. Live crawlers are at arrow points.
G. Calico scale eggs and scales.
H. Immature magnolia scales.
I. Nearly mature magnolia scales. Note that the white fluffy wax is beginning to weather away.

PLATE 151

Rose Scale and Globose Scale (Plate 152)

Some of the differences between soft and armored scale insects can be seen in the facing plate, in which both the globose scale and the rose scale are shown. The males of these soft and armored scales are superficially similar. They are both small and white. From a distance, groups of them look like a whitish flaky crust on the branches of host plants. Close examination with a magnifying lens shows that the immature male armored scale insect (rose scale) is covered with a definite waxy scale cover. The male breaks through the cover when it emerges. However, the cover remains attached to the plant for most of the season. When the winged males of soft scales (globose scale) are about ready to emerge they likewise turn white. An empty cast skin (skeleton) remains attached to the twig upon emergence. The winged males of both soft and armored scales tend to be numerous but inconspicuous, for only a few days of the year.

The females of armored and soft scales are seldom confused. Armored scale females such as those of the rose scale (C), have a characteristic scale cover, composed of waxy secretions, that incorporates the cast skins of earlier instars. The so-called "scale" in the soft scale group is the body of the female itself. No cover is produced. When the insect molts, the very delicate cast skin is broken and sloughed off as the body expands.

The rose scale, *Aulacaspis rosae* (Bouche), is a pest of brambles and roses, but has also been found on the fringe tree, *Chionanthus virginicus*, on peach, and on *Geranium* in Florida. It also occurs throughout California. The rose scale is the only species of *Aulacaspis* in North America. Infestation by this pest is not regarded as a serious problem. Canes, twigs or stems are the sites of attack on their host plants. Two or more generations occur in a single season, depending on the climate. In New York State, two generations occur. The first-generation eggs hatch in late May or early June; the second-generation eggs hatch in August. Details of the biology of the rose scale have not been studied.

The globose scale, *Lecanium prunastri* (Fonsc.), has been recognized since 1738 in Europe where it is known as the plum lecanium scale (E). By 1900 it was known to have occurred in New York, Ohio, and Pennsylvania. The globose scale can be injurious to peach and plum trees and has also been found on apricot and sweet cherry. It appears to be a pest of minor importance. The insect overwinters on the undersides of twigs and limbs in the rough crevices of the bark.

References: 67, 181, 315

A. Light infestation of rose scale, *Aulacaspis rosae*, on rose canes.
B. Male scale covers of the rose scale, an armored scale.
C. Single female scale cover of the rose scale.
D. Predominantly empty "pupal" skins of male globose scales.
E. Colony of mature female globose scales on purple plum tree.
F. Brown male globose scale "pupae" and empty pupal skins. At arrows: two males ready to emerge.
G. Female globose scales with crawlers emerging.

PLATE 152

European Elm Scale and Other Scales on Elm (Plate 153)

Elms are susceptible to infestation by a variety of scale insects in both the soft and armored scale groups. There may be as many as five or more species found attacking a single elm at the same time. Species of *Gossyparia, Pulvinaria, Lecanium, Clavaspis, Diaspidiotus, Quadraspidiotus, Chionaspis,* and *Lepidosaphes* have been observed on elm.

The European elm scale, *Gossyparia spuria* (Modeer) is a common pest of elms. It attacks no other host. It was seldom seen during the era of intensive spraying of elms with DDT, but prior to that time it was a severe pest, and is becoming more prevalent as DDT now has few legal uses. It overwinters as a first-instar nymph in the crevices of rough bark (B). Active development and extensive feeding occur in the spring. The developing female (A) feeds on the trunk of its host plant as well as on the bark of twigs and smaller branches, before it reaches maturity in early summer. Eggs laid in June hatch in July. Crawlers migrate to the rough cracks in the bark where they remain until the following spring. In section A, the arrow points to a developing female lecanium scale. The European fruit lecanium, *Lecanium corni* Bouche, is frequently present on the small twigs of trees infested with the European elm scale. The large hickory lecanium, *Lecanium caryae* Fitch, which is similar in appearence to an undetermined species pictured in section G in Plate 150, occurs on the larger limbs and branches.

The elm scurfy scale, *Chionaspis americana* Johnson, is widely distributed, is common, and is seriously injurious to elm (C). It has also been reported from *Celtis* and *Platanus*. In addition to *C. americana*, elm is also attacked by another scurfy scale, *C. furfura* (Fitch), although this species usually occurs primarily on rosaceous plants such as mountain ash, and willow.

The two species of *Chionaspis* are indistinguishable in general appearance. However, chionaspid scales can be distinguished from other genera of armored scales found on elm in the egg stage. Eggs of *C. americana* are reddish in color and oval (F). Other genera have whitish eggs. The eggs overwinter on the bark and hatch in May. Two generations occur each season. Parasite populations develop naturally in severely infested trees. They provide effective natural control, but usually not until serious damage has been done by the scale insects.

References: 12, 32, 67, 181

A. European elm scale females. Arrow points to a developing *Lecanium* female.
B. Overwintering first-instar European elm scale nymphs in crack of bark.
C. Dead elm twig encrusted with elm scurfy scale.
D. Twig showing all stages of the scurfy scale. Immature scale cover at upper arrow; mature female at lower arrow.
E. Typical elm scurfy scale covers of mature females.
F. A female cover turned up to show reddish oval eggs (see arrows).

PLATE 153

Oystershell Scale (Plate 154)

The living armored scale insect is hidden under a shell made of its own cast skins and waxy secretions. It can be exposed by gently lifting this armor. Under it, there is an animal that seems to have no resemblance to an insect. It has no legs, no eyes, no antennae. It is attached to its foodplant by hair-like mouthparts that are embedded into the host tissue for a length of three or more times that of its body. The oystershell scale and those insects illustrated in the following twelve plates are examples of such armored scale insects.

The oystershell scale, *Lepidosaphes ulmi* (L.), is probably more widely known than any other scale insect. In 1738, Reaumur noted the resemblance of this scale to a sea shell. In Europe it is still known commonly as the mussel scale. Linnaeus first described this species in 1758. A letter, dated December 1794, held among the official documents of the still active Massachusetts Society for Promoting Agriculture, gives the first known description of oystershell scale in the United States. In it, Enoch Perley included observations of its seasonal development which hold true nearly 180 years later. Oystershell scale is distributed throughout the world except for arctic and tropical climates. In the United States it occurs in every state, but more commonly in the North than in the South.

Oystershell scale is an important pest of fruit trees, shade trees, and other woody ornamental plants. It was much more common prior to the advent of synthetic organic insecticides. In 1916, 128 different species of plants were recorded as hosts. In 1925, Griswold (118) recognized two forms of the scale in Ithaca, New York, and found them locally on plants representing 19 genera in 12 families.

There are two forms of the oystershell scale. These differ in appearance and in seasonal development. The "lilac," or banded form, is slightly larger and somewhat later in developing than the "apple" or brown form (C,D).

Although well over 128 host plants are known, oystershell scale is a serious pest on relatively few of them. The hosts most commonly infested by the lilac form include lilac, ash, willow, poplar, and maple. The apple form infests apple and dogwood. Other frequently infested hosts include: boxwood, birch, beech, cotoneaster, elm, horse chestnut, linden, mountain ash, pachysandra, pear, plum, sycamore, tuliptree, viburnum, Virginia creeper, and walnut. It is typical for the oystershell scale to initially involve only certain branches or parts of a host. Entire branches may become be encrusted with scales before other sections of the plant become infested. If this pest is not controlled early, large portions of trees and shrubs are frequently killed.

The oystershell scale overwinters in the egg stage under the female scale covers. In the Northeast, there is one generation each year. The eggs hatch for a ten-to-fourteen-day period beginning in late May. On Long Island and in areas to the south of it, two generations are reported annually. In these areas, the first generation of crawlers appears in late May, and the second early in August. The time of emergence is earlier for insects living farther south. By autumn, males and females have matured and overwintering eggs are present under the scale covers.

Numerous parasites and predators have been recorded from populations of the oystershell scale. They play an important role in naturally reducing heavy populations, but usually they are too late to prevent serious damage. The twicestabbed lady beetle, *Chilocorus stigma* (Say), is an important predator, and when it is abundant in a local area, it is influential in restricting scale build-up. Generally, however, natural enemies are attracted to, and develop populations in, areas where large numbers of scales have already become established.

References: 93, 129

A. *Viburnum* sp. (at left) is near death, due to activities of the oystershell scale. Plant on right shows effects of lesser infestation.
B. Crawlers (circle) and settled nymph (arrow) initiating its waxy cover.
C. Banded or lilac form on *Syringa;* adult female scales.
D. Brown or apple form of the oystershell scale; females and male (at arrow). Note scale covers with exit hole of a parasite.
E. Four old female scale covers and numerous partially-developed females. Adult females are up to 3 mm long.

PLATE 154

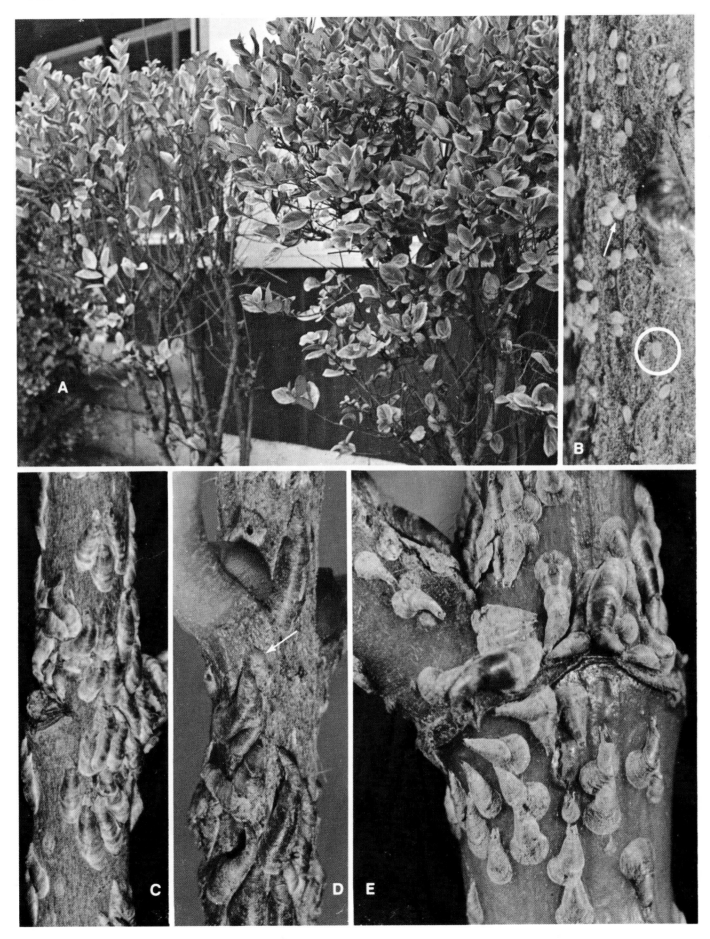

Greedy Scale and Peony Scale (Plate 155)

The greedy scale, *Hemiberlesia rapax* (Comstock), is the commonest and most widely distributed species of armored scales in California, according to E. O. Essig (93), one of California's best known entomologists. Professor Comstock (48a), who provided one of the first descriptions of this insect said, "I have named this the greedy scale on account of the great number of plants upon which the species subsists." It has been found on 45 ornamental species in Florida alone. In Florida some of its hosts are: abelia, avocado, azalea, bay, cactus, camphor, *Castanopsis* sp., chinaberry, cedar, *Elaeagnus, Euonymus*, fig, geranium, guava, gumbolimbo, holly, honeysuckle, huckleberry, juniper, loquat, magnolia, morning glory, mulberry, myrtle, oak, palm, pear, pecan, persimmon, plumeria, poisonwood, privet, sapodilla, seagrape, and tecoma. Additional hosts (found in California) include *Acacia*, almond, apple, bladderpod, boxwood, broom, *Ceanothus*, camellia, *Cestrum* chapparal broom, cherry, cissus, *Cotoneasters*, cottonwood, English holly, English ivy, English laurel, *Eucalyptus, Fuchsia, Genista*, giant sequoia, grape, hakea, heath, mountain holly, Japanese quince, California laurel, *Lavatera*, locust, manzanita, mistletoe, nightshade, olive, orange, Oregon grape, palms, passion vine, pepper tree, *Pittosporum*, pomegranate, pyracantha, quince, redbud, sage, sedum, Strawberry tree, *Strelitzia*, tan oak, umbrella tree, English walnut, willow, and yam.

The distribution of the greedy scale in the United States is as yet unknown, though it appears to be a subtropical species. It has been recorded outdoors in California, Oregon, Arizona, New Mexico and Florida. The greedy scale undoubtedly occurs along the Gulf Coast. It is a rather common insect in greenhouses in the North.

In the warmer climates, the greedy scale probably reproduces continually, several generations occurring each year. The greedy scale is closely related to the latania scale (Plate 157) and may also be confused with the Putnam scale, *Diaspidiotus ancylus*. The scale armor, or test, is usually light gray, is circular and measures about 1 to 1.5 mm in diameter (E,H,I,J) when fully grown. As in many of the armored or diaspid scales, the cover of the greedy scale shows concentric color lines when viewed from above. These rings are formed by the discarded skeletons and secretions of the juvenile form which as the insect grows are pushed upward and incorporated into the scale insect's armor.

H. rapax feeds by sucking sap and cell contents from woody stems, twigs, leaves or fruit. The yellowing of foliage, poor growth, and dead twigs or branches are all symptomatic of persistent attack by this insect (A,F,G).

Pseudaonidia paeoniae (Cockerell) is sometimes called the peony scale although it is primarily a pest of azalea, camellia and, occasionally, ligustrum. It is presumed to be a southern species, and has been observed in Florida, Georgia, Mississippi, South Carolina and Virginia.

Little is known about its biology. Eggs are lavender (C) and are probably laid in April. In parts of Virginia, the purple crawlers appear in late May. They feed on bark and in severe infestations, can kill twigs and branches. The female armor, or test, is 3–4 mm in diameter and is sometimes partially covered by flakes of bark, giving it a grayish cast. The high point of the armor, called the first exuviae, is orange-yellow (B). This feature can usually be relied upon in making accurate field identification. The camphor scale, *P. duplex* (Cockerell), is often confused with the peony scale and may occur on both the leaves and the twigs of camellia, as well as on other mutual hosts. The camphor scale was brought into the United States from Japan, and has become a pest of camphor in Texas, Mississippi and Alabama. It is a potential threat to many subtropical trees and shrubs in the southern United States and Mexico. Dekle (67) lists 43 host species in Florida. Three generations of the peony scale occur each year.

References: 48a, 67, 93, 181, 194

A. Symptoms of injury caused by greedy scale on California laurel.
B. Peony scales on bark of *Camellia*. The first exuviae (skeleton) is orange-yellow. Bark flakes partially cover part of the armor, giving the scale an effective camouflage.
C. Peony scales at crotch of *Camellia*. A cluster of eggs is located in the circle.
D. Aucuba injury caused by greedy scale.
E,H,I,J. Close-ups of greedy scales on various hosts. Inside the circle in section E are young scales, eggs and crawlers.
F,G. An English holly severely injured by greedy scales. Premature leaf drop is the major symptom of injury.

PLATE 155

Ivy Scale, or Oleander Scale (Plate 156)

The ivy scale, also called oleander scale, resembles in many respects the greedy scale (see Plate 155). However, the shell covering is 1–2 mm in diameter, lighter in color and not as globular as that of the greedy scale. The "nipple" of the shell of the ivy or oleander scale, *Aspidiotus hederae* Vallot, is located more nearly in the center than that of the greedy scale.

This species attacks the bark, leaves, and fruit of its host plants. It occurs outdoors in the warmer parts of the United States, and in greenhouses throughout the country. In the western United States, it has been reported in Arizona, California, Colorado, Nevada, New Mexico, and Utah.

Woody host plants on which this species has been found include: *Acacia*, aloe, *Aucuba*, avocado, azalea, Boston ivy, blueberry, boxwood, buddleia, buckthorn, broom, cactus, California laurel, camellia, carob, *Ceanothus*, cherry, coffeeberry, currant, daphne, dogwood, English ivy, *Elaeagnus, Eucalyptus*, ferns, *Genista*, grape, grapefruit, Grecian laurel, guava, hakea, heath, holly, holly oak, hypericum, lemon, magnolia, manzanita, maple, mistletoe, Monterey pine, mulberry, myrsine, myrtle, nightshade, olive, *Osmanthus*, orange, palms, pepper tree, pistache, poinsettia, pomegranate, privet, redbud, redwood, rose, rubber, sago palm, sumac, umbrella plant, umbrella tree, viburnum, *Vinca*, vitex, yew, yucca.

Little is known about the biology of this insect.

References: 93, 181

A. Ivy scales look like grayish spots on the leaves of *Magnolia grandiflora*.
B. Clusters of ivy scale on a variegated Virginia creeper (*Parthenocissus*) leaf.
C,F. Ivy scales on *Viburnum rhytidophyllum* leaves. On this host, the scale prefers the underside of the leaf and causes small yellowish spots which are visible from the upper surface (arrow). The scales shown in section F are covered by the leaf hairs, making them almost invisible.
D. Ivy scales on *Pittosporum*.
E. At the arrow point are two adult female ivy scales with their shells removed.
G. A close-up of ivy scale on magnolia.

PLATE 156

Subtropical Armored Scales (Plate 157)

The latania scale, *Hemiberlesia lataniae* (Signoret), is known primarily in the coastal states. It feeds on a great many plants including a wide range of ornamental plants. In California some of the latania scale's hosts are *Acacia, Cedrus, Euonymus, Fatsia, Fuchsia, Grevillea, Hedera helix, Howeia, Olea europaea, Persea, Rosa, Rubus, Salix* and *Yucca*. In Florida its most common hosts are *Casuarina* sp., loquat, palms and rose; and in Maryland this pest often feeds on holly.

H. latania is a circular armored scale (D), and is about 1.5 to 2 mm in diameter. The scale covering is gray and almost indistinguishable from the greedy scale, *H. rapax* (see Plate 155). Only a microscopic examination of specially prepared stained specimens will reveal the difference between these two species.

Female latania scales lay eggs beneath their bodies. Upon hatching from the eggs the young crawlers migrate a short distance from the parent scale. Here they settle, insert their mouthparts into the host plant and begin to feed. The legs of the crawler become functionless after it settles. In southern California, scales undergo two molts within two months, become fully mature and begin to lay eggs. Most reproduction takes place without mating. In Maryland, there are two generations of these insects per year. They overwinter as second-instar males and females on leaves or stems. (see seasonal history chart).

The majority of a scale population feeds on the twigs and branches of its host. If the population is great dieback of twigs and smaller branches occurs. No honeydew or blackening of plant parts results from the infestation as occurs with soft scales. The latania scale has many natural enemies, among them lady beetles, lacewings, predaceous mites, and tiny parasitic wasps. These provide a measure of biological control of this pest. Wasp parasites are most important. They emerge in mid-May, in mid-June, during the second week of August, and in early September in Maryland. From the Maryland base location the time of parasite emergence can be estimated for other areas. Do not apply pesticides for scale control at the time of parasite emergence.

The cocos scale, *Diaspis cocois* Lichtenstein, is a small leaf-infesting armored scale (A) which infests *Chamaerops, Cocos, Kentia, Latania, Livistonia, Phoenix* and *Roystonea* in California. This scale was found in Florida in 1961 but reported to have been eradicated. The adult female is white and circular in form, whereas the male scale, also white, is quite elongate. The armor of *Diaspis boisduvalii* Signoret looks like that of *D. cocois*, The two cannot be distinguished from each other in the field. The boisduval scale is common on palm and yucca in the subtropical areas of the United States, and is frequently found elsewhere in greenhouses, especially on orchids.

References: 67, 83, 181, 277

Seasonal history of Hemiberlesia lataniae on Holly in Maryland (after Stoetzel and Davidson)

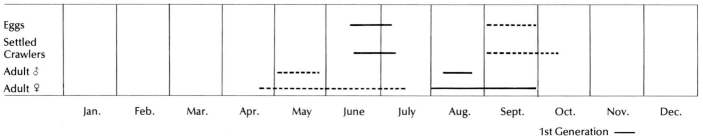

| | Jan. | Feb. | Mar. | Apr. | May | June | July | Aug. | Sept. | Oct. | Nov. | Dec. |

1st Generation ——
2nd Generation · · · ·

A. A palm frond heavily infested with *Diaspis cocois*.
B. A close-up of male (at arrow) and female *Diaspidiotus* sp. scale covers on the palm, *Livistonia*.
C. *Hemiberlesia lataniae* scales on a small branch of the handflower tree, *Chiranthodendron pentadactylon*.
D. *Hemiberlesia lataniae* on a handflower tree leaf.
E. *Hemiberlesia lataniae* females reared on a potato tuber.

PLATE 157

California Red Scale and Yellow Scale (Plate 158)

The California red scale, *Aonidiella aurantii* (Maskell), is considered to be the most important pest of citrus in the world. It also occurs on a large number of other woody plants. The insect is believed to be a native of China. It is known to occur in the Gulf states and in California.

The California red scale attacks all parts of the host plant. Symptoms of infestation include the yellowing of foliage, defoliation, and the death of twigs and branches. In extreme cases, death of the entire plant may result from the infestation. The scales feed by sucking the sap of their host plant. It is believed that a toxic substance may be introduced by the scale into plant tissues, a process which causes injury to the plant beyond that resulting from feeding alone (D,E,F).

In southern California, there are from two to four generations of the California red scale each year. More generations develop in inland areas of California than on coastal sites. The adult female does not lay eggs, but gives birth to living young. The crawlers settle on any part of the host plant and begin to feed within a day of emerging from beneath the scale cover of the female parent. There is a great deal of overlapping of generations, so all stages may be found at any time of the year.

The following are common woody ornamental hosts of the California red scale: *Acacia*—wattle; *Acer negundo*—boxelder; *Aspidistra*—iron plant; *Buxus*—boxwood; *Chaenomeles*—quince; *Citrus; Coprosma; Eucalyptus; Euonymus; Ficus*—fig; *Fuchsia; Ilex*—holly; *Juglans*—walnut; *Leptospermum*—tea tree; *Ligustrum*—privet; *Magnolia virginiana*—sweet bay; *Malus*—apple; *Mangifer indica*—mango; *Morus*—mulberry; *Olea*—olive; palms; *Passiflora*—passion vine; *Pistacia*—pistache; *Podocarpus; Pyrus*—pear; *Quercus*—oak; *Rosa*—rose; *Salix*—willow.

For many years, the yellow scale, *Aonidiella citrana* (Coquillett), was considered to be a variety of the California red scale. However, several minor anatomical differences between red scale and yellow scale have prompted taxonomists to regard California red scale and the yellow scale as separate species.

The insects have very similar life cycles, but have different habits and geographical distribution. When the yellow scale infests *Citrus* it tends to feed on the fruit and leaves instead of the twigs or branches. The California red scale, on the other hand, infests all parts of its host plants. The yellow scale is abundant in the non-coastal citrus regions, whereas the California red scale tends to be found along the Pacific coast.

The yellow scale, known only in California, attacks a number of plants other then *Citrus*. Many of these are important ornamentals (A). Its hosts are fewer than those of *A. aurantii*. They include: *Aucuba; Citrus; Daphne; Euonymus; Ficus elastica*—Indian rubber tree; *Hedera helix*—English ivy; palms; and *Pandanus utilis*—screw pine.

References: 84, 93

A. Yellow spotted leaves of privet that have been damaged by the yellow scale, *Aonidiella citrana*.

B,C. Yellow scales on the lower surface (B) and upper surface (C) of privet leaves, *Ligustrum lucidum*. Arrow points to a male.

D,E,F. Close-up of the California red scale, *Aonidiella aurantii*, on lemon fruit. Male at arrow. The red versus yellow colors are not satisfactory field identification characters.

PLATE 158

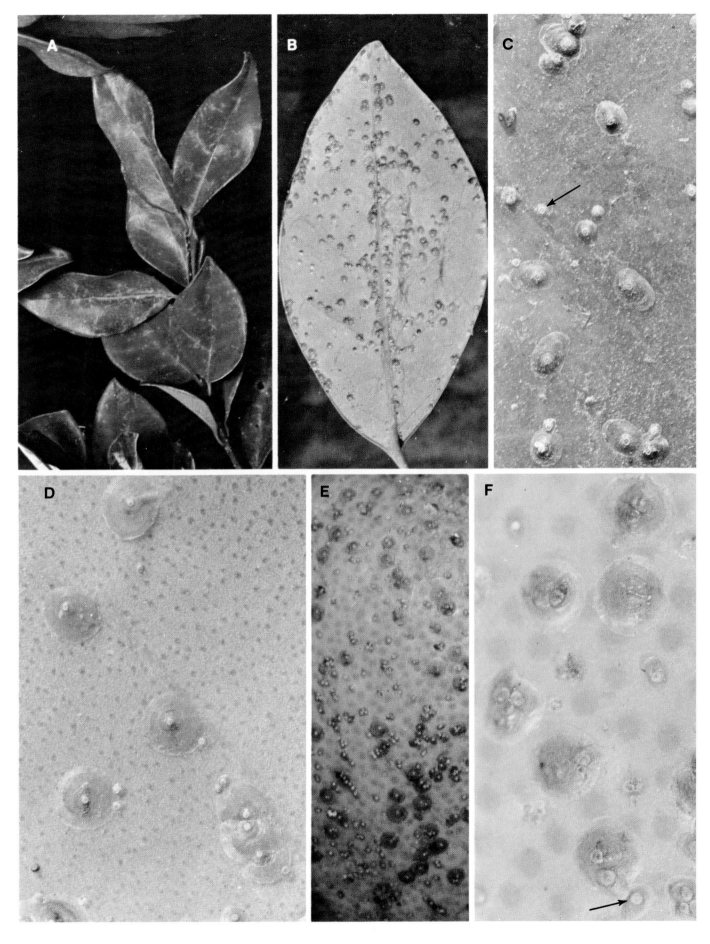

333

Subtropical Armored Scales (Plate 159)

The Florida red scale, *Chrysomphalus ficus* Ashmead (= *aonidum* (L.)), infests only the leaves of its hosts. It occurs outdoors in all of the citrus-growing areas of the world, and in greenhouses and plant conservatories everywhere. The list of hosts upon which it feeds seems endless. Dekle (67) lists about 260 genera of known host plants. The Florida red scale (B) is one of the most serious pests on citrus and ornamental plants in Florida. In California, it is reported to be of little importance as a pest of citrus, but is present on 27 genera of ornamental plants. Four to five generations occur each year. Most generations overlap. Females produce eggs over an extended period of time. Eggs hatch several hours after they are laid. All stages are present at any time during the season.

The Glover scale (D), *Lepidosaphes gloverii* (Packard), is a relative of the oystershell scale. Its range covers all citrus-growing regions. It occurs on all citrus, magnolia, euonymus, arborvitae, boxwood, ivy, cherry laurel, cypress, mulberry, myrtle, orchid, cabbage palmetto, *Podocarpus*, and privet. In California, it is reported on *Salix* and *Sciadopitys* as well as on euonymus, magnolia, and palms. It is often found in association with the purple scale and has a similar life cycle. It occurs mainly on twigs and branches but is also found on leaves.

Another cosmopolitan species found in citrus-growing areas all over the world is the purple scale (F), *Lepidosaphes beckii* (Newman). Dekle (67) has listed 43 genera of hosts in Florida, including citrus. McKenzie (181) noted that in addition to citrus in California, boxwood, eleagnus, and holly are attacked. The purple scale feeds on the bark, leaves, and fruit of its host plant. It is quite similar in appearance to the oystershell scale. Its seasonal development is continuous, and occurs in three annual, overlapping generations. The females lay from sixty to eighty eggs which may hatch over a period lasting from two to several weeks. About six to eight weeks is required for maturation of an individual scale insect.

The natural enemies of these scales include parasitic wasps, predaceous mites, and lady beetle predators.

References: 67, 181

A. Citrus foliage infested with Florida red scale.
B. Various stages of development of Florida red scales. Arrow at bottom of photograph indicates yellow-bodied scale where cover was removed. Arrow at top indicates elongate male.
C. Nearly mature and mature females of the Florida red scale. The arrow indicates a crawler.
D. Glover scale females on citrus leaf.
E. Various stages of glover scale; elongate forms are adult females (see arrow).
F. Immature females of the purple scale.

PLATE 159

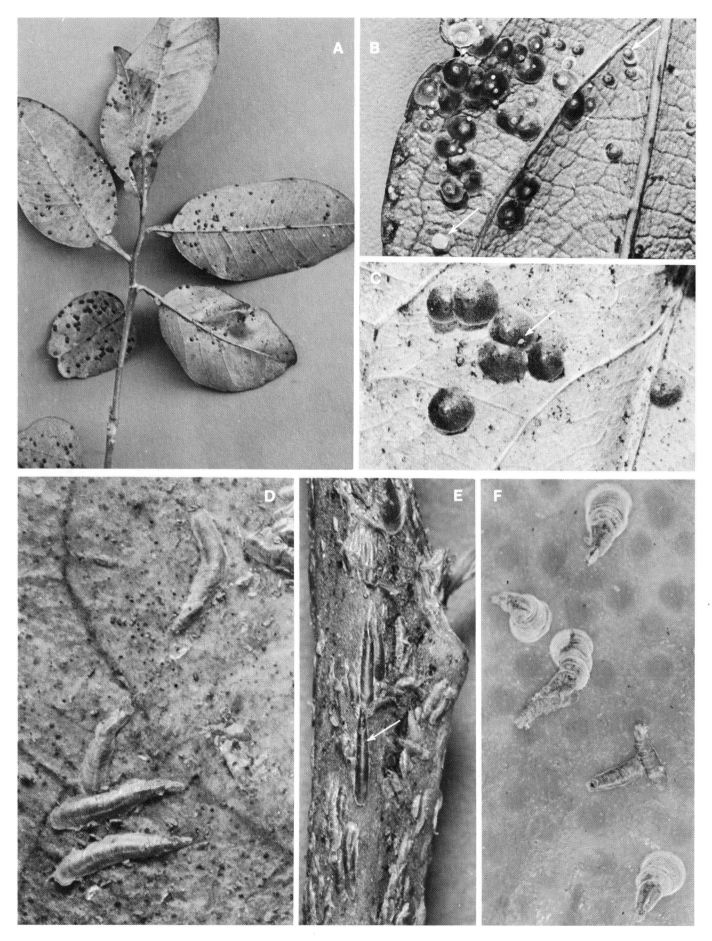

Armored Scales (Plate 160)

The dictyospermum scale, *Chrysomphalus dictyospermi* (Morgan), is found in the subtropical areas of the United States. It feeds chiefly on leaves (A), but may also be found on bark or fruit. When abundant, it brings about the slow decline and eventual death of its host. Because of their small size (less than 2 mm in diameter), the scales may be unnoticed until the infested host is beyond recovery. Some of the more common hosts of the dictyosperm scale are: *Acacia, Aralia, Araucaria*, arborvitae, *Aucuba, Avocado, Bauhinia*, boxwood, *Callistemon, Camellia*, cherry laurel, *Cinnamonum, Citrus, Clematis, Cotoneaster, Cupressus, Elaeagnus, Eucalyptus, Eugenia, Euonymus, Feijoa, Ficus, Gardenia, Ilex, Kalmia, Laurus, Ligustrum*, mulberry, myrtle, oleander, olive, *Osmanthus*, palm, *Pyracantha, Raphiolepis*, rose, *Taxus, Vinca*, willow.

In subtropical climates the generations of this scale overlap. Thus, their seasonal history is somewhat confusing. In southern California, there may be from five to six generations each year. In the spring, a generation may be completed in seven weeks.

Female dictyospermum scales lay eggs which remain under their shells or scale covers. Upon hatching, the young crawlers leave the protection of the scale cover and rove about, seeking a suitable place to settle and begin feeding. The crawlers are very tiny (less than one-half mm in length) and are yellow (Plate 163, section C, depicts a typical armored scale crawler). Several days after a crawler settles, it assumes a circular shape. It then begins to produce a fine mass of white cottony threads through pores. These white threads eventually cover the entire insect. When the insect molts, the cast skin forms the nipple-like prominence seen at the top of the female cover. With the first molt, the crawler's legs and antennae are shed. Hence, the insect becomes a sac-like creature with mouthparts as its only appendages. Upon reaching maturity, it produces eggs to bring forth another generation.

Sweet gum, *Liquidambar styraciflua*, is a primary host of *Diaspidiotus liquidambaris* (Kotinsky). The summer population of this scale insect is found in small pits on the underside of the host's leaves. These pits are often located at the junction of the leaf veins. Individuals are not easily noticed (D). An early symptom of their presence, however, are yellow spots on the leaf's upper surface (C). The affected leaf eventually forms a bluntly conical gall containing a single female scale. A second brood feeds on buds and twigs, where they overwinter as fertilized adult females. In Maryland and Ohio, eggs hatch in early June, and at this time the crawlers migrate to leaves. The main damage done by this insect is to foliage. *D. liquidambaris* has been found in the southeastern quadrant of the United States, in New York State and, less frequently, in California. The pest has also been known to occur on *Acer rubrum*.

Another armored scale, *Lindingaspis rossi* (Maskell), attacks *Araucaria, Euonymus*, oleander, olive, *Ficus, Gardenia, Camellia, Citrus, Hedera helix, Eucalyptus* and several palms. It is a tropical Australian species, and its distribution in the United States is limited to California. A related species, *Lindingaspis floridana* Ferris, is found in Florida infesting mango, avocado, *Ficus, Ligustrum*, palms, and others. The scale covers of both species look very much alike. Both live only on leaves.

References: 67, 181, 277

A. *Ficus pumila* leaves, heavily infested with *Chrysomphalus dictyospermi*.
B. Mature and immature female *Chrysomphalus dictyospermi*.
C. Early symptoms of presence of *Diaspidiotus liquidambaris* on the upper surface of a sweet gum leaf.
D. Male *Diaspidiotus liquidambaris* at the junction of veins on a sweet gum leaf.
E. Male (at arrow) and female *Lindingaspis rossi* scales on the foliage of *Araucaria*.

PLATE 160

Armored Scales (Plate 161)

Comstock described both the obscure scale and the gloomy scale in 1911 as *Aspidiotus obscura* and *A. tenebricosa*, respectively. In 1941, Ferris (103) placed both species in the genus *Melanaspis*. Thus, these two pests of shade trees are referred to under the genus *Aspidiotus* in much of the literature on the subject. Both species attack the trunk and larger limbs of young and old trees. Dieback of branches, limbs, and sometimes of entire trees occurs where these infestations are not controlled. The scale insects suck the sap from the phloem cells, depriving the tree of food manufactured in the leaves.

The obscure scale, *Melanaspis obscura* (Comstock), is widely distributed in the United States. Although it is most prevalent in the South, it is also common in certain areas of the middle Atlantic states as well as in California. The obscure scale attacks oak, chestnut, and pecan, and has been reported on beech, English walnut, willow, maple, hickory, grape, dogwood, wild myrtle, chinquapin, hackberry and the hog plum, *Spondias mombi*. In California, the pest also attacks apricot, peach and plum. In recent years, the obscure scale has been regarded as the pest most destructive to ornamental plants in at least two eastern states.

Detailed studies in Maryland by Stoetzel and Davidson (276) have provided life history data on the obscure scale. On white oaks it completes growth about mid-August, one month later than on red oaks. On pin oak, males and females overwinter until about the first of May, when they begin to mature. Eggs are laid starting in July. By late July, egg production is greatly reduced, but continues into early September. The population of crawlers peaks during July, then drops, with another slight surge occurring in August. One generation develops during the summer.

Three important factors contribute to the difficulty in effectively controlling the obscure scale. First, the insects tend to settle close together. This results in layers of scales as they grow and enlarge (C). Second, egg laying occurs over a relatively long period, and this results in an extended period of crawler activity. Third, crawlers often settle beneath old clusters of scales where eggs were laid, never exposing themselves to insecticides that may be applied for their control. The waxy scale cover of the live insect also provides protection. There are, however, numerous parasites and predators of this scale which may be effective as biological control agents.

The biology of the gloomy scale (E), *Melanaspis tenebricosa* (Comstock), is not well known. It is chiefly a pest of silver maple, *Acer saccharinum*, and red maple, *Acer rubrum*. It has also been found on sugar maple, elm, hackberry, boxelder, buckthorn, sweet gum, gallberry, *Ilex glabra*, mulberry, and soapberry, *Sapindus* sp. It is highly destructive and may kill trees if not controlled. Currently, few recommended control measures are more than partially effective. The gloomy scale is common in the southeastern quadrant of the United States, and also inhabits some of the mid-Atlantic and Midwestern states. Trees in nurseries as well as those in landscape plantings are often severely injured by this pest. Like the egg-laying, egg-hatching, and crawler activities of the obscure scale, those of the gloomy scale are long-lasting. Sometimes, populations of this pest increase to the extent that food supplies in the host become depleted. This condition along with buildup of parasites and predators eventually leads to population collapse.

References: 67, 276

A. Scale covers of the gloomy scale on a limb of red maple.
B. Clusters of the obscure scale on a pin oak limb. Note bark depressions.
C. Typical cluster of female covers of the obscure scale.
D. Individual scale covers of immature female obscure scales. The black nipple is the first-instar exuviae.
E. Nearly mature gloomy scale females on red maple. The cover of one has been lifted to expose the insect's body.
F. A "covey" of gloomy scales on red maple with covers lifted to expose bodies. Arrow points to the living scales.

PLATE 161

San Jose Scale and Walnut Scale (Plate 162)

The two species of scales shown here are widely distributed geographically and have many hosts. The San Jose scale (G), *Quadraspidiotus perniciosus* (Comstock), is highly injurious and destructive to its host plant. Until the advent of the newer organic insecticides after World War II, it was one of the most common, most destructive and most widely distributed scale insect pests of fruit, shade, and ornamental trees. It is common still throughout the United States and in many other parts of the world. Although first described from North America, the San Jose scale originated in Asia.

The literature pertaining to the San Jose scale is voluminous. The pest appeared in the United States in 1870, on a shipment of ornamental plants from the Orient. It is still a major pest and, if not controlled, is capable of killing trees.

Partially-grown males and females of the San Jose scale overwinter, mature in the spring, and produce living young. Feeding and development proceed rapidly, resulting in as many as five overlapping generations in a single season. The scales infest the fruit as well as the bark of their hosts. Twigs, limbs and stems are often completely encrusted with scales.

Well over sixty kinds of fruit and ornamental trees are infested by the San Jose scale. Pyracantha and cotoneaster are especially susceptible to severe damage. Numerous other hosts may support small populations of this scale, and provide for perpetuation of this species.

The walnut scale (D), *Quadraspidiotus juglansregiae* (Comstock), occurs throughout the United States. This insect is found primarily on deciduous trees and shrubs, although it is also known to occur on coniferous trees, such as hemlock, Virginia pine or Scots pine, and on broad-leaved evergreens. A partial host list includes: ash, birch, black locust, boxelder, buckeye, dogwood, elm, hackberry, hawthorn, hickory, holly, honeylocust, horse chestnut, Kentucky coffee tree, linden, maple, mountain ash, poplar, privet, sour cherry, sweet gum, tuliptree, and witch-hazel. It has not been reported on any of the *Juglans* except English walnut.

The walnut scale attacks the bark of the host tree, causing serious injury to the phloem, or living bark tissue. In Ohio, there are two or more generations each year. The insect overwinters as an adult. Mating occurs early in spring. In Ohio, egg laying occurs during June and July, and first-instar nymphs appear in September. Detailed studies of the biology and seasonal development of this scale are lacking. Many parasites, predators, and symbionts have been reported, but to date their precise relationships to the walnut scale are unknown.

References: 129, 181

A. Newly-settled first instar walnut scale nymphs. Note white waxy covers.
B. Second instar nymphs producing initial brown wax covers.
C. Waxy covers on mature female.
D. Walnut scale in all stages.
E. A rose stem showing typical symptoms of infestation by the San Jose scale. Dark-colored discoloration also appears on the green bark and fruit of other hosts.
F. The effects of a serious San Jose scale infestation on flowering quince twigs.
G. Second instar San Jose covers. Arrow points to one scale insect from which the cover has been removed. The fully grown scale produces a cover about 1–2 mm in diameter.

PLATE 162

Euonymus Scale (Plate 163)

The euonymus scale, *Unaspis euonymi* (Comstock), is a major pest in all temperate regions of the world except Australia. It attacks a number of hosts including *Euonymus, Camellia, Buxus, Celastrus, Daphne, Eugenia, Hedera, Hibiscus, Ilex, Jasminum, Ligustrum, Lonicera, Olea, Pachistima, Pachysandra, Solanum* and *Prunus.* Apparently, this scale was introduced from Japan or China. In the United States, it is a major pest of evergreen euonymus such as *Euonymus japonica,* and often causes complete defoliation or death of the plant. *Euonymus kiautschovica* (= *sieboldiana*) appears to resist heavy attacks of euonymus scale even when grown among heavily infested *E. japonica.* This scale is likely to be found throughout the United States and in many of the Canadian provinces.

The euonymus scale is difficult to detect until after it has caused serious damage. One symptom of a light attack is the occurrence of yellowish or whitish spots on the leaves (A,B). The female scales are usually found along the stems and leaf veins of the host plant (D,E). At times, however, the whole plant is whitened by the covers of the smaller male scales. When this occurs, the plant's leaves may drop and sometimes a normally green plant becomes bare by mid-summer. Plants growing closest to buildings seem to be damaged more than those growing where there is free air circulation. This pest frequents the stems at ground level where they are well protected.

The scales overwinter as fully-grown, fertilized, grayish females, which are easily distinguished from the smaller whitish males (D). Eggs are deposited in early spring, beneath the dark-colored female scale covering. The eggs hatch over a period of two or three weeks in early June in the Northeast, and in late May in Virginia. The nymphs crawl to other parts of the host plant, or are blown to other susceptible hosts. A second generation of crawlers develops by mid-July in Virginia. There may be up to three generations per year in the more southern locations.

Frequent treatments with certain pesticides are usually required for control. Because of apparent resistance to this pest, *E. kiautschovica* should be used as a substitute for *E. japonica* where low-maintenance plants are desired.

Reference: 42

A,B. Yellowish or whitish spots on *Euonymus* sp. caused by the euonymus scale.

C. Orangish crawlers and newly settled nymphs on stem.

D. Narrow whitish males with wider and darker females, as well as some newly settled nymphs. Females are about 2 mm long.

E. Characteristic clustering of scales along twigs and leaf midribs.

F,G. Leaves of *Euonymus japonica* heavily infested with euonymus scale. Section F shows yellowish spot symptoms as seen from the upper surface of the leaf; section G shows both male and female scales on the lower surface of the leaf.

PLATE 163

Armored Snow Scales (Plate 164)

Color is not often used by taxonomists as a basis for classifying animals. However, it is convenient to group several scale species together because of their color. Some armored scales have white covers and a few of them have been collectively called snow scales. Among these are *Unaspis citri* (Comstock), *Pinnaspis strachani* (Cooley), *P. aspidistrae* (Signoret), *Quernaspis quercus* (Comstock), and *Unaspis euonymi* (Comstock) (Plate 163).

Pinnaspis strachani, the lesser snow scale (A), is a general pest of ornamentals. It is also found on a number of subtropical plants. It has been recorded as an economic species in both Florida and California, and occurs on more than 200 plant species or cultivars. Some of its more common woody ornamental hosts include *Hibiscus, Acacia, Cassia, Citrus, Ficus, Pittosporum,* rose, *Schinus* and several palms. Although it is a common and omnivorous species, its biology has not been studied in detail. In subtropical climates, the lesser snow scale engages in continuous reproduction, and produces several generations each year. The male scale is of a different shape than the female. Section C is a photograph of empty scale covers of emerged males. The female is about 2 mm long (E) and has the form of an oyster shell. It feeds on the bark, fruit and leaves of the host plant. In Florida, many individuals of this species are killed by parasitic wasps.

The citrus snow scale, *Unaspis citri,* occurs only on *Citrus* species. Like the lesser snow scale, the male of this species is white; the female is brown, and sometimes nearly black. It, too, is found only in Florida and California.

Pinnaspis aspidistrae (Signonet), the fern scale, is common in the Southeast, particularly on *Liriope,* and in greenhouses in the North. It has numerous hosts but its biology is unknown.

Quernaspis (= *Chionaspis*) *quercus* (Comstock) occurs in New Mexico and California (D). It apparently is found only on the bark of *Quercus lobata, Q. agrifolia* and the tan oak, *Lithocarpus densiflora.* This species causes little damage to its host though the bark of some trees may appear white because of the abundance of the old male scale covers. The biology of this scale is unknown.

References: 67, 181

A. Stems of the shrub *Leucophyllum frutescens* encrusted with the lesser snow scale, *Pinnaspis strachani.*
B. A stem killed by *Pinnaspis strachani.*
C. A close-up of a cluster of lesser snow scale males. Female scales blend so well with the bark that they are not visible in this photograph.
D. Male scales of *Quernaspis quercus* on *Quercus agrifolia* in Belmont, California.
E. Hidden female scale. The arrow points to *Pinnaspis strachani.* The circle outlines an unidentified female scale. Male scales have emerged from the white scale covers.
F. Two adult female scales with their covers removed. A female *Pinnaspis strachani* is shown at the arrow point.

PLATE 164

White Peach Scale (Plate 165)

The white peach scale, *Pseudaulacaspis pentagona* (Targioni-Tozzetti), was first described in 1886 in Italy. It has been a serious pest in the United States since the early 1900's. The white peach scale is also known as the West Indian peach scale. It has been one of the most serious pests of fruits, especially peach and cherry. It is also very destructive to ornamental trees and shrubs including flowering cherry, plum, peach, privet, lilac, walnut, catalpa, chinaberry, persimmon, *Hibiscus*, chinese elm, golden raintree, honeysuckle, redbud, spiraea, dogwood, and many others. Dekle (67) lists 97 hosts in Florida. Kwansan cherry, *Prunus serrulata* Kwansan, is a favorite host of this species and has increased in popularity as an ornamental tree. White peach scale has become a major pest where this tree is grown. The white peach scale is common on the east coast of the United States, from Long Island southward. Although it has been reported as far north as Connecticut, it has not been observed in that state for two or three decades. In 1930, peach production in Florida came to a standstill because of damage done by the white peach scale. In the Carolinas and Virginia, it is an important stonefruit pest.

In northern Florida, the white peach scale has four generations each year. From the Carolinas north through Maryland there are three generations. On Long Island, New York, there are generally two generations per year, although an unusually long growing season may provide time for a third.

The white peach scale overwinters as an adult female. In North Carolina, the female begins to deposit her eggs in early April. Each female produces more than 100 eggs. The peak of the egg-hatching season for first-generation eggs is during the first week of May in North Carolina and Virginia. The peak egg-hatching season for second-generation eggs is during the first week of August; for third-generation eggs, during the first week of September. Since the eggs of any one generation are laid during a period that extends over one month, the crawlers also emerge over a similar period of time. Bennett and Brown (23) have reported that females are produced first and males later. Female embryos are coral in color; male embryos are whitish pink. The color difference remains distinct through the crawler stage until the end of the first instar. In the adult stage, the cover of the male scale is bright white (D). The female scale is larger, but is gray in color and thus less conspicuous. Infestations appear more intense during periods when males mature. Large masses of cottony secretions are quite apparent.

The white peach scale feeds primarily on the bark of the trunk and larger limbs. It is not uncommon for the bark of entire trees to be thoroughly encrusted with scales. Populations build up rapidly, resulting in the death of large branches and, frequently, entire trees.

Smith (263) observed that considerable natural mortality occurs in the first two generations in North Carolina and that the scale spreads mostly during the third generation in the fall.

Parasitic and predaceous insects are numerous. Coccinellids include the twice-stabbed lady beetle, *Chilocorus stigma* (Say), *Lindorus lophanthae* (Blaisdell), and *Exochomus childreni* Muls. in Florida. The wasp parasites *Prospaltella berlesi* (Howard) and *Aspidiotiphagus citrinus* (Craw.) along with a predaceous thrips and a mite species in the family *Belbidae* have also been reported there.

References: 23, 67, 263

A. Males of the white peach scale, *Pseudaulacaspis pentagona*, heavily encrusted on the bark of flowering cherry.

B. Female white peach scales in profile.

C. Heavily encrusted white peach scales on lilac.

D. Male and female (at arrow) white peach scales on flowering cherry.

E. A privet hedge damaged by white peach scale.

F. Catalpa trees severely injured by white peach scales.

G. A lady beetle in the act of emerging from its pupa. The larva had been feeding on the young scales.

PLATE 165

Fiorinia Scale Insects (Plate 166)

Five species of *Fiorinia* are known to occur in the United States. They are the tea scale, *F. theae* Green; the palm fiorinia scale, *F. fioriniae* (Targ.); the juniper fiorinia scale, *F. juniperi* (Bouche); the Japanese fiorinia scale, *F. japonica* Kuwana; and the hemlock fiorinia scale, *F. externa* Ferris (see Plate 36). The palm fiorinia scale and the tea scale, the two species which commonly occur in the South, are discussed here.

Dekle (67) has called the tea scale one of the ten pests considered most harmful to ornamentals in Florida nurseries. It is widely distributed throughout the deep South, and is very difficult to control. Twenty-five host species are known in Florida. Of these, camellia, Chinese holly, and burford holly are frequently infested. The following genera are hosts in Florida: *Aucuba, Callistemon, Camellia, Citrus, Cornus, Euonymus, Eurya, Gardenia, Gordonia, Ilex, Malpighia, Mangifera, Melaleuca, Osmanthus, Poncirus, Rubescens, Senecio, Symplocos,* and *Thea*.

The tea scale was first described from specimens found on the tea bush in India. It is now widely distributed in that country on tea bushes as well as on *Citrus*. In Japan, it occurs on *Eurya japonica*. In the United States, it is frequently intercepted after being discovered on nursey stock shipped northward from the South. However, it has not been reported to be established north of the Carolinas and southeastern Virginia, except in greenhouses where it is occasionally found on camellias. It has not been a serious pest in California.

This scale insect occurs on the leaves of its host (B). It is a small scale. The adult female is about 1.3 mm long; the male is two-thirds that length. Females are elongate oval, and their coloring ranges from dark brown or dark gray to almost black (D). After molting, the second-instar scale cover completely covers the insect. Male scales are narrow and snow-white in color (C). When populations of this pest become dense, long white waxy filaments are produced so profusely that the undersides of infested leaves take on a conspicuous cottony appearance (A).

Ten to sixteen yellow eggs are laid by the female, and remain beneath her body until they hatch in one to three weeks. The crawlers are also bright yellow, and settle permanently in a feeding position on the leaf, two to three days after they hatch. This species occurs on the undersides of the leaves, and requires from 40 to 65 days to complete its life cycle. A number of overlapping generations occurs in a year, resulting in the presence of all stages of the scale at any time during this period.

In Florida, the palm fiorinia scale, *F. fioriniae*, has been reported on 29 species of plants in 23 genera. These hosts are chiefly various palms and bays (*Persea, Gordonia, Camellia, Podocarpus,* and *Magnolia virginiana*). The palm fiorinia scale is not considered to be the cause of any severe economic losses in Florida. The female is elliptical, about 1.3 mm long, and has translucent yellow- to orange-brown coloring (F). Males are absent or rare; no filamentous wax is associated with this species.

Little is known of the life history of the palm fiorinia scale, but all stages may be present at the same time. This suggests the existence of a number of overlapping generations. The insects infest both the upper and lower surfaces of the leaves.

The geographical distribution of this species is unknown. It has been found in both California and Florida.

References: 67, 103, 299, 312

A. Cottony appearance and thin foliage of a camellia which is infested with tea scale.
B. Typical appearance of a tea scale infestation on a burford holly leaf.
C. Abundance of filamentous wax from male tea scales.
D. Females, and a male (at arrow) of *Fiorinia theae*, the tea scale.
E. Typical appearance of camellia infested with *Fiorinia fioriniae*.
F. Settled crawlers, immatures, and adult females of *Fiorinia fioriniae* on Persea.

PLATE 166

Fourlined Plant Bug (Plate 167)

Poecilocapsus lineatus (Fabricus) is the scientific name for the fourlined plant bug. Since the common name for this insect is so descriptive of its characteristics, the scientific name is rarely used. The fourlined plant bug is an insect of some beauty in both the adult and nymphal stages. The nymphs have a coloring that varies from bright red to yellow (D). The fore wings of the adult are yellow, but may turn bright green. However, the four stripes (which give the insect its name) always remain distinct.

The fourlined plant bug feeds upon a wide range of cultivated, herbaceous plants. The woody ornamental plants include currant, rose, weigela, forsythia, amur maple, sumac, and viburnum (B).

The biology and seasonal history of this species have not been fully explored. Eggs are laid in early summer in the Northeast but do not hatch until the following spring. Thus, this species overwinters as an egg. Eggs are laid, six to eight at one location, in slits cut by adult females in the canes of currant, weigelia and other woody plants. A single generation of the fourlined plant bug occurs for about six weeks during late May and June.

Only a few fourlined plant bugs can cause great damage to a host plant. Therefore, it is usually best to eradicate these insects if they appear on ornamental plantings. The topmost, young leaves of the host are the first to be injured. A reddish-brown spot (B) indicates a feeding injury. The color of the damaged portions of leaves attacked by this insect ranges from white to almost black, depending on the host. The sharp mouthparts of the attacking insects pierce the leaf tissue to feed. During the feeding process all of the chlorophyll is removed, and a toxic salivary secretion is injected. When a great amount of feeding occurs on a single plant, individual feeding spots may coalesce to form a large, brown blotch and/or leaf distortion.

The fourlined plant bug is widely distributed throughout the northern United States and in parts of Canada.

Neolygus viburni (Knight) is a small, yellowish-brown plant bug, 5 mm in length, that feeds upon *Viburnum lentago*. In New York State, this bug often occurs in such numbers that foliage of its host is badly injured. Its distribution ranges from Minnesota and Illinois east through Pennsylvania to Connecticut.

References: 31, 312

A,B. Injury to amur maple (A) and forsythia caused by fourlined plant bugs.

C. An adult fourlined plant bug, about 7 mm in length. The stripe color may vary from yellow to green.

D. A fourlined plant bug nymph.

PLATE 167

Plant Bugs (Plate 168)

The plant bugs shown in this plate cause two types of injury as illustrated in sections A, B, C and D. *Lygus lineolaris* (Beau.) is commonly known as the tarnished plant bug (E). It is perhaps the most numerous and harmful of the true bugs (Order, Hemiptera) in the northeastern quadrant of the United States. The adult goes into hibernation in the fall and becomes active in the early spring, about the time the first leaves begin to form. Its host plants include weeds, vegetables, fruit trees and a wide variety of ornamental flowers, shrubs and trees. In the spring, it feeds upon young tender twigs, but prefers leaves or fruit. Eggs are laid mainly on the stems and flowers of herbaceous plants. After hatching, the young nymphs move around readily, but usually remain to feed upon the plant selected by the parent until they mature. Adults are capable flyers and readily move from place to place. There may be two to five generations each year. By late summer this pest usually becomes very abundant. The illustration in section A shows plant injury attributed to the tarnished plant bug. The tarnished plant bug occurs throughout the United States. In the western United States, however, related species which cause similar injury are more numerous.

Boxelder bugs, *Leptocoris trivittatus* Say, are often an enormous nuisance around homes where *Acer negundo* is used as a shade tree. They are especially troublesome in the Mississippi River Valley. This species is known throughout the eastern United States and west to Nevada.

In the fall, boxelder bugs become gregarious and crowd together, usually on the south sides of trees, buildings and rocks exposed to the sun. After large masses of boxelder bugs congregate, they fly to nearby buildings to hibernate for the winter as adults. They are a nuisance to occupants, and are considered to be a common household pest. In the spring, boxelder bugs emerge from hibernation when buds of the boxelder trees open. In the spring, adults fly back to their host plants where they spend the active growing season.

The eggs may be laid almost anywhere on the host plant, but normally are deposited in crevices in the bark of boxelder trees. The empty shells of the egg of this pest are shown in section J. When freshly laid, the eggs are red. After hatching, the nymphs (F) make their way to the foliage. They suck the plant sap from newly developing leaves which later grow in distorted shapes (B,C). They also feed on boxelder flowers and seeds. Populations of boxelder bugs have been reported widely to develop only on the female boxelder trees.

In the warmer parts of the range of this pest, there may be two generations a year. Otherwise, one generation develops each year.

Leptocoris rubrolineatus (I) is similar to the boxelder bug, but it is found only in the states bordering the Pacific Ocean. It feeds on boxelder and other maples. Leaf distortion and discoloration (C) results from the feeding activities of *L. rubrolineatus* Barber.

Future studies may reveal greater variation in the habits of this species. A boxelder bug, presumably *L. rubrolineatus*, has been reported to feed on almond and other fruit trees in California. Adults lay their eggs on leaves and nuts. When feeding, the nymphs and adults pierce the husk of the nut with their sharp mouthparts, thereby causing a black spot to form on the kernel. The injury cannot be seen until the kernel is removed from the shell.

References: 93, 129, 170

A. Injury to *Ilex crenata* believed to have been caused by the tarnished plant bug.

B,C. Leaves of boxelder, *Acer negundo*, injured by *Leptocoris rubrolineatus*, the western boxelder bug.

D. A *Raphiolepsis* leaf injured by a plant bug. An injured leaf becomes distorted and covered with spots.

E. Adult tarnished plant bug, *Lygus lineolaris*.

F. A nymph of *Leptocoris trivittatus*.

G. An adult boxelder bug, *Leptocoris trivittatus*.

H. A milkweed bug. Notice the resemblance between this species and the boxelder bug.

I. An adult *Leptocoris rubrolineatus*.

J. Empty egg shells of *Leptocoris trivittatus*.

PLATE 168

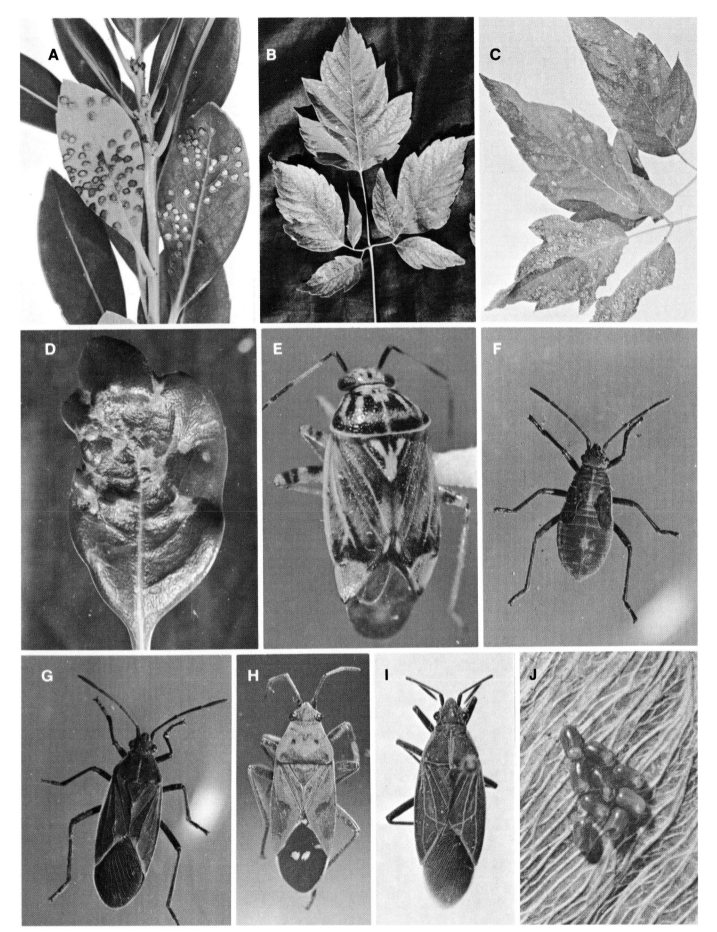

Plant Bugs (Plate 169)

The sycamore plant bug, *Plagiognathus albatus* (Van Duzee), can severely injure the leaves of *Platanus occidentalis* and *P. acerifolia* (A,B). It has also been found on *Juglans nigra* and *J. cinerea*. Little is known about the biology of this insect. On Long Island, New York, injury by this pest on sycamore becomes noticeable about the first week in July. Where the insect's mouthparts pierce the host's leaf tissue, a brown spot appears. In a short time this spot drops out. As feeding continues, the damage increases in severity. By mid-July, the entire leaf may appear tattered, yellowed, and riddled with holes (A,B). The sycamore plant bug feeds only on young leaves.

Plagiognathus albatus has been found in the eastern half of the United States and in Quebec, Canada.

Kunzeana kunzii (Gill.) is a very small leafhopper, approximately two mm in length. It is predominantly dull green and occurs in the southwestern United States. It is believed to feed primarily on legumes. Sections E and F show the injury that this pest causes to *Acacia decurrens*. *K. kunzii* feeds on the undersides of leaves. It is often abundant in northern California during October. Little is known about the biology and seasonal history of this species. This leafhopper looks somewhat like those shown on Plate 176, section B.

Reference: 157

A. *Platanus acerifolia* showing the outer leaves injured by the plant bug *Plagiognathus albatus*.
B. A London plane tree leaf showing injury typical of that caused by the sycamore plant bug.
C,D. *Plagiognathus albatus* adults on the upper and lower surfaces of a London plane tree leaf. About 5 mm long.
E,F. *Acacia decurrens* showing the yellowed, stippled foliage caused by a leafhopper, *Kunzeana kunzii*, in California.

PLATE 169

Ash Plant Bugs (Plate 170)

Tropidosteptes amoenus Reuter, a plant bug (D), is primarily an eastern species, though it is found as far west as Texas and Montana. It is likely to occur also in southern Canada. During the growing season, this species produces two generations on both *Fraxinus americana* and *F. pennsylvanica*. These insects remain on the trees from early summer until frost. As they increase to large numbers, they damage the autumn foliage.

Little is known about the seasonal history of *T. amoenus*, but it is believed that it overwinters as an egg imbedded in the bark of its host. After hatching, the young nymphs (G) feed on the undersides of the leaves. Nymphs can move rather rapidly, but are not easily motivated to do so. The leaf injury shown in section B occurred in western New York over a period of several weeks. The photograph was taken in late August and shows the severe accumulative damage.

Two plant bugs, *Tropidosteptes illitus* (Van Duzee) and *T. pacificus* (Van Duzee), cause damage to the foliage of ash in the western United States. *T. illitus* adults are uniformly light brown, and the nymphs of this species are brown. One generation occurs each year. *T. pacificus* adults (F) are black or brown with yellow markings and the nymphs are green with black spots.

They were accidentally introduced into Pennsylvania in 1973. Both species produce two generations each year.

Like the eastern species, *amoenus*, the western species lay their eggs in the thin bark of their ash tree hosts. The eggs hatch in early spring and the nymphs feed on new leaves, causing a yellow stippling. The varnish-like excrement, from the insects, spots the lower surface of infested leaves. Feeding by these pests on the leaf stem and petioles leads to wilting or curling and drying of the leaf blade. The western species of plant bugs occasionally cause defoliation of ash in the Sacramento Valley of California. However, defoliation caused by the anthracnose fungus, *Gloeosporium aridum*, is far more severe and important than that resulting from ash bug infestations. Whatever the cause of defoliation, affected trees put out a new flush of foliage after the causal agent has disappeared. By June or July, both *T. illitus* and *T. pacificus* have completed their activities for the year and are not seen until the following spring.

All three species of ash bugs limit their feeding to ash leaves.

References: 157, 290

A. *Fraxinus velutina* leaves showing injury symptoms caused by *Tropidosteptes illitus*. Note dead leaves at the growing tip. This injury occurs early in the season.

B. A nursery cultivar of *Fraxinus americana*. The mottled yellow color of the leaves is a result of feeding injury caused by *Tropidosteptes amoenus*.

C. *Fraxinus velutina* leaflets. Yellow discoloration, dead leaf margins, and excrement spots on both upper and lower leaf surfaces were caused by *Tropidosteptes illitus*.

D. *Tropidosteptes amoenus* adult; the eastern species.

E. A plant bug, western species, going through its final molt; arrow indicates black bands on its legs.

F. *Tropidosteptes pacificus* adult; western species.

G. An immature plant bug; eastern species.

PLATE 170

Plant Bug, and Leafhopper of Locust (Plate 171)

Diaphnocoris chlorionis (Say), the honeylocust plant bug (D), and *Macropsis fumipennis* (G & B), a leafhopper (E), are pests of *Gleditsia triacanthos*. These insects may be found together on the same tree, making it difficult to distinguish the injury caused by each. Early in the spring the honeylocust plant bug causes discoloration, stunting, and deformation of the foliage that persists throughout the season (A,C). Severe infestation may result in twig dieback. Adults occur from the end of May until early July. One generation occurs each year. Eggs are laid and overwinter in woody tissue, and begin to hatch in late April in central Pennsylvania.

D. chlorionis feeds on both honeylocust and black locust. It is found generally throughout the eastern half of the United States and in California. Sections A and C show the symptoms that occurred in Ithaca, New York, in late June. The same symptoms occur in early June along the Ohio River.

M. fumipennis feeds on shrubs and trees. Among its hosts are *Salix, Populus, Prunus, Quercus* and *Ulmus. Gleditsia tricanthos* appears to be a favorite. It has been found in Idaho, Colorado, Montana, the Ohio River Valley and south to Louisiana, as well as in New York State.

Other plant bugs that commonly feed upon *Gleditsia* are *Plagiognathus gleditsiae* Knight and *P. delicatus* (Uhler). As adults their color is generally reddish yellow to brown. Both of these adult insects are about 3 mm long. *P. delicatus* is found in the north central states, and in New York, Pennsylvania and Virginia. *P. gleditsiae* is reported only from Illinois and Texas.

Section B shows injury to *Juglans nigra* caused by a plant bug belonging to the genus *Plagiognathus*.

References: 157, 219

A. Injury on *Gleditsia tricanthos* caused by both *Diaphnocoris chlorionis* and *Macropsis fumipennis*. The yellow spots on the foliage are a common symptom of damage attributed to the leafhopper.
B. Injury to *Juglans nigra* caused by *Plagiognathus punctatipes*.
C. A newly formed leaflet injured by *Diaphnocoris chlorionis*.
D. The plant bug, *Diaphnocoris chlorionis*. Length is 3.7 mm.
E. The leafhopper, *Macropsis fumipennis*. Length is 4.5 mm.

PLATE 171

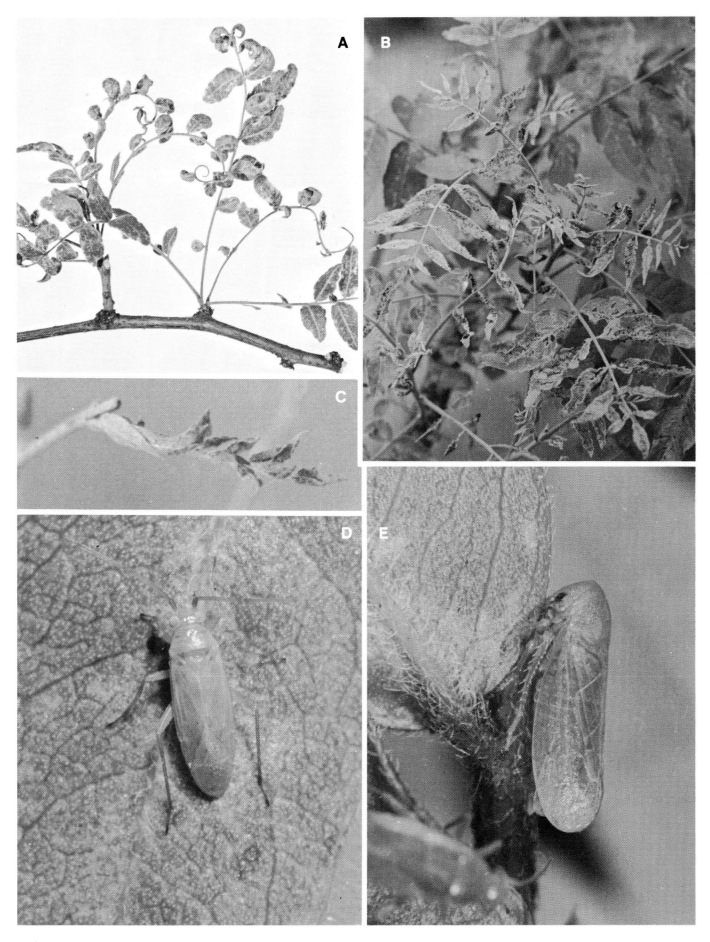

Treehoppers (Plate 172)

Treehoppers are strange-looking creatures with bizarre forms; some have been described as resembling miniature dinosaurs. They feed by inserting their sharp, needle-like mouthparts into plant tissues and sucking out cell fluids. Injury to the plant host is primarily caused by females of this species. They cut slits in the young bark in preparation for egg-laying. Eggs are then deposited in these slits in the bark.

The buffalo treehopper, *Stictocephala bubalus* (Fabricus), may be found throughout much of the United States and Canada. It lays eggs in the early fall under the bark (C) of many kinds of trees and shrubs including maple, crabapple, elm, hawthorn, cherry, locust, poplar, ash, and quince. These eggs (D) remain under the bark throughout the winter, and hatch late in the spring. The young nymphs are green and their bodies are very spiny. After hatching, they drop to the ground and feed on various weeds and grasses until they reach maturity (G) in August. They then fly to trees to lay their eggs, and remain until they are killed by cold temperatures. Oviposition is facilitated by a sharp, knife-like ovipositor which the female uses to cut slits in the bark. Eggs are forced to the right and left under the bark through the slit (C,D). Scar tissue later forms in the shape of a double crescent, a characteristic of past injury by this pest (B). The bark of such injured twigs is roughened, and thereafter never grows very vigorously. Canker and other disease-causing fungi gain entrance through these slits. Small twigs which have been thus injured may die from desiccation.

Glossonotus acuminatus (Fabricius) is common, but not abundant, in late summer (E). It is found on oak, locust, chestnut, pear, and probably many other trees and shrubs. Little is known of its biology and life history.

Platycotis vittata (Fabricius) and its relatives are distributed locally over much of the United States, but occur most commonly in southern and coastal areas. There has been one report of its collection on Vancouver Island, British Columbia.

These treehoppers overwinter as eggs and have a single annual generation in the North. In Florida, there may be two annual broods but the main brood occurs in early spring. Eggs are laid in the bark of twigs. Both the nymph and adult stages feed on twigs. Damage is minor, and is confined mostly to the small scars caused by oviposition in the twigs. Both the nymphs and adults may be found together, for they often occur in compact colonies.

In Florida, nymphs of *P. vittata* have been found on *Quercus laurifolia, Q. nigra, Q. laevis, Q. virginiana* and *Citrus mitis*. On the west coast, they have been found primarily on *Quercus agrifolia* and *Q. ilex*. In other areas, adults have been found on red oak, white oak, *Quercus marilandica, Betula nigra* and *B. alba*.

The nymphs are very colorful (F). Adults are dull grayish and are sometimes marked with stripes or spots. They usually have a frontal horn.

References: 34, 93, 184, 220

A. The bark of a red maple, *Acer rubrum*, twig with numerous oviposition scars of *Stictocephala bubalus*, the buffalo treehopper. Arrow indicates old eggshells.
B. Elm twig damaged by the buffalo treehopper. Arrow indicates a double crescent scar.
C. The same twig as that shown in section B. Bark has been peeled away from the wood to reveal egg clusters.
D. A close-up of egg clusters of the buffalo treehopper on elm. The bark has been peeled back to show the eggs.
E. An adult treehopper, *Glossonotus acuminatus*.
F. Nymphs of *Platycotis vittata* in various stages of development. Horizontal arrow indicates a newly molted nymph. Vertical arrow indicates adult.
G,H. Adult buffalo treehoppers, *Stictocephala bubalus*.

PLATE 172

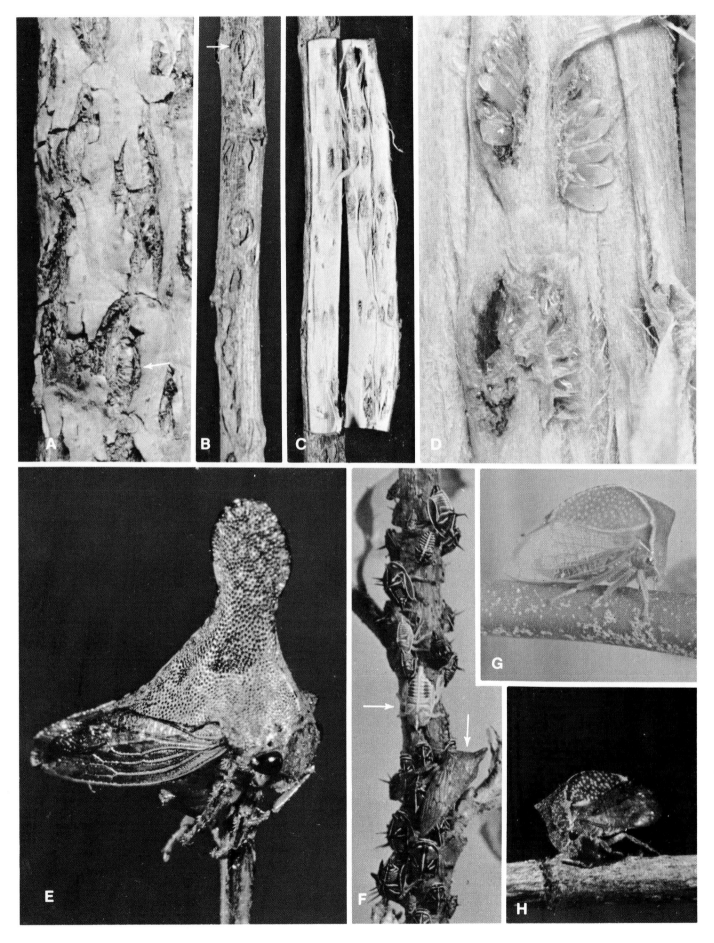

Thornbug and Relatives (Plate 173)

The thornbug, *Umbonia crassicornis* A. and S., is a treehopper that is found rather abundantly in Florida. It is considered to be a subtropical insect. The thornbug is aptly named, for as it clings to the stem of a plant it closely resembles a thorn. The naturalist takes special interest in the thornbug because of its striking color and bizarre form (see Figure 29). The male and female have different forms (C). The thornbug's shape provides a measure of protection from its enemies.

The female lays her eggs in a mass under the tender bark of twigs. The eggs hatch in about 20 days; the mother stays nearby. Upon hatching she tends to her brood, actively maintaining the colony. Nymph clusters, or colonies, range in size from 15 to 50 individuals. The young (nymphs) have three horns rather than one (B). Nymphs, as well as adults, injure plants by sucking sap from the bark of twigs. Females also cut slits in the bark as a feeding aid for newly hatched nymphs and as a place to deposit their eggs. Four generations of thornbugs occur per year. Thornbugs may injure humans too. There are reports of barefoot children having stepped on the spines of thornbugs that have dropped from trees. Wounds are slow to heal and sometimes become infected.

Some trees (*Cassia* species, for example) prematurely drop their leaves when injured by the thornbug. Dead terminal twigs often are a result of attack on *Pithecellobium* species. The thornbug produces large quantities of honeydew which becomes a nuisance when it drops on cars or outdoor living areas such as patios. Dense clusters of nymphs and adults are frequently seen on *Hibiscus* species, *Albizia lebbeck*, *Acacia* species, *Jacaranda acutifolia*, *Delonix regia*, *Callistemon* species, *Calliandra* and *Mimosa*. The range of some of the host plants exceeds the present known range of the thornbug.

Figure 29. Not a cartoon but true likenesses of treehoppers. (Drawing by Anna Botsford Comstock, Cornell University Press)

References: 189, 322

A. A cluster of thornbugs, *Umbonia crassicornis*, on *Albizia lebbeck*, commonly called woman's tongue tree. Adults are 8–10 mm long.
B. Preserved specimens. From left to right: a male, female, and two nymphal stages.
C,D,F. Mostly female thornbugs. A male is indicated by the arrow in section C.
E. An unidentified treehopper collected in New York State that also might be described as a thornbug. Note oviposition slit at arrow.

PLATE 173

Treehoppers (Plate 174)

An interesting group of insects collectively called membracids or treehoppers, injure many woody plants. They damage the host during their egg-laying stage.

Enchenopa binotata Say overwinters as an egg embedded in the bark of trees. Eggs hatch during May and early June. The nymphs congregate at the growing tips of twigs where they feed by sucking sap. During early development, the nymphs do not resemble their parents. Their bodies are black and they have white markings. There are several spine-like structures extending from their abdomens. After about five weeks, they molt and become adults (E). Adults, like nymphs, are gregarious and arrange themselves one behind the other in rows on twigs.

E. binotata begins oviposition in August and ends it in October. The eggs are laid under thin bark, in slits similar to those shown in sections B and C (see also Plate 172). After the eggs are laid, the female covers the slit with a white frothy substance (E). The froth has a sticky consistency and is laid down in ridges. After several weeks the froth appears to be a solid covering. The froth acts as an insulation from both heat and cold, and helps hold the eggs at high humidity. It has been postulated that the froth also protects the eggs from parasites.

The foodplants of *E. binotata* include hoptree, *Ptelea trifoliata;* black walnut; butternut; black locust; viburnum; redbud, *Cercis canadensis;* and bittersweet, *Celastrus scandens.* Reportedly, this insect has also been found on *Wisteria.* Its range is quite extensive, covering most of the eastern half of the United States.

Reference: 321

A. *Viburnum lentago* (hybrid). The numerous oviposition scars were caused by *Enchenopa binotata.* These scars will remain for years.
B. Oviposition slit, in the bark of *Juglans nigra.*
C. The same slit as in section B, cut open to show eggs of an unidentified treehopper.
D. Hoptree, *Ptelea trifoliata,* twigs covered with froth which has been deposited over the slits where eggs were laid.
E. Two female treehoppers, *Enchenopa binotata,* alongside froth masses.

PLATE 174

Rose Leafhopper (Plate 175)

The rose leafhopper, *Edwardsiana rosae* (Linnaeus), is widely distributed throughout the United States and southern Canada. Its chief foodplants belong to the rose family, including the cultivated rose. The rose, however, serves as the foodplant for but one of the several annual generations of this leafhopper. Nymphs of summer generations feed on *Cornus* (Plate 176), *Prunus, Crataegus, Malus, Populus, Ulmus, Acer* and others.

The fall brood of eggs is deposited within the bark of canes of wild or cultivated rose. Bush fruits such as blackberry and raspberry and are also hosts of the rose leafhopper. Egg deposition often occurs before the first frost or onset of cool weather. The presence of eggs is indicated by dark, pimple-like spots on the cane growth. In studies by Childs (46), 577 eggs were found per lineal inch of rose cane. Eggs usually hatch in the spring after the threat of frost is past. The young nymphs are white and have red eyes. They wander about the plant until they find a suitable leaf. Then they establish themselves on the underside of the leaf. If food is plentiful they may pass their entire nymphal development on the same leaf. By the fourth molt, the red coloring in the eyes disappears. The first-brood adults may vacate rose leaves for other woody plants (listed above). They insert eggs into the plant tissue on the undersides of the leaves. The eggs soon hatch and a summer generation continues to develop.

Rose leafhopper nymphs always move forward, never sideways, as is the case with many leafhoppers.

Plant injury occurs in three ways: by destruction of the chlorophyll, by removal of plant fluids and by winter egg deposition. An insect that feeds continually on an apple leaf, for example, during its nymphal development will remove or destroy from one-third to one-half of the green chlorophyll. Injured leaves often drop prematurely. Fungus diseases (often stem cankers) enter rose canes when the tissues are cut by the leafhopper's egg-laying apparatus. Such diseases often kill the less hardy cultivated rose.

Roses are a primary ornamental plant affected by the rose leafhopper (B). The feeding and egg laying of the rose leafhopper on rose may be sufficient to kill the plants. The rose leafhopper is an immigrant from Europe. It does not suffer to any great extent from the attack of predaceous and parasitic enemies, although the wasp egg parasite, *Anagrus armatus* (Ashm.), has been known to reduce populations to the level where no other control measures need be taken. Lacewings such as *Chrysopa californica* Coquillett and *Hemerobius pacificus* Banks are predators.

References: 46, 256, 307, 312

A. An adult rose leafhopper.
B. Typical leaf injury caused primarily by the feeding of nymphs.
C. A fifth-instar nymph.
D. A molted "skin" of a leafhopper nymph found on the underside of a leaf.

PLATE 175

Leafhoppers (Plate 176)

There are hundreds of species of leafhoppers that feed upon the leaves of ornamental trees and shrubs. Many are difficult to identify and most have a variety of food plants. Present taxonomic methods rely on dissection of male reproductive structures for positive identification. On the facing plate are shown typical symptoms of injury caused by leafhoppers belonging to four genera: *Edwardsiana, Empoasca, Erythroneura* and *Alebra.* Many species of all these genera are attracted to incandescent and fluorescent light at night.

Several generations of leafhoppers may occur each year. The leafhoppers are serious vectors of destructive virus and mycoplasma diseases. These diseases are more prevalent on cultivated herbaceous plants than on trees. A notable exception is phloem necrosis of elm and possibly some of the witchesbroom diseases.

The leaves of flowering dogwood become white and stippled due to the leafhopper's activities. In the northern Rocky Mountains and on the west coast *Edwardsiana commissuralis* (Stål) is the species that causes this type of injury. A species of *Erythroneura* causes similar injury to redbud, *Cercis,* in Ohio and other eastern states. Eight species of *Erythroneura* feed and lay eggs upon birch trees in New Brunswick, Canada.

The buckeye, *Aesculus californica,* is subject to severe injury by certain leafhoppers in California. The injury shown in section G is caused by a species of *Empoasca.* The California buckeye is a favorite host and is a common ornamental tree in central and northern California. Because of the dry climate, the leaves of this tree normally drop by early August. When the *Empoasca* leafhopper is present, however, leaf drop may occur one month before this time. These hoppers cause a disease condition called hopperburn. The leaves of trees suffering from hopperburn are brown at the edges, and the leaf tips curl upward. The symptoms shown in section G are manifestations of injury caused by the leafhopper and by drought. The species attacking this tree sometimes bite humans. The bite is sharp but is usually not harmful.

The potato leafhopper, *Empoasca fabae* (Harris), attacks a wide variety of ornamental plants. It produces symptoms of injury on both leaves and twigs (E,F). In northern states, this species is not a problem every year. When it is sufficiently numerous, it can cause dwarfed and distorted leaves, and can kill twigs and small branches. On birch, the potato leafhopper feeds on the terminals of tender twigs. This injury may result in dead twigs and shortened, swollen internodes as well as distortion of leaves (E). The tree's crown then becomes more dense, but the tree is weakened and becomes sickly. Leafhopper-injured trees are more subject to winter injury as is evident from dead twig terminals on damaged trees in the spring of the next year (F).

In the North, the damage to trees is caused primarily by migrating adults. Presumably, they overwinter in the South and migrate north in the spring. Adults are green, are about 3 mm long, and have a row of six white spots on their backs near their heads. Immature leafhoppers, nymphs (B), have a peculiar habit of running sideways when disturbed. In the northern states, two or more generations may occur each year. The potato leafhopper occurs in the eastern half of the United States.

Sections C and D show injury caused to *Ulmus americana* by the leafhopper, *Alebra albostriella* (Fallen). This insect is known to feed on birch, hickory, oak, elm, and maple. Some authors have given it the common name, maple leafhopper. The adult is about 4 mm long.

This leafhopper overwinters in the egg stage on twigs of its host trees. When laid, the eggs are placed singly in longitudinal slits cut by the ovipositor of the female. These slits often form an almost complete circle around the twig, which may severely injure or kill it. Eggs of a single generation hatch about the same time. In the Washington, D. C. area, eggs hatch in late April. By the time the leaves are half-grown, pale-yellow nymphs swarm on the undersides of leaves. Small white spots appear on the upper leaf surface as symptoms of feeding injury. It takes about one month for nymphs to mature to adults. The new generation of adults begins to lay eggs in early June; by the middle of July, the adults have disappeared. Eggs remain in the bark for 10 months or more.

A. albostriella is an early season leafhopper in the East. On the West Coast, it occurs during midsummer. It is not a common species in the West. The injury shown on elm (C,D) occurred in late July in Oakland, California. From Ball's (16) description, the whitish discoloration made by this pest on elm leaves is the same symptom commonly seen on *Acer palmatum.*

References: 16, 47, 70, 219, 232, 291, 292

A. The light stippled spots on the upper side of this dogwood leaf were probably caused by the feeding of *Edwardsiana* sp.
B. An immature leafhopper on a birch leaf; about 2 mm long. Note the white eyes which are characteristic of the potato leafhopper.
C. Cast skins of the leafhopper, *Alebra albostriella,* on American elm.
D. Severe injury to elm leaves by *Alebra albostriella.*
E. A birch twig showing both twig and leaf injury symptoms. Potato leafhoppers caused this injury in early summer.
F. The winter state of a birch twig injured by potato leafhopper.
G. Buckeye leaves, severely injured by an *Empoasca* leafhopper.

PLATE 176

Flower Thrips and Leafhoppers (Plate 177)

Thrips are small, active insects measuring from 1 to 2 mm in length. Adults have distinctive wings fringed with relatively long hairs and fly readily. Some species migrate north and south. The adult thrips shown in section B is believed to be *Frankliniella tritici* (Fitch), the flower thrips. This species is the most abundant and widely distributed thrips in the United States. It has many overlapping generations. Under favorable conditions a complete life cycle may occur in two weeks. Thrips feed by rasping the soft plant tissue and sucking up the plant fluid. This causes necrotic spots or blotches on flower petals (A), or rough callous tissue on leaves (Plate 184, section H). Immature thrips are yellow and are usually hidden under flower petals.

Thrips breed primarily on various grasses, weeds, clover and alfalfa. Garden flowers and flowering woody ornamentals are generally infested by thrips that have come from these plants. *F. tritici* attracts attention when it damages rose buds. White roses seem to be more attractive to migrating thrips than those of any other color. Hawthorns are often attacked by flower thrips, injuring both flowers and flower buds. Sometimes the feeding injury is so severe that the bud will not open.

Control of thrips is difficult, especially during the migration period. In the Washington, D.C., area migration occurs in May and June. Thrips are subject to predation by aphid lions, by the larvae of lacewing flies, and by other predators. Late in the growing season, these predators often prevent thrips from increasing to larger populations.

On the west coast there are several large leafhoppers (about 7 mm long) commonly called sharpshooters (D) because of their sharp, pointed heads. They are brightly colored and are active jumpers and flyers. Both young leafhoppers and adults have a characteristic habit of running sideways. They suck sap from leaves, and the loss of sap causes the leaves to curl and to become spotted in a mosaic fashion.

The aster leafhopper (F), *Macrosteles fascifrons* (Stål), is a serious virus vector. Its spreads certain viruses to various vegetable and annual flowers. Periwinkle (*Vinca*) and *Thunbergia* are woody plants susceptible to the aster yellows virus; the aster leafhopper feeds upon both. Virus disease symptoms on periwinkle include chlorotic foliage and malformed flowers. *Thunbergia* responds to the virus infection by showing dwarfed leaves and chlorotic veins, and the plant loses its normal ability to climb.

The aster leafhopper is widespread throughout North America. It migrates from south to north each year, overwintering in the egg stage in the North. Four to five generations occur during the growing season in southern Ontario. The adult is greenish-yellow and is about 4 mm long.

References: 11, 35, 214

A. A rose flower injured by thrips of the genus *Frankliniella*. White flowers usually are most severely injured.
B. An adult thrips on rose.
C. A rose leaf showing crinkled leaves thought to be caused by adult sharpshooter leafhoppers.
D. A sharpshooter leafhopper, probably *Hordina circellata* (Baker).
E. Individuals of the above species seen from the underside.
F. The aster leafhopper, sometimes called the six-spotted leafhopper, is about 4 mm long. (Photo courtesy New York State Experiment Station, Geneva.)

PLATE 177

371

Planthoppers and Plant Bugs (Plate 178)

The planthoppers shown in this plate are related to the leaf-hoppers and spittlebugs. *Metcalfa pruinosa* (Say), as seen in sections B and C, belongs to a group called flatids. They are abundant throughout the United States and southern Canada but are probably more common in the southern states. *M. pruinosa* has a long list of foodplants such as hickory and pecan, oak, elm, birch, linden, ash, privet, camellia, azalea, viburnum, magnolia, holly, seagrape, cherry, laurel, and all of the flowering fruit trees such as flowering peach. The amount of injury caused to ornamental plants is believed to be rather insignificant, although oviposition punctures may kill small twigs. The white web-like flocculent material (A) made by the nymphs affects the ornamental value of a plant.

The insect overwinters as an egg inside the twigs of its host plant. There appears to be no particular oviposition pattern as is found with the treehoppers. Eggs are found scattered singly in the bark. In the Weslaco area of Texas, eggs hatch in late March. Nymphs develop on twigs and suck sap. They also feed on fruits of trees such as *Citrus*. In the south it takes about 9 weeks for the nymphs to develop into adults. Adult activity occurs over a period of approximately two months. Adults shown in this plate were collected in New York State on August 20. There is one generation each year.

A related species, *Ormenis septentrionalis* (Spinola), occurs on woody vines, boxwood, hawthorn, holly and others. Cottony fluff conceals the white nymphs. In the states along the eastern coast, adults, which have bluish-green wings, may be found from late June through August. They are more conspicuous than injurious.

The leaffooted bug is so named because of the shape of the tibia of the hind legs. There are several species of this insect; the one illustrated in section D is *Leptoglossus phyllopus* (Linnaeus). Leaffooted bugs are primarily found in the southern half of the United States, though they have been reported on Long Island, New York, and in Iowa, Colorado and Utah.

In the South, adults have been collected in all months of the year. However, peak populations occur during the warmer months.

The mouthparts of leaffooted bugs are particularly long and are capable of penetrating the husk of nut tree fruits when the fruit is in an early stage of development. Leaffooted bugs are among those insects that cause black pit in the kernels of pecan. Nymphs are similar in shape to adults but do not acquire the leaf-shaped legs until they are nearly grown. Eggs are golden brown and are laid in a single row along a stem or leaf midrib. Each egg looks like one of a series of longitudinal segments.

These bugs are likly to be of concern to the homeowner with yard trees, primarily fruit and nut trees. They feed on *Citrus*, peach, plum, pecan, and walnut, and cause blemishes, undersized fruit, or premature fruit drop. They feed on the fruit or flowers of blueberry, *Hibiscus*, loquat, persimmon, crape myrtle, *Ligustrum* and rose. Injury is caused by both the adult and nymph.

A related species, *Leptoglossus zonatus* (Dallas), is found in southern California. It also has the leaf-shaped tibia. Its biology and feeding behavior are essentially the same as those of the eastern species.

Acanthocephala femorata (Fab.) is a larger and more robust insect than the leaffooted plant bug (E). It, too, is primarily a southern species and is one of the relatively few insects that are both predators on other insects and plant feeders. This bug feeds on the cottonworm and causes damage to the fruits of cherry, citrus, peach, plum and pecan. It also feeds on flowers and flower buds. It is a rather fearsome looking creature but is of less economic importance than any of the other bugs mentioned above.

References: 62, 78, 117, 191

A. White cottony fluff produced by a nymph of the planthopper, *Metcalfa pruinosa*.
B. A dorsal view of *Metcalfa pruinosa*. The insect is 5.5 to 8 mm long.
C. A side view of *Metcalfa pruinosa*. Note color of the eyes.
D. An adult leaffooted bug, *Leptoglossus phyllopus*, on *Schinus terebinthifolius*.
E. The plant bug, *Acanthocephala femorata*. It is about 30 mm long.

PLATE 178

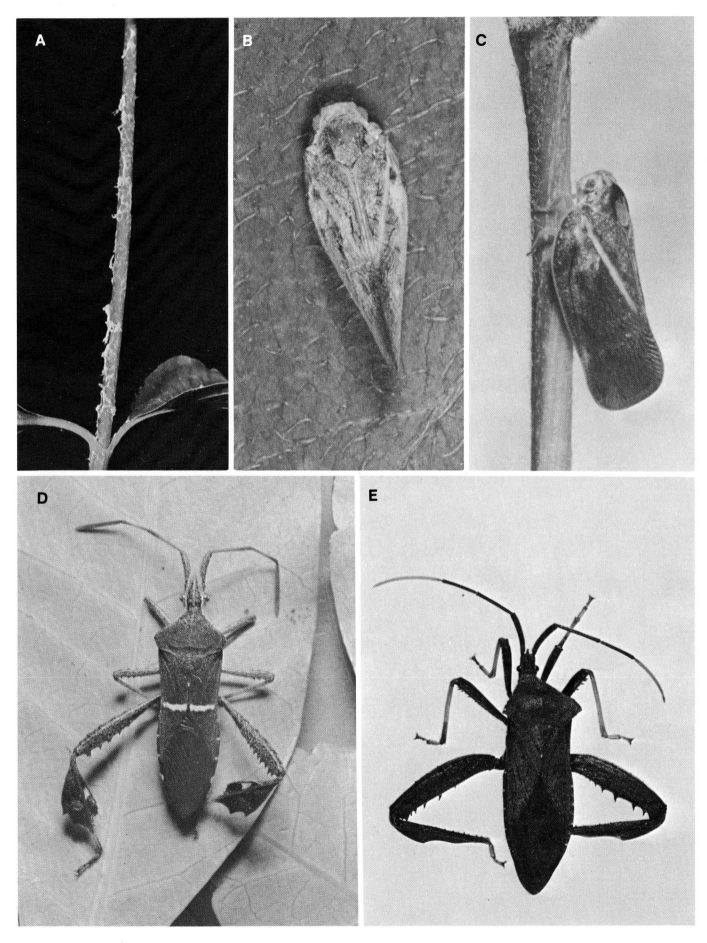

Lacebugs of Broad-leaved Evergreens (Plate 179)

In relation to injury on ornamental trees and shrubs, the *Tingidae* or lacebugs comprise the most important family in the order *Hemiptera*. In 1965 Drake and Ruhoff (79) published a monograph, "Lacebugs of the World," cataloguing 1,820 species in 236 genera. Of these, there are 3 major economic species in the genus *Stephanitis* that feed on ornamental broad-leaved evergreens in the United States.

Stephanitis pyrioides (Scott), a native of Japan, is a primary pest of azalea (D). It is found in New York and Massachusetts south to Florida and Alabama. *S. rhododendri* Horvath is a pest of rhododendron (C) and *Kalmia latifolia* and is found from southern Canada to Georgia, West Virginia, Ohio and Michigan; it is known also in Washington and Oregon. *S. takeyai* Drake and Maa, likewise a native of Japan, is a pest of andromeda (A) and *Leucothoe*. It occurs in New York, Connecticut, Rhode Island, New Jersey, Delaware and Pennsylvania.

Lacebug damage on broad-leaved evergreens is most common and severe on andromeda, azalea, laurel, pyracantha, and rhododendron. High populations of lacebugs, and consequently higher degrees of damage, occur on azalea and rhododendron when grown in sunny rather than shady locations; andromeda lacebug is damaging in both sun and shade.

The feeding of lacebugs is distinctively characteristic. It can be readily distinguished from that of other insects and mites. Lacebugs feed on the undersides of leaves but the damage is very

Figure 31. An adult cherry lacebug, *Corythucha pruni*. The wing color pattern is characteristic of this species.

apparent on the upper surface. Damage symptoms bear a strong similarity to those of leafhopper damage, but lacebugs produce varnish-like spots on the undersides of the leaves. An occasional shed skin of a leafhopper nymph is evidence of the cause of that damage. Lacebug damage may suggest mite injury from a distance. Feeding by mites causes chlorotic flecks in the leaves that are much finer than those caused by lacebugs. Close examination reveals that large numbers of contiguous cells are chlorotic where lacebugs have fed. Positive identification of lacebug damage is confirmed by the presence of brown patches or black droplets of excrement on the undersides of damaged leaves. Frequently, the cast "skins" of nymphs remain attached to the undersides of leaves. A nymph is shown in Figure 30.

Species that occur on broad-leaved evergreens overwinter as eggs. The eggs are either inserted into veins or cemented to the leaves with a brown crusty material. Eggs hatch in May in Virginia, and usually before the end of May further north. At least two generations occur each year in the North and three or more in the South. It is especially important to prevent damage on broad-leaved evergreens early in the season, since the foliage will retain the unsightly injury and be less functional for more than one year.

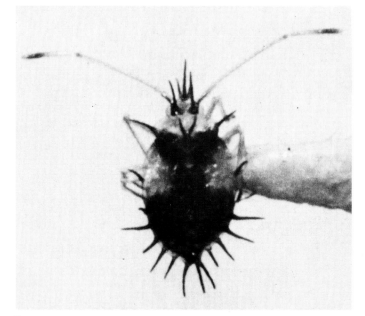

Figure 30. An immature azalea lacebug, *Stephanitis pyrioides*. Note its dark color and spines. Wings have not yet developed. (See also Plate 180)

References: 79, 252, 314

A. Lacebug injury on andromeda, caused by *Stephanitis takeyai*.
B. Varnish-like deposits from lacebugs on the undersides of andromeda leaves.
C. Leaves of rhododendron. Range of damage is from none to severe. Damage to leaves was caused by *Stephanitis rhododendri*.
D. "Varnish" spots on azalea, indicating a severe infestation. They were caused by *Stephanitis pyrioides*.
E. Typical appearance of the underside of a previously infested rhododendron leaf.
F. Early season lacebug damage to sycamore. Damage was caused by *Corythucha ciliata* (see Plate 180).

PLATE 179

Lacebugs of Deciduous Plants (Plate 180)

There are at least 27 species of lacebugs in the genus *Corythucha* that feed on deciduous trees and shrubs. Most have very specific host preferences which aid in making field identifications. The adults (A) are beautifully sculptured and resemble an intricate, lacy network. They range in size from 3 to 6 mm.

All the lacebugs of this genus overwinter as adults on their host in the bark crevices, branch crotches or similarly protective areas of their host. All generally have the same sequence of events in life cycle development. The sycamore lacebug, *Corythucha ciliata* (Say) (Plate 179, section F) shall be used as an example.

The adult lacebug arouses from hibernation about the time sycamore leaves begin to develop in spring. Eggs are attached to the underside of leaves with a brown sticky substance. Within a few days the eggs hatch and nymphs (see Figure 30 on page 374) begin feeding on the underside of the leaf. With sucking mouthparts they pierce the epidermis and withdraw fluids and cell contents causing the characteristic chlorotic flecks which are visible on the upper side of the leaf. The nymphs remotely resemble the adults. They are darker and their bodies are often covered with large, finely pointed spines. A complete cycle, from egg to adult, may develop in approximately 30 days. Several generations occur each year. The exact number depends upon the length of the growing season. In late summer all stages may be found feeding together. By this time the dark, varnish-like excrement (E) may cover most of the undersurfaces of the leaves. The western sycamore lacebug may so completely discolor the leaves that by the end of August, little or no food-manufacturing tissues are left.

The sycamore lacebug is found throughout the United States wherever sycamores or London plane trees are grown. Its natural enemies include lacewings, assassin bugs, spiders and predaceous mites.

References: 79, 193, 226, 284, 295

LACEBUGS AND THEIR HOST PLANTS

Primarily Eastern Species

Latin name	Common name	Host preference
Corythucha ciliata (Say)	sycamore lacebug*	sycamore
C. cydoniae (Fitch)	hawthorn lacebug*	Crataegus (hawthorn), pyracantha, Cydonia (quince)
C. ulmi O. & D.	elm lacebug	American elm (only)
C. juglandis (Fitch)	walnut lacebug*	butternut, black walnut, linden
C. arcuata (Say)	oak lacebug	oak species (variety *C. a. mali* Gib. found also on maples)
C. mollicula O. & D. (=canadensis Parsh.)	willow lacebug (no spines on margins)	willow
C. elegans Drake	willow and poplar lacebug	balsam poplar, quaking aspen, bigtooth aspen, willow
C. pallipes Parsh (=betula Drake =cyrta Parsh.)	birch lacebug	yellow birch, white birch, beech, eastern hophornbeam, willow spp., mountain ash, maple
C. celtidis O. & D.	hackberry lacebug	hackberry
C. aesculi O. & D.	buckeye lacebug	buckeye sp.
C. associata O. & D.	none	wild cherry
C. pruni O. & D.	cherry lacebug (Figure 31)	wild cherry
C. pergandei Heidemann	alder lacebug*	alder, also hazel, elm, birch, crabapple
C. tiliae (Walsh)	none	linden
C. bellula Gibson	none	Crataegus

Primarily Western Species

Latin name	Common name	Host preference
C. confraterna Gibson	western sycamore lacebug	sycamore
C. coelata Uhler	apple lacebug	apple
C. incurvata Uhler	California Christmas berry tingid	California Christmas berry (Plate 181)
C. heteromelecola Drake	California Christmas berry tingid	California Christmas berry
C. bullata Van Duzee	California Christmas berry tingid	California Christmas berry
C. obliqua O. D.	Ceanothus tingid	ceanothus* (Plate 181)
C. padi Drake	Choke cherry tingid	western choke cherry
C. salicata Gibson	western willow tingid	willow, apple
C. salicis O. & D.	eastern willow tingid*	willow
Gargaphia angulata Heidemann	angulate tingid	ceanothus*
Leptoypha minor McAtee	Arizona ash tingid	ash, poplar
L. costata Parshley	none	ash, hazel

* Found throughout the United States and parts of Canada.

A. An adult walnut lacebug, *Corythucha juglandis*, on the underside of a basswood leaf.

B,C. A range of injury symptoms, from a white stipple to brown blotches, caused by *Corythucha pallipes* as seen on the upper surface of mountain ash leaves.

D. Severe injury to mountain ash leaflets. View is of under-surface.

E. The lower surface of a hawthorn leaf showing the excrement spots deposited by the hawthorn lacebug, *C. cydoniae*.

F. The upper surface of the same leaf showing severe discoloration. All discolored tissue is dead.

G. The undersurface of a basswood leaf. Leaf injury and excrement spots of the walnut lacebug are apparent.

PLATE 180

Ceanothus Insects (Plate 181)

Lacebugs, or tingids, are common on certain western trees and shrubs but they have not attracted as much attention as those in the eastern United States. The western lacebugs occur predominantly on wild or native vegetation and usually are found in small populations.

Since the appearance and biology of western tingids vary little among the species, an account of only one of the tingids will be given. It is the California Christmas berry lacebug, *Corythucha incurvata* Uhler.

The adult California Christmas berry lacebug is a flattened insect with a distinctive reticulated dorsal surface which is lacelike in appearance (see plate 180). It measures about 3.3 mm in length and has a yellowish-brown back. It overwinters in the adult stage beneath the bark of the host or under fallen leaves, or other plant refuse on the ground. In the spring it returns to the foliage, where it inserts eggs into the underside of the leaf surface. In about a month the eggs hatch and the tiny nymphs insert their sucking mouthparts into the leaves and begin to remove the contents of the plant cells. The nymphs are oval, motile insects, heavily armed with large spines on the bodies (see Figure 30 on page 374 for an example of spines). All feeding is done from the undersurfaces of leaves. After five molts over a period of about six weeks, the adult stage appears. There are believed to be three annual broods each year in coastal central California.

Injury is caused by the withdrawal of plant fluids from small groups of cells in leaf tissue. This causes a coarse stippling of the leaves. When many insects congregate to feed on the same leaf a bleaching or overall yellowing of the foliage results. The nymphs produce honeydew, which drops to the foliage below and soon becomes blackened by sooty mold fungi. Many species of tingids excrete a varnish-like material which persists on the lower leaf surface, adding to the unsightliness of a lacebug-infested plant.

The ceanothus tingid (B), *C. obliqua* Osborn and Drake, is slightly larger than *C. incurvata* and has a pale dorsal surface with many small brown dots. It occurs on *Ceanothus* in California, Oregon, and Idaho.

The western willow tingid, *C. salicata* Gibson, is creamy white with several brown bands and spots on the back. It is found on willow and apple in Oregon and British Columbia.

On several species of *Ceanothus*, small white flocculent spheres are often associated with the leaves (D). This is a sign of the presence of a psyllid, *Euphalerus vermiculosus* Crawford. The cottony white material is formed by the immature psyllids, called nymphs. With rare exceptions, they always occur on the undersides of the leaves. Waxen threads are produced from the psyllid's body. The threads curl about themselves and cover the body of the nymph. A cell or cavity is formed inside this mass by the movements of the nymph. As the insect molts, its cast skins become entangled in the waxen threads and thus become a part of the flocculent covering. The waxen mass is not attached to the leaf except in a small area which surrounds the feeding site. When the nymph has completed its feeding stage, it leaves the cottony mass and develops into a free-flying adult psyllid. Noticeable injury to *Ceanothus* does not result from an infestation by *Euphalerus*. The flocculence on leaves may, however, be considered by some to be unsightly.

References: 93, 144, 226, 284

A. The brown spots on *Ceanothus* leaves are symptoms of severe injury done by Ceanothus lacebug, *Corythucha obliqua*.
B. An extremely heavy infestation of lacebugs on the leaves of *Ceanothus arboreus*.
C. Ceanothus lacebug nymphs on the underside of a *Ceanothus* leaf.
D. A twig of *Ceanothus gloriosus*. The conspicuous white cottony material on the leaves is produced by the psyllid *Euphalerus vermiculosus*.
E. A close-up of the grainy white covers of the ceanothus psyllid. The cast skins (arrow) are presumed to be from the final molt.

PLATE 181

379

Greenhouse Thrips (Plate 182)

Long a pest of certain greenhouse-grown plants, the greenhouse thrips, *Heliothrips haemorrhoidalis* (Bouche), also causes damage to outdoor-grown woody ornamentals in California, Florida and several other of the southernmost states. The list of host plants for this insect is very extensive and includes alligator pear, *Persea americana; Azalea; Citrus;* croton, *Codiaeum variegatum;* dogwood, *Cornus; Ficus; Fuchsia;* Grecian laurel, *Laurus nobilis;* mango, *Mangifera indica; Magnolia;* maple, *Acer;* palm; *Rhododendron;* St. Johnswort, *Hypericum;* toyon, *Heteromeles arbutifolia;* and *Viburnum.*

Unlike many other thrips, the greenhouse thrips feeds openly on leaves rather than on blossoms, buds or growing shoots. Shaded conditions are preferred. Hot, sunny, dry weather is not suitable for a buildup of this pest. Both immature and adult greenhouse thrips (both of which live in dense colonies) feed by puncturing plant cells with their specialized mouthparts and withdrawing cell sap. Such activity causes a flecking, bleaching, or silvering of the affected leaves. Damaged foliage becomes papery and wilts, then drops prematurely. Fully as important as direct feeding injury by *Heliothrips* is the production of vast quantities of varnish-like excrement, which collects on the foliage and creates an unsightly appearance (C).

The adult greenhouse thrips measures only about 1 mm and is dark black in color, but has a silver-like sheen. (A photograph of an adult rose thrips, which is similar in appearance to the adult greenhouse thrips appears in Plate 177, section B.) Eggs are deposited within leaf tissues and hatch in two to three weeks. Nymphal thrips are translucent and white, though they do accumulate a drop of dark acrid feces on the dorsum as a deterrent to predators. Nymphs feed for a period of only about two to three weeks. A resting stage is undergone on the foliage and about one week later the adult stage appears. Adults are active feeders and persist for some time after reaching maturity. In California five to seven generations are reported to occur each year. The thrips overwinters in the egg stage.

Although it has wings, the adult greenhouse thrips is not a strong flier. Movement from place to place therefore proceeds slowly. The writer has seen an area of damage in a planting of the ground-cover *Hypericum* grow in size day by day, as the peripheral plants came under attack by the advancing infestation of thrips.

References: 11, 246

A. Field view of greenhouse thrips injury to Grecian laurel. Commonly only one section of a large plant is injured by this pest.
B. Close-up of greenhouse thrips damage to Grecian laurel.
C. Injury to *Viburnum* by greenhouse thrips. Note bleached leaves and varnish-like spots of excrement.
D. *Rhododendron* damaged by greenhouse thrips.

PLATE 182

Privet Thrips and Mites (Plate 183)

California privet, *Ligustrum ovalifolium*, and regel privet, *L. obtusifolium regelianum*, are not among the more valuable ornamental plants. They are, however, commonly planted and used for hedges. They are attacked by two pests which are frequently overlooked: the privet thrips, *Dendrothrips ornatus* (Jablonowski); and the privet rust mite, *Aculus ligustri* (Keifer) (Plate 204, section E). The latter is a mite in the family Eriophyidae. The false spider mite, *Brevipalpus obovatus* Donnadieu, is much larger than the rust mite. It also occurs on privet and other plants, but is more conspicuous and is not easily confused with the eriophyid or thrips. None of these pests kills its host; they all can cause unsightly injury to foliage.

The larvae and adults of the privet thrips cause conspicuous chlorotic flecks and a dusty grayish appearance of their hosts' leaves (A). The privet thrips number from 20 to 30 per leaf when abundant, but are larger than the mites and cause more damage per individual. The adult privet thrips (D) is winged and is an active flier. Little is known of its life history and seasonal development. Adults lay eggs on the leaves in late spring and several generations develop during the summer until plants are rendered unfit for feeding by the thrips. The immature forms are spindle-shaped, are light yellow in color, and are wingless (E). They occur primarily on the undersides of the leaves. Adults are about 1 mm in length. Larvae are smaller but two or three times larger than the eriophyid mites. Thrips are spindle-shaped, while eriophyid mites tend to be carrot-shaped or worm-like (G,H). The privet rust mite causes the foliage to become dull green, russetted and cupped.

The privet rust mite is adapted to cool temperatures and initiates activity as soon as new leaves develop from the buds. Overwintering females migrate from under bark scales to the leaves and begin laying eggs. Numerous overlapping generations occur from early spring into early summer. Eriophyids may number more than 2,000 per leaf on more than 70 per cent of the foliage. During a cool summer, some mites may be active, but generally, activity is nil until fall. Privet rust mite is common and widespread, from California east to New York and Massachusetts, and south at least through Virginia and Tennessee.

All eriophyid mites have but two pairs of legs. Only one other group of arthropods, the hair follicle mites, is similar. All other mites have four pairs of legs and all other arthropods except the spiders have three or more pairs of legs. Since the eriophyid mites are so small, their needle-like mouthparts are able to penetrate only the plant cells near the surface. Consequently the damage appears as russeting rather than as coarse chlorotic flecks. Positive identification of the species is difficult and is based on body setae, configuration of the genital cover flap, and body microtubules (H).

Predaceous mites in the family Phytoseiidae are common among infestations of the privet rust mite, but do not occur in sufficient numbers to keep pace with the reproductive rate of the rust mite. Predaceous mites are known to have greater effectiveness when their prey are at low population levels.

References: 86, 312

A,B. Privet leaf damage caused by the privet thrips.
C. Adults and eggs (at arrows) of the privet rust mite. These mites cannot be seen without magnification.
D. Adult privet thrips, *Dendrothrips ornatus*.
E. Privet thrips larvae.
F. Thrips injury to *Ligustrum ovalifolium*. Note immature thrips at arrows.
G. Diagram of the eriophyid *Phyllocoptes variabilis* shows body shape, and two pairs of legs (arrow). Actual size is about 0.2 mm.
H. Diagram of *Eriophyes maculatus*. Genital coverflap (at arrow) is critical for species identification.

PLATE 183

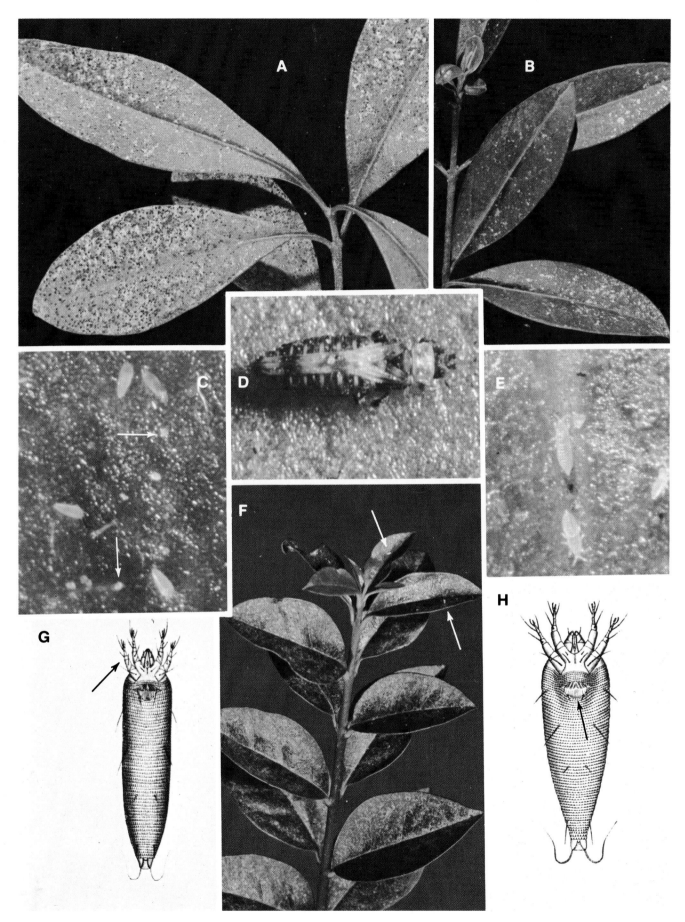

Thrips (Plate 184)

The Cuban laurel, *Ficus retusa*, particularly the popular variety *nitida*, is subject to severe injury by the Cuban laurel thrips, *Gynaikothrips ficorum* (Marchal). It has been found in the United States only in California, Florida, Hawaii and Texas.

Severe infestations of this thrips greatly reduce the ornamental value of the host plants but apparently do not cause serious or lasting injury. Adults and nymphs feed on the tender expanding leaves, causing purplish red spots on the undersurfaces and leaving them severely curled or rolled and distorted (A). The curled leaves are ineffective photosynthetically and soon turn yellow and drop prematurely.

In California five generations of the Cuban laurel thrips occur each year. On hot days the adults are active and rapid fliers. They are black and about 1 mm long. Breeding is almost continuous. The female lays her eggs (C) on the upper surface of leaves already curled. Here eggs hatch and develop with some protection from adverse weather conditions. All stages may be found on a single leaf. Under optimum conditions, the complete development of one generation may occur in as little as 30 days. Populations are most abundant from October through December.

The Cuban laurel thrips is of tropical origin. The potential role of major predators from the Carribean region are now being studied in California for control of this pest. The common native predators such as lady beetles and lacewings are not effective. Other species of *Ficus* such as *F. aurea*, *F. benjamina*, and *F. hilli* appear to be secondary hosts and are attacked if the insects are extremely abundant. *G. ficorum* also has been recorded on *Viburnum* and *Citrus* of Florida.

The toyon thrips *Rhynchothrips ilex* (Moulton), is of importance in California where toyon or Christmas berry, an evergreen shrub, is used widely as an ornamental. Although the insect has been collected from a number of other plants it is believed that the toyon thrips reproduces only on toyon. Damage to the host is caused by both adults and nymphs. By rasping the newly expanding foliage with their mouthparts they effectively prevent the leaves from developing normally. The result is misshapen and badly distorted terminal growth (D,E). Damage may be so severe that parts of the leaf may die or turn black, or the entire leaf may fall. Injury by the toyon thrips is more serious in coastal locations than in inland California.

The adult thrips (see Plate 183) is black, narrow and 1 mm long with silvery-white wings folded lengthwise over the abdomen. In late winter and early spring the adults leave the deformed foliage they damaged the year before, and begin laying eggs on new unfolding leaves. The pale yellow larvae, after hatching, feed on the new growth. When mature, the larvae drop to the ground, tunnel into the soil, and pupate there. Upon reaching the adult stage these individuals return to the toyon plants where a partial second generation develops. By late summer, breeding and reproduction cease. The adults remain in hiding on the foliage until the next year.

Thrips of other species on other plants, and in other geographical areas, may cause similar injury. Several species of thrips, particularly those of the genus *Frankliniella*, cause widespread injury to the blossoms, growing shoots, and other vegetative parts of many woody ornamental plants throughout the United States. All are very small insects—less than 1.5 mm in length—and look like tiny black or straw-colored slivers of wood as they move about on plants. Thrips are most numerous during late spring and mid-summer. In the western states their destructiveness to ornamentals increases dramatically when uncultivated vegetation begins to dry up, forcing the thrips to migrate by flight to areas where artificial watering maintains plants in an attractive state during the remainder of the growing season. The plants susceptible to thrips injury are too numerous to list here, but rose, peony, privet, and herbaceous plants such as daisy, gladiolus, and chrysanthemum are among the favored hosts.

Generally thrips prefer to feed in sites such as flower buds, open blossoms, vegetative growing points, and behind leaf sheaths, where a measure of protection to the insects is provided by the tightness of plant parts. Where flower feeding is done, the blossoms become streaked with discolored areas and bloom life is shortened. If growing points are attacked, the foliage, as it opens out, may be twisted (F) or otherwise distorted, and may become flecked with yellow or scarred (G,H). Foliage may also become bleached or silvered due to the feeding activities of thrips (see Plate 183). Thrips cause damage by rupturing plant cells with their cone-like rasping mouthparts and imbibing the plant sap that escapes.

The adult flower thrips lays eggs by inserting them into plant tissue. The tiny immature thrips feed in the same manner as the adults. On completion of the juvenile stage, a resting stage is undergone on the plant or in or on the soil below. The entire life cycle, from egg to egg, may require as little as three weeks for some species. As many as eight generations occur annually.

References: 11, 71, 233, 265

A. The growing tip of *Ficus retusa* var. *nitida*, showing how the Cuban laurel thrips injures its host.
B. A close-up of the curled undersides of leaves injured by thrips.
C. An injured Cuban laurel leaf opened to show eggs (circle), and young thrips. Sections A,B, and C all show damage done by the Cuban laurel thrips, *Gynaikothrips ficorum*.
D. The young and growing twig of toyon injured by *Rhynchothrips ilex*.
E. Several toyon leaves showing degrees of thrips injury.
F. *Viburnum odoratissimum* twig with leaves injured by thrips feeding on the underside.
G. A photograph of the underside of *Viburnum odoratissimum* leaves showing brown callous scar tissue. The callus is a response to the injury caused by thrips.
H. A close-up of the scar tissue on a single leaf. Sections F, G, and H show injury by thrips believed to have been caused by members of the genus *Frankliniella*.

PLATE 184

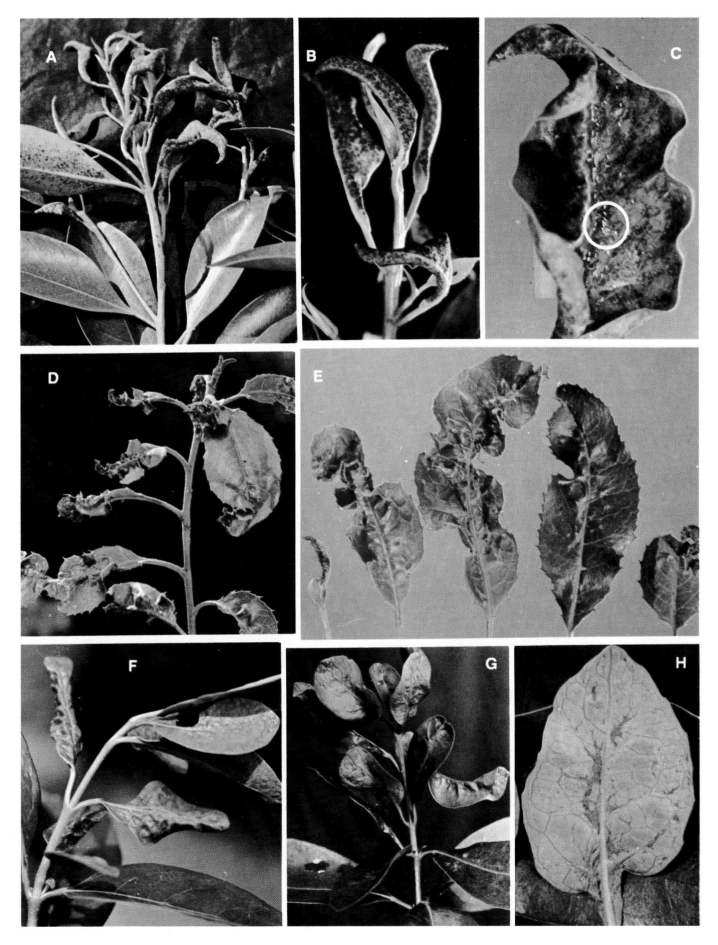

Oak Galls (Plates 185—189)

Wherever oaks occur they are attacked by a group of tiny insects which are sometimes called gallflies. They cause deformities, known as galls or gallnuts, of various shapes, sizes and colors on leaves, twigs, bark, flowers, buds, acorns and even the roots of the tree. The galls are better known than the insects that produce them. These so-called gallflies may be true flies or minute non-stinging wasps. Muesebeck et al (206a) list 717 species of "gall" wasps which attack oaks in North America. A few midges (flies) cause galls on oak leaves (Plate 187, sections A and B).

The galls are believed to be caused by powerful plant growth-regulating chemicals or other stimuli produced by the insect itself. The inner walls of the gall are rich in protein, and thus provide the larvae with an abundance of concentrated food. The larva is somewhat protected from parasites and predators by the abnormal plant tissue that surrounds it.

Each gallfly incites its own distinctive gall formation which is unlike those caused by other gallfly species. It is from the shape and appointments of these galls that the insect that produced it can be identified. Some galls of oak are globular, others are dish-shaped, and still others look like thorns or spiny balls. The size may vary from 1 mm to over 50 mm. Galls are so commonly associated with oaks that many people regard them as typical structures of the plant. It is of interest that some of the earlier botanical drawings of oaks actually show galls as representative of the normal plant.

A characteristic of many gallflies is a phenomenon known as alternation of generations. The offspring of a gallfly may produce galls quite unlike that produced by the parent but identical to those produced by their grandparents. In addition, individual gallflies of these two generations often vary in body structure to the extent that they appear to be two distinct insect species. An example of this phenomenon is the gallwasp *Dryocosmus dubiosus* (Fullaway) which infests California live oak, *Quercus agrifolia* (Plate 186).

D. dubiosus overwinter on the ground in fallen galls like those shown in Plate 186, section E. In the early spring, they emerge, fly to the trees and lay eggs in the male flowers. Instead of a normal flower, a tiny sac-like gall forms in its place. Development proceeds quickly within the gall and the insect soon leaves its "home" and lays eggs in the veins of live oak leaves. Some three months later, a tiny green gall with a spine on each end appears on the lower leaf surface. The gall becomes brown when mature and soon drops to the ground where the insect overwinters. This cycle is repeated every year (see Figure 32). It would be very difficult for the casual observer to surmise that the flower gall had any connection with the leaf gall, yet the same species of insect caused them both.

The oak apple is familiar to most young boys who have found and popped open the dried hollow galls, some of which are as large as apples. Actually there are several species of wasps that cause oak apples. (The most common one is *Amphibolips confluens* Harris.) The life history of these species is not fully known. It is known, however, that each has two broods, one consisting of only females and the other both sexes. The large galls are attached to the midrib or petiole of a leaf and are filled with a spongy mass that is easily sliced with a knife. However, the single larva in each "apple" is inside a small and very hard center capsule (Plate 187, section D). When the gall dries, the spongy center becomes a mass of fibers radiating from the center of the larval capsule to the now thin and papery shell of the gall. This insect does no serious damage to its host.

The jumping oak gall, caused by *Neuroterus saltatorius* H. Edwards, produces tiny globular, seed-like galls on leaves of various oaks. The galls—each of which contains a single larva—drop to the ground when they have matured. The activity of the live insect inside actually makes the gall move or jump. The leaf-infesting form found on certain oaks in the west may at times become so numerous as to cause injury to the host.

The vast majority of oak galls are of no particular economic significance. Twig galls, however, may cause severe injury and bring about the demise of a tree. The horned oak gall, caused by *Callirhytis cornigera* (O.S.), and the gouty oak gall, formed by *Callirhytis punctata* (O.S.), may be particularly injurious or even fatal to shade trees. *C. cornigera* occurs from southern Canada to Georgia and attacks the twigs of pin, scrub, black, black jack, and water oak. *C. punctata* is found in the same general geographical area but attacks twigs of scarlet, red, pin, and black oaks. The galls of these two species may be up to 50 mm in diameter. They often grow together to form a mass of a foot or more in length that extends along the length of a small branch. They are solid and woody with many larval cells near the center.

The horned oak gall is similar to the gouty oak gall but has horns protruding through the surface. These horns develop the second or third year after the eggs are laid, when the larvae inside are nearing their full size (Plate 189, section C). A single adult wasp emerges from each horn. The biology of the insect that forms these two galls is complicated. The following is a biological account of the horned oak gall wasp in the Niagara Falls, New York, area.

In May and June tiny parthenogenic female wasps emerge from the fully developed twig galls. These females lay eggs on the outstanding veins on the underside of the leaf. The eggs hatch and the larvae cause tiny galls which protrude from the veins. The galls appear as small, oblong blisters and are noticeable from late May through June. In early July this generation matures and both male and female wasps fly from these galls. After mating the females lay eggs in the young oak twigs. Galls do not usually begin to form until the following spring. Nearly two years, or more, are required for the wasps living in the woody gall to mature. The branches of a heavily infested tree may droop from the weight of these knotty excrescences (see Figures 33 and 34).

Other cynipid wasps often reared from twig galls are *Eurytoma auriceps* Walsh (a parasite), and *Synergus* spp. (a commensal). *Callirhytis seminator* Harris makes the wool sower gall. It is 30 to 50 mm in diameter, and is found on oaks of the white oak group (see Plate 186, section B).

References: 77, 93, 99, 142, 186, 309, 310

A. The leaves of valley oak, *Quercus lobata*, with galls caused by the cynipid wasp, *Andricus kingi*. Galls also occur on blue oak and Oregon oak.

B. A close-up of the galls shown in section A. White galls redden as they mature. Galls in this photograph are of about natural size.

C. The upper leaf surface of white oak with galls of the cynipid wasp *Neuroterus saltatorius*. (See also Plate 186, section A.)

D. A close-up of the galls shown in section C. View is of underside of leaf. The leaf has been magnified about 5 times.

PLATE 185

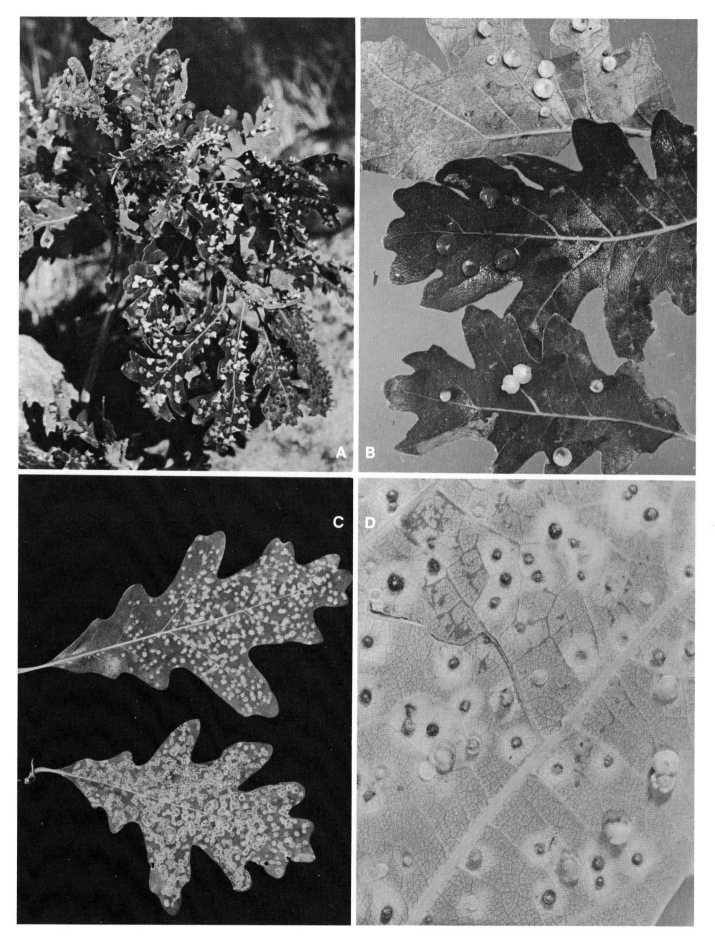

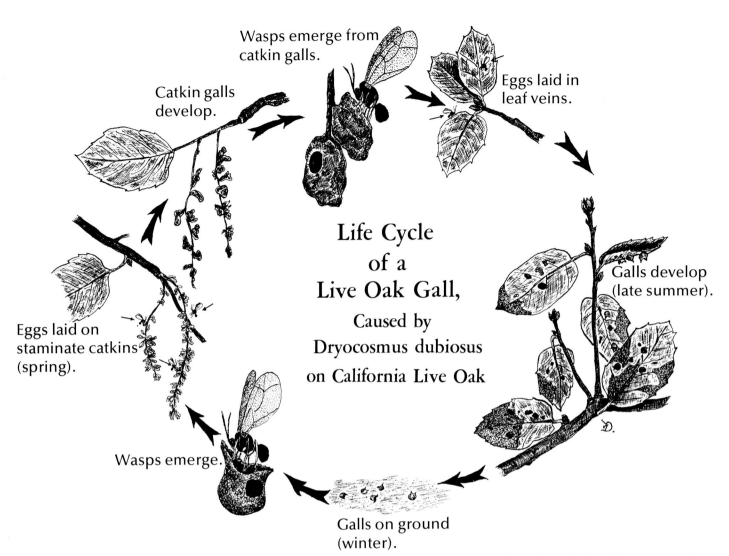

Wasps emerge from catkin galls.

Catkin galls develop.

Eggs laid in leaf veins.

Life Cycle
of a
Live Oak Gall,
Caused by
Dryocosmus dubiosus
on California Live Oak

Galls develop (late summer).

Eggs laid on staminate catkins (spring).

Wasps emerge.

Galls on ground (winter).

Figure 32. A pictorial life cycle of the gall wasp, *Dryocosmus dubiosus*. This species goes through one complete cycle, involving two generations, each year. (Drawing by R. Dirig)

A. Galled and deformed valley oak leaves. Galls were caused by a cynipid wasp, *Neuroterus saltatorius* (*decipiens* form). A western gall.

B. The wool sower gall, caused by *Callirhytis seminator,* on white oak. An eastern gall. Left: wool pulled apart to show seed-like structures, each of which contains a gall insect.

C. The hedgehog gall, formed by *Acraspis* (=*Andricus*) *erinacei,* on the upper and lower surface of a white oak leaf. Three stages of growth are shown. An eastern gall.

D. Coast live oak leaves showing symptoms of injury by the gall wasp, *Dryocosmus dubiosus.* A western gall.

E. The undersides of leaves from the same tree shown in section D.

PLATE 186

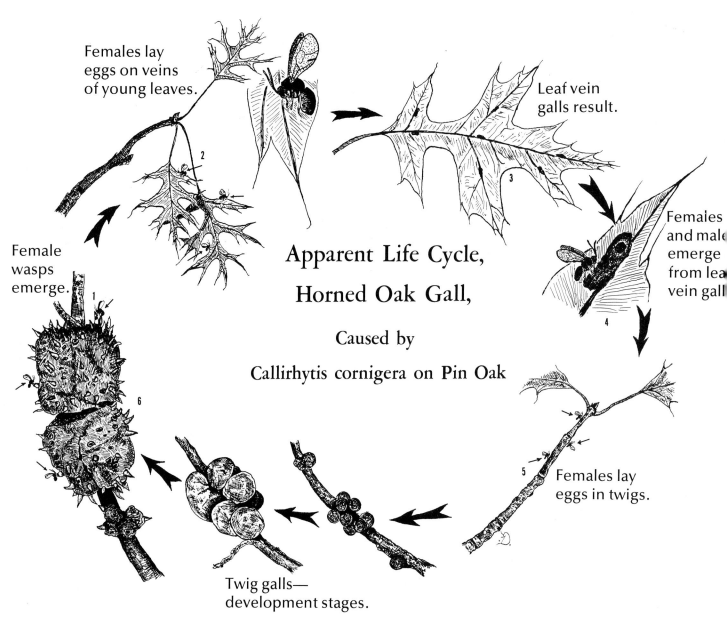

Females lay
eggs on veins
of young leaves.

Leaf vein
galls result.

Apparent Life Cycle,
Horned Oak Gall,

Caused by

Callirhytis cornigera on Pin Oak

Female
wasps
emerge.

Females
and male
emerge
from lea
vein gall

Females lay
eggs in twigs.

Twig galls—
development stages.

Figure 33. A pictorial life cycle of the gall wasp, *Callirhytis cornigera.* In May female gall wasps emerge from twig galls (1) and fly to oak foliage (2), where they deposit their eggs in the leaf veins. The larvae cause vein galls (3) to form. During mid-summer the insects in the vein galls mature and emerge as wasps (4), both male and female. After mating the females lay eggs in oak twigs (5). Twig galls form slowly at the place where eggs were laid, reaching maximum size (6) in about two years. (Drawing by R. Dirig)

A. A midge gall, *Macrodiplosis erubescens* (O.S.), sometimes called the vein pocket gall on pin oak.
B. Gall tissue removed to show the maggot-like larvae of *Macrodiplosis erubescens.*
C. Oak potato gall caused by *Neuroterus quercusbatatus* (=*batatus*).
D. Oak apples on red oak. A gall cut open to show the larvae of *Amphibolips confluenta* in the center (note arrow). The gall turns brown as it ages.

PLATE 187

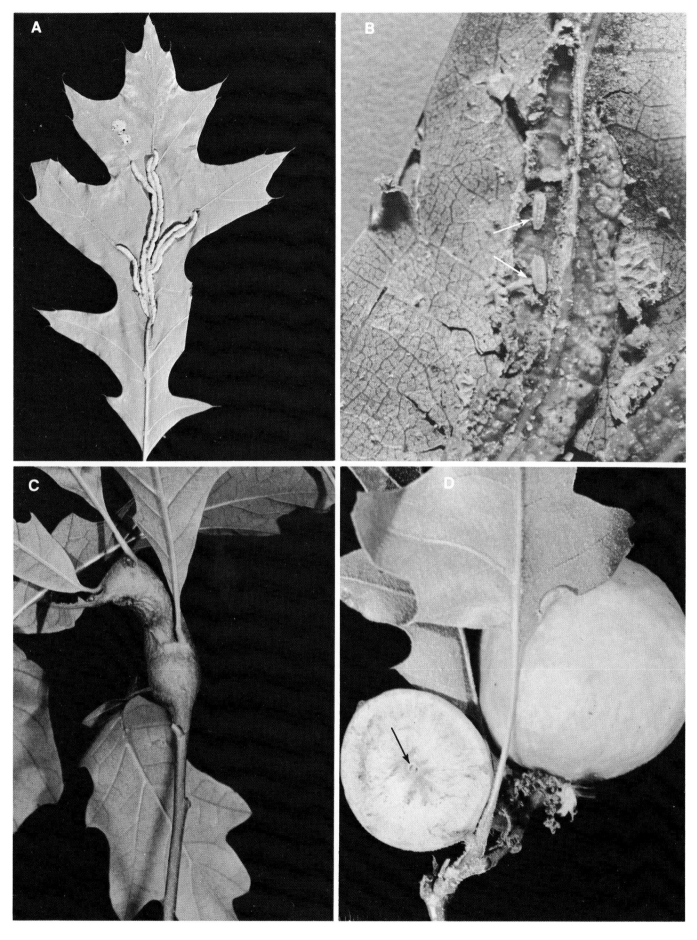

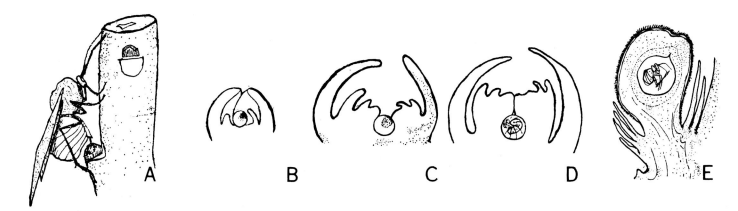

Figure 34. The sequence of bud gall development: (A) an adult gall wasp lays an egg in an immature bud; (B) the position of the egg inside the bud scales; (C) as the bud grows the plant cells enclose the egg; (D) the egg hatches and the larva develops, stimulating the growth of abnormal plant tissue; (E) gall tissue has now replaced the bud and the insect will soon cut a channel to the outside. (Drawings modified from G. S. Winterringer, Illinois State Museum Story of Illinois Series, No. 12, with permission)

A. Valley oak with star-shaped galls on undersides of leaves. Galls were caused by the cynipid wasp, *Antron* (=*Dryophanta*) *douglasi* (Ashm.), a western species. Galls also occur on blue oak and California scrub oak.
B. A woody twig gall on *Quercus wislizenii*. Gall was caused by the cynipid wasp, *Callirhytis perdens*. A bird has punctured parts of the gall to get to the insects. A western gall.
C. A single gall caused by *Antron douglasi*. Gall is of natural size.
D. A red oak tree. Most of its leaves have been replaced by "roly-poly" galls.
E. A woolly leaf gall on *Quercus engelmannii*. Gall was caused by the cynipid wasp, *Andricus fullawayi* Beut.
F. A close-up of the galls on the tree in section D. Galls were caused by a minute wasp.

PLATE 188

A. Young horned oak galls on pin oak twigs. Photograph was taken in the spring.
B. Gouty oak galls on pin oak twigs. One gall has been cut open to show the developing larvae.
C. Mature horned oak galls with horns. Where horns have been broken off, the adult wasp has emerged.
D. A pin oak tree heavily infested by gall makers. Photograph was taken in the winter.
E,F. Damage to twigs of black oak, *Quercus velutina*, caused by the gall wasp, *Callirhytis crypta*.

PLATE 189

Leaf Galls (Plate 190)

Galls are pathologically developed plant tissues induced by the stimulus of a parasitic organism. The stimulus is believed to be a growth-regulating chemical produced by the parasite. If the parasite leaves the host or dies, normal cells are again produced. Each gall-making species causes an escrescence structurally different from all others. Thus one can identify the gall-making organism without actually seeing it, by observing the structure of the gall and by noting the species of the host plant.

About 95 percent of the known types of galls of the world are caused by nematodes, mites and insects. The remaining 5 percent are caused by bacteria, fungi and viruses. Galls may occur on any of the active growing parts of plants, from root tips to the growing points of shoots. The facing plate shows leaf galls induced by an aphid, by a fly and by a mite, respectively. Plates 191–200 show examples of some of the most common galls of woody plants.

The galls in section E are elm cockscomb galls caused by the aphid *Colopha ulmicola* (Fitch). In many respects these galls do resemble a cockscomb. The galls are not all the same size or shape but in general they are about 25 mm long, 6 mm high, and are irregularly gashed and toothed. Newly matured galls are reddish along the sides and top, especially if they have exposure to the sun. As the galls age, they turn a dull brown color and may become dry and hard. On the underside of the leaf there is a long, slit-like opening. If this orifice is opened when it is still fresh, one female aphid and a number of her young will be found. The young aphids are able to leave the gall through the orifice and are sometimes seen crawling about on the outside of the leaf. These aphid nymphs are pale white, with blackish legs and antennae. They are related to the *Eriosoma* aphids (Plate 123) and undoubtedly have a secondary though as yet unknown host. The galls are produced in early summer. By midsummer the aphids have left elm for secondary hosts.

Elm cockscomb galls occur on *Ulmus americana* and *U. fulva* wherever these trees grow. A similar cockscomb-type gall occurs in the West on elm foliage and is produced in the spring by the stem mothers of the pear root aphid, *Eriosoma languinosa* (Hartig). The summer host is pear. These aphids do little harm to the plant, but attract attention because of the leaf galls they produce.

Eriophyes ulmi Gar, a mite, produces a gall (D) on leaves of American elm, *Ulmus americana*. The presence of the galls causes some curling and deformation of the foliage. The gall always occurs on the upper leaf surface, but has an opening on the underside of the leaf. The mites feed and reproduce inside the gall, migrating to new growth as new leaves develop. The mite illustrated in section D is the early summer form. Many eriophyid mites have a summer form which is annulate and wormlike, and a winter form much coarser in structure. In either form they cannot be seen readily without visual magnification because of their very small size (0.2 mm). This gall is likely to be found wherever elms grow. If numerous, it can disfigure the leaves somewhat, but is seldom considered to be seriously injurious.

The ash midrib gall midge, *Contarinia canadensis* Felt, causes a disfiguring leaf gall (A,B,C) on American ash, *Fraxinus americana*. The galls vary in size from 10 to 30 mm. They are succulent and thick-walled, and each has a small cavity that is occupied by one or more white maggots.

The adult midge of this species lays its eggs in the vein of very young ash leaflets in the spring. The gall forms soon after the egg is laid. Little is known about the biology and habits of this insect or how it overwinters. Galls produced by this midge occur on forest as well as shade trees. They are, however, not very common. As with most galls, their unique appearance is often cause for concern of tree owners and others curious about unusual growths on plants. *C. canadensis* is known only from the eastern half of the United States and Canada.

References: 96, 99, 142, 186

A,B,C. Ash midrib gall caused by the midge *Contarinia canadensis*.
D. Elm leaves with bladder-type galls caused by the mite *Eriophyes ulmi*.
E. An elm cockscomb gall, caused by *Colopha ulmicola*, on American elm. The newly mature gall has a reddish "comb."

PLATE 190

Leaf and Petiole Galls (Plate 191)

In the spring, the leaves of various species of hickory, including pecan, are deformed with peculiar tumor-like growths. These are of various shapes and sizes and occur on leaf blades, petioles and, occasionally, on rapidly growing twigs. When these galls occur on a tree in large numbers they may seriously affect its vitality and cause major dieback of branches. They are caused by aphid-like insects in the family Phylloxeridae (=*Chermidae*, Adelgidae). Most of the gall insects discussed here belong to the genus *Phylloxera*. Insects in this family are commonly called aphids, but are merely related to true aphids.

The eggs of *Phylloxera* "aphids" overwinter in cracks and crevices on the bark of the host tree. Coincident with the opening of buds in the spring, these eggs begin to hatch. The young "aphids" all develop into females and are called stem mothers. They settle on the leaf stems and midribs of leaflets and begin feeding. Plant reaction to the feeding results in the formation of a gall. Plant tissues grow around the feeding stem mother until structures such as those shown in sections A and B are formed. The galls are hollow. Inside them, the stem mother deposits eggs. In New York State, the eggs hatch in early June, and by the end of June the progeny are fully grown and have wings. If the gall is nut-like (B), it splits open the way the shucks of the hickory nut do, and the mature "aphids" are free to move outside. An orifice forms at the apex of succulent galls to allow the insects to exit. Several generations of *Phylloxera* occur on summer hosts, but few biological studies of summer broods have been made. In the early fall winged forms return to hickory to deposit their eggs and prepare the species for survival through the winter.

The aphid *Gobaishia ulmifusa* Walsh and Riley causes hollow galls on the upper leaf surfaces of slippery elm, *Ulmus fulva*. The gall is an elongate sack or pouch (E) often more than 35 mm long, although sometimes much smaller. Its walls are leathery in texture and are thin. If she has produced young, there may be a great number of immature aphids present. The galls may be found in June. Usually only one occurs per leaf.

These galls are known to occur on slippery elm in New England, New York, Illinois, Minnesota, Ohio, Kansas, Indiana and Colorado.

References: 96, 98, 99, 142

A. Galls on a hickory leaf. Galls were caused by insects of the genus *Phylloxera*, probably the leaf stem gall aphid, *P. caryaecaulis*. This species produces galls on both petioles and midveins of the leaflets. For proper orientation, this photograph should be viewed from the fold of the book. Arrow indicates the exit orifice.
B. A nut-like gall caused by a *Phylloxera* at the base of the petiole of *Carya ovata*.
C. An elm leaf gall cut open to show the huge population of phylloxerid "aphids" inside.
D,F. A gall cut open to show the single wingless female aphid, *Gobaishia ulmifusa*, before the appearance of progeny.
E. A gall on the leaf of *Ulmus fulva* caused by the aphid *Gobaishia ulmifusa*.

PLATE 191

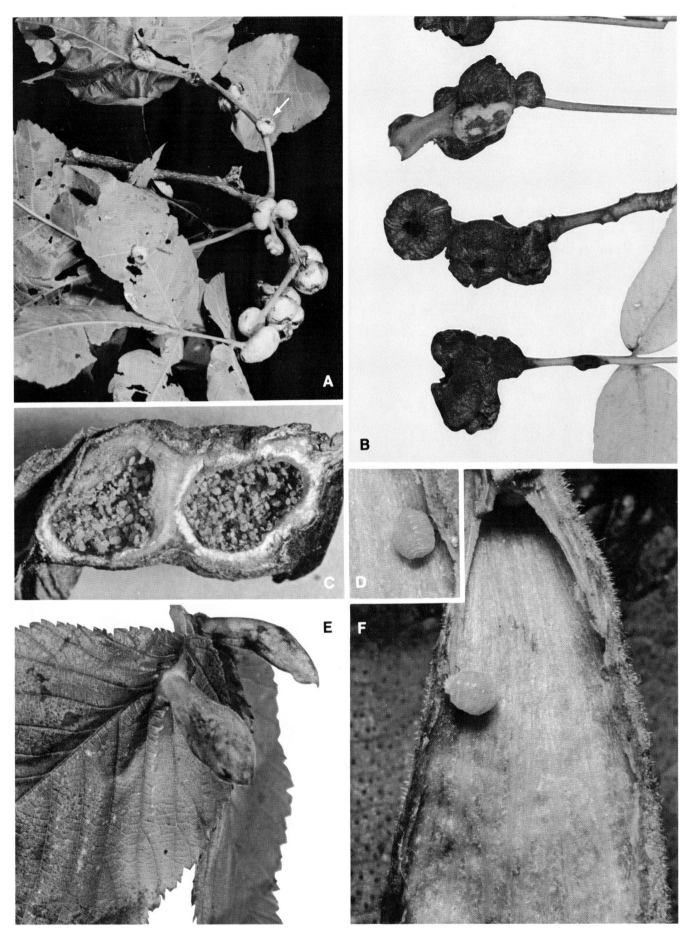

Aphid and Psyllid Galls (Plate 192)

The witch-hazel leaf gall aphid, *Hormaphis hamamelidis* (Fitch), and the spring witch-hazel bud gall aphid, *Hamamelistes spinosus* Shimmer (Plate 118), are common on witch-hazel, *Hamamelis* sp., and their alternate host, birch (*Betula*). Both overwinter in the egg stage on the twigs of witch-hazel.

H. hamamelidis may also be called the witch-hazel cone gall aphid. It causes conical galls to form on the upper sides of the leaves early in spring when young nymphs begin feeding. A single aphid initiates the gall formation by the plant. The aphid grows to maturity rapidly, contained within the developing gall. The adult female produces great numbers of young aphids that pack the hollow interior of the gall. When the young mature, they develop wings and then emerge through the opening or orifice (C) on the undersides of the leaves. These aphids fly in late spring and early summer to the foliage of birch, where several wingless generations occur during the summer. With the approach of autumn, the last generation is winged, and migration back to witch-hazel occurs. Eggs are laid on the twigs where they spend the winter and the life cycle is completed.

The cone galls are green, sometimes tipped with red (B). They are about 1 cm high and are fully developed by June (somewhat earlier in the latitude of Washington, D. C.). The galls persist on the leaves for the remainder of the season, but are empty. The galls are unsightly, but are not notably injurious or deleterious to the trees. The presence and feeding of these aphids on birch does not stimulate abnormal growth reactions nor gall formations.

So far as is known, all of the horticultural cultivars of witch-hazel are equally susceptible to attack by these aphids. *H. hamamelidis* occurs in the northeastern quadrant of the United States from Illinois to the East Coast, south to North Carolina, and north to Canada.

The hackberry galls shown on this plate (D,E,F,G) were found in Louisiana. They are caused by a psyllid in the genus *Pachypsylla*. Little is known of the biology, habits, and occurrence of species in the genus, in the Gulf States. For more discussion on psyllids, see the text for Plate 194.

Reference: 227

A. A witch-hazel branch with leaf galls caused by the aphid *Hormaphis hamamelidis*.
B. Galls on the upper leaf surface of witch-hazel.
C. The gall opening on the undersurface of a witch-hazel leaf.
D. Hackberry leaves with crater-shaped *Pachypsylla* galls on the upper surface.
E. Crater-shaped galls. View is of undersurface of the leaf.
F,G. Apple or quince-shaped galls on hackberry. View is of underside of leaf. In section F the top of a gall has been removed to expose a young *Pachypsylla* nymph.

PLATE 192

Laurel Psyllid (Plate 193)

The laurel psyllid, *Trioza alacris* Flor, is an Old World insect. It was first reported in the United States in Oakland, California, in 1911. As nearly as can be determined, the insect was introduced into America on nursery stock originating in Belgium. In Europe this insect feeds on Grecian laurel, *Laurus nobilis*, and on English laurel, *Prunus laurocerasus*, yet in the United States only the former host is attacked. This is surprising in view of the fact that English laurel is a far more common plant in California than is Grecian laurel. The insect is known to occur in the New World only in California and New Jersey.

Damage to *Laurus nobilis* foliage is characterized by the rolling inward of the leaf margins to form a gall within which the immature psyllids develop (D). Some thickening of the affected leaf portions occurs. When newly formed, the galls are the same color as the unaffected leaves. Later, however, they turn reddish and eventually brown or black as the leaf tissue dies (B). Defoliation of part or all of the plant has been reported when infestations are severe. Some blackening of foliage occurs as a consequence of sooty mold fungi colonizing the honeydew produced by the insects. In addition, the cast skins of the mature nymphs persist on the foliage and contribute to the unsightliness of infested laurel plants.

Trioza overwinters in the adult stage on the plant. In early spring, egg laying begins on the newly growing terminal leaves. Eggs are pale yellow when newly deposited, and are covered with a grayish white powder. Like most psyllid eggs, those of *Trioza* are attached to the leaf surface by a slender tube called a stipe. This appendage is necessary to maintain a proper moisture balance in the egg; incubation will not proceed if the eggs are removed from the leaf surface and transferred to another substrate.

On hatching, the tiny, flattened nymphs insert their mouthparts into leaves to withdraw plant sap. This feeding causes the curling and thickening of the foliage; eventually a secure gall is formed into which the nymphs move to continue feeding. Nymphs are yellow to orange. Their bodies are covered by white cottony wax. At maturity they leave the galls, attach themselves to the surface of an open leaf, and transform into the winged adult stage. There are several generations each year of the laurel psyllid, the last one maturing in the fall of the year. During most of the growing season all stages of the psyllid are commonly found at the same time on the same tree.

References: 51, 90, 93

A. Field view of Grecian laurel plant, showing sites of infestation of the laurel psyllid.
B. Galled leaf margins, and discoloration of leaves, caused by the laurel psyllid.
C. Severely galled terminal of *Laurus nobilis*. Note nymphs of *Trioza* inside partly opened gall.
D. Close-up of rolled leaf margins, and cast skins of last-instar psyllid nymphs.
E,F. Cast skins of *Trioza* nymphs on leaves of Grecian laurel.

PLATE 193

Hackberry Psyllids (Plate 194)

Hackberry trees and shrubs are not planted as frequently as most other woody plants. They are used extensively as windbreaks and shade trees in the Midwest and as an occasional specimen tree in landscape plantings in the East. Wherever they occur, hackberry psyllids are also likely to be found. Adults look much like miniature cicadas. The adult psyllid is four to five mm in length and has hind legs adapted for springing from a resting position into flight. For this reason insects in the family Psyllidae are also called jumping plant lice.

Seven species of *Pachypsylla* have been reported to attack hackberry. The three most common species are the hackberry blister gall maker, *P. celtidisvesicula* Riley; the hackberry nipple gall maker, *P. celtidismamma* (Riley); and the hackberry bud gall psyllid, *P. celtidisgemma* Riley. The life cycle and habits of the hackberry blister gall maker and the hackberry nipple gall maker are similar. The bud gall psyllid, however, has a different life cycle.

The hackberry blister gall (E) measures 3 to 4 mm in diameter and is only slightly raised from the leaf surface. The hackberry nipple gall (G) is about 4 mm in diameter, and is nearly 6 mm high. both species overwinter as adults in the crevices of rough bark, or—all too often—inside houses. One generation of these insects occurs each year. Mating and egg laying occur over a period of weeks beginning when new leaves unfold from the buds. Eggs hatch in a week to 10 days and nymphs begin to feed on the leaves. At the feeding site, rapid and abnormal plant growth takes place on the leaf, and a pouch or gall forms around the nymph(s). They live inside the galls throughout the summer and emerge as adults in September. The emerging adults can be extremely annoying to people in late summer. They sometimes alight by the hundreds on cars, buildings, and even on objects in homes near large hackberry trees. The host trees apparently do not suffer seriously from the galls, although severe infestations over a period of years may weaken them. Hackberry blister gall is most common on tree forms of hackberry, whereas the nipple gall tends to be more prevalent on shrubby types. The nipple gall has been reported to cause premature leaf drop on tree forms in Illinois.

The same trees infested with leaf galls may support a large population of hackberry bud gall psyllids. *P. celtidisgemma* adults occur for two or three weeks during the latter part of June. Eggs are laid on the leaves and nymphs crawl to the newly formed buds where gall formation occurs. By fall, nymphs have molted to the fifth instar which remains in the gall throughout the winter and early spring. Both the leaf and bud-inhabiting psyllids feed on plant cells with piercing-sucking mouthparts. Even when bud galls are abundant, damage to host plants is not severe. A sufficient number of buds generally remains uninfested for the tree to maintain its vigor.

Parasites are common and important in the natural control of hackberry psyllids. The chalcid wasp, *Psyllaephagus pachypsyllae* (Howard), has been reported to destroy 30 percent of the bud gall nymphs. Studies of the nipple gall have shown 47 to 51 percent of the nymphs destroyed by the internal parasites *Torymus pachypsyllae* (Ashmead), *Psyllaephagus pachypsyllae*, *Eurytoma semivanae*, and three other less abundant species. The weevil, *Conotrachelus buchanani* Schoof, was found to be predaceous on psyllids. It also feeds in the galls.

Reference: 52

A. Psyllid eggs on the undersurface of a newly developed hackberry leaf.
B. Hackberry psyllid eggs magnified; note eyespots of embryo (arrow).
C. Newly emerged nymphs prior to initiation of gall formation.
D. A female psyllid beside her eggs.
E. Hackberry blister galls on foliage. View is of upper leaf surfaces.
F. Lower surfaces of same leaves shown in section E.
G. Galls caused by *Pachypsylla celtidismamma* on underside of hackberry leaf.

PLATE 194

Yaupon Psyllid (Plate 195)

The feeding of many psyllid species causes galls to form on their host plant. *Metaphalaria ilicis* (Ashmead) causes a leaf gall on yaupon, *Ilex vomitoria,* a holly which the southeastern Indians at one time used ceremoniously.

The biology of this psyllid is incompletely known. It is believed to occur only on *I. vomitoria* and to have one generation each year. In northern Florida the adult may be found in late December and January (F). Galls form on young leaves during the summer, causing them to be reduced in size and grossly distorted (B). By early December the galled portion of the leaf turns red. Inside the galls, several psyllid nymphs feed on the succulent tissue (E). One or more ball-like structures slightly larger than a nymph are found inside the gall. They are covered with white wax-like material. If punctured, clear fluid will run out and the ball collapses. This is assumed to be honeydew excreted by the psyllids.

This insect is known to occur along the coastal plain from North Carolina to Florida and along the Gulf Coast to Louisiana.

A. Yaupon twigs with galls on the youngest leaves. Galls were caused by *Metaphalaria ilicis.*
B,C. A close-up view of several galls.
D,E. Galls cut open to show the young psyllids. The arrow in section D points to a ball of honeydew.
F. An adult *Metaphalaria ilicis.* About 3 mm long.

PLATE 195

Psyllid Gall of Persea (Plate 196)

Trioza magnoliae Ashmead, a psyllid, is a common inhabitant of Florida, and occurs in Georgia, Alabama, and Mexico. It has also been reported from New Jersey. F. W. Mead (190) summarized the known information on this species in 1963. This psyllid was described by Ashmead in 1881 and discussed in 1914 by Crawford (52) in a monograph on New World species of Psyllidae.

The principal host of *T. magnoliae* is red bay, *Persea borbonia*. It has also been found on other species of *Persea*: silk bay, *P. humilis;* swamp bay, *P. palustris;* and shore bay, *P. littoralis.* Large unsightly galls form on the leaves, but apparently cause little damage to the tree, since a large proportion of leaves remain unaffected. The galls are about 25 mm in length, and are green. They are, however, covered with a whitish to bluish bloom (A). Galls first form on the leaf margins and as they grow cause the leaf blade to roll and the mid-vein to curl (B). The psyllids are enclosed in the pouchlike gall. The gall's hollow interior also contains shed skins, white waxy material, and drops of honeydew. When the galls mature, a slit opens along the side of the gall permitting the adult psyllids to emerge. In Florida nymphs have been found from April to June, and in November and December. The majority of adults emerge in mid-May.

Adults are typical psyllids in appearance. They look like miniature cicadas. They are about 4 mm in length, and have a greenish to light brown coloring. Sometimes brown stripes appear on the thorax. Little is known about the biological details of this insect.

References: 52, 190

A. Young bay leaves with galls caused by the psyllid *Trioza magnoliae*. Such symptoms are often found by late March in central Florida. The galls shown in this photograph range from 4 to 11 mm in length.
B. Leaf malformations on red bay caused by *T. magnoliae*.
C. Newly developing galls as seen in late March.
D. Appearance of red bay leaves infested with *Trioza magnoliae*, a psyllid gall maker.
E. Gall cut open to reveal nymphs.

PLATE 196

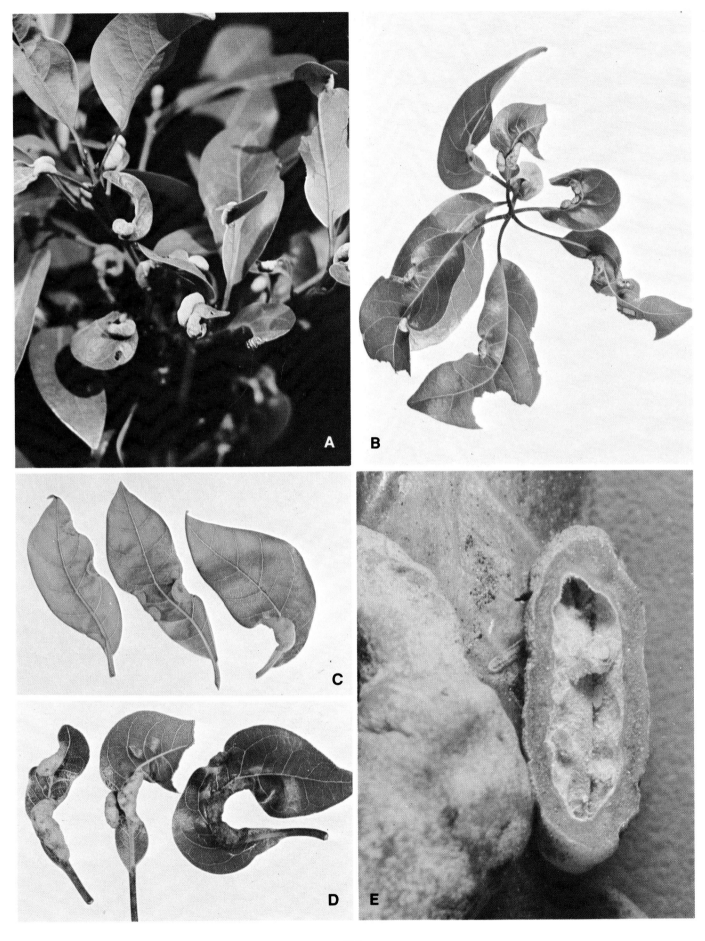

Honeylocust Pod Gall (Plate 197)

Honeylocust trees, especially the thornless varieties such as the Imperial and Shademaster, are being widely planted in various parts of the United States. At one time these trees were thought to be relatively free of insect pests. Now, however, several insects and mites are known to damage these shade trees.

The honeylocust pod gall midge, *Dasineura gleditschiae* (O.S.), causes leaf deformation: leaflets become globular or pod-like (C). Within each pod-like gall are one to several small, whitish (or slightly yellowish) larvae that are about 6 mm long (E). The larvae mature and pupate within the pods and then emerge as small delicate flies or midges that are about 3 mm long. The male is generally black. The female is black with a red abdomen. Adult midges first appear when new growth begins in the spring. The female lays microscopic kidney-shaped, lemon-colored eggs in the young leaflets. The larvae hatch in a day or two and start to feed immediately, at the same time causing the leaf to develop into a pod. In Connecticut, from five to seven generations may occur in a single year. The insect apparently overwinters as an adult somewhere outside the pod.

Galled leaflets may dry up and drop prematurely. Repeated attacks may cause death of small branches, but normally new shoots form at the base of the dead twigs. The trees are not killed, but lose their ornamental qualities in yard or street tree plantings. Pod gall midge is likely to be found wherever ornamental cultivars of honeylocust are grown.

Reference: 250

A,B,D. General damage caused by the honeylocust pod gall midge, *Dasineura gleditschiae*.
C. Well developed pod-like galls replace the leaflets.
E. Gall opened to reveal the maggot-like larvae.

PLATE 197

Leaf and Bud Galls (Plate 198)

Some insects cause leaf spot symptoms on attached plants that look much like those caused by fungus diseases. Such is the case of the cecidomyid fly, *Cecidomyia ocellaris* (Osten Sacken), on red maple *Acer rubrum*. A gall is produced which superficially looks like a fungus leaf spot (A).

The biology of the fly is poorly known but the female is believed to lay single eggs at various locations on the undersides of red maple leaves. Upon hatching, a pouch gall forms around the developing larva. The gall is small (about 1 mm in diameter) and on the upper surface it appears to be a black elevated spot. The undersurface appears to be closed when viewed without the aid of optical equipment. The gall maker larva is found inside the pit-like gall. The spot or affected area is about 8 mm in diameter and varies in color, depending upon the stage of development. The larva is a typical maggot in form. It is about 1.5 mm long when fully grown and is nearly colorless. When larval growth is completed, it drops to the ground, and burrows in for a short distance to pupate. Several generations are believed to occur each year, beginning about mid-May in central New York State. J. H. Comstock, while the United States Entomologist (1881), wrote that the maple leaf spot gall "occurs so abundantly that I have repeatedly seen trees when every leaf was infested." Fifty or more galls have been found on a single leaf. Foliage injury does result from the existence of these galls, but actual damage would be difficult to measure.

C. ocellaris is assumed to be distributed over the natural range of its only host, *Acer rubrum*. Infestations may not occur every year but cycles of high and low populations might be expected.

Several gall-making sawflies of the genus *Pontania* cause fleshy, subspherical galls on the leaves of willow. These galls may be found wherever willows grow. *P. hyalina* Norton is thought to be an eastern species. It causes bright red excrescences (C) which often occur in two parallel rows, one row on either side of the midvein. The gall is 7 to 10 mm long and projects through both surfaces of the leaf.

P. californica Marlatt and *P. parva* (Cresson) are western species. The galls produced by these species are of about the same size and color. Little is known about the biology of these sawflies. The amount of damage caused by them is negligible.

Another fly, *Rhabdophaga strobiloides* Walsh, produces the willow cone gall (D). The adult fly is gnat-like in appearance. It appears in late April or early May and deposits a single egg in the swelling terminal bud. When the egg hatches, the bud ceases to develop normally into a twig. Instead, it continues to get larger and larger. It reaches a maximum length of 25 mm by early July. The larva remains in a cavity inside the gall through the winter. In early spring it transforms to a pupa. A fully developed fly emerges shortly thereafter. The gall may be found on several species of willows throughout the northeastern and north-central states, and as far south as Maryland and Virginia. Distribution records are not complete. Injury to the host plant is minimal. Control may be effected by removing and destroying the galls by the end of summer.

References: 93, 96, 129, 186, 256, 318

A. Maple leaf spot galls on red maple. Galls were caused by *Cecidomyia ocellaris*, a midge. Three color phases are shown. Each spot is about 8 mm in diameter.
B. Undersurface of a red maple leaf showing the pouch opening of the maple leaf spot gall.
C. A fleshy willow leaf gall on *Salix*, sp. (*fragilis* or *blanda*). The gall was caused by *Pontania hyalina*, a sawfly. The discolored leaves at the bottom of the photograph are not part of the gall symptom, but are a symptom of a fungus disease.
D. Willow cone galls.

PLATE 198

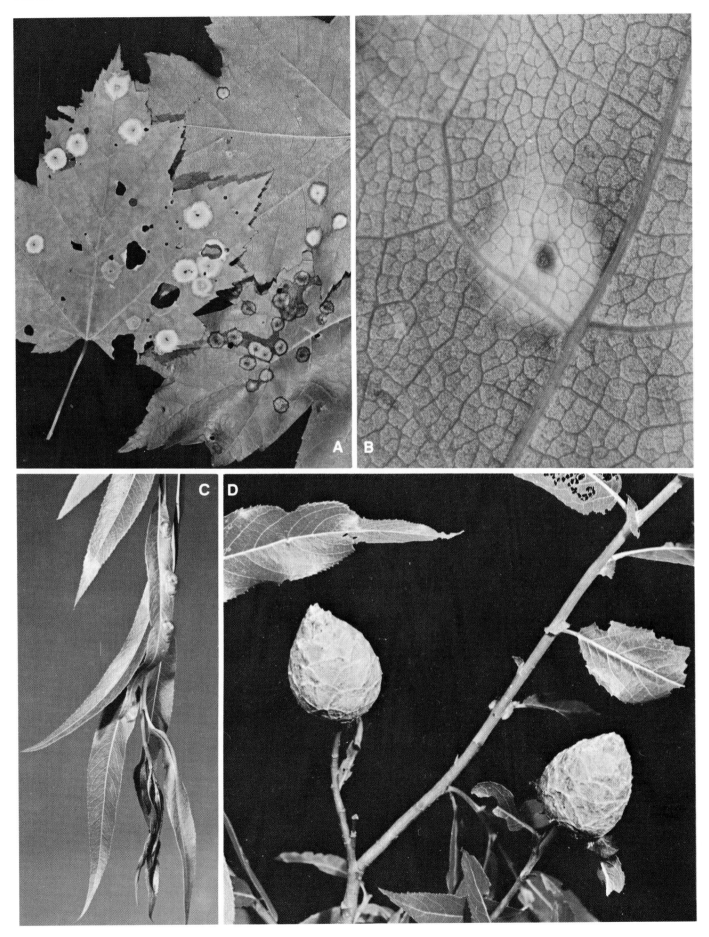

Dogwood Club Gall (Plate 199)

The dogwood club gall is caused by the larva of *Mycodiplosis clavula* (Beut.), which is a small fly, or midge. These galls may be found throughout the normal range of the flowering dogwood, *Cornus florida,* from Connecticut to Florida.

M. clavula is primarily an eastern species. Its larvae, or maggots, overwinter on the ground. They are protected by sod, decayed grass and duff. Pupation occurs in the spring, and in Connecticut, adults emerge from the pupae in June. They emerge much earlier in the Carolinas and Georgia. The midges are quite small, and are delicate and extremely shy. They deposit their eggs in the tiny terminal leaves. Upon hatching the maggots work their way into the newly developing twig at the base of the petiole. Occasionally, they enter the leaf near the base of the midrib and mine through the petiole to the twig. The first symptom of their presence is a wilted, deformed leaf. As the maggots grow, a cavity develops in the twig and the surrounding tissue swells, giving the clubbed appearance. The number of maggots which may be found inside a single gall ranges from one to sixty. As the maggots mature, they become yellow or orange (D). More than one gall may occur on a single twig. The galls vary in length from less than 10 mm to 50 mm or more. They taper at both ends. During the late summer or early fall, the maggots inside the gall make one or more exit holes and drop to the ground to overwinter.

A heavy infestation of club gall midges may seriously stunt a tree. A light infestation in a large tree will hardly be noticed. Galled twigs with their terminal leaves usually die prematurely. The leaves may cling to the tree for a year or more. Most of the flower and leaf buds that develop beyond the apex of the gall, die, thus greatly reducing the number of flowers the following spring.

A small chalcid parasite of the maggot has been identified as *Platygaster* sp. The degree of control caused by this parasite is unknown.

Reference: 251

A. Twigs of *Cornus florida*. Galls were caused by the midge *Mycodiplosis clavula.*
B. A dead twig with galls that have remained on the tree for several years.
C. A fresh gall cut open to show the developing maggots. When fully grown, maggots are about 2 mm long.
D. A close-up view of the maggots.

PLATE 199

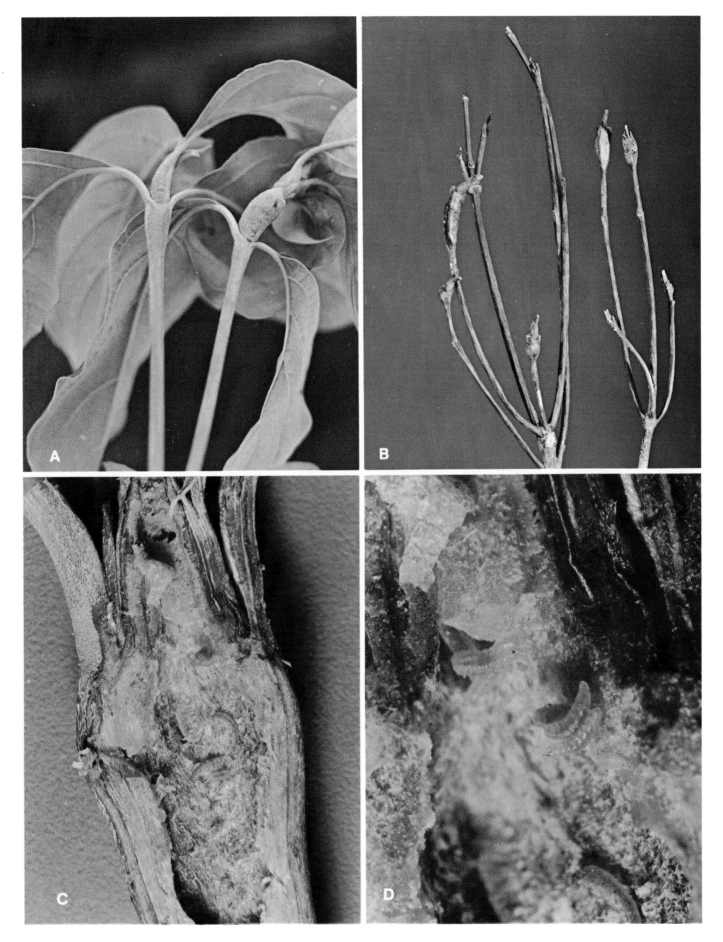

Stem Galls (Plate 200)

No fewer than 40 kinds of galls are produced on roses by gall wasps. The galls occur on roots, twigs, leaves and buds. Each gall-forming insect chooses one particular site on the plant for the deposition of its eggs. The location of egg deposition subsequently becomes the site of a unique gall.

The mossy rose gall maker, *Diplolepis rosae* (Linnaeus), causes a large spherical hairy mass (D), which is 25 mm or more in diameter to form on year-old rose twigs in the spring. The galls are light green and moss-like at first. Later they turn brown. Inside each gall is a cluster of hard kernel-like cells from which the moss-like filaments originate. Each cell contains the larva of a tiny gall wasp. The adults emerge the spring following gall development. One generation occurs each year.

The long rose gall (C), formed by *Diplolepis dichlorcerus* Harris, is spindle-shaped and is covered with many spines. The gall ranges in length from 12 to 50 mm; its diameter may reach 20 mm.

Mossy rose galls and long rose galls are commonly found on the East Coast but they also occur elsewhere. In Utah, Idaho and Oregon the gall wasp, *Diplolepis bassetti* Beautm., causes a mossy, filamentous gall that is much smaller than the mossy rose gall.

Spindle-shaped swellings along the stems of *Ceanothus* are caused by *Periploca ceanothiella* (Cosens), the ceanothus stem gall moth. This pest has a stunting effect on the new growth, since galls may number more than 20 per lineal foot of growth. More serious damage, however, occurs on the bloom, which may be reduced to about one-fourth its normal size. Some twigs may be killed as a result of the injury. This pest is of particular concern in California. Its distribution in the United States probably corresponds to the distribution of *Ceanothus*. Specimens of this insect have been reported, however, in Kansas, New York, Ontario, and Texas as well as in California. Research data from Munro (207) in southern California have shown striking differences in susceptibility to stem gall moth, based on the relative abundance of galls observed on species and cultivars of *Ceanothus*:

Severely infested	Not infested
Ceanothus griseus	*C. americanus*
C. griseus horizontalis	*C. parryi*
Moderately infested	*C. papillosus*
C. cyaneus	*C. impressus*
C. thyrsiflorus	*C. foliosus*
C. 'Ray Hartman'	*C. insularia*
C. 'Marie Simon'	*C. cuneatus*
Lightly infested	*C. ramulosus fascicularia*
C. arboreus	*C. gloriosus*
C. oliganthus	*C. gloriosus exaltatus*
C. diversifolius	*C. rigidus albus*
C. lemmonii	*C. purpureus*
C. integerrimus	*C. prostratus*
C. leucodermis	*C. verrucosus*
C. lobbianus	*C. spinosus*
C. 'Treasure Island'	*C. jepsonii*
C. 'Sierra Blue'	*C. masonii*
C. 'Royal Blue'	*C. megacarpus*
C. 'Mountain Haze'	*C. greggi perplexus*
C. 'Mary Lake'	*C. 'Blue Cloud'*
C. 'Concha'	*C. 'Lester Rowntree'*

The ceanthus stem gall moth overwinters in the larval stage in its gall on the plant. Pupation and moth emergence from the galls take place during the spring and early summer. Eggs are laid on the plants by the adults and the newly hatched larvae tunnel directly into the buds and flower inflorescences, causing the formation of galls. There is never more than one larva in each gall and only a single generation of the ceanthus stem gall moth occurs each year.

References: 99, 207

A. *Ceanothus thyrsiflorus* twig showing the galls and the resultant dwarfed and dead foliage.

B. A gall cut open to show the larva and pupa of *Periploca ceanothiella*.

C. The long rose gall, *Diplolepis dichlorcerus*.

D,E. The gall and winter coloration of the mossy rose gall, which is caused by *Diplolepis rosae*.

PLATE 200

Spider Mites on Deciduous Hosts (Plate 201)

The family Tetranychidae, or spider mites, contains dozens of species which attack shade trees and other woody ornamental plants. The most injurious or common in taxonomic order include: the clover mites, *Bryobia arborea* Morgan and Anderson, and *B. praetiosa* Koch; the European red mite, *Panonychus ulmi* (Koch); the hickory spider mites, *Eotetranychus caryae* Reeves and *E. hickoriae* (McGregor); the linden spider mites, *E. tiliarum* (Herman) and *E. uncatus* Garman; the elm spider mite, *E. matthyssei* Reeves; the honeylocust spider mite, *E. multidigituli* (Ewing); the willow spider mites, *Schizotetranychus schizopus* (Zacher) and *S. garmani* (Pritchard and Baker); the oak red mite, *Oligonychus bicolor* (Banks); the maple spider mite, *O. aceris* (Shimer); the platanus mite, *O. platani* (McGregor); the four-spotted mite, *Tetranychus canadensis* (McGregor); the Atlantic spider mite, *T. atlanticus* McGregor; the two-spotted mite, *T. urticae* Koch; and numerous others.

The oak mite (A), when present, is found only on the upper leaf surfaces of oak, chestnut, birch, beech, and elm. It seldom seriously damages its host, and is conspicuous only when most of the foliage is infested. The maple spider mite occurs only on the undersides of the leaves. It is usually not injurious. Some species of mites tend to be active in the spring. These include the clover mites, the European red mite, and the willow mites. The spider mites on oak, elm, linden, honeylocust; hickory, mountain ash, and sycamore produce active populations in midsummer. Others are active generally throughout the growing season and may or may not increase markedly in midsummer.

Each spider mite has a pair of needle-like stylets, or "teeth" called chelicerae, which rupture cells of the host leaf tissue. The mouth of the spider mite then is pushed into the torn cells, and the cell sap is drawn up while the stylets probe deeper. The feeding action causes fine flecking or stippling of the foliage (B). Where large populations exist, injured and chlorotic areas coalesce. Large portions of the leaf, and sometimes even the entire leaf, become yellow or bronzed in appearance (D). It is not uncommon to find thousands of egg shells and cast skins on a single leaf. Many of the spider mites produce mats of webbing over the surface on which they live and feed. A single female and progeny may occupy only 25 square mm of leaf surface in a single generation.

All spider mites undergo similar developmental stages. These are: the egg stage, the six-legged "larva" stage, the protonymph and deutonymph stages, and the adult female and male stage. Most species overwinter in the egg stage, although a few hibernate as adult females. The presence of dust and dirt on foliage tends to favor an increase in mite populations. Many generations occur in a single season, which accounts for the very rapid buildup of extremely large damaging populations.

Spider mites vary in size from 0.25 to 1 mm and in color from translucent pale yellow and pale green to dark green and red (E). Since the sophisticated microscopes necessary for positive identification are rarely available in the field, tentative identification is reasonably accurate if based upon mite size, color, location on the plant, and host.

There are no known insect parasites of mites. Insect predators include lady beetles (especially *Stethorus* spp.), certain thrips, and an anthocorid bug. *Stethorus punctillum* Weise populations are capable of virtually eliminating both European red mite infestations on apple, and spruce mite infestations on arborvitae. However, the decimation of mites occurs after the infestation peaks. *Stethorus* adults were observed to lay eggs among increasing populations of mites, but not when populations were declining and foliage had been severely damaged. Predaceous mites, notably many species in the family Phytoseiidae, are commonly found among spider mite and eriophyid mite colonies. They are reported to be most effective in limiting spider mites which are present at low population densities. (See also Plates 43 and 202).

References: 2, 86, 211, 234, 240, 288

A. Red oak leaves severely injured by the mite, *Oligonychus bicolor*.

B,C. A close-up of a portion of the upper side of a red oak leaf on which are the empty white eggshells of mites (B) and the viable eggs ready to hatch (C). Note the leaf discoloration.

D. Pyracantha leaves totally "bleached" by the feeding of spider mites.

E. An adult mite, *Oligonychus bicolor*, and four newly laid eggs. The arrow indicates an eriophyid mite to show relative sizes.

F. A sycamore leaf, *Platanus racemosa*, with little of its normal color left after attack by the mite *Oligonychus platani*. Some of the red mites are faintly visible in the lower right corner.

G. An *Amelanchier arborea* leaf injured by the mite *Oligonychus mcdanieli*.

PLATE 201

Spider Mites on Evergreens and Honeylocust (Plate 202)

The spruce mite, *Oligonychus ununguis* (Jacobi), and the southern red mite, *Oligonychus ilicis* (McGregor), are similar in habits but are quite distinct in host preferences. Therefore it is appropriate to discuss these two economically important pests together. A related species, the boxwood mite, *Eurytetranychus buxi* (Garman), is similar to these two, but is found only on boxwood. All three attack evergreens.

The spruce mite is found only on conifers: hemlock, spruce, arborvitae, chamaecyparis, juniper and, occasionally, pine. There are a few other closely related species of spider mites which occur on these hosts also, but the spruce mite is most important. The spruce mite is a serious pest. It is widespread in distribution and can develop enormous populations rapidly. Immature and adult mites feed by rupturing cells in the foliage and withdrawing the cell contents. As a result the needles are covered with tiny chlorotic flecks. Continued feeding causes most of the foliage to become stippled and yellow or white (A). Copious webbing is produced on the foliage, and collects much dust and dirt. The feeding habits and the appearance of damage caused by the spruce mite are quite similar to those of the southern red mite, except that webbing is greatly reduced or absent for the latter.

The southern red mite is found on broad-leaved evergreens throughout the Southeast, as well as in New England, New York, Ohio, and the Great Lakes states. It is especially prolific in the South, particularly on Japanese holly, azalea, and camellia. It also attacks laurel, rhododendron, other hollies, and boxwood, and has been reported from numerous other hosts. The southern red mite is highly destructive and is one of the most common, serious pests throughout the South.

The boxwood mite attacks boxwood (C), especially varieties of European and American boxwood, *Buxus sempervirens*. Japanese boxwood, *B. microphylla* is rarely infested. The boxwood mite occurs throughout the United States and apparently is tolerant of a wide range of climatic conditions. Feeding injury gives the foliage a whitish or yellowish peppered or scratched appearance.

The spruce mite and southern red mite are quite similar in appearance. They are usually a dark reddish color. The spruce mite may also be deep dark green. The legs and front part of the body of each are buff or tan colored. The boxwood mite is greenish with orange-colored, longer legs, and is more spider-like in appearance. Young mites are much lighter in hue. Most of the coloration of spider mites results from the accumulation of food material and waste in the body. Therefore, coloration is most pronounced just prior to molting in nymphs and in more mature adults.

The three mite species discussed here are similar in seasonal development. They are most prolific in cooler weather. They reproduce rapidly and feed predominantly during spring and fall—not, as is commonly believed, during hot, dry weather. The maximum effects of the injury they have done appear coincidentally with the first hot spells of summer. It is suspected that spruce mite and southern red mite eggs aestivate, or remain dormant, during prolonged hot spells in summer. Since hot weather favors predators, a suppression of mite populations takes place. The boxwood mite occurs primarily during May and June. It is not as active in the summer or fall.

All three species overwinter in the egg stage (D,E,F,G), primarily on the foliage. Eggs of the spruce mite and southern red mite hatch in late March or in April, depending on the climate. Boxwood mite eggs hatch in early May and population development occurs more slowly. Numerous overlapping generations of the spruce and southern red mites occur until the host plant is nearly devoid of food material for the mites, or until the weather becomes excessively hot. Reproduction rates rise again in the fall. Several generations of the boxwood mite occur in the spring and early summer. It is important to apply control measures early in the season or in the fall to prevent unsightly damage to foliage, which remains on the plant for more than one growing season.

The honeylocust spider mite, *Eotetranychus multidigituli* (Ewing), is a serious pest of *Gleditsia triacanthos*, its only known host. It often causes all of the foliage of its host to turn brownish by early July (I). It has been reported in New England, New York and Ohio, as far west as Illinois and as far south as Louisiana and North Carolina.

Adult female mites overwinter in bark crevices and under bud scales. Egg laying on the foliage begins as early as mid-April in Illinois. An individual mite can develop from egg to adult in four days in the summer and in eleven days in cooler weather. Populations build up rapidly. By mid-summer, populations collapse if injury is severe. Then, new growth becomes conspicuously green on branch terminals of infested trees. When infestations are light, mites continue to reproduce until autumn when females move to the bark to hibernate.

Natural enemies of mites are common and important, although they cannot be relied upon to prevent injury to the host plants. Predaceous mites, thrips, and lady beetles are important predators. There are no known insect parasites of mites. Lady beetles in the genus *Stethorus* are extremely efficient predators and clean up declining populations of spider mites. Control measures applied too late to prevent infestations of mites are often deleterious to *Stethorus*.

References: 234, 240

A. Hemlock injury caused by the spruce mite, *Oligonychus ununguis*.
B. The larva of a spruce mite just after egg hatch (two photographs).
C. Boxwood mite injury on American boxwood.
D. Southern red mite eggs on the undersides of Japanese holly leaves.
E. Typical appearance of spruce mite eggs: recently laid (at arrow), ready to hatch (mottled eggs), and eggshells.
F. A close-up of southern red mite eggs.
G. Spruce mite egg (center) and clear, empty eggshells.
H. Boxwood mite injury on leaves of English boxwood.
I. Honeylocust leaflets injured by the honeylocust spider mite, *Euotetranychus multidigituli*.

PLATE 202

Gall Mites and Bud Mites (Plate 203)

Some mites in the Eriophyidae family are called leaf vagrants (Plate 204) because they feed freely on the foliage of plants. Leaf vagrants may be called rust mites if their damage causes russetting of the leaves. Other mites in the same family incite the proliferation of plant tissue and produce galls (Plates 205, 206). Still others infest buds of plants (Plate 203, 204) and cause internal bud injury. A number of species induce their host plants to produce blisters on the foliage (Plate 207, 208). Thus, eriophyid mites are commonly referred to as rust mites, gall mites, bud mites, and blister mites. Fortunately, the appearance of the plant reaction to these mites provides, along with the host type, a visual means of identification of many species. All eriophyid mites measure less than 0.5 mm in length. If one is not familiar with them, they can be easily overlooked, even with a 10X magnifier, and even if one is consciously trying to observe them.

Certain gall mites and bud mites are described and shown here and on pages 424-432.

Trembling aspen, *Populus tremuloides*, produces large growths on twigs and branches (A) in response to the feeding activities of an as-yet-undescribed species of eriophyid mite. Two other species of mites which occur on poplar have been identified, though their life histories are not known. *Eriophyes parapopuli* Keifer causes proliferation of poplar buds, resulting in irregular galls 13 mm or larger in diameter. *E. populi* has been reported to cause the same type of damage to buds.

Eriophyes betulae Steb. occurs on birch and causes proliferation of bud tissue like that shown in section B. A growth similar to that shown in section A may also result from its activities.

On hackberry, *Celtis occidentalis*, a witches-broom gall is occasionally found and associated with the presence of an eriophyid mite, probably *Eriophyes celtis* Kendall, and a powdery mildew fungus, *Sphaerotheca phytophila*. Trees become quite unsightly in appearance (G). The life history and habits of this eriophyid mite are also unknown. A common, and equally unsightly gall, produced by *Eriophyes fraxinoflora* Felt, is the ash flower gall. *E. fraxinoflora* causes tremendous proliferation of flower buds on the male ash trees.

The taxus bud mite (E), *Cecidophyes psilaspis* (Nalepa), is occasionally a serious pest of yew. It causes blasting and death of buds. It has been damaging to taxus on Long Island, New York. Its origin is Northern Europe. It is a pest capable of becoming more prevalent in the United States if infested plants or propagated materials are distributed in the nursery trade.

Adult taxus bud mites crawl between the bud scales where they overwinter. Feeding and reproduction occur during the late summer and fall. Secondary infectious organisms cause the decay of the buds. As many as 1000 mites may live in a single bud. Buds do not grow in the spring. Buds that are lightly infested do grow, but injury to plant tissue in the buds results in distorted needle and twig growth in the spring. When new buds are formed in the summer, mites migrate to infest them and carry on the life cycle.

References: 99, 155, 156, 271

A. *Populus tremuloides* with massive bud proliferation galls caused by an as-yet-unnamed eriophyid mite.
B. *Eriophyes betulae* bud gall on birch. (Black and white photograph)
C. Male flower buds on taxus; uninfested natural growth.
D. Blasted bud severely infested with taxus bud mite. x5
E. Immature (white) and adult (orange) taxus bud mites.
F. Typical appearance of blasted buds infested with taxus bud mite.
G. Witches-broom growth found on hackberry and caused by an eriophyid mite.
H. A close-up view of a witches-broom growth caused by eriophyid mites on hackberry.

PLATE 203

Rust Mites and Bud Mites (Plate 204)

The privet rust mite, *Aculus* (=*Vasates*) *ligustri* (Keifer), was described from *Ligustrum* species in Pasadena, California in 1938. This mite is known to occur from New England and New York south at least into Virginia. It is also known from California. *A. ligustri* seems to prefer cool weather; the heaviest populations occur in the spring and fall. Mites, however, may be found on leaves, usually on the undersurfaces, and on green stems throughout the year. The new leaves of infested *Ligustrum ovalifolium* curl and turn brown. The leaves of infested *L. armurense* become severely cupped and drop from the bush while still green (G). Also found on privet is a false spider mite, *Brevipalpus obovatus* (Donnadieu), commonly called the privet mite. It is slightly larger (.25 mm) than an eriophyid but only barely visible to the unaided eye. It occurs on the leaves of privet, azalea, Boston ivy, and other plant species. This pest is known primarily in Connecticut and in the Central Atlantic states.

The eriophyid bud mites *Phytocoptella avellanae* (Nalepa), and *Cecidophyopsis vermiformis* (Nalepa) injure both flower and vegetative buds of filbert. These species can occur wherever European filberts or their hybrids grow. The mites make their way into the newly forming buds during the summer and feed internally on the undeveloped bud tissue. Reproduction takes place inside the infested bud. The feeding of the mites causes the bud to enlarge. If the mite population is large enough the bud will be killed, and the number of nuts produced during the following year will be reduced. Normal and swollen buds are shown in section F.

An eriophyid mite of camellia was described by Keifer in 1945 and named *Cosetacus* (=*Aceria*) *camelliae*. This mite inhabits buds, especially the flower buds. Symptoms of its presence are not detectable until early February (in northern California), when flower buds with heavy infestations show brown edges on the bud scales (A). If reproduction of the mites is not retarded, the flower buds turn brown and drop before blooming. The mite feeds on the inner side of the bud scale and sometimes on the developing flower petals. It cannot be readily seen without the aid of a microscope or a 20X hand-lens. The mite is colorless, and is sometimes described as carrot-shaped. The immature and mature mites and the eggs of this species are shown (magnified about 50 times) in section C. This mite probably occurs in the southeastern states as well as in California. It causes leaves to appear rusty. Little is known about its biology.

Reference: 155

A,B,D. Brown bud scale symptoms on camellia buds caused by the eriophyid mite, *Cosetacus* (=*Aceria*) *camelliae*.

C. Inside of a camellia bud scale showing a high population of *Cosetacus camelliae*. All stages are present. Highly magnified.

E. A highly magnified photograph of *Aculus ligustri*, a mite.

F. Normal buds and "big buds" of filbert. The large buds have been damaged by the feeding of eriophyid mites inside the bud.

G. *Ligustrum armurense* showing symptoms of injury caused by the eriophyid mite *Aculus ligustri* or by a closely related species.

PLATE 204

Gall Mites of Maple (Plate 205)

Mites that cause plants to produce bladder or spindle galls, or the dense masses of hairy or bead-like growths called erinea are extremely small (about 0.15 mm) and belong to the family Eriophyidae. Several species of eriophyid mites induce maples to produce three types of galls. They are bladder, spindle and erineum galls. The brilliant red color often associated with the bladder galls makes them spectacular and conspicuous (A). Consequently, they cause much concern among tree owners, who are not aware that the colorful growths on the foliage are not detrimental to the health of the tree. Early spring foliage is affected, particularly those leaves next to the trunk and larger branches. As immature mites inside the galls become adults they move from the galls to newly developing leaves and initiate more galls. Mite activity decreases as the growing season progresses. Sufficient foliage unaffected by galls is produced during a growing season to sustain the tree without serious harm.

The maple spindle gall occurs most frequently on sugar maple (B) and is caused by *Vasates aceris-crumena* (Riley). The maple bladder gall mite, *Vasates quadripedes* (Shimer), is most common on silver maple (A) and also is common on red maple. Sometimes, distortion of leaves occurs with heavy infestations. Both spindle and bladder galls occur on the upper leaf surfaces. Several species of erineum-producing mites cause red or green patches on the lower and upper sides of maple leaves (C, D). These include *Eriophyes* (=*Aceria*) *elongatus* Hodgkiss, a red erineum, *E. modestus* Hodgkiss, a green erineum, and *Aculops maculatus* (Hodgkiss), among others. Erineum galls may look like felt patches (D) or, when magnified, like the beaded surface on a movie projection screen. Norway maple and boxelder also are attacked by species of eriophyid mites.

Generally, maple gall mites overwinter as adults under bark scales where they are able to withstand severe weather conditions. Early in the spring they move to the unfolding leaves and begin feeding. Mites that cause bladder galls and spindle galls feed on the undersides of the leaves. Initially, a slight depression results. The leaf then rapidly produces a pouch-like gall at that spot enclosing the mite. An opening remains on the underside of the leaf. The mite continues to feed and lays numerous eggs within the gall. Reproduction is prolific and as mites mature, they leave the gall and crawl to new leaves to continue infesting new foliage. By July mite activity on the foliage ceases.

H. E. Hodgkiss (134) published a comprehensive paper on the maple gall mites in 1930. There has been no other extensive study of the biology and habits of the group. However, H. H. Keifer's thorough studies (156) of eriophyid mites have provided an excellent basis for understanding the classification and relationships of the maple gall mites. Hodgkiss found and described three species of eriophyids from silver maple; eight species from sugar maple, including one which produced a green erineum; five species from red maple; three species from boxelder; three species from Norway maple; and one species from mountain maple. Nine species of eriophyids that attack maples in Europe were also described. Keifer has added new descriptions more recently, but has been unable to corroborate certain of Hodgkiss' findings.

Eriophyid mites infest other tree species and produce galls similar in appearance to those which occur on maple. *Eriophyes parulmi* (Keifer) produces a spindle gall on several *Ulmus* species that is similar to the maple spindle gall. Similarly shaped galls are found on cherry and linden. Erineum galls also commonly occur on beech (see Plate 206) and poplar.

References: 134, 155

A. *Vasates quadripedes* galls (commonly called maple bladder galls) on silver maple.
B. Spindle gall, caused by *Vasates aceris-crumena*, on sugar maple.
C. *Eriophyes* (=*Aceria*) *elongatus* erineum gall on the upper surface of sugar maple.
D. *Eriophyes aceris* erineum gall on the lower surface of silver maple.
E. *Eriophyes elongatus* erineum gall on sugar maple.
F. *Eriophyes aceris.* Left: underside of leaf with erineum; right: upper surface with leaf depressions.

PLATE 205

Eriophyid Mites That Cause Erineum and Blister Galls (Plate 206)

Many species of mites in the family Eriophyidae are called leaf vagrants because they live freely on the surfaces of leaves (Plates 183, 204). Leaf vagrants may be called rust mites, if this damage causes russetting of the leaves. Still other eriophyid mites cause the host plant to produce a variety of abnormal growths or galls. In some cases leaf blisters and erinea occur where mites have fed. Representative types of leaf abnormalities associated with several eriophyid mites are illustrated in this plate.

The wart-like galls on hickory, *Carya* sp., (A) are caused by an as yet unidentified eriophyid species collected in Ottawa, Canada. A similar gall formation is produced by mountain ash, *Sorbus* sp., infested with eriophyids. Leaf blisters on mountain ash (B,E) are caused by *Plataculus pyramidicus* Keifer, which may be the species shown in section B. However, the pear leaf blister mite also infests mountain ash as well as pear. American beech, *Fagus grandifolia,* commonly produces light green to yellowish erineum galls on the upper and lower leaf surfaces (C). Other trees—such as the European white elm, *Ulmus laevis*—exhibit the same type of erineum gall. Under high magnification (F) the erineum gall appears as a contiguous mass of bead-like growths (See Plate 205, section E). Normally the mites are concealed within or under the erineum mats. When the galls turn brown and start to dry, mites move out over the leaves (see arrows).

Hairy or felt-like erineum galls are also common on alder (D). An immature eriophyid mite is shown in section H. The extremely small size of these mites makes them barely discernible with a 10X hand lens. Another type of gall induced by eriophyid mites is the marginal fold gall. Mites which feed along the edges of leaves are common on plants such as wild cherry, sour gum, and hawthorn, *Crataegus* (G).

Eriophyid mites are host specific. Hundreds of species have been described and many are yet unknown. Very careful studies by well-qualified specialists on mite classification are necessary to determine the species of eriophyid mites encountered on trees and shrubs. In many cases their biologies and habits are complex and all too often unknown, leaving a tremendous amount of biological information yet to be discovered.

Reference: 155

A. Unidentified mite gall on hickory, *Carya* sp.
B,E. Eriophyid mite galls on mountain ash, *Sorbus* sp.
C. The yellow, felt-like pads are erineum mite galls on *Fagus grandifolia* (see Plate 205).
D. Felt-like patches caused by eriophyid mites on *Alnus* sp.
F. A magnified view of the felt-like gall of the beech leaf shown in section C.
G. Marginal fold gall on hawthorn, *Crataegus.*
H. Immature eriophyid mite.

PLATE 206

Eriophyid Mites That Cause Blister, Erineum, and Pouch Galls (Plate 207)

One unique type of injury produced by certain eriophyids is the leaf blister (A). A number of species are associated with pomaceous host plants. They cause serious injury to the foliage of pear and apple, frequently browning and curling nearly 100 percent of the foliage on infested trees. These species are also reported to attack *Amelanchier, Cotoneaster, Crataegus,* and *Sorbus.* The pear blister mite, *Phytoptus pyri* Pgst. (A) is common and injurious. Blister mites on pear and apple have been recognized for a long time as fruit pests and were first reported in the United States in 1872. They were especially widespread and abundant in major pear-growing areas of the United States and Canada in the late 1800's and early 1900's. Now they occur predominantly on fruit trees around the home, where few pest control measures are applied.

The pear and apple blister mites overwinter under the bud scales and migrate to the leaves as they develop in the spring. Mite feeding occurs on the undersurfaces of the leaves. The epidermis ruptures where feeding occurs and mites enter the opening to deposit eggs. As eggs hatch, more and more mites destroy increasing numbers of cells. A pimple-like swelling appears on the upper surface and develops into a blister which enlarges up to 3 mm in diameter. Many blisters coalesce, discoloring large contiguous patches on the leaves. As internal leaf tissue deteriorates, infested areas become brown or black, then shrink and dry out.

Eriophyes tiliae (Pgst.) incites an erineum gall (B,D) on little leaf linden, *Tilia cordata.* It is not known to attack the native linden, *T. americana. E. tiliae* has been reported from New York and California, but little is known of its life history and habits. It is likely to be similar to species found on beech, elm, maple, alder, and other plants.

The black walnut leaf pouch gall is very common and is representative of numerous similar eriophyid mites which have two structurally different forms, i.e., protogynes and deutogynes. The protogynes incite the formation of pouch galls on the leaves (C,E). Deutogynes incite erineum patches and swellings on the leaf petioles (F,G). In the eastern United States deutogynes from petioles have been described as *Eriophyes cinereae.* In the west, deutogynes and protogynes have been described respectively as *Eriophyes brachytarsus* Keifer (see Plate 208, section C) and *E. amiculus* Keifer. Recent studies have shown that both are different morphological forms of the same species. Deutogynes overwinter and are present in the erineum galls on the petiole early in the season. As the season progresses, deutogynes disappear and protogynes appear to incite and inhabit pouch galls on the leaves. In late summer and fall protogynes give rise to deutogynes which then overwinter.

White erineum patches (H) on the foliage of boxelder, *Acer negundo,* occur in the presence of *Eriophyes* (=*Aceria*) *negundi* Hodgkiss. This mite is widespread throughout much of the United States. Several other species of eriophyid mites also have been reported from boxelder.

Numerous species of predatory mites have been associated with eriophyids, most commonly, *Seius* spp. They not only feed on leaf vagrants and erineum mites, but frequently enter galls to prey upon mites as they develop inside.

References: 155, 196

A. Leaf blister mite on pear.
B,D. Erineum gall on little leaf linden.
C,E. Black walnut pouch gall.
F,G. Black walnut leaf petiole galls caused by the mite *Eriophyes caulis.*
H. Erineum galls caused by *Eriophyes negundi* on boxelder.

PLATE 207

Eriophyid Mites (Plate 208)

Several eriophyid mite species attack walnut (see also Plate 207). In the West, the walnut blister mite, *Eriophyes* (=*Aceria*) *erineus* (Nalepa), has been recognized as a pest of Persian (English) walnut for many years. It is of about the same shape and size as those mites shown in Plate 183, section C. This pest causes yellow, densely hairy and felt-like erineum pads (B) to form on the undersurfaces of leaflets. On the upper surface, a blister-like swelling is evident. The pads continue to grow as the mites multiply, and sometimes eventually cover the entire undersurface of the leaf. The mites overwinter in the vegetative buds. As soon as the first signs of growth occur in the bud the following spring, the mites become active. In the East, there are related species that affect black walnut and butternut. On butternut they produce a yellow, felt-like, erineum pad on the upper side of the leaf (A). When a leaflet is covered with these galls, its effectiveness as a food producer for the plant is greatly reduced. The mites also feed on the nut husk causing a russetting of its surface.

An eriophyid mite, *Eriophyes* (=*Aceria*) *nyssae* (Trotter), produces yellow, pimple-like blisters on the upper leaf surfaces of black tupelo, *Nyssa sylvatica* (E). Little is known about its biology and habits. It is believed to be present throughout much of the southeastern United States.

The cause of a disease condition on oak branches (D) has not been definitely established, but eriophyid mites as well as bacteria and viruses are suspected to be possible causes. Bud proliferation that may be shown to be related to eriophyid mite infestation occurs on many woody plants. Section D shows hundreds of dead buds on oak around the rough, calloused areas as an example of this type of problem. Bud formation was induced, but buds died before they were able to grow. Control of this condition can often be effected by removal of the affected part well below the evidence of symptoms.

There are hundreds of eriophyid mites that feed on all kinds of trees and shrubs. Each causes characteristic symptoms on its particular host. Because of their minute size, relatively few have yet been collected or studied. Much remains to be learned about eriophyid mites, their habits, and the cause-effect relationship between the mites and their hosts.

References: 155, 198

A. Butternut leaves and nuts affected by eriophyid mites. An erineum gall is produced on the upper side of the leaf.
B. The same butternut leaves shown in section A. Erineum galls were caused by the mite *Eriophyes cineraea*.
C. Galls of the walnut purse gall mite, *Eriophyes brachytarsus* (see also Plate 207). These galls are about 5 mm in diameter.
D. Bud proliferation on the branch of an oak, possibly induced by eriophyid mites.
E. Leaf galls caused by *Eriophyes nyssae* on black tupelo, *Nyssa sylvatica*.

PLATE 208

Katydid, Grasshopper, and Periodical Cicada (Plate 209)

Some of our most common and universally known insects are katydids and grasshoppers. The broad-winged katydid, *Microcentrum rhombifolium* (Saussure), is a minor pest of trees and shrubs that feeds on both leaves and flowers. It is a slow moving, rather heavy-bodied insect capable of only short flights. When fully grown it may measure up to 47 mm from the head to end of the wing tip. Katydids may be found throughout much of the United States but are rare in the northernmost states. They are usually of little economic importance, though occasionally, they do defoliate young citrus trees and ornamental plants. The injury sustained by the host usually takes the form of chewed-out, semi-circular holes along the leaf margins. In warmer areas of the United States broad-winged katydids may be found from March through November.

The eggs are laid in a characteristic manner (B,C) either on twigs or leaves. When the young hatch they usually feed upon the nearest foliage. Their green bodies provide excellent camouflage. The wings of an adult (A) look much like a leaf. They are arboreal and are only rarely found on the ground.

Grasshoppers are omnivorous feeders. The eastern lubber grasshopper, *Romalea microptera* (Bauv.) is common all along the south Atlantic and Gulf Coasts. During the summer literally thousands of these grasshoppers may be seen sunning themselves on the roads of Florida and Georgia. The eastern lubber is one of the largest grasshoppers in the United States. With a heavy body and short, stubby wings, it is incapable of flight (D). It is sluggish and clumsy, has weak hind legs and can leap only short distances.

Lubber grasshoppers overwinter in the egg stage in the ground. In Florida they begin to hatch in February. The nymphs are almost solid black, with yellow and occasionally red markings. Young nymphs are gregarious. Fifty to 100 may be found on a single plant. They mature in June and begin laying eggs by early July. These eggs do not hatch until the following spring.

Adults may be seen through August. One generation occurs each year.

The periodical cicada, *Magicicada septendecim* (Linnaeus), is a native North American species. It is the longest-lived insect in North America. In many rural areas people view its appearance superstitiously. Even before the white man colonized America, the Indians thought its periodic appearance had an evil significance.

There are two distinct races of periodical cicadas. The southern race has a 13-year life cycle; the northern race, a 17-year cycle. They are found widely distributed over the eastern half of the United States and occur nowhere else in the world.

In some of the southern areas, cicadas begin to emerge from the ground in late April. In northern areas, emergence begins in late May or early June. The fact that cicadas have either a 13- or 17-year life cycle should not be interpreted to mean that cicadas are seen only at 13- or 17-year intervals. These insects emerge somewhere almost every year. The various populations are described as broods. Most of the broods are separated geographically, but some overlap. Twenty-three broods have been located. Some are quite small; others have apparently been eradicated by man. The appearance of all broods can be accurately predicted. Emergence of some of the larger broods is a striking event; thousands seem to appear overnight and begin singing at dawn. Only the male has a sound-producing apparatus.

Adult cicadas (E) do not feed on leaves. If they feed at all it is by sucking sap from the young twigs. The severe injury to host plants is the result of the cicada's egg-laying habits. The female has a saw-like egg-laying apparatus which she uses to cut the bark of twigs and to splinter the sapwood. In the splintered sapwood, she lays 24 to 48 eggs. A single female may make up to 20 of these splinter pockets (E) and lay up to 600 eggs. The adult lives for about 20 to 23 days. After hatching, the nymphs drop to the ground, burrow into the soil, and search out a suitable root from which to suck sap. This is the beginning of a 13- or 17-year underground existence.

There are many natural enemies of the cicada. Insect-feeding birds appreciably reduce their numbers. Predatory insects and mites attack the eggs, and a fungus disease kills some adults.

The annual or dog-day cicada, *Tibicen linnei* (S. & G.), is a close eastern relative of the periodical cicada and appears each year in July and August. There are nine species of cicadas in New York State. In Kansas and Colorado, there are about 25 species; on the Pacific coast they are even more numerous. *Tibicen cinctifera* (Uhler) is one of the more destructive species in California, Arizona and New Mexico. With the exception of the periodical cicada, *M. septendecim*, little is known about cicadas.

Egg punctures can be extremely damaging to nursery stock as well as specimen plants. Twigs and small branches with many bark slits wilt and die, or are broken off by winds. The symmetry of ornamental plants, may be destroyed. Common deciduous forest trees may be damaged, and ornamentals such as azaleas are sometimes killed by the cicada's activities.

References: 117, 225

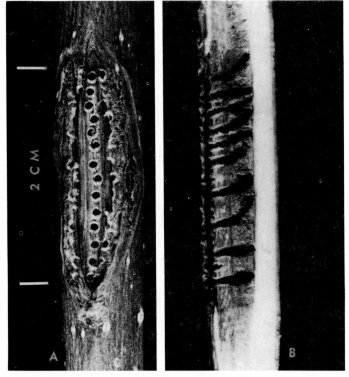

Figure 35. Three-year-old yellow poplar twigs damaged by the egg-laying organ of a tree cricket. Eggs have hatched, leaving the excavated holes and a severely damaged twig. B. A twig in sagital section showing the full length of egg chambers. (Also see plate 172.) Photos courtesy U.S. Forest Service.

A. A broad-winged katydid, *Microcentrum rhombifolium*, on a *Bougainvillea* twig. Arrow points to eggs lined up in typical fashion.
B. A twig with a double row of katydid eggs.
C. Azalea leaves with katydid eggs.
D. The eastern lubber grasshopper, *Romalea microptera*.
E. Periodical cicadas, *Magicicada septendecim*. Note cut bark where eggs have been laid (at arrow).

PLATE 209

Hymenopterous Plant Pests (Plate 210)

The giant hornet, *Vespa crabro germana* (Christ), is the largest hornet found in the United States (E). It resembles the well known cicada killer wasp but is stouter, hairier, and more reddish brown. It injures plants not by feeding but by chewing bark from twigs and branches for use in building its nest. This results in severe girdling of branches (A) which in turn causes the death of the distal portion of the branches. The injury occurs most extensively in August and September when large colonies of hornets have developed. Squirrels are often falsely accused of causing this damage (see Plate 212).

The trees and shrubs most frequently attacked by the giant hornet are lilac, birch, willow, boxwood, mountain ash, poplar, and, occasionally, rhododendron. Giant hornets may be found all along the Atlantic Coast from Massachusetts to Georgia. Their presence has also been reported in Pennsylvania and Ohio. Nests may be located up to 100 yards away from injured plants. The nests usually are located in partitions of buildings, tree holes, or holes in the ground.

The work of leafcutter bees, *Megachile* sp., are usually little more than a curiosity. The bee is black and looks like a small bumblebee. The female cuts circular pieces of foliage (D) usually from rose and uses the discs as a lining and plug for her egg cells. The bees are solitary insects but they make numerous cells in hollowed out twigs and other protected places. These bees are known throughout the United States.

A group of wasp-like insects commonly called horntails, *Tremex columba Linnaeus*, (F) are more of a naturalist's curiosity than a pest. *T. columba* derives its common name from the horn-like tail at the end of its abdomen. Adults are active early in the summer. They are also called pigeon tremex.

The larva of this species infests maple, elm, oak, hickory, sycamore, beech, apple and pear. It is whitish, and is deeply segmented with fleshy, poorly formed, thoracic legs. It grows to a length of about 50 mm. Larvae bore round tunnels of about the size of a lead pencil through the heartwood of host trees. They maintain no opening to the outside.

The adult female horntail has the unusual ability to thrust her sharp ovipositor into solid wood to a depth of 13 mm, where she deposits a single egg. The ovipositor frequently becomes wedged in the wood. In such cases, the trapped female dies. The female prefers to lay her eggs in unhealthy and dying trees. Several races of horntails occur. They are found primarily in the northern part of the United States from coast to coast.

The extremely large parasite, *Megarhyssa lunator*, lays its eggs in horntail larval galleries. The female has an ovipositor nearly eight cm long. She drills it deep into wood infested with horntail larvae. Often the ovipositor cannot be withdrawn from the tree and the female dies.

References: 257, 280

A. Fresh injury to a birch twig caused by the giant hornet, *Vespa crabro germana*, sometimes called European hornet.
B. Year-old injury to birch caused by the European hornet.
C. A close-up view to show texture of the wood after the European hornet has removed birch bark.
D. Rose leaves. Note typical circular cuts made by leafcutter bees.
E. The adult European hornet.
F. An adult horntail, *Tremex columba*.
G. Side view of a living horntail.

PLATE 210

Slugs and Snails (Plate 211)

Slugs and snails often devour the foliage of plants in a manner similar to that of insects. They leave a trail of mucus that glistens in light for extended periods even after it dries. They produce large holes in fruit, flowers, roots and tubers, as well as in foliage, when they feed. On woody plants, they feed only upon the foliage. The woody ornamentals that lie on the ground—like cotoneaster and vines—are most susceptible. Certain snails are reported to be particularly injurious to citrus trees and privet shrubs.

Slugs and snails are terrestrial relatives of oysters and clams. A slug is a snail without a visible shell. Both slugs and snails have tentacles or feelers on their heads. Each has a file-like mouthpart that rasps at the soft plant tissue and draws particles into its mouth opening. Feeding occurs primarily at night; during the day both slugs and snails remain concealed, usually on the ground where it is dark and damp. A large mucous or slime gland is located behind the mouth of slugs. There are, however, many mucous glands interspaced over much of the body that serve to keep the entire body surface moist.

The spotted garden slug, *Limax maximus* Linnaeus, is an introduced species from Europe (C). Urban and suburban gardens are its most common haunts. It may be found from Massachusetts to Virginia and west to Oregon and California.

Eggs are laid in damp places in masses of 25 or more (B). The newly hatched slug is dull white. Under favorable conditions it may grow to a length of 25 mm in a month. When it is fully grown it is brown. It takes more than a year for slugs to grow to maturity. When mature they are from 80 to 120 mm long.

The spotted garden slug feeds on foliage and flowers close to the ground. The snail shown in section A is probably *Cepaea nemoralis* (Linnaeus). It is an introduced species and is known in Massachusetts, New York, New Jersey, Virginia, Tennessee, Pennsylvania and Wisconsin. It has been recorded in Ontario, Canada, and is believed to occur in California.

Helix aspersa Muller, sometimes called the brown garden snail, is one of the edible European snails. It is seldom, if ever, used for that purpose in the United States. This species can be a noxious pest in many areas where the humidity remains high for at least part of the year. It feeds upon such plants as boxwood, rose, hibiscus, magnolia and peach. When fully grown, the yellowflecked brown shell is wrinkled and may reach 38 mm in diameter. The eggs are round and white, and are laid in masses about 25 mm beneath the soil surface. From 10 to 20 eggs may be laid at a time. Young snails grow slowly. They often require two to three years to reach maturity. The brown garden snail is believed to be found throughout most of the deep South as well as in Arizona and California. It was successfully eradicated in Florida during the 1960's.

Natural enemies of snails and slugs include toads, several parasitic flies, and carabid and lampyrid beetles.

References: 3, 37, 69, 151, 168

A. A fully grown snail believed to be *Capaea nemoralis*. (Black and white photo)
B. Eggs of the gray garden slug, *Deroceras reticulatum* Muller. The species is common throughout much of the United States. (Photo courtesy N.Y. State Agricultural Experiment Station, Geneva, N.Y.)
C. The spotted garden slug, *Limas maximus*.
D. Clematis leaves supporting two snails believed to be *Helix aspersa*. The foliage shows typical slug and snail injury.
E. Some snails feed gregariously. This often localizes the plant injury. Note that many of the leaf stems remain as stubs, evidence of snail injury.

PLATE 211

Tree Injury by Birds and Small Mammals (Plate 212)

Occasionally birds and small mammals damage trees and shrubs in city residential areas or, more commonly, in suburbs. The most common offenders are woodpeckers, squirrels, mice and rabbits.

Of the woodpeckers, the sapsuckers are of most concern. These birds rarely, if ever, dig through bark to capture wood-boring insects but rather to feed on the cambium and sap in the phloem. Sapsucker feeding results in a distinct pattern of uniformly drilled holes through the bark (A,B,C). These holes are arranged characteristically in horizontal rings and are sometimes aligned in vertical rows. The holes may be round or rectangular and the injury may be slight or severe. The birds usually select a favorite tree and feed on it repeatedly year after year. Apple orchards have been destroyed by these birds. Fungus diseases often gain access to a tree by way of the bird's beak. Fungus spores are sometimes blown or washed into the tree wounds. The shake defect phenomenon (the separation of annual rings in lumber) of concern to foresters has been attributed in part to initial damage by sapsuckers.

The tree species most commonly attacked by sapsuckers are hemlock, pine, red spruce, fir, Douglas fir, *Acer rubrum*, sugar maple, aspen, beech, birch, larch, willow, magnolia, apple, *Acacia, Grevillea, Casuarina* and certain palms.

Sapsuckers are handsome birds. The red-breasted sapsucker, *Sphyrapicus varius ruber* (Gmelin), is common in the Northwest and in British Columbia. The yellow-bellied sapsucker (A), *S. varius varius* (Linnaeus), is common throughout much of the United States from New England to California. The yellow-bellied sapsucker is reported to winter in the South and to spend the summer in the North.

Squirrels—particularly the red squirrel, *Tamiasciurus hudsonicus* Erxlenen—are fond of maple sap in the spring. With their chisel-like teeth, they make V-shaped wounds (E) on bark, and then lap up the sap. Dust and fungus spores become trapped in this sticky sap. If canker disease fungi colonize the wound, a large scar develops and the tree may die or never again grow vigorously.

In the spring and again in late autumn, the gray squirrel, *Sciurus carolinensis*, occasionally strips bark from a variety of conifer and hardwood trees. Some bark is probably eaten but most seems to be used in the construction of nests. Severe tree damage may result.

Squirrels also eat the buds of maple, elm, beech, ironwood, birch, willow, poplar and spruce in the spring. Professor Deuber of Yale Univeristy observed two pairs of squirrels, in a little more than one day, cut 2,886 twigs from elm trees to obtain the seeds (Becker, 20). These seeds made up their entire diet during the latter part of May and early June. One way to avoid such tree damage is to trap the offending squirrels and relocate them in rural areas; however, this in no way assures the survival of the animal.

Rabbits, *Sylvilagus* sp., and mice—particularly the field mouse, *Microtus pennsylvanicus* Ord—may girdle trees and shrubs by eating the bark during the winter. Rabbits girdle trees at the snow line which at times may be several feet above the base of the tree or shrub (D). Mice girdle plants under the snow (I). Bark is not ordinarily mouse food but if normal food is scarce and the mouse population is high, trees and shrubs may be seriously damaged. Both rabbits and mice feed on thin-barked trees and shrubs such as holly, ligustrum, pine, birch, apple, and young maple.

People injure trees, sometimes thoughtlessly. A young alder (H) served as a support for a pellet gun target. The damage, shown as bark scars, was caused by BB's.

References: 58, 200

A. The yellow-bellied sapsucker, a member of the woodpecker family, injures many kinds of coniferous and deciduous trees. Sapsuckers range throughout North America. (Drawing courtesy United States Forest Service)
B. Sapsucker damage to birch.
C. Sapsucker bird damage to *Acacia decurrens*. Pitch flows as a defense mechanism of the tree.
D. Girdling damage on *Ligustrum* caused by rabbits during the winter.
E,G. The V-shaped notches on maple bark are caused by squirrels that bite the bark to get sap.
F,H. Pellet gun injury to alder. Note (at arrow) pellet embedded in the bark.
I. Girdling injury to a young maple caused by mice.

PLATE 212

441

Sources of Information on Pest Control

Most of the states and provinces in the United States and Canada have governmental agencies or educational services that provide pest control recommendations and technical assistance with pest problems. Pest-control recommendations frequently change as pesticide regulations are developed and our understanding of the biology of pests expands. Non-chemical means of pest control also become more practical as biological information increases. Research laboratories and institutions that develop pest-control recommedations include agricultural and forest experiment stations, colleges of agriculture and forestry (often located at state or provincial universities), and state, provincial, or federal departments of agriculture.

Information, technical assistance, and recommendations are available directly from county, state, or federal Extension Services. The Cooperative Extension Service and various state Extension Divisions are represented by local county extension agents or agricultural advisors. The local county or city extension offices should be contacted for assistance related to plant culture, maintenance, protection, and recommendations for pest control. They serve not only commercial agriculture interests, but consumers, home horticulturists, and other residents within their governmental units. Leaflets, bulletins, and other publications on the subject of pest control are generally available from the extension agents' offices.

It is best to direct inquiries to local representatives. An extension or agricultural agent is usually listed in the telephone directory under the *city* or *county government*, but sometimes under the *United States Department of Agriculture*. In Canada, call or write your nearest federal or provincial Forestry Office.

Other sources of information include botanical gardens, arboretums, horticultural consultants, arborists, nurserymen, garden store managers, and garden editors of newspapers and magazines.

Land-Grant Institutions and Agricultural Experiment Stations in the United States

For help in finding who is the local extension representative write to the Extension Entomologist or Plant Pathologist at the College of Agriculture of your State University or to your State Experiment Station.

Alabama: Auburn University, Auburn 36830.
Alaska: University of Alaska, Fairbanks 99701; Experiment Station, Palmer 99645.
Arizona: University of Arizona, Tucson 85721.
Arkansas: University of Arkansas, Fayetteville 72701; Cooperative Extension Service, P.O. Box 391, Little Rock 72203.
California: University of California, Berkeley 94720; Riverside 92502; Davis 95616.

Colorado: Colorado State University, Fort Collins 80521.
Connecticut: University of Connecticut, Storrs 06268; Connecticut Agricultural Experiment Station, New Haven 06504.
Delaware: University of Delaware, Newark 19711.
Florida: University of Florida, Gainesville 32611.
Georgia: University of Georgia, Athens 30601; Agricultural Experiment Station, Experiment 30212; Coastal Plain Station, Tifton 31794.
Hawaii: University of Hawaii, Honolulu 96822.
Idaho: University of Idaho, Extension Service, Boise 83702; Agricultural Experiment Station, Moscow 83843.
Illinois: University of Illinois, Urbana 61801.
Indiana: Purdue University, Lafayette 47907.
Iowa: Iowa State University, Ames 50010.
Kansas: Kansas State University, Manhattan 66506.
Kentucky: University of Kentucky, Lexington 40506.
Louisiana: Louisiana State University, University Station, Baton Rouge 70803.
Maine: University of Maine, Orono 04473.
Maryland: University of Maryland, College Park 20742.
Massachusetts: University of Massachusetts, Amherst 01002.
Michigan: Michigan State University, East Lansing 48823.
Minnesota: University of Minnesota, St. Paul 55101.
Mississippi: Mississippi State University of Applied Arts & Sciences, Mississippi State 39762.
Missouri: University of Missouri, Columbia 65201.
Montana: Montana State University, Bozeman 59715.
Nebraska: University of Nebraska, Lincoln 68503.
Nevada: University of Nevada, Reno 89507.
New Hampshire: University of New Hampshire, Durham 03824.
New Jersey: Rutgers, The State University, New Brunswick 08903.
New Mexico: New Mexico State University, Las Cruces 88003.
New York: Cornell University, Ithaca 14853, Agricultural Experiment Station, Geneva 14456.
North Carolina: North Carolina State University, Raleigh 27607.
North Dakota: North Dakota State University, Fargo 58102.
Ohio: Ohio State University, Columbus 43210; Ohio Agricultural Research & Development Center, Wooster 44691.
Oklahoma: Oklahoma State University, Stillwater 74074.
Oregon: Oregon State University, Corvallis 97331.
Pennsylvania: Pennsylvania State University, University Park 16802.
Puerto Rico: University of Puerto Rico, Mayaguez.
Rhode Island: University of Rhode Island, Kingston 02881.
South Carolina: Clemson University, Clemson 29631.
South Dakota: South Dakota State University, Brookings 57006.
Tennessee: University of Tennessee, Knoxville 37901.
Texas: Texas A & M University System, College Station 77841; Agricultural Experiment Station, Lubbock 79414.
Utah: Utah State University, Logan 84321.

Vermont: University of Vermont, Burlington 05401.
Virginia: Virginia Polytechnic Institute and State University, Blacksburg 24061.
Virgin Islands: College of the Virgin Islands, St. Croix Campus 00850.
Washington: Washington State University, Pullman 99163; Western Washington Research and Extension Center, Puyallup 98371.
West Virginia: West Virginia University, Morgantown 26506.
Wisconsin: University of Wisconsin, Madison 53706.
Wyoming: University of Wyoming, Laramie 82070.

Regional Pest-Control Information in Canada

British Columbia: Pacific Forest Research Centre, Canadian Forestry Service, Dept. of the Environment, 506 West Burnside Road, Victoria, British Columbia; Council of Forest Industries of B.C., 1500 Guinness Tower, 1055 West Hastings St., Vancouver, British Columbia.
Maritime Provinces: Maritimes Forest Research Centre, Canadian Forestry Service, Dept. of the Environment, P.O. Box 4000, College Hill, Fredericton, New Brunswick.
Newfoundland: Newfoundland Forest Research Centre, Canadian Forestry Service, Dept. of the Environment, P.O. Box 6028, St. John's, Newfoundland.
Ontario: Great Lakes Forest Research Centre, Canadian Forestry Service, Dept. of the Environment, P.O. Box 490, 1189 Queen St. East, Sault Ste. Marie, Ontario; Pest Control Unit, Environmental Protection Branch, Ontario Ministry of Natural Resources, Queen's Park, Toronto, Ontario.
Prairie Provinces: Entomology & Pesticides Section, Crop Protection & Pest Control Branch, Alberta Dept. of Agriculture, Agricultural Building, Edmonton, Alberta; Northern Forest Research Centre, Canadian Forestry Service, Dept. of the Environment, 5320 - 122 Street, Edmonton, Alberta; Extension Entomologist, Extension Services Branch, Manitoba Dept. of Agriculture, 711 Norquay building, Winnipeg, Manitoba; Northern Forest Research Centre, Canadian Forestry Service, Dept. of the Environment, 501 University Crescent, Fort Garry, Winnipeg, Manitoba; Pest Control Specialist, Plant Industry Division, Sask. Dept. of Agriculture, Administrative Building, Regina, Saskatchewan; P.F.R.A. Tree Nursery, Canada Dept. of Regional Economic Expansion, Indian Head, Saskatchewan.
Quebec: Laurentian Forest Research Centre, Canadian Forestry Service, Dept. of the Environment, P.O. Box 3800, 1080 Route du Vallon, Ste. Foy, Quebec 10, Quebec.
Other Federal Sources: Information Division, Canada Dept. of Agriculture, Ottawa, Ontario; Canadian Forestry Service, Forest Pest Management Institute, P.O. Box 490, Sault Ste. Marie, Ontario P6A 5M7.

Selected References

1. Anderson, R. F. 1960. Forest and shade tree entomology. John Wiley & Sons, Inc., N.Y. 428 pp.
1a. Anderson, John F., and H.K. Kaya. 1974. Parasitism of the elm spanworm by *Telenomus alsophilae* and *Actia ontario* in Connecticut. Memoirs, Conn. Ent. Soc.
2. Anonymous. 1953. Insects of importance in New Jersey nurseries. N.J. Dept. of Agr., Div. Plant Industry, Circ. 390. 175 pp.
3. Anonymous. 1959. Land slugs and snails and their control. Farmers' Bul. 1895, USDA.
4. Anonymous. 1960. Pests and diseases of trees and shrubs. Wisc. State Dept. of Agr. Bul. 351. 87 pp.
5. Anonymous. 1960. The elm leaf beetle. USDA Leaflet #184. 4 pp.
6. Anonymous. 1961. Mimosa webworm and its control. Purdue Univ. Dept. Ent. Agr. Ext. Service Mimeo E-11. 2 pp.
7. Anonymous. 1965–74. Cooperative insect reports. USDA Weekly Publication of APHIS.
8. Armitage, H. M. 1944. Twenty-fifth annual report. Bureau of Ent. and Plant Quarantine. Calif. State Dept. Agr. Bul. 33(4): 228–275.
9. Arnott, D. A. 1957. Occurrence of *Trirhabda pilosa* Blakee (Coleoptera: Chrysomelidae) on sagebrush in British Columbia, with notes on life history. Proc. British Columbia Ent. Soc. 53:14–15.
10. Baerg, W. J. 1947. The biology of the maple leaf scale. Univ. of Ark. Agr. Exp. Sta. Bul. 470. 14 pp.
11. Bailey, S. F. 1938. Thrips of economic importance in California. Calif. Agr. Exp. Sta. Circ. 346. 77 pp.
12. Baker, W. L. 1972. Eastern forest insects. USDA Forest Service, Misc. Pub. #1175. 642 pp.
13. Balch, R. E. 1952. Studies of the balsam woolly aphid, *Adelges piceae* Ratz., and its effects on balsam fir. Canada Dept. Agr. Publ. 867. 76 pp.
14. Balch, R. E., and G. R. Underwood. 1950. The life history of *Pineus pinifoliae* (Fitch) (Homoptera: Phylloxeridae) and its effects on white pine. Can. Ent. 82 (6): 117–123.
15. Balduf, W. V. 1929. The life history of the goldenrod beetle, *Trirhabda canadensis* Kirby (Coleoptera: Chrysomelidae). Ent. News 40 (20): 35–39.
16. Ball, E. D. 1926. The life histories of two leafhoppers, a study in adaptation. J. Econ. Ent. 19:95–99.
17. Barrett, R. E. 1932. An annotated list of the insects and arachnids affecting the various species of walnuts or members of the genus *Juglans*. Calif. Univ., Pubs., Ent. 5:275–309.
18. Barter, G. W. 1957. Studies of the bronze birch borer, *Agrilus anxius* Gory. in New Brunswick. Can. Ent. 89(1):12–36.
19. Beal, J. A. 1952. Forest insects of the southeast: with special reference to the species occurring in the Piedmont Plateau of North Carolina. Duke Univ. School of Forestry Bul. 14. 168 pp.
20. Becker, W. B. 1938. Leaf-feeding insects of shade trees. Mass. Agr. Exp. Sta. Bul. No. 353. 82 pp.
21. Beckwith, R. C. 1963. An oak leaf tier, *Croesia semipurpurana* (Lepidoptera: Tortricidae) in Connecticut. Ann. Ent. Soc. of Am. 56 (6):741–744.
22. Beirne, B. P. 1956. Leafhoppers (Homoptera: Cicadellidae) of Canada and Alaska. Can. Ent. 88 Suppl. 2. 180 pp.
23. Bennett, F. D., and S. W. Brown. 1958. Life history and sex determination in the diaspine scale, *Pseudaulcaspis pentagona* (Targ.) (Coccidea). Can. Ent. 110 (6): 317–352.
24. Blake, D. H. 1931. Revision of the species of beetles of the genus *Trirhabda* north of Mexico. Proc. U.S. Natl. Museum 79(2):1–36.
25. Blakeslee, E. B. 1915. American plum borer. USDA Bul. 262. 13 pp.
26. Bobb, M. L., J. A. Weidhaas, Jr., and L. F. Ponton. 1973. White peach scale: life history and control studies. Jour. Econ. Ent. 66(6): 1290–1292.
27. Boerg, W. J. 1947. The biology of the maple leaf scale. Ark. Col. Agr. Bul. 470. 14 pp.
28. Borror, D. J., and R. E. White. 1970. A field guide to the insects. Houghton Mifflin, Boston. 404 pp.
29. Bratley, H. E. 1932. The oleander caterpillar, *Syntomedia Epilais* Walker. Fla. Ent. 15(4):57–67.
30. Britton, W. E. 1923. Guide to the insects of Connecticut. Part IV, The Hemiptera or sucking insects of Connecticut. Conn. State Geol. & Nat'l. Hist. Survey Bul. No. 34. pp. 335–345.
31. Britton, W. E., and M. P. Zappe. 1927. Some insect pests of nursery stock in Connecticut. Conn. Agr. Exp. Sta. Bul. 292:119–173. illus.
32. Britton, W. E., and R. B. Friend. 1935. Insect pests of elms in Connecticut. Conn. Agr. Exp. Sta. Bul. 369:265–307.
33. Brooks, H. L., and L. O. Warren. 1964. Biology of a pine bark aphid, *Cinara watsoni* and its response to temperature. Jour. Kansas Ent. Soc. 37:310–316.
34. Brown, L. R., and C. O. Eads. 1965. A technical study of insects affecting the oak tree in southern California. Calif. Agr. Exp. Sta. Bul. 810. 105 pp.
35. Brown, L. R., and C. O. Eads. 1965. A technical study of insects affecting the sycamore tree in southern California. Calif. Agr. Exp. Sta. Bul. 818. 38 pp.
36. Brown, L. R., and C. O. Eads. 1967. Insects affecting ornamental conifers in southern California. Calif. Agr. Exp. Sta. Bul. 834. 72 pp.
37. Burch, J. B. 1962. How to know the eastern land snails. Wm. C. Brown Co., Dubuque, Iowa. 214 pp.
38. Burke, H. E., and F. B. Herbert. 1920. California oak worm. USDA Farmers' Bul. 1076. 14 pp.
39. Burke, H. E., and A. G. Boving. 1929. The Pacific flathead borer. USDA Tech. Bul. 83. 35 pp.
40. Burns, D. P. 1971. Yellow poplar weevil. USDA Forest Pest Leaflet 125. 5 pp.
41. Cannon, W. N., Jr. 1970. Distribution records of the locust leafminer, *Odontota* [*Chalepus*] *dorsalis* (Thun.), in the United States. Rep. Ntheast. For. Exp. Sta. 1970 (34).
42. Cantelo, W. W. 1953. Life history and control of euonymus scale in Massachusetts. Mass. Agr. Exp. Sta. Bul. 471. 31 pp.
43. Cary, L. R. 1923. Plant-house aleyrodes, *Aleyrodes vaporariorum* Westw. Maine Agr. Exp. Sta. Rept. pp. 125–144.
44. Chamberlin, W. J. 1915–20. Flat-headed borers which attack orchard trees and cane fruits in Oregon. Third Crop Pest and Hort. Rept. Oregon Agr. Expt. Sta. pp. 103–108.
44a. Champlain, A. B. 1924. *Adirus trimaculatus* Say: a rose pest. Jour. Econ. Ent. 17(6): 648–650.
45. Chellman, C. W. 1971. Insects, diseases, and other problems of Florida's trees. Florida Dept. of Agr. Bul. #196. 156 pp.
46. Childs, Leroy. 1918. The life history and control of the rose leafhopper. Oregon Agr. Expt. Sta. Bul. 148. 32 pp.
47. Christian, P. J. 1953. A revision of the North American species of *Typhlocyba* and its allies. U. Kansas Sci. Bul. 35(9):1103–1277.
48. Clark, R. C., and A. G. Raske. 1974. The birch casebearer. Newfoundland Forestry Notes No. 7. 5 pp.
48a. Comstock, J. H. 1916. Reports on scale insects. Cornell Univ. Agr. Exp. Sta. Bul. 372 pp.

49. Côté, W. A., and D. C. Allen. 1973. Biology of the maple trumpet skeletonizer. *Epinotia aceriella* (Lepidoptera: Olethreutidae) in New York. Canadian Entomologist 105(3):463–470.

50. Craighead, F. C. 1950. Insect enemies of eastern forests. USDA Misc. Pub. 657. 679 pp.

51. Crawford, D. L. 1912. A new insect pest (*Trioza alacris* Flor.) Monthly Bull. Calif. State Commission Hort. 1(3):86–87.

52. Crawford, D. L. 1914. A monograph of the jumping plant-lice or Psyllidae of the new world. Smithsonian Inst., USNM Bul. 85. 186 pp.

53. Creighton, J. T. 1929. The biology and life history of the palm-leaf skeletonizer (palm leaf miner), *Homaledra sabelella* Chambers. Unpublished manuscript. Univ. of Fla.

54. Cumming, M. E. P. 1953. Notes on the life history and seasonal development of the pine needle scale, *Phenacaspis pinifolia* (Fitch) (Homoptera: Diaspididae). Canadian Ent. 85(9):347–352.

55. Cumming, M. E. P. 1959. The biology of *Adelges cooleyi* (Gill) (Homoptera: Phylloxeridae). Can. Ent. 91(10):601–617.

56. Cumming, M. E. P. 1962. The biology of *Pineus similis* (Gill) (Homoptera: Phylloxeridae) on spruce. Can. Ent. 94:395–408.

57. Cumming, M. E. P. 1968. The life history and morphology of *Adelges lariciatus* (Homoptera: Phylloxeridae). Can. Ent. 100(2):113–126.

58. Davidson, A. M., and W. Adams. 1973. The grey squirrel and tree damage. Quar. Journ. of Forestry 67 (3):237–247.

59. Davidson, John A. 1964. The genus *Abgrallaspis* in North America (Homoptera: Diaspididae). Ann. Ent. Soc. Am. 57(5):638–643.

60. Davidson, J. A., and C. W. McComb. 1958. Notes on the biology and control of *Fiorinia externa* Ferris. J. Econ. Ent. 51:405–406.

61. Davidson, R. H., and L. M. Peairs. 1966. Insect pests of farm, garden, and orchard. John Wiley & Sons, Inc., N.Y. 675 pp.

61a. Davis, Donald R. 1964. Bagworm moths of the Western Hemisphere. U.S. National Museum Bul. 244, Washington, D. C. 233 pp.

62. Dean, H. A., and J. C. Bailey. 1961. A flatid planthopper, *Metcalfa pruinosa*, Jour. Econ. Ent. 54:1104–1106.

63. DeBach, P. (ed.). 1964. Biological control of insect pests and weeds. Reinhold, N.Y. 844 pp.

64. DeBoo, R. F. 1966. Investigations of the importance, biology, and control of *Eucosma gloriola* Heinrich (Lepidoptera: Olethreutidae) and other shoot and tip moths of conifers in New York. Ph.D. thesis, Cornell Univ. 185 pp.

65. DeBoo, R. F., and J. A. Weidhaas. 1967. Phenological notes on a non-migrating population of *Pineus floccus* (Homoptera: Chermidae). Can. Ent. 99(7):765–766.

66. DeBoo, R. F., W. L. Sippell, and H. R. Wong. 1971. The eastern pineshoot borer, *Eucosma gloriola* (Lepidoptera: Tortricidae), in North America. Can. Ent. 103:1473–1486.

67. Dekle, G. W. 1965. Florida armored scale insects, in arthropods of Florida and neighboring land areas. Vol. 3. Fla. Dept. of Agr., Div. of Plant Industry. 265 pp.

68. Dekle, G. W. 1966. Azalea leafminer (*Gracillaria azaleella* Brants) (Lepidoptera: Gracillariidae). Fla. Dept. of Agr. Ent. Cir. #55.

69. Dekle, G. W. 1969. The brown garden snail (*Helix aspersa* Muller). Fla. Dept. of Agr. Ent. Cir. #83.

70. DeLong, D. M. 1965. Ecological aspects of North American leafhoppers and their role in agriculture. Bul. Ent. Soc. Amer. 11:9–26.

71. Denmark, H. A. 1967. Cuban laurel thrips, *Gynaikothrips ficorum*, in Florida. Fla. Dept. of Agr. Ent. Cir. #59.

72. Denmark, H. A. 1969. A Podocarpus aphid. *Neophyllaphis podocarpi* Tak. Fla. Dept. of Agr. Ent. Cir. #84.

73. Denton, R. E., and Scott Tunnock. 1972. Larch casebearer in western larch forests. USDA Forest Pest Leaflet 96. 8 pp.

74. Dickson, R. C. 1950. The Fuller rose beetle. Calif. Agr. Exp. Sta. Bul. 719. 8 pp.

75. Dietz, H. F., and H. Morrison. 1916. The Coccidae or scale insects of Indiana. Eighth Ann. Rept. Indiana State Entomologist. pp. 195–321.

76. Donley, D. E., and D. P. Burns. 1965. The tulip tree scale. USDA Forest Pest Leaflet 92. 5 pp.

77. Doutt, R.L. 1959. Heterogony in *Dyrocosmus* (Hymenoptera: Cynipidae). Ann. Ent. Soc. Amer. 52(1):69–74.

78. Dozier, H. L. 1928. The Fulgoridae or planthoppers of Mississippi, including those of possible occurrence; a taxonomic, biological, ecological, and economic study. Tech. Bul. Miss. Agr. Exp. Sta. 14:112–114.

79. Drake, C. J., and F. A. Ruhoff. 1965. Lacebugs of the world: a catalogue. U.S. National Museum Bul. 243. 634 pp.

80. Drooz, A. T. 1956. The larch sawfly. USDA Forest Pest Leaflet 8. 4 pp.

81. Drooz, A. T. 1960. White pine shoot borer (*Eucosma gloriola* Heinrich). Jour. Econ. Ent. 53(2):248–251.

82. Dyar, H. G. 1897. On the larvae of certain sawflies (*Tenthredinidae*). Journal of the N.Y. Entomological Society. Vol. 5, pp. 18–30.

83. Eaton, C. B. 1955. The Saratoga spittle bug. USDA Forest Pest Leaflet 3. 4 pp.

84. Ebeling, W. 1959. Subtropical fruit pests. Univ. of Calif. Div. of Agr. Sci. 436 pp.

84a. Edmunds, G. F., Jr. 1973. Ecology of black pineleaf scale (Homoptera: Diaspididae). Environ. Ent. 2(5): 765–777.

85. Engelhardt, G. P. 1946. The North American clearwing moths of the family Aegeriidae. Smithsonian U.S. Nat. Museum Bulletin 190. 222 pp.

86. English, L. L. 1962. Illinois trees and shrubs: their insect enemies. Ill. Natural History Circ. 47. 92 pp.

87. Essig, E. O. 1912. Plant lice affecting citrus trees. Calif. State Comm. Hort. Monthly Bul. 1(4):115–133.

88. Essig, E. O. 1913. Injurious and beneficial insects of California. Calif. State Comm. Hort. Monthly Bul. 2(1,2):1–351.

89. Essig, E. O. 1916. The soft bamboo scale. Calif. State Commission Hort. Monthly Bul. 5(2):72–73.

90. Essig, E. O. 1917. The tomato and laurel Psyllids. Jour. Econ. Ent. 10(4):433–444.

91. Essig, E. O. 1932. A genus and species of the family Aphididae new to North America. Univ. of Calif. Publ. in Ent. 6(1):1–8.

92. Essig, E. O. 1945. The pit-making Pittosporum scale. Calif. State Dept. of Agr. Bul. 34(3):134–136.

93. Essig, E. O. 1958. Insects and mites of Western North America. The Macmillan Co., N.Y. 1050 pp.

94. Ewan, H. G. 1957. Jack-pine sawfly. USDA Forest Pest Leaflet 17. 4 pp.

95. Fedde, G. F. 1973. Impact of the balsam woolly aphid (Homoptera: Phylloxeridae) on cone and seed produced by Fraser fir. Can. Ent. 105(5):673–680.

96. Felt, E. P. 1906. Insects affecting park and woodland trees. N.Y.S. Museum Memoir 8. 877 pp. 2 vols.

97. Felt, E. P., and L. H. Joutell. 1904. Monograph of the genus Saperda. N.Y.S. Museum Bul. 74. 86 pp.

98. Felt, E. P. 1924. Manual of tree and shrub insects. L. H. Bailey, Ed. The Macmillan Company, N.Y. 382 pp.

99. Felt, E. P. 1940. Plant galls and gall-makers. Comstock Publ. Co., Ithaca, N.Y. 364 pp.

100. Fenton, F. A. 1917. Observations on *Lecanium corni* Bouche, and *Physokermes piceae* Schr. Canad. Ent. 49:309–320.

101. Fenton, F. A. 1939. Control of shade tree borers. Oklahoma Agricultural & Mechanical College Exp. Sta. Circ. No. 84. 28 pp.

102. Ferris, G. F. 1950. Atlas of the scale insects of North America. Ser, V. The Pseudococcidae (Part I). Stanford Univ. Press, Stanford, Calif. 278 pp.

103. Ferris, G. F. 1953. Atlas of the scale insects of North America. Vol. VI. Stanford Univ. Press, Stanford, Calif.

104. Fitzgerald, T. D. 1973. Coexistence of three species of bark-mining *Marmara* (Lepidoptera: Gracillariidae) on green ash and descriptions of new species. Ann. Ent. Soc. of Am. 66(2):457–464.

105. Fisher, W. S. 1942. A revision of the North American species of Buprestid beetles belonging to the tribe Chrysobothrini. USDA Misc. Pub. No. 470. 274 pp.

106. Flint, W. P., and M. D. Farrar. 1940. Protecting shade trees from insect damage. Ill. Agr. Exp. Sta. and Ext. Service Circular 509. 60 pp.

107. Forbush, E. H., and C. H. Fernald. 1896. The gypsy moth. Mass. State Board of Agriculture, Boston. 495 pp.

108. Frankie, G. W. 1969. Investigations on the ecology of the cypress bark moth, *Laspeyresia cupressana* (Kearfott) (Lepidoptera: Olethreutidae). Ph.D. thesis, Univ. of California, Berkeley. 126 pp.

109. Frankie, G. W., and C. S. Koehler. 1967. Cypress bark moth on Monterey cypress. Calif. Agr. 21(1):6–7.

110. Freeman, T. H. 1960. Needle-mining Lepidoptera of pine in North America. Can. Ent. v. 92, Suppl. 160. 51 pp.

111. Frost, S. W. 1923. A study of the leaf-mining Diptera of North America. N.Y. (Cornell) Agr. Exp. Sta. Mem. 78. 228 pp.

112. Frost, S. W. 1924. The leaf-mining habit in the Coleoptera. Ent. Soc. Amer. Ann. 17(4):457–467.

113. Garman, P. 1923. Notes on the life history of the spruce mite. Conn. Agr. Exp. Sta. Bul. 247:240–242.

114. Gillette, C. P. 1909. American snowball louse *Aphis viburnicola*. Ent. News, Vol. XX, No. 6, June, pp. 280–285.

115. Gimpel, W. F., Jr., D. R. Miller and J. A. Davidson. 1974. A systematic revision of the wax scales, genus *Ceroplastes*, in the U.S. (Ho-

moptera; Coccoidea; Coccidae). Misc. Bul. 841 Univ. of Md. Agr. Exp. Sta.

116. Green, C. T. 1914. The cambium miner in river birch. Jour. Agr. Research 1(7):471–474.

117. Griffiths, J. T., and W. L. Thompson. 1957. Insects and mites found on Florida citrus. Fla. Agr. Exp. Sta., Bul. 591. 96 pp.

118. Griswold, G. H. 1937. Common insects of the flower garden. Cornell Ext. Bul. 371. 59 pp.

119. Haegele, R. W. 1936. The elm leaf beetle. Univ. Idaho Extension Circ. 52. 8 pp.

120. Hansell, D. E., Editor. 1970. Handbook of hollies. Am. Hort. Magazine, Vol. 49(4):234–255.

121. Hanson, J. B., and D. M. Benjamin. 1967. Biology of *Phytobia setosa*, a cambium miner of sugar maple. J. Econ. Ent. 60(5):1351–1355.

122. Hantsbarger, W. M., and J. W. Brewer. 1970. Insect pests of landscape plants. Colo. State Univ. Coop. Ext. Bul. 472A. 65 pp.

123. Harris, J. W., and H. C. Coppel. 1967. The poplar-and-willow borer, Sternochetus (=*Cryptorhynchus*) *lapathi* (Coleoptera: Curculionidae) in British Columbia. Canadian Ent. 99(4):411–418.

124. Harville, J. P. 1955. Ecology and population dynamics of the California oak moth. Microentomology 20:83–166.

125. Hay, C. J., and R. C. Morris. 1961. Carpenterworm. USDA Forest Pest Leaflet 64. 8 pp.

125a. Heinrich, C. 1956. American moths of the subfamily Phycitinae. U.S. National Museum Bul. 207. Smithsonian Institution, Washington, D.C. 58 pp.

126. Heinrichs, E. A., E. E. Burgess, and E. L. Matheny, Jr. 1973. Control of leaf-feeding insects on yellow-poplar. Jour. of Econ. Ent.66(5):1240–1241.

127. Herrick, G. W. 1923. The maple casebearer. Cornell Univ. Agr. Exp. Sta. Bul. 417.

128. Herrick, G. W. 1931. The magnolia scale (*Neolecanium comuparvum* Thro). Ann. Ent. Soc. Amer. 24(2):302–305. illus.

129. Herrick, G. W. 1935. Insect enemies of shade trees. Comstock Publ. Co., Ithaca, N.Y. 417 pp.

130. Herrick, G. W., and T. Tanaka. 1926. The spruce gall aphid. Cornell Univ. Agr. Exp. Sta. Bul. #454. 17 pp.

131. Hess, A. D. 1940. Biology and control of the round-headed apple-tree borer, *Saperda candida* Fabricius. N.Y. State Agr. Exp. Sta. Bul. 688, pp. 5–93.

132. Hille Ris Lambers, D. 1966. Notes on California aphids, with description of new genera and new species (Homoptera: Aphididae). Hilgardia 37 (15):569–623.

133. Hixson, Ephriam. 1941. The walnut Datana. Oklahoma A & M College Exp. Sta. Bul. B - 246.

134. Hodgkiss, H. E. 1930. The Eriophyidae of N.Y. II. The maple mites. N.Y. Agr. Exp. Sta. Tech. Bul. 163. 45 pp.

135. Hoerner, J. L. 1936. Western rose Curculio. Colo. Agr. Exp. Sta. Bul. 432. 19 pp.

136. Hosley, N. W. 1938, Damage to forest trees by wild mammals. Tree Pest Leaflet 30. Mass. Forest & Park Assoc. 4 pp.

137. Hottes, F. C., and T. H. Frison. 1931. The plant lice of Aphiidae of Illinois. Ill. Natural History Survey Bulletin. Vol. XIX, Article III, pp. 121–447.

138. Hough, W. S. 1925. Biology and control of Comstock's mealybug on the umbrella catalpa. Va. Agr. Exp. Sta. Tech. Bul. 29. 27 pp.

139. Howard, L. D., and F. H. Chittenden. 1916. The bagworm, an injurious shade tree insect. USDA Farmers Bul. 701. 11 pp.

140. Hussy, N. H. 1952. A contribution to the bionomics of the green spruce aphid, *Neomyzaphis abietina* Walker. Scott. Forestry 6, 121–130.

141. Hutchings, C. B. 1924. The lesser oak carpenter worm and its control. Canada Dept. of Agr. Ent. Branch Circ. 23.

142. Hutchins, Ross E. 1969. Galls and gall insects. Dodd, Mead, & Co., N.Y. 128 pp.

143. Jaynes, Richard A. 1969. Handbook of North American nut trees. Northern Nut Growers Assoc. 421 pp.

144. Jensen, D. D. 1957. Parasites of the Psyllidae. Hilgardia 27(2):71–99.

145. Jensen, G. L., and C. S. Koehler. 1969. Biological studies of *Scythropus californicus* on Monterey pine in Northern California. Ann. Ent. Soc. of Amer. 62(1):117–120.

146. Johnson, N. E. 1965. Reduced growth associated with infestations of Douglas fir seedlings by *Cinara* sp. (Homoptera: Aphidae). Can. Ent. 97(2):113–119.

147. Johnson, S. A. 1906. The cottony maple scale. Colo. Agr. Exp. Sta. Press Bul. 27. 4 pp.

148. Johnson, W. T. The Asiatic oak weevil and other insects causing damage to chestnut foliage in Maryland. Jour. Econ. Ent. 49(5):717–718.

149. Johnson, W. T., and M. L. Russell. 1962. The black citrus aphid *Toxoptera aurantii* (Fonscolombe) in Maryland. Proc. Ent. Soc. of Washington 64(2):90.

150. Jones, T. H., and J. V. Schaffner. 1959. Cankerworms. USDA Leaflet 183.

151. Judge, F. D. 1972. Aspects of the biology of the gray garden slug (*Deroceras reticulatum* Muller). Search, Vol. 2 (19):1–18. N.Y. State Agric. Exp. Sta.

152. Kattoulas, M. E., and C. S. Koehler. 1965. Studies on the biology of the irregular pine scale. Jour. Econ. Ent. 58(4):727–730.

153. Keen, F. P. 1952. Insect enemies of western forests. USDA Misc. Publ. 273. 271 pp.

154. Keifer, H. H. 1936. California Micro-lepidoptera VIII. Bull. So. Calif. Acad. Sci. 35(1):9–29.

155. Keifer, H. H. 1946. A review of North American economic Eriophyid mites. Jour. Econ. Ent.39(5):563–570.

156. Keifer, H. H. 1938–1975. Eriophyid studies. Vol. I–XXVI (1938–1959) Bul. Calif. Dept. of Agr. Vol. XXVII–XXVIII (1959) Bur. Ent., Calif. Dept. of Agr., Occasional Papers 1 & 2. B Series 1–21 (1969–1974) Bur. Ent. Calif. Dept. of Agr. Special Publications. C Series 1–9 (1969–1974) Bur. Ent. Calif. Dept. of Agr. Special Publications.

157. Knight, Harry H. 1941. The plant bugs or Miridae of Illinois. Ill. Nat. Hist. Survey. Vol. 22 (Art. 1). 234 pp.

158. Koehler, C. S., and M. Tauber. 1964. *Periploca nigra,* a major cause of dieback of ornamental juniper in California. Jour. Econ. Ent. 57(4):563–566.

159. Koehler, C. S., M. E. Kattoulas, and G. W. Frankie. 1966. Biology of *Psylla uncatoides*. Jour. Econ. Ent. 59(5):1097–1100.

160. Kotinsky, Jacob. 1921. Insects injurious to deciduous shade trees and their control. USDA Farmers' Bul. 1169. 100 pp.

161. Kuitert, L. C. 1958. Insect pests of ornamental plants. Fla. Agr. Exp. Sta. Bul. 595. 51 pp.

162. Kuitert, L. C. 1967. Observations on the biology, bionomics, and control of white peach scale, *Pseudaulacaspis pentagona* (Targ.) Proc. Fla. St. Hort. Soc. Vol. 80:376–381.

163. Kulp, L. A. 1968. The taxonomic status of dipterous holly leaf miners (Diptera: Agromyzidae). Univ. of Md. Agr. Exp. Sta. Bul. A-55:4.

164. Latta, R. 1937. The rhododendron white fly and its control. USDA Circ. 429. 8 pp.

165. Leonard, M. D. 1963. A list of aphids of New York. Proc. Rochester Acad. of Science, Vol. 10, No. 6, pp. 289–428.

166. Leonard, M. D. and T. L. Bissell. 1970. A list of the aphids of District of Columbia, Maryland and Virginia. Univ. of Md. Agr. Sta. MP770. 129 pp.

167. Lindquist, O. H. 1971. The Adelgids (Homoptera) on forest trees in Ontario with key to galls on spruce. Proc. Ent. Soc. of Ontario Vol. 102, 23–27.

168. Lovett, A. L., and A. B. Black. 1920. The gray garden slug (with notes on allied forms). Bul. Ore. Agr. Exp. Sta. 170. 43 pp.

169. Lowe, J. H. 1965. Biology and dispersal of *Pineus pinifoliae* (F). Unpublished thesis, Yale Univ. 104 pp. illus.

170. Lugger, Otto. 1900. Buds injurious to our cultivated plants. Univ. of Minn. Agr. Exp. Sta. Bul. 69. 257 pp. illus.

171. MacAloney, H. J. 1961. Pine tortoise scale. USDA Forest Pest Leaflet 57. 7 pp.

172. MacAloney, H. J., and D. C. Schmiege. 1962. Identification of conifer insects by type of tree injury, Lake States. Lake States Forest Exp. Sta. Paper #100, USDA.

173. MacAloney, H. J., and H. G. Ewan. 1964. Identification of hardwood insects by type of tree injury, North Central Region. U.S. Forest Service Research Paper LS-11. 70 pp.

174. MacAloney, H. J., and L. F. Wilson. 1964. The red-headed pine sawfly. USDA Forest Pest Leaflet 14. 5 pp.

175. McConnell, H. S. 1949. A new North American species of *Pulvinaria*. Proc. Ent. Soc. Wash. 51(1):29–34.

176. McConnell, H. S., and J. A. Davidson. 1959. Observations on the life history and morphology of *Kermes pubescens* Bogue (Homoptera: Coccoidea: Dactylopiidae). Ann. Ent. Soc. Amer.52:463.

177. McDaniel, E. I. 1930. Soft scales injurious to deciduous ornamentals. Michigan Agr. Exp. Sta. Circ. Bul. 133. 17 pp.

178. McDaniel, E. I. 1933. Important leaf feeding and gall making insects infesting Michigan's deciduous trees and shrubs. Michigan Agr. Exp. Sta. Spec. Bul. No. 243. 70 pp.

179. McDaniel, E. I. 1933. Some wood borers attacking the trunks and

limbs of deciduous trees and shrubs. Michigan Agr. Exp. Sta. Spec. Bul. No. 238. 36 pp.

180. McDaniel, E. I. 1937. Controlling sucking insects on conifers. Michigan Ext. 175:21–22.

181. McKenzie, H. L. 1956. The armored scale insects of California. Bul. Calif. Insect Survey. Vol. V. Univ. of Calif. Press. 209 pp.

182. McKenzie, H. L. 1967. Mealybugs of California. Univ. of Calif. Press. Berkeley. 526 pp.

183. Madsen, H. F., and S. C. Hoyt. 1957. *Schizura ipomaeae* Dbldy. attacking plums in California. Jour. Econ. Ent. 50(3):284–287.

184. Madsen, H. F., and M. M. Barnes. 1959. Pests of pear in California. Calif. Agr. Exp. Sta. Circ. 478. 40 pp.

185. Mains, E. B. 1958. North American entomogenous species of *Cordyceps*. Mycologia 50(2):169–222.

186. Mani, M. S. 1964. Ecology of plant galls. Junk Publishers, The Hague. 434 pp.

187. Marcovitch, S. 1916. The red rose beetle. Office of the Minnesota State Entomologist Circ. 36. 4 pp.

188. Matheson, Robert. 1917. The poplar and willow borer. Cornell Agr. Exp. Sta. Bul. 388.

189. Mead, F. W. 1962. The thorn bug, *Umbonia crassicornis*. Ent. Circular No. 8, Florida Dept. of Agriculture.

190. Mead, F. W. 1963. A Psyllid, *Trioza magnoliae* (Ashmead) (Homoptera: Psyllidae). Fla. Dept. Agr., Div. Pl. Ind., Ent. Circ. #15. 2 pp.

191. Mead, F. W. 1969. Citrus flatid planthopper, *Metcalfa pruinosa* (Say) (Homoptera: Flatidae). Fla. Dept. of Agr. Ent. Circular No. 85.

192. Mead, F. W. 1970. *Ctenodactylomia watsoni* Felt, a gall midge pest of seagrape, *Coccoloba uvifera* L., in Florida (Diptera: Cecidomyiidae). Fla. Dept. of Agr. Ent. Circular No. 97.

193. Mead, F. W. 1972. The hawthorn lace bug *Corythucha cydoniae* (Fitch) in Florida (Hemiptera: Tingidae). Florida Dept. of Agr. and Consumer Services. Ent. Circ. No. 127.

194. Merrill, G. B. 1953. A revision of the scale insects of Florida. State Plant Board of Fla. Bul. 1. 143 pp.

195. Merrill, G. B., and J. Chaffin. 1923. Scale-insects of Florida. Fla. State Plant Board Quarterly Bul. 7(4):177–298.

196. Metcalf, C. L., W. P. Flint, and R. L. Metcalf. 1951. Destructive and useful insects. McGraw-Hill, N.Y. 1071 pp.

197. Michelbacher, A. E., and S. Hitchcock. 1956. Frosted scale on walnuts. Calif. Agr. 10(4):11–14.

198. Michelbacher, A. E., and J. C. Ortega. 1958. A technical study of insects and related pests attacking walnuts. Calif. Agr. Exp. Sta. Bul. 764. 86 pp.

199. Middleton, Wm. 1922. Sawflies injurious to rose foliage. USDA Farmers Bul. 1252. 14 pp.

200. Mills, E. M. 1938. Tree injury by squirrels. Mass. Agr. Exp. Sta. Bul. No. 353. 2 pp.

201. Mitchell, R. G., G. D. Amman, and W. E. Waters. 1970. Balsam woolly aphid. USDA Forest Pest Leaflet #118. 10 pp.

202. Mordvilko, A. 1924. *Eriosoma lanigera*, biology and distribution. Trans. Dept. of Applied Ent., Leningrad Vol. XII, No 3. 110 pp.

203. Morris, R. F. 1967. Factors inducing diapause in *Hyphantria cunea*. Canadian Ent. 99(5):522–529.

204. Mote, D. C. 1936. Strawberry root weevil control in Oregon. Oregon State Agr. Exp. Sta. Circ. 115.

205. Moulton, D. 1907. The Monterey pine scale, *Physokermes insignicola* (Craw.). Proc. Davenport Acad. Sci. 12:1–25.

206. Moznette, G. G. 1922. The avocado: its insect enemies. USDA Farmers Bul. 1261. 31 pp.

206a. Muesebeck, C. F. W., K. V. Krombein and H. K. Townes. 1951. Hymenoptera of America North of Mexico. USDA Agr. Monograph No. 2. 1420 pp.

207. Munro, J. A. 1963. Biology of the *Ceanothus* stem-gall moth, *Periploca ceanothiella* (Cosens). Jour. of Research on the Lepidoptera. 1(3):183–190.

208. Munro, J. A. 1965. Occurrence of *Psylla uncatoides* on *Acacia* and *Albizia* with notes on control. Jour. Econ. Ent. 58(6):1171–1172.

209. Needham, J. G., S. W. Frost, and B. H. Tothill. 1928. Leaf-mining insects. Williams & Wilkins, Baltimore. 351 pp.

210. Neiswander, C. R. 1941. *Coryphista meadii*: a new pest of Japanese barberry. Jour. Econ. Ent. 34(3):386–389.

211. Neiswander, R. B. 1966. Insect and mite pests of trees and shrubs. Ohio Agricultural Research and Development Center Research Bul. 983. 54 pp.

212. Nichols, J. O. 1961. The gypsy moth in Pennsylvania. Penna. Dept. Agr. Misc. Bul. 4404. 82 pp.

213. Nichols, J. O. 1968. Oak mortality in Pennsylvania. Jour. of Forestry. 66(9):681–684.

214. Nielson, M. W. 1968. The leafhopper vectors of phytopathogenic viruses. USDA, ARS Tech. Bul. 1382. 386 pp.

215. Nord, J. C., D. G. Grimble and F. B. Knight. 1972. Biology of *Saperda inornata* [*S. concolor*] (Coleoptera: Cerambycidae) in trembling aspen, *Populus tremuloides*. Ann. Ent. Soc. Amer. 65(1):127–35.

216. Nordin, G. L., and J. E. Appleby. 1969. Bionomics of the juniper webworm. Ent. Soc. of Am. Ann. 62(2):287–292.

217. Oliver, A. D. 1964. A behavioral study of two races of the fall webworm, *Hyphantria cunea* (Lepidoptera: Arctiidae) in Louisiana. Ann. Ent. Soc. Amer. 57:192–194.

218. Ollieu, M. M. 1971. Damage to southern pines in Texas by *Pissoides nemorensis*. Jour. Econ. Ent. 64(6):1456–1459.

219. Osborn, Herbert. 1928. The leafhoppers of Ohio. Biol. Survey Bul. 14. Vol. 3, No. 4.

220. Osborn, Herbert. 1940. The Membracidae of Ohio. Ohio Biol. Surv. Bul. 37. Vol. 7(2):51–101. illus.

221. Parker, D. L., and M. W. Moyer. 1972. Biology of a leafroller, *Archips negundanus* in Utah (Lepidoptera: Tortricidae). Ann. Ent. Soc. of Am. 65(6):1415–1418.

222. Parr, T. 1940. *Asterolecanium variolosum* Ratzeburg, a gall-forming coccid, and its effect upon the host tree. Yale Univ. School of Forestry Bul. No. 46. 49 pp.

223. Parrott, P. J., and B. B. Fulton. 1915. The cherry and hawthorn sawfly leafminer. N.Y.S. Agr. Exp. Sta. Bul. 411, pp. 551–580.

224. Payne, J. A., W. L. Tedders, G. E. Cosgrove, and D. Foard. 1972. Larval mine characteristics of four species of leafmining Lepidoptera in pecan. Ann. Ent. Soc. Amer. 65(1):74–84.

225. Pechuman, L. L. 1968. The periodical cicada, Brood VII (Homoptera: Cicadidae: Magicicada). Trans. Amer. Ent. Soc. 94:137–153.

226. Pemberton, C. 1911. The California Christmas-berry tingid. Jour. Econ. Ent. 4(3):339–343.

227. Pergande, Theodore. 1901. The life history of two species of plant-lice. USDA Division of Ent. Tech. Series No. 9.

228. Pergande, Theodore. 1912. The life history of the alder blight aphis. USDA Bur. of Ent. Tech. Series No. 24, pp. 1–28.

229. Peterson, L. O., and R. F. DeBoo. 1969. Pine needle scale in the prairie provinces. Canada Dept. of Fisheries and Forestry, Note MS-L-5. 9 pp.

230. Peterson, L. O. T. 1958. The boxelder twig borer, *Proteoteras willingana* (Kearfott), (Lepidoptera: Olethreutidae) Can. Entomologist 90(11):639–646.

231. Pollet, D. K. 1972. The morphology, biology, and control of *Ceroplastes ceriferus* (Fab.) and *C. sinensis* Del Guer. in Virginia including a redescription of *C. floridensis* Comstock (Homoptera: Coccoidae: Coccidae). Ph.D. thesis, VPI & S.U. 208 pp.

232. Poos, F. W., and N. H. Wheeler. 1943. Studies on host plants of the leafhoppers of the genus *Empoasca*. USDA Tech. Bul. 850. 51 pp.

233. Pritchard, A. E. 1949. Calif. greenhouse pests and their control. Calif. Agr. Exp. Sta. Bul. 713. 71 pp.

234. Pritchard, A. E., and E. W. Baker. 1955. A revision of the spider mite family Tetranychidae. Pac. Coast Ent. Soc. Mem. Ser. Vol. 2. 472 pp.

235. Pritchard, A. E., and J. A. Powell. 1959. *Pyramidobela angelarum* Keifer on ornamental *Buddleia* in the San Francisco Bay area. Pan-Pac. Entomol. 35(2):82.

236. Pritchard, A. E., and R. E. Beer. 1950. Biology and control of *Asterolecanium* scales on oak in California. Jour. Econ. Ent. 43(4):494–497.

237. Quaintance, A. L., And A. C. Baker. 1914. Classification of the Aleyrodidae. Tech. Ser., 24, 1, 1913, II. Bur. Ent. USDA.

238. Quednau, F. W. 1967. Ecological observations on *Chrysocharis laricinellae* (Hymenoptera: Eulophidae), a parasite of the larch casebearer (*Coleophora laricella*). Can. Ent. 99(6):631–641.

239. Rabkin, F. B., and R. R. Lejune. 1954. Some aspects of the biology and dispersal of the pine tortoise scale. Can. Ent. 86(12)570–575.

240. Reeves, R. M. 1963. Tetranychidae infesting woody plants in New York State and a life history study of the elm spider mite, *Eotetranychus matthyssei* n. sp. Cornell Univ. Agr. Exp. Sta. Mem. 380. 99 pp.

241. Richards, W. R. 1967. The *Pterocomma* of Canada and Greenland with notes on the phyletic position of the Pterocommatini (Homoptera: Aphidiidae). Can. Ent. 99:1015–1040.

242. Rings, Roy W. 1973. Contributions to the bionomics of green fruitworms: the life history of *Lithophane antennata*. Jour. Econ. Ent. 66(2):364–368.

243. Rosenthal, S. S., G. W. Frankie, and C. S. Koehler. 1969. Biological studies of *Argyresthia franciscella* and *A. cupressella* on ornamental Cupressaceae. Ann. Ent. Soc. Amer. 62(1):109–112.

244. Ross, D. A. 1962. Bionomics of the maple leaf cutter, *Paraclemensia acerifoliella* (Fitch), (Lepidoptera: Incurvariidae). Can. Ent. 94 (10):1053–1063.

245. Russell, L. M. 1941. A classification of the scale insect genus *Asterolecanium*. USDA Misc. Publ. 424. 322 pp.

246. Russell, H. M. 1912. The greenhouse thrips. USDA Bur. Ent. Circ. 151. 9 pp.

247. Sanders, J. G. 1905. The cottony maple scale. USDA Bur. Ent. Circ. 64. 6 pp.

248. Schmiege, D. C. 1970. Hemlock sawfly. USDA Forest Pest Leaflet 31. 4 pp.

249. Schneski, Wm. 1966. Biology and control of the balsam twig aphid, *Mindarus abietinus* Koch. Unpublished research, Cornell Univ., Ithaca, N.Y.

250. Schread, J. C. 1959. Pod gall of honeylocust. Conn. Agr. Exp. Sta. Circ. 206. 4 pp.

251. Schread, J. C. 1964. Dogwood club gall. Conn. Agr. Exp. Sta. Circ. No. 225.

252. Schread, J. C. 1968. Control of lacebugs on broadleaved evergreens. Conn. Agr. Exp. Sta. Bul. 684.

253. Schread, J. C. 1970. Control of scale insects and mealybugs on ornamentals. Conn. Agr. Exp. Sta. Bul. 710. 27 pp.

254. Schread, J. C. 1971. Leafminers and their control. Conn. Agr. Exp. Sta. Bul. 693. 19 pp.

255. Schread, J. C. 1971. Control of borers in trees and woody ornamentals. Conn. Agr. Exp. Sta., Circ. No. 241. 11 pp.

256. Schuh, J., and D. C. Mote. 1948. Insect pests of nursery and ornamental trees and shrubs in Oregon. Oregon Agr. Exp. Sta. Bul. 449. 164 pp.

257. Shaw, F. R., and J. A. Weidhaas, Jr. 1956. Distribution and habits of the giant hornet in North America. Jour. Econ. Ent. 49(2):275.

258. Shenefelt, Roy D., and D. M. Benjamin. 1955. Insects of Wisconisn forests. Univ. of Wisconsin Ext. Circ. 500.

259. Shigo, A. L. 1970. Beech bark disease. USDA Forest Pest Leaflet 75. 7 pp.

260. Silver, G. T. 1957. Studies on the arborvitae leaf miners in New Brunswick (Lepidoptera: Yponomeutidae and Gelechiidae). Can. Ent. 89, 171–182.

261. Simanton, F. L. 1916. The terrapin scale, an important insect enemy of peach orchards. USDA Bul. 351. 96 pp.

262. Slingerland, M. V. 1906. The bronze birch borer. Cornell Agr. Exp. Sta. Bul. 234.

263. Smith, C. F. 1969. Controlling peach scale. Research and Farming. N. Car. Agr. Exp. Sta. 28:12.

264. Smith, F. F. 1955. Notes on the biology and control of *Pseudocneorhinus bifasciatus*. Jour. Econ. Ent. 48(5):628.

265. Smith, F. F. 1962. Controlling insects on flowers. USDA Info. Bul. 237. 78 pp.

266. Smith, F. F., and J. H. Fisher. 1930. The boxwood leaf miner. Pa. Dept. of Agr. Bul. Vol. 13(12):1–14.

267. Smith, R. H. 1941. Spraying for the sycamore scale. Western Shade Tree Conf. Proc. 8:30–39.

268. Smith, R. H. 1944. Insects and mites injurious to sycamore trees in western North America. Arborist's News 9:9–15.

269. Smith, R. H. 1944. Bionomics and control of the nigra scale, *Saissetia nigra*. Hilgardia 16(5):255–288.

270. Smith, R. H. 1945. Scale important pests of sycamore trees. Pacific Coast Nurseryman 3:7, 8, 13.

271. Snetsinger, R., and E. B. Himelick. 1957. Observations on witches'-broom of hackberry. Plant Dis. Reptr. 41(6):541–544.

272. Solomon, J. D., and W. W. Neel. 1972. Emergence behavior and rhythms in the carpenterworm moth, *Prionoxystus robiniae*. Ann. of the Ent. Soc. of America 65(6):1296–1299.

273. Speers, C. F., and J. L. Rauschenberger. 1971. Pales weevil. USDA Forest Pest Leaflet 104. 6 pp.

274. Spencer, K. A. 1969. The Agromyzidae of Canada and Alaska. Mem. Ent. Soc. of Canada. No. 64. 311 pp.

275. Sreenivasam, D. D., D. M. Benjamin, and D.D. Walgenbach. 1972. The bionomics of the pine tussock moth. Res. Bul 282, Univ. of Wisconsin.

276. Stoetzel, M. B., and J. A. Davidson. 1971. Biology of the obscure scale, *Melanapsis obscura* (Homoptera: Diaspidae), on pin oak in Maryland. Ann. Ent. Soc. Amer. 64(1):45–50.

277. Stoetzel, M. B. and J. A. Davidson. 1974. Biology, morphology and taxonomy of immature stages of 9 species in the Aspidiotini (Homoptera: Diaspididae) Ann. Ent. Soc. of America. 67(3):475–509.

278. Streu, H. T., and L. M. Vasvary. 1970. Pests of holly in the eastern United States. Nat. Horticulture Magazine Vol. 39(4):234–255 revised. Handbook of Hollies.

279. Struble, G. R., and P. C. Johnson. 1964. Black pine leaf scale. USDA Forest Pest Leaflet 91. 6 pp.

280. Stillwell, M. A. 1967. The pigeon tremex, *Tremex columba* (Hymenoptera: Siricidae), in New Brunswick. Can. Ent. 99(7):685–689.

281. Symons, T. B., and E. H. Cory. 1910. The terrapin scale. Md. Agr. Expt. Sta. Bul. 149.

282. Tashiro, H. 1973. Evaluation of soil applied insecticides on insects of white birch in nurseries. Search Agriculture 3(9):1–10. N. Y. State. Agr. Exp. Sta. Geneva.

283. Thatcher, R. C. 1967. Pine sawfly, *Neodiprion excitans*. USDA Forest Pest Leaflet 105. 4 pp.

284. Thompson, B. G., and K. L. Wong. 1933. Western willow tingid, *Corythuca salicata* Gibson, in Oregon. Jour. Econ. Ent. 26(6):1090–1095.

285. Thompson, Hugh E. 1962. Controlling the elm calligrapha beetles. Kansas Agr. Exp. Sta. Circ. 385. 7 pp.

286. Tilden, J. W. 1951. The insect associates of *Baccharis pilularis* De Candolle. Microentomology 16(1):149–185.

287. Turnock, W. J. 1953. Some aspects of the life history and ecology of the pitch nodule maker, *Petrova albicapitana* (Busck) (Lepidoptera: Olethreutidae). Can. Ent. 85(7):233–243.

288. Tuttle, D. M., and E. W. Baker. 1968. Spider mites of the southwestern United States and a revision of the family Tetranychidae. Univ. of Arizona Press, 143 pp.

289. Underhill, G. W. 1935. The pecan tree borer in dogwood. Jour. Econ. Ent. Vol. 28, No. 2 (April), pp. 393–396.

290. Usinger, R. L. 1945. Biology and control of ash plant bugs in California. Jour. Econ. Ent. 38(5):585–591.

291. Varty, I. W. 1967. *Erythroneura* leafhoppers from birches in New Brunswick. Can. Ent. 99(6):570–573.

292. Varty, I. W. 1967. Leafhoppers of the subfamily Typhlocybinae from birches. Can. Ent. 99(2):170–180.

293. Volck, W. H. 1907. The California tussock-moth. Calif. Agr. Exp. Sta. Bul. 183:191–216.

294. Volck, W. H. 1956, March. Strawberry root weevils—control them! Utah State Coop. Ext. Bul., Leaflet 7.

295. Wade, O. 1917. The sycamore lace-bug (*Corythucha ciliata* Say) Okla. Agr. Exp. Sta. Bul. 116. 16 pp.

296. Wagener, N. W. 1936. The cypress bark canker and other western cypress diseases. Western Shade Tree Conf. Proceedings 3:79–85.

297. Wallace, P. P. 1945. Biology and control of the dogwood borer *Thamnosphecia (Synanthedon) Scitula* Harris. Conn. Agr. Exp. Sta. Bul. 488:373–395.

298. Wallesz, D. P., and D. M. Benjamin. 1960. The biology of the pine webworm, *Tetralopha robustella* in Wisconsin. Jour. of Econ. Ent. 53(4):587–589.

299. Wallner, W. E. 1965. The biology and control of Fiorinia hemlock scale *Fiorinia externa* Ferris. Ph.D. thesis, Cornell University. 166 pp.

300. Wallner, W. E. 1969. Insects affecting woody ornamental shrubs and trees. Michigan State Univ. Extension Bul. 530. 45 pp.

301. Walton, B. C. J. 1960. The life cycle of the hackberry gall-former, *Pachypsylla celtidisgemma* (Homoptera: Psyllidae). Ent. Soc. Amer. Ann. 53(2):265–277.

302. Warren, L. O., and M. Tadic. 1970. The fall webworm, *Hyphantria cunea* (Dryry). Univ. of Ark. Agr. Exp. Sta. Bul. 795. 106 pp.

303. Watson, J. R. 1915. The woolly whitefly. Florida Agr. Exp. Sta. Bul. 126, pp. 81–102.

304. Weaver, C. R., and D. R. King. 1954. Meadow spittlebug. Ohio Agr. Exp. Sta. Res. Bul. 741. 99 pp.

305. Weidhaas, J. A., Jr., and Frank R. Shaw. 1956. Control of the Taxus mealybug with notes on its biology. Jour. Econ. Ent. 49(2):273–274.

306. Weidhaas, J. A., Jr. 1959. Investigations of the effects of some modern pesticides on certain coccinellid predators of aphids and mites in Massachusetts. Ph.D. dissertation, Univ. of Mass. 259 pp.

307. Weigel, C. A., and L. G. Baumhofer. 1948. Handbook on insect enemies of flowers and shrubs. USDA Misc. Publ. No. 626. 115 pp.

308. Weiss, H. B., and R. B. Lott. 1922. The juniper webworm, *Dichomeris marginellus* Fabr. Ent. News 33:80–82.

309. Weld, L. H. 1957. Cynipid galls of the Pacific slope. Privately published, Ann Arbor, Michigan. 64 pp.

310. Weld, L. H. 1959. Cynipid galls of the eastern United States. Privately published. Ann Arbor, Michigan. 124 pp.

311. Wellhouse, W. H. 1922. The insect fauna of the genus *Crataegus*. Cornell Univ. Agr. Exp. Sta. Memoir 56.

449

312. Westcott, Cynthia. 1964. The gardener's bug book. Doubleday & Co., N.Y. 625 pp.

313. Westcott, Cynthia (Editor). 1960. Handbook on biological control of plant pests. Plants and gardens, Vol. 16, No. 3. Brooklyn Botanic Garden, N.Y. 97 pp.

314. White, R. P., and C. C. Hamilton. 1935. Diseases and insect pests of rhododendron and azalea. N.J. Agr. Exp. Sta. Cir. 350.

315. Williams, M. L., and Michael Kosztarab. 1972. Morphology and systematics of the Coccidae of Virginia with notes on their biology. Homoptera: Coccoidae. Va. Polytech. Inst. & State Univ. Res. Div. Bul. 74. 215 pp.

316. Wilson, L. F. 1962. Yellow-headed spruce sawfly. USDA Forest Pest Leaflet 69. 4 pp.

317. Wilson, L. F. 1966. Introduced pine sawfly. USDA Forest Pest Leaflet 99. 4 pp.

318. Wilson, L. F. 1968. Life history and habits of the pine cone willow gall midge, *Rhabdophaga strobiloides* (Diptera: Cecidomyiidae), in Michigan. Can. Ent. 100(4):430–433.

319. Wilson, L. F. 1970. The red-headed pine sawfly. USDA Forest Pest Leaflet 14. 6 pp.

320. Wilson, L. F., and D. C. Schmiege. 1970. Pine root collar weevil. USDA Forest Pest Leaflet 39. 7 pp.

321. Wood, T. K. 1968. The chemical composition, host plant variation and overwintering survival value of the egg froth of the Membracid *Enchenopa binotata* Say. Unpublished thesis, Cornell University.

322. Woollerman, E. H. 1970. The locust borer. USDA Forest Service Forest Pest Leaflet 71. 8 pp.

Glossary

Abiotic—Without life or ever being alive.

Adventitious buds—Refers to the many lateral buds of twigs and branches. Their formation and continued growth is usually stimulated by pruning or by insects.

Aestivation—To rest, sleep or be inactive during the hot summer months. An aestivating insect may be inactive over a period of one or two months.

Anal shield—A hard plate on the terminal segment of a caterpillar and certain other immature insects.

Asexual—Literally meaning without sex. Reproducing without the union of sperm and egg.

Biotic—Relating to living things.

Bud blast—A developed bud that may appear to have died suddenly. Dead buds may be partially opened.

Chlorosis—A common symptom of disease marked by yellow or blanched leaves.

Chrysalis—The pupa of a butterfly.

cm—Centimeter, a unit of measure in length or diameter. 2½ cm = 1 inch.

Commensalism—A relation between two kinds of organisms in which both live together but neither one at the expense of the other.

Cornicles—Dorsal tubular appendages on the posterior part of the abdomen of certain aphids.

Crawler—An immature stage of an adelgid or scale insect. The active crawling stage.

Cultivar—A cultural variety of an economic plant, maintained by asexual propagation or controlled breeding.

Deutogyne—A reproductive stage of certain eriophyid mites. A distinct female which characterizes one of the alternate generations. (See Protogyne.)

Diapause—A period of rest in the life of an insect where growth is nil and metabolic activity is low.

Dieback—The dying backwards from bud tip to branch.

Distal—Farthest from the body or main stem.

Dorsal—Relating to the upper surface; the back.

Epidermis—The outer layer of a plant tissue; or the layer of an insect that produces the cuticula of an insect's exoskeleton.

Erineum—A gall made up of tiny plant hairs with round heads. The gall develops in the form of a velvety and sometimes glossy pad. These galls are caused by eriophyid mites.

Eriophyid—Any of a group of tiny mites characterized by having a slender body and two pairs of legs, rather than four.

Excrescence—A gall or abnormal growth that disfigures a plant. A tumor.

Exfoliate—To cast off or flake off as bark.

Exocarp—The outer layer of a fruit; the fleshy part of a peach or husk of a walnut or hickory nut.

Exoskeleton—The external skeleton of insects and other arthropods. The exoskeleton is discarded (molted) at various times. The molted skeleton is sometimes called a "skin."

Exuviae—The cast exoskeleton (skin) of an insect or other arthropod.

Flocculence—A woolly, sometimes fuzzy, covering of a soft waxy substance often resembling wool.

Frass—Wood fragments mixed with excrement produced by an insect.

Free-living—Living on and free to move about as opposed to living within a gall, under bark or in a leaf mine.

Gall—An abnormal growth or excrescence on a plant. May be caused by insects, mites, bacteria or other living entities. A plant tumor.

Generation—A measurement of time relative to birth and reproductive stage of an individual. The period between the birth of one generation and that of the next.

Honeydew—A sweet sticky fluid excreted by aphids, certain scales, mealybugs, whiteflies and some leafhoppers.

Instar—The stage of an insect between molts.

Internode—The part of a stem between two successive nodes. (See node.)

Kernel—The edible portion of a nut or seed.

Larva—An immature stage, between egg and pupa of an insect with complete metamorphosis. A caterpillar, maggot or grub are examples.

Life cycle—The series of changes in the form of life beginning with the egg, ending in the adult reproductive stage.

Mesophyll—The middle or internal components of a leaf. See parenchyma.

Micron—A unit of length. 1000 microns = 1 mm. (See mm.)

Midrib—The central vein of a leaf.

Molt—A process of shedding the exoskeleton (sometimes improperly called a "skin").

mm—Millimeter, a unit of measure in length or diameter. Twenty-five mm = 1 inch.

Morphologist—A scientist who studies the form and structure of living organisms.

Mouthparts—The structures of an insect that aid in obtaining food.

Necrosis—The death of tissue.

Node—A slightly enlarged portion of a stem where leaves and buds arise, and where branches and twigs originate.

Nymph—A young insect with simple metamorphosis. A young leafhopper or true bug (Hemiptera) is called a nymph.

Orifice—An opening in a plant part, often a gall, for the exit of insects developing inside.

Ovipositor—The external egg-laying apparatus of an insect.

Ovisac—An extension of the body wall, or specialized structure of a female, where certain kinds of insects deposit their eggs.

Parasite—An animal, or plant, that lives in or on another living organism (host) for at least a part of its life cycle. The host is injured by the relationship.

Parenchyma—Soft tissue between the epidermal layers of a leaf.

Parthenogenesis—Reproduction without fertilization.

Pathogenic—Disease producing.

Petiole—The leaf stem or stalk that attaches to a twig.

Pheromone—A complicated biochemical substance produced by insects to communicate with the same species through the sense of smell.

Prolegs—Fleshy abdominal legs of certain insect larvae.

Protogyne—A reproductive stage of certain eriophyid mites; a male-like female. One of the two forms of the same mite species. (See deutogyne.)

Pseudogall—A false gall; appearing like a gall but not necessarily an abnormal growth.

Pupa—A resting stage of an insect; the stage between the larva and adult in insects with complete metamorphosis.

Rasping mouthparts—Insect mouthparts for filing or rasping plant tissue; typical of thrips mouthparts.

Russetting—A brownish superficial roughening of the "skin" of fruits, leaves and other plant parts.

Scale insect—A group of insects characterized as having a hard convex covering over their body with no visible appendages or segmentation. Usually small, ranging from 1 to 5 mm in length or diameter.

Sessile—Term used to describe insects, in certain stages, that are normally immobile.

Setaceous—Bristle-like in form or texture.

Sign—The actual organism, skeleton or other parts of a pest, used to associate or identify the cause of a symptom.

Skeletonize—Term used to describe the feeding pattern of certain leaf-feeding insects. Only the veins or basic matrix remain.

Snout beetle—A weevil. An insect with a long proboscis or snout bearing chewing mouth-parts.

Sooty mold—A dark, often black, fungus growing in insect honeydew.

Spiracle—The external opening of the respiratory organ of "air-breathing" insects.

Stomata—Tiny openings in leaves where respiration or exchange of oxygen and carbon dioxide take place, and water vapor is lost.

Stylet—A needle-like part of the piercing-sucking mouthparts of an insect or mite.

Symptom—The injury or plant response to an offender.

Taxonomist—A scientist especially trained in the classification of plants or animals.

Test—The external shell or covering of many invertebrate animals.

Thorax—The middle region of an insect's body where the legs and wings are attached.

Ventral—The lower surface or undersurface; situated on the abdominal side of the body.

Witches-broom—An abnormal cluster of twigs about a common focus. A brush-like growth of small branches on trees and shrubs.

Index of Insects, Mites and Other Animals

This listing includes the scientific and common names of the animal species discussed. The pages listed in boldface type indicate the location of the principal description.

455

This index should enable the horticulturist, forester and home gardener, not trained in entomology, to locate the text and illustrations useful in pest identification. The pages listed in boldface type indicate where most of the biological and distribution information is given. The **Reader's Aide to Identification of Insects** on page 9 is a quick index to the plates.

Designed by Richard E. Rosenbaum.
Composed by Dix Typesetting Co. Inc. in 9/10 Mergenthaler VIP Optima Medium with Optima Black display.
Color separations, plates, and printing by Simpson/Milligan Printing Co., Inc.
Printed offset on Potlatch Vintage Velvet, 70 pound basis.
Bound by John H. Dekker and Sons, Inc. in Columbia Bayside Linen, with stamping in All Purpose foil.
Endpapers are Multicolor Antique Gold.